C++:

A Beginner's Guide

C++:
A Beginner's Guide

Herbert Schildt

McGraw-Hill/Osborne

New York   Chicago   San Francisco
Lisbon   London   Madrid   Mexico City   Milan
New Delhi   San Juan   Seoul   Singapore   Sydney   Toronto

McGraw-Hill/Osborne
2600 Tenth Street
Berkeley, California 94710
U.S.A.

To arrange bulk purchase discounts for sales promotions, premiums, or fund-raisers, please contact **McGraw-Hill**/Osborne at the above address. For information on translations or book distributors outside the U.S.A., please see the International Contact Information page immediately following the index of this book.

C++: A Beginner's Guide

234567890 DOC DOC 019876543

ISBN 0-07-219467-7

Publisher   Brandon A. Nordin
Vice President & Associate Publisher   Scott Rogers
Acquisitions Editor   Ann Sellers
Project Editor   Patty Mon
Acquisitions Coordinator   Tim Madrid
Technical Editor   Greg Guntle
Copy Editor   Jan Jue
Proofreader   Susie Elkind
Indexer   Sheryl Schildt
Computer Designers   Michelle Galicia, Lauren McCarthy
Illustrators   Michael Mueller, Lyssa Wald
Series Design   Gary Corrigan
Cover Design   Greg Scott
Cover Illustration   Kevin Curry

This book was composed with Corel VENTURA™ Publisher.

About the Author

Herbert Schildt is the world's leading programming author. He is an authority on the C, C++, Java, and C# languages, and is a master Windows programmer. His programming books have sold more than 3 million copies worldwide and have been translated into all major foreign languages. He is the author of numerous bestsellers, including *C++: The Complete Reference, C#: The Complete Reference, Java 2: The Complete Reference, C#: A Beginner's Guide, Java 2: A Beginner's Guide,* and *C: The Complete Reference.* Schildt holds a master's degree in computer science from the University of Illinois. He can be reached at his consulting office at (217) 586-4683.

Contents at a Glance

Contents

Preface

C++ is the preeminent language for the development of high-performance software. It is also the language that defines the modern syntax and style that have influenced all subsequent languages. For example, both Java and C# are descended from C++. Moreover, C++ is the universal language of programming, in which nearly all professional programmers have at least passing competency. By learning C++, you will be establishing a solid foundation that will enable you to pursue any aspect of programming today.

The purpose of this book is to teach you the fundamentals of C++ programming. It uses a step-by-step approach complete with numerous examples, self-tests, and projects. It assumes no previous programming experience. The book starts with the basics, such as how to compile and run a C++ program. It then discusses the keywords, features, and constructs that comprise the C++ language. By the time you finish, you will have a firm grasp of the essentials of C++ programming.

It is important to state at the outset that this book is just a starting point. C++ is a large, sophisticated language, and successful C++ programming involves more than just the keywords, operators, and syntax that define the language. It also involves the use of an extensive set of class and function libraries that aid in the development of programs. Although several of the library elements are discussed in this book, because of space limitations, most are not. To be a top-notch C++

programmer implies mastery of C++ libraries, too. After completing this book, you will have the knowledge to explore the libraries and all other aspects of C++.

How This Book Is Organized

This book presents an evenly paced tutorial in which each section builds upon the previous one. It contains 12 modules, each discussing an aspect of C++. This book is unique because it includes several special elements that reinforce what you are learning.

Goals

Each module begins with a set of goals that tell you what you will be learning.

Mastery Check

Each module concludes with a Mastery Check, a self-test that lets you test your knowledge. The answers are in Appendix A.

1-Minute Drills

At the end of each major section, 1-Minute Drills are presented that test your understanding of the key points of the preceding section. The answers to these questions are at the bottom of the page.

Ask the Expert

Sprinkled throughout the book are special "Ask the Expert" boxes. These contain additional information or interesting commentary about a topic. They use a Question/Answer format.

Projects

Each module contains one or more projects that show you how to apply what you are learning. These are real-world examples that you can use as starting points for your own programs.

No Previous Programming Experience Required

This book assumes no previous programming experience. Thus, if you have never programmed before, you can use this book. Of course, in this day and age, most readers will have at least a little prior programming experience. For many, this previous experience will be in Java or C#. As you will learn, C++ is the parent of both of these languages. Therefore, if you already know Java or C#, then you will be able to learn C++ easily.

Required Software

To compile and run the programs in this book, you will need a modern C++ compiler, such as a recent version of Microsoft's Visual C++ or Borland's C++ Builder.

Don't Forget: Code on the Web

Remember, the source code for all of the examples and projects in this book is available free-of-charge on the Web at **www.osborne.com**.

For Further Study

C++: A Beginner's Guide is your gateway to the Herb Schildt series of programming books. Here are some others that you will find of interest.

To learn more about C++, try

C++: The Complete Reference
C++ From the Ground Up
Teach Yourself C++
STL Programming From the Ground Up
C++ Programmer's Reference

To learn about Java programming, we recommend the following:

Java 2: A Beginner's Guide
Java 2: The Complete Reference
Java 2 Programmer's Reference

To learn about C#, Herb offers these books:

C#: A Beginner's Guide
C#: The Complete Reference

To learn about Windows programming, we suggest the following Schildt books:

Windows 98 Programming From the Ground Up
Windows 2000 Programming From the Ground Up
MFC Programming From the Ground Up
The Windows Programming Annotated Archives

If you want to learn about the C language, which is the foundation of all modern programming, then the following titles will be of interest:

C: The Complete Reference
Teach Yourself C

When you need solid answers, fast, turn to Herbert Schildt, the recognized authority on programming.

Module 1

C++ Fundamentals

The Goals of This Module

- Understand the history behind C++
- See how C++ relates to C, C#, and Java
- Learn the three principles of object-oriented programming
- Create, compile, and run C++ programs
- Use variables
- Use operators
- Work with the if and for statements
- Apply code blocks
- Know the C++ keywords
- Understand identifiers
- Use functions

If there is one language that defines the essence of programming today, it is C++. It is the preeminent language for the development of high-performance software. Its syntax has become the standard for professional programming languages, and its design philosophy reverberates throughout computing. C++ is also the language from which both Java and C# are derived. Simply stated, to be a professional programmer implies competency in C++. It is the gateway to all of modern programming.

The purpose of this module is to introduce C++, including its history, its design philosophy, and several of its most important features. By far, the hardest thing about learning a programming language is the fact that no element exists in isolation. Instead, the components of the language work together. This interrelatedness makes it difficult to discuss one aspect of C++ without involving others. To help overcome this problem, this module provides a brief overview of several C++ features, including the general form of a C++ program, some basic control statements, and operators. It does not go into too many details, but rather concentrates on the general concepts common to any C++ program.

A Brief History of C++

The history of C++ begins with C. The reason for this is easy to understand: C++ is built upon the foundation of C. Thus, C++ is a superset of C. C++ expanded and enhanced the C language to support object-oriented programming (which is described later in this chapter). C++ also added several other improvements to the C language, including an extended set of library routines. However, much of the spirit and flavor of C++ is directly inherited from C. Therefore, to fully understand and appreciate C++, you need to understand the "how and why" behind C.

C: The Beginning of the Modern Age of Programming

The invention of C defines the beginning of the modern age of programming. Its impact should not be underestimated because it fundamentally changed the way programming was approached and thought about. Its design philosophy and syntax have influenced every major language since. C was one of the major, revolutionary forces in computing.

C was invented and first implemented by Dennis Ritchie on a DEC PDP-11 using the UNIX operating system. C is the result of a development process that started with an older language called BCPL. BCPL was developed by Martin Richards. BCPL influenced a language called B, which was invented by Ken Thompson and which led to the development of C in the 1970s.

Prior to the invention of C, computer languages were generally designed either as academic exercises or by bureaucratic committees. C was different. It was designed, implemented, and developed by real, working programmers, reflecting the way they approached the job of programming. Its features were honed, tested, thought about, and rethought by the people who actually used the language. As a result, C attracted many proponents and quickly became the language of choice of programmers around the world.

C grew out of the *structured programming* revolution of the 1960s. Prior to structured programming, large programs were difficult to write because the program logic tended to degenerate into what is known as "spaghetti code," a tangled mass of jumps, calls, and returns that is difficult to follow. Structured languages addressed this problem by adding well-defined control statements, subroutines with local variables, and other improvements. Using structured languages, it became possible to write moderately large programs.

Although there were other structured languages at the time, such as Pascal, C was the first to successfully combine power, elegance, and expressiveness. Its terse, yet easy-to-use syntax coupled with its philosophy that the programmer (not the language) was in charge quickly won many converts. It can be a bit hard to understand from today's perspective, but C was a breath of fresh air that programmers had long awaited. As a result, C became the most widely used structured programming language of the 1980s.

The Need for C++

Given the preceding discussion, you might be wondering why C++ was invented. Since C was a successful computer programming language, why was there a need for something else? The answer is *complexity*. Throughout the history of programming, the increasing complexity of programs has driven the need for better ways to manage that complexity. C++ is a response to that need. To better understand the correlation between increasing program complexity and computer language development, consider the following.

Approaches to programming have changed dramatically since the invention of the computer. For example, when computers were first invented, programming was done by using the computer's front panel to toggle in the binary machine instructions. As long as programs were just a few hundred instructions long, this approach worked. As programs grew, assembly language was invented so that programmers could deal with larger, increasingly complex programs by using symbolic representations of the machine instructions. As programs continued to grow, high-level languages were developed to give programmers more tools with which to handle the complexity.

The first widely used computer language was, of course, FORTRAN. While FORTRAN was a very impressive first step, it is hardly a language that encourages clear, easy-to-understand programs. The 1960s gave birth to structured programming, which is the method of programming encouraged by languages such as C. With structured languages it was, for the first time, possible to write moderately complex programs fairly easily. However, even with structured programming methods, once a project reaches a certain size, its complexity exceeds what a programmer can manage. By the late 1970s, many projects were near or at this point.

In response to this problem, a new way to program began to emerge: *object-oriented programming* (OOP). Using OOP, a programmer could handle larger, more complex programs. The trouble was that C did not support object-oriented programming. The desire for an object-oriented version of C ultimately led to the creation of C++.

In the final analysis, although C is one of the most liked and widely used professional programming languages in the world, there comes a time when its ability to handle complexity is exceeded. Once a program reaches a certain size, it becomes so complex that it is difficult to grasp as a totality. The purpose of C++ is to allow this barrier to be broken and to help the programmer comprehend and manage larger, more complex programs.

C++ Is Born

C++ was invented by Bjarne Stroustrup in 1979, at Bell Laboratories in Murray Hill, New Jersey. He initially called the new language "C with Classes." However, in 1983 the name was changed to C++.

Stroustrup built C++ on the foundation of C, including all of C's features, attributes, and benefits. He also adhered to C's underlying philosophy that the programmer, not the language, is in charge. At this point, it is critical to understand that Stroustrup did not create an entirely new programming language. Instead, he enhanced an already highly successful language.

Most of the features that Stroustrup added to C were designed to support object-oriented programming. In essence, C++ is the object-oriented version of C. By building upon the foundation of C, Stroustrup provided a smooth migration path to OOP. Instead of having to learn an entirely new language, a C programmer needed to learn only a few new features before reaping the benefits of the object-oriented methodology.

When creating C++, Stroustrup knew that it was important to maintain the original spirit of C, including its efficiency, flexibility, and philosophy, while at the same time adding support for object-oriented programming. Happily, his goal was accomplished. C++ still provides the programmer with the freedom and control of C, coupled with the power of objects.

Although C++ was initially designed to aid in the management of very large programs, it is in no way limited to this use. In fact, the object-oriented attributes of C++ can be effectively applied to virtually any programming task. It is not uncommon to see C++ used for projects such as editors, databases, personal file systems, networking utilities, and communication programs. Because C++ shares C's efficiency, much high-performance systems software is constructed using C++. Also, C++ is frequently the language of choice for Windows programming.

The Evolution of C++

Since C++ was first invented, it has undergone three major revisions, with each revision adding to and altering the language. The first revision was in 1985 and the second in 1990. The third occurred during the C++ standardization process. Several years ago, work began on a standard for C++. Toward that end, a joint ANSI (American National Standards Institute) and ISO (International Standards Organization) standardization committee was formed. The first draft of the proposed standard was created on January 25, 1994. In that draft, the ANSI/ISO C++ committee (of which I was a member) kept the features first defined by Stroustrup and added some new ones. But, in general, this initial draft reflected the state of C++ at the time.

Soon after the completion of the first draft of the C++ standard, an event occurred that caused the standard to be greatly expanded: the creation of the Standard Template Library (STL) by Alexander Stepanov. The STL is a set of generic routines that you can use to manipulate data. It is both powerful and elegant. But it is also quite large. Subsequent to the first draft, the committee voted to include the STL in the specification for C++. The addition of the STL expanded the scope of C++ well beyond its original definition. While important, the inclusion of the STL, among other things, slowed the standardization of C++.

It is fair to say that the standardization of C++ took far longer than anyone had expected. In the process, many new features were added to the language, and many small changes were made. In fact, the version of C++ defined by the ANSI/ISO C++ committee is much larger and more complex than Stroustrup's original design. The final draft was passed out of committee on November 14, 1997, and an ANSI/ISO standard for C++ became a reality in 1998. This is the specification for C++ that is usually referred to as *Standard C++*.

The material in this book describes Standard C++. This is the version of C++ supported by all mainstream C++ compilers, including Microsoft's Visual C++ and Borland's C++ Builder. Thus, the code and information in this book are fully portable.

How C++ Relates to Java and C#

As most readers will know, two new computer languages have appeared: Java and C#. Java was developed by Sun Microsystems, and C# was created by Microsoft. Because there is sometimes confusion about how these two languages relate to C++, a brief discussion of their relationship is in order.

C++ is the parent for both Java and C#. Although both Java and C# added, removed, and modified various features, in total the syntax for these three languages is nearly identical. Furthermore, the object model used by C++ is similar to the ones used by Java and C#. Finally, the overall "look and feel" of these languages is very similar. This means that once you know C++, you can easily learn Java or C#. The opposite is also true. If you know Java or C#, learning C++ is easy. This is one reason that Java and C# share C++'s syntax and object model; it facilitated their rapid adoption by legions of experienced C++ programmers.

The main difference between C++, Java, and C# is the type of computing environment for which each is designed. C++ was created to produce high-performance programs for a specific type of CPU and operating system. For example, if you want to write a program that runs on an Intel Pentium under the Windows operating system, then C++ is the best language to use.

Java and C# were developed in response to the unique programming needs of the online environment of the Internet. (C# was also designed to simplify the creation of software components.) The Internet is connected to many different types of CPUs and operating systems. Thus, the ability to produce cross-platform, portable programs became an overriding concern.

The first language to address this need was Java. Using Java, it is possible to write a program that runs in a wide variety of environments. Thus, a Java program can move about freely on the Internet. However, the price you pay for portability is efficiency, and Java programs execute more slowly than do C++ programs. The same is true for C#. In the final analysis, if you want to create high-performance software, use C++. If you need to create highly portable software, use Java or C#.

One final point: Remember that C++, Java, and C# are designed to solve different sets of problems. It is not an issue of which language is best in and of itself. Rather, it is a question of which language is right for the job at hand.

1-Minute Drill

- From what language is C++ derived?

- What was the main factor that drove the creation of C++?

- C++ is the parent of Java and C#. True or false?

Object-Oriented Programming

Central to C++ is object-oriented programming (OOP). As just explained, OOP was the impetus for the creation of C++. Because of this, it is useful to understand OOP's basic principles before you write even a simple C++ program.

Object-oriented programming took the best ideas of structured programming and combined them with several new concepts. The result was a different and better way of organizing a program. In the most general sense, a program can be organized in one of two ways: around its *code* (what is happening) or around its *data* (who is being affected). Using only structured programming techniques, programs are typically organized around code. This approach can be thought of as "code acting on data."

- C++ is derived from C.
- Increasing program complexity was the main factor that drove the creation of C++.
- True.

Ask the Expert

Question: How do Java and C# create cross-platform, portable programs, and why can't C++ do the same?

Answer: Java and C# can create cross-platform, portable programs and C++ can't because of the type of object code produced by the compiler. In the case of C++, the output from the compiler is machine code that is directly executed by the CPU. Thus, it is tied to a specific CPU and operating system. If you want to run a C++ program on a different system, you need to recompile it into machine code specifically targeted for that environment. To create a C++ program that would run in a variety of environments, several different executable versions of the program are needed.

Java and C# achieve portability by compiling a program into a pseudocode, intermediate language. In the case of Java, this intermediate language is called *bytecode*. For C#, it is called *Microsoft Intermediate Language* (MSIL). In both cases, this pseudocode is executed by a runtime system. For Java, this runtime system is called the Java Virtual Machine (JVM). For C#, it is the Common Language Runtime (CLR). Therefore, a Java program can run in any environment for which a JVM is available, and a C# program can run in any environment in which the CLR is implemented.

Since the Java and C# runtime systems stand between a program and the CPU, Java and C# programs incur an overhead that is not present in the execution of a C++ program. This is why C++ programs usually run faster than the equivalent programs written in Java or C#.

Object-oriented programs work the other way around. They are organized around data, with the key principle being "data controlling access to code." In an object-oriented language, you define the data and the routines that are permitted to act on that data. Thus, a data type defines precisely what sort of operations can be applied to that data.

To support the principles of object-oriented programming, all OOP languages, including C++, have three traits in common: encapsulation, polymorphism, and inheritance. Let's examine each.

1

Encapsulation

Encapsulation is a programming mechanism that binds together code and the data it manipulates, and that keeps both safe from outside interference and misuse. In an object-oriented language, code and data can be bound together in such a way that a self-contained *black box* is created. Within the box are all necessary data and code. When code and data are linked together in this fashion, an *object* is created. In other words, an object is the device that supports encapsulation.

Within an object, code or data or both may be *private* to that object or *public*. Private code or data is known to and accessible by only another part of the object. That is, private code or data cannot be accessed by a piece of the program that exists outside the object. When code or data is public, other parts of your program can access it even though it is defined within an object. Typically, the public parts of an object are used to provide a controlled interface to the private elements of the object.

C++'s basic unit of encapsulation is the *class*. A class defines the form of an object. It specifies both the data and the code that will operate on that data. C++ uses a class specification to construct *objects*. Objects are instances of a class. Thus, a class is essentially a set of plans that specifies how to build an object.

The code and data that constitute a class are called *members* of the class. Specifically, *member variables*, also called *instance variables*, are the data defined by the class. *Member functions* or just *functions* are the code that operates on that data. *Function* is C++'s term for a subroutine.

Ask the Expert

Question: I have heard the term *method* applied to a subroutine. Is a method the same as a function?

Answer: In general, the answer is yes. The term *method* was popularized by Java. What a C++ programmer calls a function, a Java programmer calls a method. C# programmers also use the term method. Because it is becoming so widely used, sometimes the term method is also used when referring to a C++ function.

Polymorphism

Polymorphism (from Greek, meaning "many forms") is the quality that allows one interface to access a general class of actions. A simple example of polymorphism is found in the steering wheel of an automobile. The steering wheel (the interface) is the same no matter what type of actual steering mechanism is used. That is, the steering wheel works the same whether your car has manual steering, power steering, or rack-and-pinion steering. Thus, turning the steering wheel left causes the car to go left no matter what type of steering is used. The benefit of the uniform interface is, of course, that once you know how to operate the steering wheel, you can drive any type of car.

The same principle can also apply to programming. For example, consider a *stack* (which is a first-in, last-out list). You might have a program that requires three different types of stacks. One stack is used for integer values, one for floating-point values, and one for characters. In this case, the algorithm that implements each stack is the same, even though the data being stored differs. In a non–object-oriented language, you would be required to create three different sets of stack routines, with each set using different names. However, because of polymorphism, in C++ you can create one general set of stack routines that works for all three situations. This way, once you know how to use one stack, you can use them all.

More generally, the concept of polymorphism is often expressed by the phrase "one interface, multiple methods." This means that it is possible to design a generic interface to a group of related activities. Polymorphism helps reduce complexity by allowing the same interface to specify a *general class of action*. It is the compiler's job to select the *specific action* (that is, method) as it applies to each situation. You, the programmer, don't need to do this selection manually. You need only remember and utilize the general interface.

Inheritance

Inheritance is the process by which one object can acquire the properties of another object. This is important because it supports the concept of hierarchical classification. If you think about it, most knowledge is made manageable by hierarchical (that is, top-down) classifications. For example, a Red Delicious apple is part of the classification *apple,* which in turn is part of the *fruit* class, which is under the larger class *food.* That is, the *food* class possesses certain qualities (edible, nutritious, and so on) which also, logically, apply to its subclass, *fruit*. In addition to these qualities, the *fruit* class has specific characteristics (juicy, sweet, and so on) that distinguish it from other food. The *apple* class defines those qualities specific to an apple (grows on trees, not tropical, and so on). A Red Delicious apple would, in turn, inherit all the qualities of all preceding classes and would define only those qualities that make it unique.

Without the use of hierarchies, each object would have to explicitly define all of its characteristics. Using inheritance, an object need only define those qualities that make it unique within its class. It can inherit its general attributes from its parent. Thus, it is the inheritance mechanism that makes it possible for one object to be a specific instance of a more general case.

1-Minute Drill

● Name the principles of OOP.

● What is the basic unit of encapsulation in C++?

● What is the commonly used term for a subroutine in C++?

Ask the Expert

Question: You state that object-oriented programming (OOP) is an effective way to manage large programs. However, it seems that OOP might add substantial overhead to relatively small ones. As it relates to C++, is this true?

Answer: No. A key point to understand about C++ is that it *allows* you to write object-oriented programs, but *does not require* you to do so. This is one of the important differences between C++ and Java/C#, which employ a strict object-model in which every program is, to at least a small extent, object oriented. C++ gives you the option. Furthermore, for the most part, the object-oriented features of C++ are transparent at runtime, so little (if any) overhead is incurred.

● Encapsulation, polymorphism, and inheritance are the principles of OOP.
● The class is the basic unit of encapsulation in C++.
● *Function* is the commonly used term for a subroutine in C++.

A First Simple Program

Now it is time to begin programming. Let's start by compiling and running the short sample C++ program shown here:

```
/*
   This is a simple C++ program.

   Call this file Sample.cpp.
*/

#include <iostream>
using namespace std;

// A C++ program begins at main().
int main()
{
  cout << "C++ is power programming.";

  return 0;
}
```

You will follow these three steps:

1. Enter the program.

2. Compile the program.

3. Run the program.

Before beginning, let's review two terms: source code and object code. *Source code* is the human-readable form of the program. It is stored in a text file. *Object code* is the executable form of the program created by the compiler.

Entering the Program

The programs shown in this book are available from Osborne's web site: **www.osborne.com**. However, if you want to enter the programs by hand, you are free to do so. Typing in the programs yourself often helps you remember the key concepts. If you choose to enter a program by hand, you must use a text editor, not a word processor. Word processors typically store format information along with text. This format information will confuse the C++ compiler. If you are using a Windows platform, then you can use WordPad, or any other programming editor that you like.

The name of the file that holds the source code for the program is technically arbitrary. However, C++ programs are normally contained in files that use the file extension **.cpp**. Thus, you can call a C++ program file by any name, but it should use the **.cpp** extension. For this first example, name the source file **Sample.cpp** so that you can follow along. For most of the other programs in this book, simply use a name of your own choosing.

Compiling the Program

How you will compile **Sample.cpp** depends upon your compiler and what options you are using. Furthermore, many compilers, such as Microsoft's Visual C++ and Borland's C++ Builder, provide two different ways for compiling a program: the command-line compiler and the Integrated Development Environment (IDE). Thus, it is not possible to give generalized instructions for compiling a C++ program. You must consult your compiler's instructions.

The preceding paragraph notwithstanding, if you are using either Visual C++ or C++ Builder, then the easiest way to compile and run the programs in this book is to use the command-line compilers offered by these environments. For example, to compile **Sample.cpp** using Visual C++, you will use this command line:

```
C:\...>cl -GX Sample.cpp
```

The -GX option enhances compilation. To use the Visual C++ command-line compiler, you must first execute the batch file VCVARS32.BAT, which is provided by Visual C++. (Visual Studio .NET also provides a ready-to-use command prompt environment that can be activated by selecting Visual Studio .NET Command Prompt from the list of tools shown under the Microsoft Visual Studio .NET entry in the Start | Programs menu of the taskbar.) To compile **Sample.cpp** using C++ Builder, use this command line:

```
C:\...>bcc32 Sample.cpp
```

The output from a C++ compiler is executable object code. For a Windows environment, the executable file will use the same name as the source file, but have the **.exe** extension. Thus, the executable version of **Sample.cpp** will be in **Sample.exe**.

Run the Program

After a C++ program has been compiled, it is ready to be run. Since the output from a C++ compiler is executable object code, to run the program, simply enter its name at the command prompt. For example, to run **Sample.exe**, use this command line:

```
C:\...>Sample
```

When run, the program displays the following output:

```
C++ is power programming.
```

If you are using an Integrated Development Environment, then you can run a program by selecting Run from a menu. Consult the instructions for your specific compiler. For the programs in this book, it is usually easier to compile and run from the command line.

One last point: The programs in this book are console based, not window based. That is, they run in a Command Prompt session. C++ is completely at home with Windows programming. Indeed, it is the most commonly used language for Windows development. However, none of the programs in this book use the Windows Graphic User Interface (GUI). The reason for this is easy to understand: Windows programs are, by their nature, large and complex. The overhead required to create even a minimal Windows skeletal program is 50 to 70 lines of code. To write Windows programs that demonstrate the features of C++ would require hundreds of lines of code each. In contrast, console-based programs are much shorter and are the type of programs normally used to teach programming. Once you have mastered C++, you will be able to apply your knowledge to Windows programming with no trouble.

The First Sample Program Line-by-Line

Although **Sample.cpp** is quite short, it includes several key features that are common to all C++ programs. Let's closely examine each part of the program. The program begins with the lines

```
/*
   This is a simple C++ program.

   Call this file Sample.cpp.
*/
```

This is a *comment*. Like most other programming languages, C++ lets you enter a remark into a program's source code. The contents of a comment are ignored by the compiler. The purpose of a comment is to describe or explain the operation of a program to anyone reading its source code. In the case of this comment, it identifies the program. In more complex programs, you will use comments to help explain what each feature of the program is for and how it goes about doing its work. In other words, you can use comments to provide a "play-by-play" description of what your program does.

In C++, there are two types of comments. The one you've just seen is called a *multiline comment*. This type of comment begins with a /* (a slash followed by an asterisk). It ends only when a */ is encountered. Anything between these two comment symbols is completely ignored by the compiler. Multiline comments may be one or more lines long. The second type of comment (single-line) is found a little further on in the program and will be discussed shortly.

The next line of code looks like this:

```
#include <iostream>
```

The C++ language defines several *headers,* which contain information that is either necessary or useful to your program. This program requires the header **<iostream>**, which supports the C++ I/O system. This header is provided with your compiler. A header is included in your program using the **#include** directive. Later in this book, you will learn more about headers and why they are important.

The next line in the program is

```
using namespace std;
```

This tells the compiler to use the **std** *namespace.* Namespaces are a relatively recent addition to C++. Although namespaces are discussed in detail later in this book, here is a brief description. A namespace creates a declarative region in which various program elements can be placed. Elements declared in one namespace are separate from elements declared in another. Namespaces help in the organization of large programs. The **using** statement informs the compiler that you want to use the **std** namespace. This is the namespace in which the entire Standard C++ library is declared. By using the **std** namespace, you simplify access to the standard library. (Since namespaces are relatively new, your compiler may not yet support them. If this is the case, see Appendix C, which describes an easy work-around.)

The next line in the program is

```
// A C++ program begins at main().
```

This line shows you the second type of comment available in C++: the *single-line comment*. Single-line comments begin with // and stop at the end of the line. Typically, C++ programmers use multiline comments when writing larger, more detailed commentaries, and single-line comments when short remarks are needed. This is, of course, a matter of personal style.

The next line, as the preceding comment indicates, is where program execution begins.

```
int main()
```

All C++ programs are composed of one or more functions. As explained earlier, a function is a subroutine. Every C++ function must have a name, and the only function that any C++ program must include is the one shown here, called **main( )**. The **main( )** function is where program execution begins and (most commonly) ends. (Technically speaking, a C++ program begins with a call to **main( )** and, in most cases, ends when **main( )** returns.) The opening curly brace on the line that follows **main( )** marks the start of the **main( )** function code. The **int** that precedes **main( )** specifies the type of data returned by **main( )**. As you will learn, C++ supports several built-in data types, and **int** is one of them. It stands for integer.

The next line in the program is

```
cout << "C++ is power programming.";
```

This is a console output statement. It causes the message **C++ is power programming** to be displayed on the screen. It accomplishes this by using the output operator <<. The << operator causes whatever expression is on its right side to be output to the device specified on its left side. **cout** is a predefined identifier that stands for console output and generally refers to the computer's screen. Thus, this statement causes the message to be output to the screen. Notice that this statement ends with a semicolon. In fact, all C++ statements end with a semicolon.

The message "C++ is power programming." is a *string*. In C++, a string is a sequence of characters enclosed between double quotes. Strings are used frequently in C++.

The next line in the program is

```
return 0;
```

This line terminates **main( )** and causes it to return the value 0 to the calling process (which is typically the operating system). For most operating systems, a return value of 0 signifies that the program is terminating normally. Other values indicate that the program is terminating because of some error. **return** is one of C++'s keywords, and it is used to return a value from a function. All of your programs should return 0 when they terminate normally (that is, without error).

The closing curly brace at the end of the program formally concludes the program.

Handling Syntax Errors

If you have not yet done so, enter, compile, and run the preceding program. As you may know from previous programming experience, it is quite easy to accidentally type something incorrectly when entering code into your computer. Fortunately, if you enter something incorrectly into your program, the compiler will report a *syntax error* message when it tries to compile it. Most C++ compilers attempt to make sense out of your source code no matter what you have written. For this reason, the error that is reported may not always reflect the actual cause of the problem. In the preceding program, for example, an accidental omission of the opening curly brace after **main( )** may cause the compiler to report the **cout** statement as the source of a syntax error. When you receive syntax error messages, be prepared to look at the last few lines of code in your program in order to find the error.

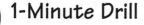

1-Minute Drill

● Where does a C++ program begin execution?

● What is **cout**?

● What does **#include <iostream>** do?

● A C++ program begins execution with **main( )**.
● **cout** is a predefined identifier that is linked to console output.
● It includes the header **<iostream>**, which supports I/O.

Ask the Expert

Question: In addition to error messages, my compiler offers several types of warning messages. How do warnings differ from errors, and what type of reporting should I use?

Answer: In addition to reporting fatal syntax errors, most C++ compilers can also report several types of warning messages. Error messages report things that are unequivocally wrong in your program, such as forgetting a semicolon. Warnings point out suspicious but technically correct code. You, the programmer, then decide whether the suspicion is justified.

Warnings are also used to report such things as inefficient constructs or the use of obsolete features. Generally, you can select the specific type of warnings that you want to see. The programs in this book are in compliance with Standard C++, and when entered correctly, they will not generate any troublesome warning messages.

For the examples in this book, you will want to use your compiler's default (or "normal") error reporting. However, you should examine your compiler's documentation to see what options you have at your disposal. Many compilers have sophisticated features that can help you spot subtle errors before they become big problems. Understanding your compiler's error reporting system is worth your time and effort.

A Second Simple Program

Perhaps no other construct is as fundamental to programming as the variable. A *variable* is a named memory location that can be assigned a value. Further, the value of a variable can be changed during the execution of a program. That is, the content of a variable is changeable, not fixed.

The following program creates a variable called **length**, gives it the value 7, and then displays the message **The length is** 7 on the screen.

```
// Using a variable.

#include <iostream>
using namespace std;              Declare a variable.

int main()
{
  int length; // this declares a variable

  length = 7; // this assigns 7 to length ◄——— Assign length a value.

  cout << "The length is ";
  cout << length; // This displays 7 ◄——— Output the value in length.

  return 0;
}
```

As mentioned earlier, the names of C++ programs are arbitrary. Thus, when you enter this program, select a filename to your liking. For example, you could give this program the name **VarDemo.cpp**.

This program introduces two new concepts. First, the statement

```
int length; // this declares a variable
```

declares a variable called **length** of type integer. In C++, all variables must be declared before they are used. Further, the type of values that the variable can hold must also be specified. This is called the *type* of the variable. In this case, **length** may hold integer values. These are whole number values whose range will be at least −32,768 through 32,767. In C++, to declare a variable to be of type integer, precede its name with the keyword **int**. Later, you will see that C++ supports a wide variety of built-in variable types. (You can create your own data types, too.)

The second new feature is found in the next line of code:

```
length = 7; // this assigns 7 to length
```

As the comment suggests, this assigns the value 7 to **length**. In C++, the assignment operator is the single equal sign. It copies the value on its right side into the variable on its left. After the assignment, the variable **length** will contain the number 7.

The following statement displays the value of **length**:

```
cout << length; // This displays 7
```

In general, if you want to display the value of a variable, simply put it on the right side of << in a **cout** statement. In this specific case, because **length** contains the number 7, it is this number that is displayed on the screen. Before moving on, you might want to try giving **length** other values and watching the results.

Using an Operator

Like most other computer languages, C+ supports a full range of arithmetic operators that enable you to manipulate numeric values used in a program. They include those shown here:

+	Addition
–	Subtraction
*	Multiplication
/	Division

These operators work in C++ just like they do in algebra.

The following program uses the * operator to compute the area of a rectangle given its length and the width.

```
// Using an operator.

#include <iostream>
using namespace std;

int main()
{
  int length; // this declares a variable
  int width;  // this declares another variable
  int area;   // this does, too

  length = 7; // this assigns 7 to length
  width = 5;  // this assigns 5 to width
```

```
   area = length * width; // compute area
```

Assign the product of **length** and **width** to **area**.

```
   cout << "The area is ";
   cout << area; // This displays 35

   return 0;
}
```

This program declares three variables: **length**, **width**, and **area**. It assigns the value 7 to **length** and the value 5 to **width**. It then computes the product and assigns that value to **area**. The program outputs the following:

```
The area is 35
```

In this program, there is actually no need for the variable **area**. For example, the program can be rewritten like this:

```
// A simplified version of the area program.

#include <iostream>
using namespace std;

int main()
{
  int length; // this declares a variable
  int width;  // this declares another variable

  length = 7; // this assigns 7 to length
  width = 5;  // this assigns 5 to width

  cout << "The area is ";
  cout << length * width; // This displays 35

  return 0;
}
```

Output **length * width** directly.

In this version, the area is computed in the **cout** statement by multiplying **length** by **width**. The result is then output to the screen.

One more point before we move on: It is possible to declare two or more variables using the same declaration statement. Just separate their names by commas. For example, **length**, **width**, and **area** could have been declared like this:

```
int length, width, area; // all declared using one statement
```

Declaring two or more variables in a single statement is very common in professionally written C++ code.

1-Minute Drill

- Must a variable be declared before it is used?
- Show how to assign the variable **min** the value 0.
- Can more than one variable be declared in a single declaration statement?

Reading Input from the Keyboard

The preceding examples have operated on data explicitly specified in the program. For example, the area program just shown computes the area of a rectangle that is 7 by 5, and these dimensions are part of the program itself. Of course, the calculation of a rectangle's area is the same no matter what its size, so the program would be much more useful if it would prompt the user for the dimensions of the rectangle, allowing the user to enter them using the keyboard.

To enable the user to enter data into a program from the keyboard, you will use the >> operator. This is the C++ input operator. To read from the keyboard, use this general form

cin >> *var*;

Here, **cin** is another predefined identifier. It stands for *console input* and is automatically supplied by C++. By default, **cin** is linked to the keyboard, although it can be redirected to other devices. The variable that receives input is specified by *var*.

- Yes, in C++ variables must be declared before they are used.
- `min = 0;`
- Yes, two or more variables can be declared in a single declaration statement.

Here is the area program rewritten to allow the user to enter the dimensions of the rectangle:

```
/*
   An interactive program that computes
   the area of a rectangle.
*/

#include <iostream>
using namespace std;

int main()
{
  int length; // this declares a variable
  int width;  // this declares another variable

  cout << "Enter the length: ";
  cin >> length; // input the length

  cout << "Enter the width: ";
  cin >> width;  // input the width

  cout << "The area is ";
  cout << length * width; // display the area

  return 0;
}
```

> Input the value of **length** from the keyboard.

> Input the value of **width** from the keyboard.

Here is a sample run:

```
Enter the length: 8
Enter the width: 3
The area is 24
```

Pay special attention to these lines:

```
cout << "Enter the length: ";
cin >> length; // input the length
```

The **cout** statement prompts the user. The **cin** statement reads the user's response, storing the value in **length**. Thus, the value entered by the user (which must be an integer in this case) is put into the variable that is on the right side of the **>>** (in this case, **length**). Thus, after the **cin** statement executes, **length** will contain the rectangle's length. (If the user enters a nonnumeric response, **length** will be zero.) The statements that prompt and read the width work in the same way.

Some Output Options

So far, we have been using the simplest types of **cout** statements. However, **cout** allows much more sophisticated output statements. Here are two useful techniques. First, you can output more than one piece of information using a single **cout** statement. For example, in the area program, these two lines are used to display the area:

```
cout << "The area is ";
cout << length * width; // This displays 35
```

These two statements can be more conveniently coded, as shown here:

```
cout << "The area is " << length * width;
```

This approach uses two output operators within the same **cout** statement. Specifically, it outputs the string "The area is" followed by the area. In general, you can chain together as many output operations as you like within one output statement. Just use a separate **<<** for each item.

Second, up to this point, there has been no occasion to advance output to the next line—that is, to execute a carriage return–linefeed sequence. However, the need for this will arise very soon. In C++, the carriage return–linefeed sequence is generated using the *newline* character. To put a newline character into a string, use this code: \n (a backslash followed by a lowercase *n*). To see the effect of the \n, try the following program:

```
/*
   This program demonstrates the \n code, which
   generates a new line.
*/
#include <iostream>
using namespace std;
```

1

```cpp
int main()
{
  cout << "one\n";
  cout << "two\n";
  cout << "three";
  cout << "four";

  return 0;
}
```

This program produces the following output:

```
one
two
threefour
```

The newline character can be placed anywhere in the string, not just at the end. You might want to try experimenting with the newline character now, just to make sure you understand exactly what it does.

1-Minute Drill

- What is C++'s input operator?
- To what device is **cin** linked by default?
- What does **\n** stand for?

Another Data Type

In the preceding programs, variables of type **int** were used. However, a variable of type **int** can hold only whole numbers. Thus, it cannot be used when a fractional component is required. For example, an **int** variable can hold the value 18, but not the value 18.3. Fortunately, **int** is only one of several data types defined by C++. To allow numbers with fractional components, C++ defines two main flavors of floating-point types: **float** and **double**, which

---

- The input operator is >>.
- **cin** is linked to the keyboard by default.
- The **\n** stands for the newline character.

represent single- and double-precision values, respectively. Of the two, **double** is probably the most commonly used.

To declare a variable of type **double**, use a statement similar to that shown here:

```
double result;
```

Here, **result** is the name of the variable, which is of type **double**. Because **result** has a floating-point type, it can hold values such as 88.56, 0.034, or –107.03.

To better understand the difference between **int** and **double**, try the following program:

```
/*
   This program illustrates the differences
   between int and double.
*/

#include <iostream>
using namespace std;

int main() {
  int ivar;    // this declares an int variable
  double dvar; // this declares a floating-point variable

  ivar = 100; // assign ivar the value 100

  dvar = 100.0; // assign dvar the value 100.0

  cout << "Original value of ivar: " << ivar << "\n";
  cout << "Original value of dvar: " << dvar << "\n";

  cout << "\n"; // print a blank line
```

Output a blank line.

```
  // now, divide both by 3
  ivar = ivar / 3;
  dvar = dvar / 3.0;

  cout << "ivar after division: " << ivar << "\n";
  cout << "dvar after division: " << dvar << "\n";

  return 0;
}
```

The output from this program is shown here:

```
Original value of ivar: 100
Original value of dvar: 100

ivar after division: 33
dvar after division: 33.3333
```

As you can see, when **ivar** is divided by 3, a whole-number division is performed and the outcome is 33—the fractional component is lost. However, when **dvar** is divided by 3, the fractional component is preserved.

There is one other new thing in the program. Notice this line:

```
cout << "\n"; // print a blank line
```

It outputs a newline. Use this statement whenever you want to add a blank line to your output.

Ask the Expert

Question: Why does C++ have different data types for integers and floating-point values? That is, why aren't all numeric values just the same type?

Answer: C++ supplies different data types so that you can write efficient programs. For example, integer arithmetic is faster than floating-point calculations. Thus, if you don't need fractional values, then you don't need to incur the overhead associated with types **float** or **double**. Also, the amount of memory required for one type of data might be less than that required for another. By supplying different types, C++ enables you to make the best use of system resources. Finally, some algorithms require (or at least benefit from) the use of a specific type of data. C++ supplies a number of built-in types to give you the greatest flexibility.

FtoM.cpp

Project 1-1: Converting Feet to Meters

Although the preceding sample programs illustrate several important features of the C++ language, they are not very useful. You may not know much about C++ at this point, but you can still put what you have learned to work to create a practical program. In this project, we will create a program that converts feet to meters. The program prompts the user for the number of feet. It then displays that value converted into meters.

A meter is equal to approximately 3.28 feet. Thus, we need to use floating-point data. To perform the conversion, the program declares two **double** variables. One will hold the number of feet, and the second will hold the conversion to meters.

Step-by-Step

1. Create a new C++ file called **FtoM.cpp**. (Remember, in C++ the name of the file is arbitrary, so you can use another name if you like.)

2. Begin the program with these lines, which explain what the program does, include the **<iostream>** header, and specify the **std** namespace.

```
/*
   Project 1-1

   This program converts feet to meters.

   Call this program FtoM.cpp.
*/

#include <iostream>
using namespace std;
```

3. Begin **main( )** by declaring the variables **f** and **m**:

```
int main() {
  double f; // holds the length in feet
  double m; // holds the conversion to meters
```

4. Add the code that inputs the number of feet:

```
cout << "Enter the length in feet: ";
cin >> f; // read the number of feet
```

5. Add the code that performs the conversion and displays the result:

```
m = f / 3.28; // convert to meters
cout << f << " feet is " << m << " meters.";
```

6. Conclude the program, as shown here:

```
   return 0;
}
```

7. Your finished program should look like this:

```
/*
   Project 1-1

   This program converts feet to meters.

   Call this program FtoM.cpp.
*/

#include <iostream>
using namespace std;

int main() {
  double f; // holds the length in feet
  double m; // holds the conversion to meters

  cout << "Enter the length in feet: ";
  cin >> f; // read the number of feet

  m = f / 3.28; // convert to meters
  cout << f << " feet is " << m << " meters.";

  return 0;
}
```

8. Compile and run the program. Here is a sample run:

```
Enter the length in feet: 5
5 feet is 1.52439 meters.
```

9. Try entering other values. Also, try changing the program so that it converts meters to feet.

1-Minute Drill

● What is C++'s keyword for the integer data type?

● What is **double**?

● How do you output a newline?

Two Control Statements

Inside a function, execution proceeds from one statement to the next, top to bottom. It is possible, however, to alter this flow through the use of the various *program control statements* supported by C++. Although we will look closely at control statements later, two are briefly introduced here because we will be using them to write sample programs.

The if Statement

You can selectively execute part of a program through the use of C++'s conditional statement: the **if**. The **if** statement works in C++ much like the IF statement in any other language. For example, it is syntactically identical to the **if** statements in C, Java, and C#. Its simplest form is shown here:

if(*condition*) *statement*;

where *condition* is an expression that is evaluated to be either true or false. In C++, true is nonzero and false is zero. If the condition is true, then the statement will execute. If it is false, then the statement will not execute. For example, the following fragment displays the phrase **10 is less than 11** on the screen because 10 is less than 11.

```
if(10 < 11) cout << "10 is less than 11";
```

However, consider the following:

```
if(10 > 11) cout << "this does not display";
```

● The integer data type is **int**.
● **double** is the keyword for the double floating-point data type.
● To output a newline, use **\n**.

In this case, 10 is not greater than 11, so the **cout** statement is not executed. Of course, the operands inside an **if** statement need not be constants. They can also be variables.

C++ defines a full complement of relational operators that can be used in a conditional expression. They are shown here:

Operator	Meaning
<	Less than
<=	Less than or equal
>	Greater than
>=	Greater than or equal
==	Equal to
!=	Not equal

Notice that the test for equality is the double equal sign.

Here is a program that illustrates the **if** statement:

```
// Demonstrate the if.

#include <iostream>
using namespace std;

int main() {
  int a, b, c;

  a = 2;
  b = 3;

  if(a < b) cout << "a is less than b\n";     ⬅ An if statement.

  // this won't display anything
  if(a == b) cout << "you won't see this\n";

  cout << "\n";

  c = a - b; // c contains -1

  cout << "c contains -1\n";
  if(c >= 0) cout << "c is non-negative\n";
  if(c < 0) cout << "c is negative\n";
```

```
cout << "\n";

c = b - a; // c now contains 1
cout << "c contains 1\n";
if(c >= 0) cout << "c is non-negative\n";
if(c < 0) cout << "c is negative\n";

return 0;
}
```

The output generated by this program is shown here:

```
a is less than b

c contains -1
c is negative

c contains 1
c is non-negative
```

The for Loop

You can repeatedly execute a sequence of code by creating a *loop*. C++ supplies a powerful assortment of loop constructs. The one we will look at here is the **for** loop. If you are familiar with C# or Java, then you will be pleased to know that the **for** loop in C++ works the same way it does in those languages. The simplest form of the **for** loop is shown here:

for(*initialization; condition; increment*) *statement;*

Here, *initialization* sets a loop control variable to an initial value. *condition* is an expression that is tested each time the loop repeats. As long as *condition* is true (nonzero), the loop keeps running. The *increment* is an expression that determines how the loop control variable is incremented each time the loop repeats.

The following program demonstrates the **for**. It prints the numbers 1 through 100 on the screen.

```
// A program that illustrates the for loop.

#include <iostream>
using namespace std;

int main()
{                        This is a for loop.
  int count;

  for(count=1; count <= 100; count=count+1)
    cout << count << " ";

  return 0;
}
```

In the program, **count** is initialized to 1. Each time the loop repeats, the condition

```
count <= 100
```

is tested. If it is true, the value is output and **count** is increased by one. When **count** reaches a value greater than 100, the condition becomes false, and the loop stops running.

In professionally written C++ code, you will almost never see a statement like

```
count=count+1
```

because C++ includes a special increment operator that performs this operation more efficiently. The increment operator is **++** (two consecutive plus signs). The **++** operator increases its operand by 1. For example, the preceding **for** statement will generally be written like this:

```
for(count=1; count <= 100; count++)
  cout << count << " ";
```

This is the form that will be used throughout the rest of this book.

C++ also provides a decrement operator, which is specified as − −. It decreases its operand by 1.

1-Minute Drill

● What does the **if** statement do?

● What does the **for** statement do?

● What are C++'s relational operators?

Using Blocks of Code

Another key element of C++ is the *code block*. A code block is a grouping of two or more statements. This is done by enclosing the statements between opening and closing curly braces. Once a block of code has been created, it becomes a logical unit that can be used any place that a single statement can. For example, a block can be a target for **if** and **for** statements. Consider this **if** statement:

```
if(w < h) {
  v = w * h;
  w = 0;
}
```

Here, if **w** is less than **h**, then both statements inside the block will be executed. Thus, the two statements inside the block form a logical unit, and one statement cannot execute without the other also executing. The key point here is that whenever you need to logically link two or more statements, you do so by creating a block. Code blocks allow many algorithms to be implemented with greater clarity and efficiency.

Here is a program that uses a block of code to prevent a division by zero:

```
// Demonstrate a block of code.

#include <iostream>
using namespace std;

int main() {
  double result, n, d;
```

● **if** is C++'s conditional statement.
● The **for** is one of C++'s loop statements.
● The relational operators are ==, !=, <, >, <=, and >=.

```
   cout << "Enter value: ";
   cin >> n;

   cout << "Enter divisor: ";
   cin >> d;

   // the target of this if is a block
   if(d != 0) {
      cout << "d does not equal zero so division is OK" << "\n";
      result = n / d;
      cout << n << " / " << d << " is " << result;
   }

   return 0;
}
```

> The target of this **if** is the entire block.

Here is a sample run:

```
Enter value: 10
Enter divisor: 2
d does not equal zero so division is OK
10 / 2 is 5
```

In this case, the target of the **if** statement is a block of code and not just a single statement. If the condition controlling the **if** is true (as it is in the sample run), the three statements inside the block will be executed. Try entering a zero for the divisor and observe the result. In this case, the code inside the block is bypassed.

Ask the Expert

Question: Does the use of a code block introduce any runtime inefficiencies? In other words, do the { and } consume any extra time during the execution of my program?

Answer: No. Code blocks do not add any overhead whatsoever. In fact, because of their ability to simplify the coding of certain algorithms, their use generally increases speed and efficiency.

As you will see later in this book, blocks of code have additional properties and uses. However, the main reason for their existence is to create logically inseparable units of code.

Semicolons and Positioning

In C++, the semicolon signals the end of a statement. That is, each individual statement must end with a semicolon. As you know, a block is a set of logically connected statements that is surrounded by opening and closing braces. A block is *not* terminated with a semicolon. Since a block is a group of statements, with a semicolon after each statement, it makes sense that a block is not terminated by a semicolon; instead, the end of the block is indicated by the closing brace.

C++ does not recognize the end of the line as the end of a statement—only a semicolon terminates a statement. For this reason, it does not matter where on a line you put a statement. For example, to C++

```
x = y;
y = y + 1;
cout << x << " " << y;
```

is the same as

```
x = y;  y = y + 1;  cout << x << " " << y;
```

Furthermore, the individual elements of a statement can also be put on separate lines. For example, the following is perfectly acceptable:

```
cout << "This is a long line.  The sum is : " << a + b + c +
        d + e + f;
```

Breaking long lines in this fashion is often used to make programs more readable. It can also help prevent excessively long lines from wrapping.

Indentation Practices

You may have noticed in the previous examples that certain statements were indented. C++ is a free-form language, meaning that it does not matter where you place statements relative to each other on a line. However, over the years,

1

a common and accepted indentation style has developed that allows for very readable programs. This book follows that style, and it is recommended that you do so as well. Using this style, you indent one level after each opening brace and move back out one level after each closing brace. There are certain statements that encourage some additional indenting; these will be covered later.

1-Minute Drill

● How is a block of code created? What does it do?

● In C++, statements are terminated by a _____.

● All C++ statements must start and end on one line. True or false?

FtoMTable.cpp

Project 1-2: Generating a Table of Feet to Meter Conversions

This project demonstrates the **for** loop, the **if** statement, and code blocks to create a program that displays a table of feet-to-meters conversions. The table begins with 1 foot and ends at 100 feet. After every 10 feet, a blank line is output. This is accomplished through the use of a variable called **counter** that counts the number of lines that have been output. Pay special attention to its use.

Step-by-Step

1. Create a new file called **FtoMTable.cpp**.

2. Enter the following program into the file:

```
/*
    Project 1-2

    This program displays a conversion table of feet to meters.

    Call this program FtoMTable.cpp.
*/
```

● A block is started by a {. It is ended by a }. A block creates a logical unit of code.
● semicolon
● False.

```
#include <iostream>
using namespace std;

int main() {
  double f; // holds the length in feet
  double m; // holds the conversion to meters
  int counter;

  counter = 0;
```
Line counter is initially set to zero.

```
  for(f = 1.0; f <= 100.0; f++) {
    m = f / 3.28; // convert to meters
    cout << f << " feet is " << m << " meters.\n";

    counter++;
```
Increment the line counter with each loop iteration.

```
    // every 10th line, print a blank line
    if(counter == 10) {
```
If **counter** is 10, output a blank line.

```
      cout << "\n"; // output a blank line
      counter = 0; // reset the line counter
    }
  }

  return 0;
}
```

3. Notice how **counter** is used to output a blank line after each ten lines. It is initially set to zero outside the **for** loop. Inside the loop, it is incremented after each conversion. When **counter** equals 10, a blank line is output, **counter** is reset to zero, and the process repeats.

4. Compile and run the program. Here is a portion of the output that you will see. Notice that results that don't produce an even result include a fractional component.

```
1 feet is 0.304878 meters.
2 feet is 0.609756 meters.
3 feet is 0.914634 meters.
4 feet is 1.21951 meters.
5 feet is 1.52439 meters.
6 feet is 1.82927 meters.
7 feet is 2.13415 meters.
8 feet is 2.43902 meters.
9 feet is 2.7439 meters.
10 feet is 3.04878 meters.
```

```
11 feet is 3.35366 meters.
12 feet is 3.65854 meters.
13 feet is 3.96341 meters.
14 feet is 4.26829 meters.
15 feet is 4.57317 meters.
16 feet is 4.87805 meters.
17 feet is 5.18293 meters.
18 feet is 5.4878 meters.
19 feet is 5.79268 meters.
20 feet is 6.09756 meters.

21 feet is 6.40244 meters.
22 feet is 6.70732 meters.
23 feet is 7.0122 meters.
24 feet is 7.31707 meters.
25 feet is 7.62195 meters.
26 feet is 7.92683 meters.
27 feet is 8.23171 meters.
28 feet is 8.53659 meters.
29 feet is 8.84146 meters.
30 feet is 9.14634 meters.

31 feet is 9.45122 meters.
32 feet is 9.7561 meters.
33 feet is 10.061 meters.
34 feet is 10.3659 meters.
35 feet is 10.6707 meters.
36 feet is 10.9756 meters.
37 feet is 11.2805 meters.
38 feet is 11.5854 meters.
39 feet is 11.8902 meters.
40 feet is 12.1951 meters.
```

5. On your own, try changing this program so that it prints a blank line every
25 lines.

Introducing Functions

A C++ program is constructed from building blocks called *functions*. Although
we will look at the function in detail in Module 5, a brief overview is useful
now. Let's begin by defining the term *function*: a function is a subroutine that
contains one or more C++ statements.

Each function has a name, and this name is used to call the function. To call a function, simply specify its name in the source code of your program, followed by parentheses. For example, assume some function named **MyFunc**. To call **MyFunc**, you would write

```
MyFunc();
```

When a function is called, program control is transferred to that function, and the code contained within the function is executed. When the function's code ends, control is transferred back to the caller. Thus, a function performs a task for other parts of a program.

Some functions require one or more *arguments,* which you pass when the function is called. Thus, an argument is a value passed to a function. Arguments are specified between the opening and closing parentheses when a function is called. For example, if **MyFunc( )** requires an integer argument, then the following calls **MyFunc( )** with the value 2:

```
MyFunc(2);
```

When there are two or more arguments, they are separated by commas. In this book, the term *argument list* will refer to comma-separated arguments. Remember, not all functions require arguments. When no argument is needed, the parentheses are empty.

A function can return a value to the calling code. Not all functions return values, but many do. The value returned by a function can be assigned to a variable in the calling code by placing the call to the function on the right side of an assignment statement. For example, if **MyFunc( )** returned a value, it could be called as follows:

```
x = MyFunc(2);
```

This statement works as follows. First, **MyFunc( )** is called. When it returns, its return value is assigned to **x**. You can also use a call to a function in an expression. For example,

```
x = MyFunc(2) + 10;
```

In this case, the return value from **MyFunc( )** is added to 10, and the result is assigned to **x**. In general, whenever a function's name is encountered in a statement, it is automatically called so that its return value can be obtained.

To review: an *argument* is a value passed into a function. A *return value* is data that is passed back to the calling code.

Here is a short program that demonstrates how to call a function. It uses one of C++'s built-in functions, called **abs( )**, to display the absolute value of a number. The **abs( )** function takes one argument, converts it into its absolute value, and returns the result.

```
// Use the abs() function.

#include <iostream>
#include <cstdlib>
using namespace std;

int main()
{
  int result;

  result = abs(-10);      This calls the abs( )
                          function and assigns its
                          return value to result.

  cout << result;

  return 0;
}
```

Here, the value –10 is passed as an argument to **abs( )**. The **abs( )** function receives the argument with which it is called and returns its absolute value, which is 10 in this case. This value is assigned to **result**. Thus, the program displays "10" on the screen.

Notice one other thing about the preceding program: it includes the header **<cstdlib>**. This is the header required by **abs( )**. Whenever you use a library function, you must include its header.

In general, there are two types of functions that will be used by your programs. The first type is written by you, and **main( )** is an example of this type of function. Later, you will learn how to write other functions of your own. As you will see, real-world C++ programs contain many user-written functions.

The second type of function is provided by the compiler. The **abs( )** function used by the preceding program is an example. Programs that you write will generally contain a mix of functions that you create and those supplied by the compiler.

When denoting functions in text, this book has used and will continue to use a convention that has become common when writing about C++. A function will have parentheses after its name. For example, if a function's name is **getval**, then it will be written **getval( )** when its name is used in a sentence. This notation will help you distinguish variable names from function names in this book.

The C++ Libraries

As just explained, **abs( )** is provided with your C++ compiler. This function and many others are found in the *standard library*. We will be making use of library functions in the example programs throughout this book.

C++ defines a large set of functions that are contained in the standard function library. These functions perform many commonly needed tasks, including I/O operations, mathematical computations, and string handling. When you use a library function, the C++ compiler automatically links the object code for that function to the object code of your program.

Because the C++ standard library is so large, it already contains many of the functions that you will need to use in your programs. The library functions act as building blocks that you simply assemble. You should explore your compiler's library documentation. You may be surprised at how varied the library functions are. If you write a function that you will use again and again, it too can be stored in a library.

In addition to providing library functions, every C++ compiler also contains a *class library,* which is an object-oriented library. However, you will need to wait until you learn about classes and objects before you can make use of the class library.

1-Minute Drill

● What is a function?

● A function is called by using its name. True or false?

● What is the C++ standard function library?

● A function is a subroutine that contains one or more C++ statements.
● True.
● The C++ standard function library is a collection of functions supplied by all C++ compilers.

The C++ Keywords

There are 63 keywords currently defined for Standard C++. These are shown in Table 1-1. Together with the formal C++ syntax, they form the C++ programming language. Also, early versions of C++ defined the **overload** keyword, but it is obsolete. Keep in mind that C++ is a case-sensitive language, and it requires that all keywords be in lowercase.

Identifiers

In C++, an *identifier* is a name assigned to a function, variable, or any other user-defined item. Identifiers can be from one to several characters long. Variable names can start with any letter of the alphabet or an underscore. Next comes a letter, a digit, or an underscore. The underscore can be used to enhance the readability of a variable name, as in **line_count**. Uppercase

asm	auto	bool	break
case	catch	char	class
const	const_cast	continue	default
delete	do	double	dynamic_cast
else	enum	explicit	export
extern	false	float	for
friend	goto	if	inline
int	long	mutable	namespace
new	operator	private	protected
public	register	reinterpret_cast	return
short	signed	sizeof	static
static_cast	struct	switch	template
this	throw	true	try
typedef	typeid	typename	union
unsigned	using	virtual	void
volatile	wchar_t	while	

Table 1-1 The C++ Keywords

and lowercase are seen as different; that is, to C++, **myvar** and **MyVar** are separate names. There is one important identifier restriction: you cannot use any of the C++ keywords as identifier names. In addition, predefined identifiers such as **cout** are also off limits.

Here are some examples of valid identifiers:

Test	x	y2	MaxIncr
up	_top	my_var	simpleInterest23

Remember, you cannot start an identifier with a digit. Thus, **98OK** is invalid. Good programming practice dictates that you use identifier names that reflect the meaning or usage of the items being named.

1-Minute Drill

● Which is the keyword, **for**, **For**, or **FOR**?

● A C++ identifier can contain what type of characters?

● Are **index21** and **Index21** the same identifier?

● The keyword is **for**. In C++, all keywords are in lowercase.
● A C++ identifier can contain letters, digits, and the underscore.
● No, C++ is case sensitive.

☑ *Mastery Check*

1. It has been said that C++ sits at the center of the modern programming universe. Explain this statement.

2. A C++ compiler produces object code that is directly executed by the computer. True or false?

3. What are the three main principles of object-oriented programming?

4. Where do C++ programs begin execution?

5. What is a header?

6. What is **<iostream>**? What does the following code do?

   ```
   #include <iostream>
   ```

7. What is a namespace?

8. What is a variable?

9. Which of the following variable names is/are invalid?

   a. count

   b. _count

   c. count27

   d. 67count

   e. if

10. How do you create a single-line comment? How do you create a multiline comment?

11. Show the general form of the **if** statement. Show the general form of the **for** loop.

12. How do you create a block of code?

13. The moon's gravity is about 17 percent that of Earth's. Write a program that displays a table that shows Earth pounds and their equivalent moon weight. Have the table run from 1 to 100 pounds. Output a newline every 25 pounds.

☑ Mastery Check

14. A year on Jupiter (the time it takes for Jupiter to make one full circuit around the Sun) takes about 12 Earth years. Write a program that converts Jovian years to Earth years. Have the user specify the number of Jovian years. Allow fractional years.

15. When a function is called, what happens to program control?

16. Write a program that averages the absolute value of five values entered by the user. Display the result.

Module 2

Introducing Data Types and Operators

The Goals of This Module

- Learn the C++ data types
- Know the type modifiers
- Use literals
- Create initialized variables
- Reexamine the arithmetic operators
- Learn the relational and logical operators
- Explore the assignment operator
- Use compound assignments
- Understand type conversion in assignments
- Understand type conversion in expressions
- Use the cast

At the core of a programming language are its data types and operators. These elements define the limits of a language and determine the kind of tasks to which it can be applied. As you might expect, C++ supports a rich assortment of both data types and operators, making it suitable for a wide range of programming.

Data types and operators are a large subject. We will begin here with an examination of C++'s foundational data types and its most commonly used operators. We will also take a closer look at variables and examine the expression.

Why Data Types Are Important

The data type of a variable is important because it determines the operations that are allowed and the range of values that can be stored. C++ defines several types of data, and each type has unique characteristics. Because data types differ, all variables must be declared prior to their use, and a variable declaration always includes a type specifier. The compiler requires this information in order to generate correct code. In C++ there is no concept of a "type-less" variable.

A second reason that data types are important to C++ programming is that several of the basic types are closely tied to the building blocks upon which the computer operates: bytes and words. Thus, C++ lets you operate on the same types of data as does the CPU itself. This is one of the ways that C++ enables you to write very efficient, system-level code.

The C++ Data Types

C++ provides built-in data types that correspond to integers, characters, floating-point values, and Boolean values. These are the ways that data is commonly stored and manipulated by a program. As you will see later in this book, C++ allows you to construct more sophisticated types, such as classes, structures, and enumerations, but these too are ultimately composed of the built-in types.

At the core of the C++ type system are the seven basic data types shown here:

Type	Meaning
char	Character
wchar_t	Wide character
int	Integer

Type	Meaning
float	Floating point
double	Double floating point
bool	Boolean
void	Valueless

C++ allows certain of the basic types to have modifiers preceding them. A modifier alters the meaning of the base type so that it more precisely fits the needs of various situations. The data type modifiers are listed here:

signed
unsigned
long
short

The modifiers **signed**, **unsigned**, **long**, and **short** can be applied to **int**. The modifiers **signed** and **unsigned** can be applied to the **char** type. The type **double** can be modified by **long**. Table 2-1 shows all valid combinations of the basic types and the type modifiers. The table also shows the guaranteed minimum range for each type as specified by the ANSI/ISO C++ standard.

Type	Minimal Range
char	−127 to 127
unsigned char	0 to 255
signed char	−127 to 127
int	−32,767 to 32,767
unsigned int	0 to 65,535
signed int	Same as **int**
short int	−32,767 to 32,767
unsigned short int	0 to 65,535
signed short int	Same as **short int**
long int	−2,147,483,647 to 2,147,483,647
signed long int	Same as **long int**
unsigned long int	0 to 4,294,967,295
float	1E−37 to 1E+37, with six digits of precision
double	1E−37 to 1E+37, with ten digits of precision
long double	1E−37 to 1E+37, with ten digits of precision

Table 2-1   All Numeric Data Types Defined by C++ and Their Minimum Guaranteed Ranges as Specified by the ANSI/ISO C++ Standard

It is important to understand that minimum ranges shown in Table 2-1 are just that: *minimum* ranges. A C++ compiler is free to exceed one or more of these minimums, and most compilers do. Thus, the ranges of the C++ data types are implementation dependent. For example, on computers that use two's complement arithmetic (which is nearly all), an integer will have a range of at least −32,768 to 32,767. In all cases, however, the range of a **short int** will be a subrange of an **int**, which will be a subrange of a **long int**. The same applies to **float**, **double**, and **long double**. In this usage, the term *subrange* means a range narrower than or equal to. Thus, an **int** and **long int** can have the same range, but an **int** cannot be larger than a **long int**.

Since C++ specifies only the minimum range a data type must support, you should check your compiler's documentation for the actual ranges supported. For example, Table 2-2 shows typical bit widths and ranges for the C++ data types in a 32-bit environment, such as that used by Windows 2000.

Let's now take a closer look at each data type.

Type	Bit Width	Typical Range
char	8	−128 to 127
unsigned char	8	0 to 255
signed char	8	−128 to 127
int	32	−2,147,483,648 to 2,147,483,647
unsigned int	32	−2,147,483,648 to 2,147,483,647
signed int	32	0 to 4,294,967,295
short int	16	−32,768 to 32,767
unsigned short int	16	−32,768 to 32,767
signed short int	16	0 to 65,535
long int	32	Same as **int**
signed long int	32	Same as **signed int**
unsigned long int	32	Same as **unsigned int**
float	32	1.8E−38 to 3.4E+38
double	32	2.2E−308 to 1.8E+308
long double	64	2.2E−308 to 1.8E+308
bool	N/A	True or false
wchar_t	16	0 to 65,535

Table 2-2   Typical Bit Widths and Ranges for the C++ Data Types in a 32-Bit Environment

Integers

As you learned in Module 1, variables of type **int** hold integer quantities that do not require fractional components. Variables of this type are often used for controlling loops and conditional statements, and for counting. Because they don't have fractional components, operations on **int** quantities are much faster than they are on floating-point types.

Because integers are so important to programming, C++ defines several varieties. As shown in Table 2-1, there are short, regular, and long integers. Furthermore, there are signed and unsigned versions of each. A signed integer can hold both positive and negative values. By default, integers are signed. Thus, the use of **signed** on integers is redundant (but allowed) because the default declaration assumes a signed value. An unsigned integer can hold only positive values. To create an unsigned integer, use the **unsigned** modifier.

The difference between signed and unsigned integers is in the way the high-order bit of the integer is interpreted. If a signed integer is specified, then the C++ compiler will generate code that assumes that the high-order bit of an integer is to be used as a *sign flag*. If the sign flag is 0, then the number is positive; if it is 1, then the number is negative. Negative numbers are almost always represented using the *two's complement* approach. In this method, all bits in the number (except the sign flag) are reversed, and then 1 is added to this number. Finally, the sign flag is set to 1.

Signed integers are important for a great many algorithms, but they have only half the absolute magnitude of their unsigned relatives. For example, assuming a 16-bit integer, here is 32,767:

    0 1 1 1 1 1 1 1   1 1 1 1 1 1 1 1

For a signed value, if the high-order bit were set to 1, the number would then be interpreted as −1 (assuming the two's complement format). However, if you declared this to be an **unsigned int**, then when the high-order bit was set to 1, the number would become 65,535.

To understand the difference between the way that signed and unsigned integers are interpreted by C++, try this short program:

```
#include <iostream>
/* This program shows the difference between
   signed and unsigned integers. */

using namespace std;
```

```
int main()
{
  short int i; // a signed short integer
  short unsigned int j; // an unsigned short integer

  j = 60000;
  i = j;
  cout << i << " " << j;

  return 0;
}
```

> 60,000 is within the range of an **unsigned short int**, but is typically outside the range of a **signed short int**. Thus, it will be interpreted as a negative value when assigned to **i**.

The output from this program is shown here:

```
-5536 60000
```

These values are displayed because the bit pattern that represents 60,000 as a short unsigned integer is interpreted as –5,536 as short signed integer (assuming 16-bit short integers).

C++ allows a shorthand notation for declaring **unsigned**, **short**, or **long** integers. You can simply use the word **unsigned**, **short**, or **long**, without the **int**. The **int** is implied. For example, the following two statements both declare unsigned integer variables:

```
unsigned x;
unsigned int y;
```

Characters

Variables of type **char** hold 8-bit ASCII characters such as A, z, or G, or any other 8-bit quantity. To specify a character, you must enclose it between single quotes. Thus, this assigns X to the variable **ch**:

```
char ch;
ch = 'X';
```

You can output a **char** value using a **cout** statement. For example, this line outputs the value in **ch**:

```
cout << "This is ch: " << ch;
```

This results in the following output:

```
This is ch: X
```

The **char** type can be modified with **signed** or **unsigned**. Technically, whether **char** is signed or unsigned by default is implementation-defined. However, for most compilers **char** is signed. In these environments, the use of **signed** on **char** is also redundant. For the rest of this book, it will be assumed that **char**s are signed entities.

The type **char** can hold values other than just the ASCII character set. It can also be used as a "small" integer with the range typically from −128 through 127 and can be substituted for an **int** when the situation does not require larger numbers. For example, the following program uses a **char** variable to control the loop that prints the alphabet on the screen:

```
// This program displays the alphabet.

#include <iostream>
using namespace std;

int main()
{
  char letter;

  for(letter = 'A'; letter <= 'Z'; letter++)
    cout << letter;

  return 0;
}
```

Use a **char** variable to control a **for** loop.

The **for** loop works because the character A is represented inside the computer by the value 65, and the values for the letters A to Z are in sequential, ascending order. Thus, **letter** is initially set to 'A'. Each time through the loop, **letter** is incremented. Thus, after the first iteration, **letter** is equal to 'B'.

The type **wchar_t** holds characters that are part of large character sets. As you may know, many human languages, such as Chinese, define a large number of characters, more than will fit within the 8 bits provided by the **char** type. The **wchar_t** type was added to C++ to accommodate this situation. While we won't be making use of **wchar_t** in this book, it is something that you will want to look into if you are tailoring programs for the international market.

Ask the Expert

Question: Why does C++ specify only minimum ranges for its built-in types rather than stating these precisely?

Answer: By not specifying precise ranges, C++ allows each compiler to optimize the data types for the execution environment. This is part of the reason that C++ can create high-performance software. The ANSI/ISO C++ standard simply states that the built-in types must meet certain requirements. For example, it states that an **int** will "have the natural size suggested by the architecture of the execution environment." Thus, in a 32-bit environment, an **int** will be 32 bits long. In a 16-bit environment, an **int** will be 16 bits long. It would be an inefficient and unnecessary burden to force a 16-bit compiler to implement **int** with a 32-bit range, for example. C++'s approach avoids this. Of course, the C++ standard does specify a minimum range for the built-in types that will be available in all environments. Thus, if you write your programs in such a way that these minimal ranges are not exceeded, then your program will be portable to other environments. One last point: Each C++ compiler specifies the range of the basic types in the header <climits>.

1-Minute Drill

● What are the seven basic types?

● What is the difference between signed and unsigned integers?

● Can a **char** variable be used like a little integer?

● **char**, **wchar_t**, **int**, **float**, **double**, **bool**, **void** are the seven basic types.
● A signed integer can hold both positive and negative values. An unsigned integer can hold only positive values.
● Yes.

Floating-Point Types

Variables of the types **float** and **double** are employed either when a fractional component is required or when your application requires very large or small numbers. The difference between a **float** and a **double** variable is the magnitude of the largest (and smallest) number that each one can hold. Typically, a **double** can store a number approximately ten times larger than a **float**.

Of the two, **double** is the most commonly used. One reason for this is that many of the math functions in the C++ function library use **double** values. For example, the **sqrt( )** function returns a **double** value that is the square root of its **double** argument. Here, **sqrt( )** is used to compute the length of the hypotenuse given the lengths of the two opposing sides.

```
/*
   Use the Pythagorean theorem to find
   the length of the hypotenuse given
   the lengths of the two opposing sides.
*/

#include <iostream>
#include <cmath>    ◄─────────────    The <cmath> header is needed
using namespace std;                  for the sqrt( ) function.

int main() {
  double x, y, z;

  x = 3;
  y = 4;

  z = sqrt(x*x + y*y);   ◄─────────    The sqrt( ) function is part
                                       of C++'s math library.
  cout << "Hypotenuse is " << z;

  return 0;
}
```

The output from the program is shown here:

```
Hypotenuse is 5
```

One other point about the preceding example: Because **sqrt( )** is part of the C++ standard function library, it requires the standard header **<cmath>**, which is included in the program.

The **long double** type lets you work with very large or small numbers. It is most useful in scientific programs. For example, the **long double** type might be useful when analyzing astronomical data.

The bool Type

The **bool** type is a relatively recent addition to C++. It stores Boolean (that is, true/false) values. C++ defines two Boolean constants, **true** and **false**, which are the only two values that a **bool** value can have.

Before continuing, it is important to understand how true and false are defined by C++. One of the fundamental concepts in C++ is that any nonzero value is interpreted as true and zero is false. This concept is fully compatible with the **bool** data type because when used in a Boolean expression, C++ automatically converts any nonzero value into **true**. It automatically converts zero into **false**. The reverse is also true; when used in a non-Boolean expression, **true** is converted into 1, and **false** is converted into zero. The convertibility of zero and nonzero values into their Boolean equivalents is especially important when using control statements, as you will see in Module 3.

Here is a program that demonstrates the **bool** type:

```
// Demonstrate bool values.

#include <iostream>
using namespace std;

int main() {
  bool b;

  b = false;
  cout << "b is " << b << "\n";

  b = true;
  cout << "b is " << b << "\n";

  // a bool value can control the if statement
  if(b) cout << "This is executed.\n";

  b = false;
  if(b) cout << "This is not executed.\n";
```

A single **bool** value can control an **if** statement.

```
// outcome of a relational operator is a true/false value
cout << "10 > 9 is " << (10 > 9) << "\n";

return 0;
}
```

The output generated by this program is shown here:

```
b is 0
b is 1
This is executed.
10 > 9 is 1
```

There are three interesting things to notice about this program. First, as you can see, when a **bool** value is output using **cout**, 0 or 1 is displayed. As you will see later in this book, there is an output option that causes the words "false" and "true" to be displayed.

Second, the value of a **bool** variable is sufficient, by itself, to control the **if** statement. There is no need to write an **if** statement like this:

```
if(b == true) ...
```

Third, the outcome of a relational operator, such as <, is a Boolean value. This is why the expression **10 > 9** displays the value 1. Further, the extra set of parentheses around **10 > 9** is necessary because the << operator has a higher precedence than the >.

void

The **void** type specifies a valueless expression. This probably seems strange now, but you will see how **void** is used later in this book.

1-Minute Drill

● What is the primary difference between **float** and **double**?

● What values can a **bool** variable have? To what Boolean value does zero convert?

● What is **void**?

● The primary difference between **float** and **double** is in the magnitude of the values they can hold.

● Variables of type **bool** can be either **true** or **false**. Zero converts to **false**.

● **void** is a type that stands for valueless.

Mars.cpp

Project 2-1: Talking to Mars

At its closest point to Earth, Mars is approximately 34,000,000 miles away. Assuming there is someone on Mars that you want to talk with, what is the delay between the time a radio signal leaves Earth and the time it arrives on Mars? This project creates a program that answers this question. Recall that radio signals travel at the speed of light, approximately 186,000 miles per second. Thus, to compute the delay, you will need to divide the distance by the speed of light. Display the delay in terms of seconds and also in minutes.

Step-by-Step

1. Create a new file called **Mars.cpp**.

2. To compute the delay, you will need to use floating-point values. Why? Because the time interval will have a fractional component. Here are the variables used by the program:

```
double distance;
double lightspeed;
double delay;
double delay_in_min;
```

3. Give **distance** and **lightspeed** initial values, as shown here:

```
distance = 34000000.0; // 34,000,000 miles
lightspeed = 186000.0; // 186,000 per second
```

4. To compute the delay, divide **distance** by **lightspeed**. This yields the delay in seconds. Assign this value to **delay** and display the results. These steps are shown here:

```
delay = distance / lightspeed;

cout << "Time delay when talking to Mars: " <<
        delay << " seconds.\n";
```

5. Divide the number of seconds in **delay** by 60 to obtain the delay in minutes; display that result using these lines of code:

```
delay_in_min = delay / 60.0;
```

6. Here is the entire **Mars.cpp** program listing:

```cpp
/*
    Project 2-1

    Talking to Mars
*/

#include <iostream>
using namespace std;

int main() {
  double distance;
  double lightspeed;
  double delay;
  double delay_in_min;

  distance = 34000000.0; // 34,000,000 miles
  lightspeed = 186000.0; // 186,000 per second

  delay = distance / lightspeed;

  cout <<  "Time delay when talking to Mars: " <<
          delay << " seconds.\n";

  delay_in_min = delay / 60.0;

  cout <<  "This is " << delay_in_min << " minutes.";

  return 0;
}
```

7. Compile and run the program. The following result is displayed:

```
Time delay when talking to Mars: 182.796 seconds.
This is 3.04659 minutes.
```

8. On your own, display the time delay that would occur in a bidirectional conversation with Mars.

Literals

Literals refer to fixed, human-readable values that cannot be altered by the program. For example, the value 101 is an integer literal. Literals are also commonly referred to as *constants*. For the most part, literals and their usage are so intuitive that they have been used in one form or another by all the preceding sample programs. Now the time has come to explain them formally.

C++ literals can be of any of the basic data types. The way each literal is represented depends upon its type. As explained earlier, *character* literals are enclosed between single quotes. For example, 'a' and '%' are both character literals.

Integer literals are specified as numbers without fractional components. For example, 10 and –100 are integer constants. *Floating-point* literals require the use of the decimal point followed by the number's fractional component. For example, 11.123 is a floating-point constant. C++ also allows you to use scientific notation for floating-point numbers.

All literal values have a data type, but this fact raises a question. As you know, there are several different types of integers, such as **int**, **short int**, and **unsigned long int**. There are also three different floating-point types: **float**, **double**, and **long double**. The question is: How does the compiler determine the type of a literal? For example, is 123.23 a **float** or a **double**? The answer to this question has two parts. First, the C++ compiler automatically makes certain assumptions about the type of a literal and, second, you can explicitly specify the type of a literal, if you like.

By default, the C++ compiler fits an integer literal into the smallest compatible data type that will hold it, beginning with **int**. Therefore, assuming 16-bit integers, 10 is **int** by default, but 103,000 is **long**. Even though the value 10 could be fit into a **char**, the compiler will not do this because it means crossing type boundaries.

By default, floating-point literals are assumed to be **double**. Thus, the value 123.23 is of type **double**.

For virtually all programs you will write as a beginner, the compiler defaults are perfectly adequate. In cases where the default assumption that C++ makes about a numeric literal is not what you want, C++ allows you to specify the exact type of numeric literal by using a suffix. For floating-point types, if you follow the number with an *F*, the number is treated as a **float**. If you follow it with an *L*, the number becomes a **long double**. For integer types, the *U* suffix stands for **unsigned** and the *L* for **long**. (Both the *U* and the *L* must be used to specify an **unsigned long**.) Some examples are shown here:

Data Type	Examples of Constants
int	1 123 21000 –234
long int	35000L –34L
unsigned int	10000U 987U 40000U
unsigned long	12323UL 900000UL
float	123.23F 4.34e–3F
double	23.23 123123.33 –0.9876324
long double	1001.2L

Hexadecimal and Octal Literals

As you probably know, in programming it is sometimes easier to use a number system based on 8 or 16 instead of 10. The number system based on 8 is called *octal*, and it uses the digits 0 through 7. In octal, the number 10 is the same as 8 in decimal. The base-16 number system is called *hexadecimal* and uses the digits 0 through 9 plus the letters *A* through *F,* which stand for 10, 11, 12, 13, 14, and 15. For example, the hexadecimal number 10 is 16 in decimal. Because of the frequency with which these two number systems are used, C++ allows you to specify integer literals in hexadecimal or octal instead of decimal. A hexadecimal literal must begin with 0x (a zero followed by an x). An octal literal begins with a zero. Here are some examples:

```
hex = 0xFF; // 255 in decimal
oct = 011; // 9 in decimal
```

Ask the Expert

Question: You showed how to specify a char literal. Is a wchar_t literal specified in the same way?

Answer: No. A wide-character constant (that is, one that is of type **wchar_t**) is preceded with the character *L*. For example:

```
wchar_t wc;
wc = L'A';
```

Here, **wc** is assigned the wide-character constant equivalent of A. You will not use wide characters often in your normal day-to-day programming, but they are something that might be of importance if you need to internationalize your program.

String Literals

C++ supports one other type of literal in addition to those of the predefined data types: the string. A *string* is a set of characters enclosed by double quotes. For example, "this is a test" is a string. You have seen examples of strings in some of the **cout** statements in the preceding sample programs. Keep in mind one important fact: although C++ allows you to define string constants, it does not have a built-in string data type. Instead, as you will see a little later in this book, strings are supported in C++ as character arrays. (C++ *does* provide a string type in its class library.)

Character Escape Sequences

Enclosing character constants in single quotes works for most printing characters, but a few characters, such as the carriage return, pose a special problem when a text editor is used. In addition, certain other characters, such as the single and double quotes, have special meaning in C++, so you cannot use them directly. For these reasons, C++ provides the *character escape sequences,* sometimes referred to as *backslash character constants,* shown in Table 2-3, so that you can enter them into a program. As you can see, the **\n** that you have been using is one of the escape sequences.

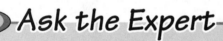

Ask the Expert

Question: Is a string consisting of a single character the same as a character literal? For example, is "k" the same as 'k'?

Answer: No. You must not confuse strings with characters. A character literal represents a single letter of type **char**. A string containing only one letter is still a string. Although strings consist of characters, they are not the same type.

2

The following sample program illustrates a few of the escape sequences:

```
// Demonstrate some escape sequences.

#include <iostream>
using namespace std;

int main()
{
  cout << "one\ttwo\tthree\n";
  cout << "123\b\b45";

  return 0;
}
```

The **\b\b** will backspace over the 2 and 3.

The output is shown here:

```
one     two     three
145
```

Here, the first **cout** statement uses tabs to position the words "two" and "three". The second **cout** statement displays the characters 123. Next, two backspace characters are output, which deletes the 2 and 3. Finally, the characters 4 and 5 are displayed.

Code	Meaning
\b	Backspace
\f	Form feed
\n	Newline
\r	Carriage return
\t	Horizontal tab
\"	Double quote
\'	Single quote character
\\	Backslash
\v	Vertical tab
\a	Alert
\?	?
\N	Octal constant (where N is an octal constant)
\xN	Hexadecimal constant (where N is a hexadecimal constant)

Table 2-3 The Character Escape Sequences

1-Minute Drill

● By default, what is the type of the literal 10? What is the type of the literal 10.0?

● How do you specify 100 as a **long int**? How do you specify 100 as an **unsigned int**?

● What is \b?

A Closer Look at Variables

Variables were introduced in Module 1. Here we will take a closer look at them. As you learned, variables are declared using this form of statement:

  type var-name;

where *type* is the data type of the variable and *var-name* is its name. You can declare a variable of any valid type. When you create a variable, you are creating an instance of its type. Thus, the capabilities of a variable are determined by its type. For example, a variable of type **bool** stores Boolean values. It cannot be used to store floating-point values. Furthermore, the type of a variable cannot change during its lifetime. An **int** variable cannot turn into a **double** variable, for example.

Initializing a Variable

You can assign a value to a variable at the same time that it is declared. To do this, follow the variable's name with an equal sign and the value being assigned. This is called a *variable initialization*. Its general form is shown here:

  type var = value;

Here, *value* is the value that is given to *var* when *var* is created.

● 10 is an **int** and 10.0 is a **double**.
● 100 as a **long int** is 100L. 100 as an **unsigned int** is 100U.
● \b is the escape sequence that causes a backspace.

Here are some examples:

```
int count = 10; // give count an initial value of 10
char ch = 'X';  // initialize ch with the letter X
float f = 1.2F; // f is initialized with 1.2
```

When declaring two or more variables of the same type using a comma separated list, you can give one or more of those variables an initial value. For example,

```
int a, b = 8, c = 19, d; // b and c have initializations
```

In this case, only **b** and **c** are initialized.

Dynamic Initialization

Although the preceding examples have used only constants as initializers, C++ allows variables to be initialized dynamically, using any expression valid at the time the variable is declared. For example, here is a short program that computes the volume of a cylinder given the radius of its base and its height:

```
// Demonstrate dynamic initialization.

#include <iostream>
using namespace std;

int main() {
  double radius = 4.0, height = 5.0;

  // dynamically initialize volume
  double volume = 3.1416 * radius * radius * height;

  cout << "Volume is " << volume;

  return 0;
}
```

volume is dynamically initialized at runtime.

Here, three local variables—**radius**, **height**, and **volume**—are declared. The first two, **radius** and **height**, are initialized by constants. However, **volume** is initialized dynamically to the volume of the cylinder. The key point here is that the initialization expression can use any element valid at the time of the initialization, including calls to functions, other variables, or literals.

Operators

C++ provides a rich operator environment. An *operator* is a symbol that tells the compiler to perform a specific mathematical or logical manipulation. C++ has four general classes of operators: *arithmetic, bitwise, relational,* and *logical.* C++ also has several additional operators that handle certain special situations. This chapter will examine the arithmetic, relational, and logical operators. We will also examine the assignment operator. The bitwise and other special operators are examined later.

Arithmetic Operators

C++ defines the following arithmetic operators:

Operator	Meaning
+	Addition
−	Subtraction (also unary minus)
*	Multiplication
/	Division
%	Modulus
++	Increment
− −	Decrement

The operators +, −, *, and / all work the same way in C++ as they do in algebra. These can be applied to any built-in numeric data type. They can also be applied to values of type **char**.

The % (modulus) operator yields the remainder of an integer division. Recall that when / is applied to an integer, any remainder will be truncated; for example, 10/3 will equal 3 in integer division. You can obtain the remainder of this division by using the % operator. For example, 10 % 3 is 1. In C++, the % can be applied only to integer operands; it cannot be applied to floating-point types.

The following program demonstrates the modulus operator:

```cpp
// Demonstrate the modulus operator.

#include <iostream>
using namespace std;

int main()
{
  int x, y;

  x = 10;
  y = 3;
  cout << x << " / " << y << " is " << x / y <<
      " with a remainder of " << x % y << "\n";

  x = 1;
  y = 2;
  cout << x << " / " << y << " is " << x / y << "\n" <<
        x << " % " << y << " is " << x % y;

  return 0;
}
```

The output is shown here:

```
10 / 3 is 3 with a remainder of 1
1 / 2 is 0
1 % 2 is 1
```

Increment and Decrement

Introduced in Module 1, the **++** and the **– –** are the increment and decrement operators. They have some special properties that make them quite interesting. Let's begin by reviewing precisely what the increment and decrement operators do.

The increment operator adds 1 to its operand, and the decrement operator subtracts 1. Therefore,

```cpp
x = x + 1;
```

is the same as

```
x++;
```

and

```
x = x - 1;
```

is the same as

```
--x;
```

Both the increment and decrement operators can either precede (prefix) or follow (postfix) the operand. For example,

```
x = x + 1;
```

can be written as

```
++x; // prefix form
```

or as

```
x++; // postfix form
```

In this example, there is no difference whether the increment is applied as a prefix or a postfix. However, when an increment or decrement is used as part of a larger expression, there is an important difference. When an increment or decrement operator precedes its operand, C++ will perform the operation prior to obtaining the operand's value for use by the rest of the expression. If the operator follows its operand, then C++ will obtain the operand's value before incrementing or decrementing it. Consider the following:

```
x = 10;
y = ++x;
```

In this case, y will be set to 11. However, if the code is written as

```
x = 10;
y = x++;
```

then **y** will be set to 10. In both cases, **x** is still set to 11; the difference is when it happens. There are significant advantages in being able to control when the increment or decrement operation takes place.

The precedence of the arithmetic operators is shown here:

Highest	++ − −
	− (unary minus)
	* / %
Lowest	+ −

Operators on the same precedence level are evaluated by the compiler from left to right. Of course, parentheses may be used to alter the order of evaluation. Parentheses are treated by C++ in the same way that they are by virtually all other computer languages: they force an operation, or a set of operations, to have a higher precedence level.

Ask the Expert

Question: Does the increment operator ++ have anything to do with the name C++?

Answer: Yes! As you know, C++ is built upon the C language. C++ adds to C several enhancements, most of which support object-oriented programming. Thus, C++ represents an incremental improvement to C, and the addition of the ++ (which is, of course, the increment operator) to the name C is a fitting way to describe C++.

Stroustrup initially named C++ "C with Classes," but at the suggestion of Rick Mascitti, he later changed the name to C++. While the new language was already destined for success, the adoption of the name C++ virtually guaranteed its place in history because it was a name that every C programmer would instantly recognize!

Relational and Logical Operators

In the terms *relational operator* and *logical operator*, *relational* refers to the relationships that values can have with one another, and *logical* refers to the ways in which true and false values can be connected together. Since the relational operators produce true or false results, they often work with the logical operators. For this reason, they will be discussed together here.

The relational and logical operators are shown in Table 2-4. Notice that in C++, *not equal to* is represented by != and *equal to* is represented by the double equal sign, ==. In C++, the outcome of a relational or logical expression produces a **bool** result. That is, the outcome of a relational or logical expression is either **true** or **false**.

Note

For older compilers, the outcome of a relational or logical expression will be an integer value of either 0 or 1. This difference is mostly academic, though, because C++ automatically converts **true** into 1 and **false** into 0, and vice versa as explained earlier.

The operands for a relational operator can be of nearly any type as long as they can be meaningfully compared. The operands to the logical operators must

Relational Operators

Operator	Meaning
>	Greater than
>=	Greater than or equal to
<	Less than
<=	Less than or equal to
==	Equal to
!=	Not equal to

Logical Operators

Operator	Meaning
&&	AND
||	OR
!	NOT

Table 2-4 The Relational and Logical Operators in C++

produce a true or false result. Since any nonzero value is true and zero is false, this means that the logical operators can be used with any expression that evaluates to a zero or nonzero result. Thus, any expression other than one that has a **void** result can be used.

The logical operators are used to support the basic logical operations AND, OR, and NOT, according to the following truth table:

p	q	p AND q	p OR q	NOT p
False	False	False	False	True
False	True	False	True	True
True	True	True	True	False
True	False	False	True	False

Here is a program that demonstrates several of the relational and logical operators:

```cpp
// Demonstrate the relational and logical operators.

#include <iostream>
using namespace std;

int main() {
  int i, j;
  bool b1, b2;

  i = 10;
  j = 11;
  if(i < j) cout << "i < j\n";
  if(i <= j) cout << "i <= j\n";
  if(i != j) cout << "i != j\n";
  if(i == j) cout << "this won't execute\n";
  if(i >= j) cout << "this won't execute\n";
  if(i > j) cout << "this won't execute\n";

  b1 = true;
  b2 = false;
  if(b1 && b2) cout << "this won't execute\n";
  if(!(b1 && b2)) cout << "!(b1 && b2) is true\n";
  if(b1 || b2) cout << "b1 || b2 is true\n";

  return 0;
}
```

The output from the program is shown here:

```
i < j
i <= j
i != j
!(b1 && b2) is true
b1 || b2 is true
```

Both the relational and logical operators are lower in precedence than the arithmetic operators. This means that an expression like 10 > 1+12 is evaluated as if it were written 10 > (1+12). The result is, of course, false.

You can link any number of relational operations together using logical operators. For example, this expression joins three relational operations:

```
var > 15 || !(10 < count) && 3 <= item
```

The following table shows the relative precedence of the relational and logical operators:

Highest	!
	> >= < <=
	== !=
	&&
Lowest	||

XOR.cpp

Project 2-2: Construct an XOR Logical Operation

C++ does not define a logical operator that performs an exclusive-OR operation, usually referred to as XOR. The XOR is a binary operation that yields true when one and only one operand is true. It has this truth table:

p	q	p XOR q
False	False	False
False	True	True
True	False	True
True	True	False

Some programmers have called the omission of the XOR a flaw. Others argue that the absence of the XOR logical operator is simply part of C++'s streamlined design, which avoids redundant features. They point out that it is easy to create an XOR logical operation using the three logical operators that C++ does provide.

In this project, you will construct an XOR operation using the **&&**, ||, and **!** operators. You can decide for yourself if the omission of an XOR logical operator is a design flaw or an elegant feature!

Step-by-Step

1. Create a new file called **XOR.cpp**.

2. Assuming two Boolean values, p and q, a logical XOR is constructed like this:

   (p || q) && !(p && q)

Let's go through this carefully. First, p is ORed with q. If this result is true, then at least one of the operands is true. Next, p is ANDed with q. This result is true if both operands are true. This result is then inverted using the NOT operator. Thus, the outcome of !(p && q) will be true when either p, q, or both are false. Finally, this result is ANDed with the result of (p || q). Thus, the entire expression will be true when one but not both operands is true.

3. Here is the entire **XOR.cpp** program listing. It demonstrates the XOR operation for all four possible combinations of true/false values.

```
/*

   Project 2-2

   Create an XOR using the C++ logical operators.

*/

#include <iostream>
#include <cmath>

using namespace std;

int main()
{
  bool p, q;
```

```
p = true;
q = true;

cout << p << " XOR " << q << " is " <<
    ( (p || q) && !(p && q) ) << "\n";


p = false;
q = true;

cout << p << " XOR " << q << " is " <<
    ( (p || q) && !(p && q) ) << "\n";


p = true;
q = false;

cout << p << " XOR " << q << " is " <<
    ( (p || q) && !(p && q) ) << "\n";


p = false;
q = false;

cout << p << " XOR " << q << " is " <<
    ( (p || q) && !(p && q) ) << "\n";


return 0;
}
```

4. Compile and run the program. The following output is produced:

```
1 XOR 1 is 0
0 XOR 1 is 1
1 XOR 0 is 1
0 XOR 0 is 0
```

5. Notice the outer parentheses surrounding the XOR operation inside the **cout** statements. They are necessary because of the precedence of C++'s operators. The << operator is higher in precedence than the logical operators. To prove this, try removing the outer parentheses, and then attempt to compile the program. As you will see, an error will be reported.

1-Minute Drill

● What does the **%** operator do? To what types can it be applied?

● How do you declare an **int** variable called **index** with an initial value of 10?

● Of what type is the outcome of a relational or logical expression?

The Assignment Operator

You have been using the assignment operator since Module 1. Now it is time to take a formal look at it. The *assignment operator* is the single equal sign, **=**. The assignment operator works in C++ much as it does in any other computer language. It has this general form:

var = expression;

Here, the value of the expression is given to *var*.

The assignment operator does have one interesting attribute: it allows you to create a chain of assignments. For example, consider this fragment:

```
int x, y, z;

x = y = z = 100; // set x, y, and z to 100
```

This fragment sets the variables **x**, **y**, and **z** to 100 using a single statement. This works because the **=** is an operator that yields the value of the right-hand expression. Thus, the value of **z = 100** is 100, which is then assigned to **y**, which in turn is assigned to **x**. Using a "chain of assignment" is an easy way to set a group of variables to a common value.

● The **%** is the modulus operator, which returns the remainder of an integer division. It can be applied to integer types.
● `int index = 10;`
● The result of a relational or logical expression is of type **bool**.

Compound Assignments

C++ provides special *compound assignment* operators that simplify the coding of certain assignment statements. Let's begin with an example. The assignment statement shown here:

```
x = x + 10;
```

can be written using a compound assignment as

```
x += 10;
```

The operator pair += tells the compiler to assign to **x** the value of **x** plus 10.

Here is another example. The statement

```
x = x - 100;
```

is the same as

```
x -= 100;
```

Both statements assign to **x** the value of **x** minus 100.

There are compound assignment operators for most of the binary operators (that is, those that require two operands). Thus, statements of the form

var = var op expression;

can be converted into this compound form:

var op = expression;

Because the compound assignment statements are shorter than their noncompound equivalents, the compound assignment operators are also sometimes called the *shorthand assignment* operators.

The compound assignment operators provide two benefits. First, they are more compact than their "longhand" equivalents. Second, they can result in more efficient executable code (because the operand is evaluated only once). For these reasons, you will often see the compound assignment operators used in professionally written C++ programs.

Type Conversion in Assignments

When variables of one type are mixed with variables of another type, a *type conversion* will occur. In an assignment statement, the type conversion rule is easy: The value of the right side (expression side) of the assignment is converted to the type of the left side (target variable), as illustrated here:

```
int x;
char ch;
float  f;

ch = x;    /* line 1 */
x = f;     /* line 2 */
f = ch;    /* line 3 */
f = x;     /* line 4 */
```

In line 1, the left high-order bits of the integer variable **x** are lopped off, leaving **ch** with the lower 8 bits. If **x** were between –128 and 127, **ch** and **x** would have identical values. Otherwise, the value of **ch** would reflect only the lower-order bits of **x**. In line 2, **x** will receive the nonfractional part of **f**. In line 3, **f** will convert the 8-bit integer value stored in **ch** to the same value in the floating-point format. This also happens in line 4, except that **f** will convert an integer value into floating-point format.

When converting from integers to characters and long integers to integers, the appropriate number of high-order bits will be removed. In many 32-bit environments, this means that 24 bits will be lost when going from an integer to a character, and 16 bits will be lost when going from an integer to a short integer. When converting from a floating-point type to an integer, the fractional part will be lost. If the target type is not large enough to store the result, then a garbage value will result.

A word of caution: Although C++ automatically converts any built-in type into another, the results won't always be what you want. Be careful when mixing types in an expression.

Expressions

Operators, variables, and literals are constituents of *expressions*. You might already know the general form of an expression from other programming experience or from algebra. However, a few aspects of expressions will be discussed now.

Type Conversion in Expressions

When constants and variables of different types are mixed in an expression, they are converted to the same type. First, all **char** and **short int** values are automatically elevated to **int**. This process is called *integral promotion*. Next, all operands are converted "up" to the type of the largest operand, which is called *type promotion*. The promotion is done on an operation-by-operation basis. For example, if one operand is an **int** and the other a **long int**, then the **int** is promoted to **long int**. Or, if either operand is a **double**, the other operand is promoted to **double**. This means that conversions such as that from a **char** to a **double** are perfectly valid. Once a conversion has been applied, each pair of operands will be of the same type, and the result of each operation will be the same as the type of both operands.

Converting to and from bool

As mentioned earlier, values of type **bool** are automatically converted into the integers 0 or 1 when used in an integer expression. When an integer result is converted to type **bool**, 0 becomes **false** and nonzero becomes **true**. Although **bool** is a fairly recent addition to C++, the automatic conversions to and from integers mean that it has virtually no impact on older code. Furthermore, the automatic conversions allow C++ to maintain its original definition of true and false as zero and nonzero.

Casts

It is possible to force an expression to be of a specific type by using a construct called a *cast*. A cast is an explicit type conversion. C++ defines five types of casts. Four allow detailed and sophisticated control over casting and are described later in this book after objects have been explained. However, there is one type of cast that you can use now. It is C++'s most general cast because it can transform any type into any other type. It was also the only type of cast that early versions of C++ supported. The general form of this cast is

(type) expression

where *type* is the target type into which you want to convert the expression. For example, if you wish to make sure the expression **x/2** is evaluated to type **float**, you can write

```
(float) x / 2
```

Casts are considered operators. As an operator, a cast is unary and has the same precedence as any other unary operator.

There are times when a cast can be very useful. For example, you may wish to use an integer for loop control, but also perform computation on it that requires a fractional part, as in the program shown here:

```
// Demonstrate a cast.

#include <iostream>
using namespace std;

int main(){
  int i;

  for(i=1; i <= 10; ++i )
    cout << i << "/ 2 is: " << (float) i / 2 << '\n';

  return 0;
}
```

The cast to **float** causes a fractional component to be displayed.

Here is the output from this program:

```
1/ 2 is: 0.5
2/ 2 is: 1
3/ 2 is: 1.5
4/ 2 is: 2
5/ 2 is: 2.5
6/ 2 is: 3
7/ 2 is: 3.5
8/ 2 is: 4
9/ 2 is: 4.5
10/ 2 is: 5
```

Without the cast (**float**) in this example, only an integer division would be performed. The cast ensures that the fractional part of the answer will be displayed.

Spacing and Parentheses

An expression in C++ can have tabs and spaces in it to make it more readable. For example, the following two expressions are the same, but the second is easier to read:

```
x=10/y*(127/x);

x = 10 / y * (127/x);
```

Parentheses increase the precedence of the operations contained within them, just like in algebra. Use of redundant or additional parentheses will not cause errors or slow down the execution of the expression. You are encouraged to use parentheses to make clear the exact order of evaluation, both for yourself and for others who may have to figure out your program later. For example, which of the following two expressions is easier to read?

```
x = y/3-34*temp+127;

x = (y/3) - (34*temp) + 127;
```

RegPay.cpp

Project 2-3: Compute the Regular Payments on a Loan

In this project, you will create a program that computes the regular payments on a loan, such as a car loan. Given the principal, the length of time, number of payments per year, and the interest rate, the program will compute the payment. Since this is a financial calculation, you will need to use floating-point data types for the computations. Since **double** is the most commonly used floating-point type, we will use it in this project. This project also demonstrates another C++ library function: **pow( )**.

To compute the payments, you will use the following formula:

$$\text{Payment} = \frac{\text{IntRate} * (\text{Principal} / \text{PayPerYear})}{1 - ((\text{IntRate} / \text{PayPerYear}) + 1)^{-\text{PayPerYear} * \text{NumYears}}}$$

where IntRate specifies the interest rate, Principal contains the starting balance, PayPerYear specifies the number of payments per year, and NumYears specifies the length of the loan in years.

Notice that in the denominator of the formula, you must raise one value to the power of another. To do this, you will use **pow( )**. Here is how you will call it:

result = pow(*base, exp*);

pow( ) returns the value of *base* raised to the *exp* power. The arguments to **pow( )** are **double** values, and **pow( )** returns a value of type **double**.

Step-by-Step

1. Create a new file called **RegPay.cpp**.

2. Here are the variables that will be used by the program:

```
double Principal;      // original principal
double IntRate;        // interest rate, such as 0.075
double PayPerYear;     // number of payments per year
double NumYears;       // number of years
double Payment;        // the regular payment
double numer, denom;   // temporary work variables
double b, e;           // base and exponent for call to Pow()
```

Notice how each variable declaration is followed by a comment that describes its use. This helps anyone reading your program understand the purpose of each variable. Although we won't include such detailed comments for most of the short programs in this book, it is a good practice to follow as your programs become longer and more complicated.

3. Add the following lines of code, which input the loan information:

```
cout << "Enter principal: ";
cin >> Principal;

cout << "Enter interest rate (i.e., 0.075): ";
cin >> IntRate;
```

```
cout << "Enter number of payments per year: ";
cin >> PayPerYear;

cout << "Enter number of years: ";
cin >> NumYears;
```

4. Add the lines that perform the financial calculation:

```
numer = IntRate * Principal / PayPerYear;

e = -(PayPerYear * NumYears);
b =  (IntRate / PayPerYear) + 1;

denom = 1 - pow(b, e);

Payment = numer / denom;
```

5. Finish the program by outputting the regular payment, as shown here:

```
cout <<  "Payment is " << Payment;
```

6. Here is the entire **RegPay.cpp** program listing:

```
/*
   Project 2-3

   Compute the regular payments for a loan.

   Call this file RegPay.cpp
*/

#include <iostream>
#include <cmath>
using namespace std;

int main() {
   double Principal;     // original principal
   double IntRate;       // interest rate, such as 0.075
   double PayPerYear;    // number of payments per year
   double NumYears;      // number of years
   double Payment;       // the regular payment
   double numer, denom;  // temporary work variables
   double b, e;          // base and exponent for call to Pow()
```

```
cout << "Enter principal: ";
cin >> Principal;

cout << "Enter interest rate (i.e., 0.075): ";
cin >> IntRate;

cout << "Enter number of payments per year: ";
cin >> PayPerYear;

cout << "Enter number of years: ";
cin >> NumYears;

numer = IntRate * Principal / PayPerYear;

e = -(PayPerYear * NumYears);
b =  (IntRate / PayPerYear) + 1;

denom = 1 - pow(b, e);

Payment = numer / denom;

cout <<  "Payment is " << Payment;

return 0;
}
```

Here is a sample run:

```
Enter principal: 10000
Enter interest rate (i.e., 0.075): 0.075
Enter number of payments per year: 12
Enter number of years: 5
Payment is 200.379
```

7. On your own, have the program display the total amount of interest paid over the life of the loan.

☑Mastery Check

1. What type of integers are supported by C++?

2. By default, what type is 12.2?

3. What values can a **bool** variable have?

4. What is the long integer data type?

5. What escape sequence produces a tab? What escape sequence rings the bell?

6. A string is surrounded by double quotes. True or false?

7. What are the hexadecimal digits?

8. Show the general form for initializing a variable when it is declared.

9. What does the % do? Can it be used on floating-point values?

10. Explain the difference between the prefix and postfix forms of the increment operator.

11. Which of the following are logical operators in C++?

    A. &&

    B. ##

    C. ||

    D. $$

    E. !

12. How can

    ```
    x = x + 12;
    ```

    be rewritten?

13. What is a cast?

14. Write a program that finds all of the prime numbers between 1 and 100.

Module 3

Program Control Statements

The Goals of This Module

- **Learn more about** if
- **Examine** switch
- **Reexamine the** for
- **Understand** while
- **Use** do-while
- **Employ** break
- **Use** continue
- **Utilize nested loops**
- **Examine the** goto

This module discusses the statements that control a program's flow of execution. There are three categories of program control statements: *selection* statements, which include the **if** and the **switch**; *iteration* statements, which include the **for**, **while**, and **do-while** loops; and *jump* statements, which include **break**, **continue**, **return**, and **goto**. Except for **return**, which is discussed later in this book, the remaining control statements, including the **if** and **for** statements to which you have already had a brief introduction, are examined here.

The if Statement

Module 1 introduced the **if** statement. Now it is time to examine it in detail. The complete form of the **if** statement is

```
if(expression) statement;
else statement;
```

where the targets of the **if** and **else** are single statements. The **else** clause is optional. The targets of both the **if** and **else** can be blocks of statements. The general form of the **if** using blocks of statements is

```
if(expression)
{
   statement sequence
}
else
{
   statement sequence
}
```

If the conditional expression is true, the target of the **if** will be executed; otherwise, the target of the **else**, if it exists, will be executed. At no time will both be executed. The conditional expression controlling the **if** may be any type of valid C++ expression that produces a true or false result.

The following program demonstrates the **if** by playing a simple version of the "guess the magic number" game. The program generates a random number, prompts for your guess, and prints the message ** **Right** ** if you guess the magic number. This program also introduces another C++ library function, called **rand( )**, which returns a randomly selected integer value. It requires the **<cstdlib>** header.

```
// Magic Number program.

#include <iostream>
#include <cstdlib>
using namespace std;

int main()
{
  int magic;  // magic number
  int guess;  // user's guess

  magic = rand(); // get a random number

  cout << "Enter your guess: ";
  cin >> guess;

  if(guess == magic) cout << "** Right **";

  return 0;
}
```

> If the guess matches the "magic number", the message is displayed.

This program uses the **if** statement to determine whether the user's guess matches the magic number. If it does, the message is printed on the screen.

Taking the Magic Number program further, the next version uses the **else** to print a message when the wrong number is picked:

```
// Magic Number program: 1st improvement.

#include <iostream>
#include <cstdlib>
using namespace std;

int main()
{
  int magic;  // magic number
  int guess;  // user's guess

  magic = rand(); // get a random number

  cout << "Enter your guess: ";
```

```
  cin >> guess;

  if(guess == magic) cout << "** Right **";
  else cout << "...Sorry, you're wrong.";

  return 0;
}
```

Indicate a wrong answer, too.

The Conditional Expression

Sometimes newcomers to C++ are confused by the fact that any valid C++ expression can be used to control the **if**. That is, the type of conditional expression need not be restricted to only those involving the relational and logical operators, or to operands of type **bool**. All that is required is that the controlling expression evaluate to either a true or false result. As you should recall from the previous module, a value of 0 is automatically converted into **false**, and all non-zero values are converted to **true**. Thus, any expression that results in a 0 or non-zero value can be used to control the **if**. For example, this program reads two integers from the keyboard and displays the quotient. To avoid a divide-by-zero error, an **if** statement, controlled by the second number, is used.

```
// Use an int value to control the if.

#include <iostream>
using namespace std;

int main()
{
  int a, b;

  cout << "Enter numerator: ";
  cin >> a;
  cout << "Enter denominator: ";
  cin >> b;

  if(b) cout << "Result: " << a / b << '\n';
  else cout << "Cannot divide by zero.\n";

  return 0;
}
```

Notice that **b** alone is sufficient to control this **if** statement. No relational operator is needed.

Here are two sample runs:

```
Enter numerator: 12
Enter denominator: 2
Result: 6

Enter numerator: 12
Enter denominator: 0
Cannot divide by zero.
```

Notice that **b** (the divisor) is tested for zero using **if(b)**. This approach works because when **b** is zero, the condition controlling the **if** is false and the **else** executes. Otherwise, the condition is true (non-zero) and the division takes place. It is not necessary (and would be considered bad style by many C++ programmers) to write this **if** as shown here:

```
if(b == 0) cout << a/b << '\n';
```

This form of the statement is redundant and potentially inefficient.

Nested ifs

A *nested if* is an **if** statement that is the target of another **if** or **else**. Nested **ifs** are very common in programming. The main thing to remember about nested **ifs** in C++ is that an **else** statement always refers to the nearest **if** statement that is within the same block as the **else** and not already associated with an **else**. Here is an example:

```
if(i) {
  if(j) result = 1;
  if(k) result = 2;
  else result = 3; // this else is associated with if(k)
}
else result = 4; // this else is associated with if(i)
```

As the comments indicate, the final **else** is not associated with **if(j)** (even though it is the closest **if** without an **else**), because it is not in the same block. Rather, the final **else** is associated with **if(i)**. The inner **else** is associated with **if(k)** because that is the nearest **if**.

You can use a nested **if** to add a further improvement to the Magic Number program. This addition provides the player with feedback about a wrong guess.

```cpp
// Magic Number program: 2nd improvement.

#include <iostream>
#include <cstdlib>

using namespace std;

int main()
{
  int magic;  // magic number
  int guess;  // user's guess

  magic = rand(); // get a random number

  cout << "Enter your guess: ";
  cin >> guess;

  if (guess == magic) {
    cout << "** Right **\n";
    cout << magic << " is the magic number.\n";
  }
  else {
    cout << "...Sorry, you're wrong.";
    if(guess > magic) cout <<" Your guess is too high.\n";
    else cout << " Your guess is too low.\n";
  }

  return 0;
}
```

Here, a nested **if** provides feedback to the player.

The if-else-if Ladder

A common programming construct that is based upon nested **ifs** is the **if-else-if** *ladder,* also referred to as the **if-else-if** *staircase.* It looks like this:

if(*condition*)
  statement;
else if(*condition*)
  statement;

     else if(*condition*)
        statement;
      .
      .
      .
     else
        statement;

The conditional expressions are evaluated from the top downward. As soon as a true condition is found, the statement associated with it is executed, and the rest of the ladder is bypassed. If none of the conditions is true, then the final **else** statement will be executed. The final **else** often acts as a default condition; that is, if all other conditional tests fail, then the last **else** statement is performed. If there is no final **else** and all other conditions are false, then no action will take place.

The following program demonstrates the **if-else-if** ladder:

```
// Demonstrate an if-else-if ladder.
#include <iostream>
using namespace std;

int main()
{
  int x;

  for(x=0; x<6; x++) {
    if(x==1) cout << "x is one\n";
    else if(x==2) cout << "x is two\n";
    else if(x==3) cout << "x is three\n";
    else if(x==4) cout << "x is four\n";
    else cout << "x is not between 1 and 4\n";
  }

  return 0;
}
```

An **if-else-if** ladder.

The program produces the following output:

```
x is not between 1 and 4
x is one
x is two
```

```
x is three
x is four
x is not between 1 and 4
```

As you can see, the default **else** is executed only if none of the preceding **if** statements succeeds.

1-Minute Drill

● The condition controlling the **if** must use a relational operator? True or false?

● To what **if** does an **else** always associate?

● What is an **if-else-if** ladder?

The switch Statement

The second of C++'s selection statements is the **switch**. The **switch** provides for a multiway branch. Thus, it enables a program to select among several alternatives. Although a series of nested **if** statements can perform multiway tests, for many situations the **switch** is a more efficient approach. It works like this: the value of an expression is successively tested against a list of constants. When a match is found, the statement sequence associated with that match is executed. The general form of the **switch** statement is

```
switch(expression) {
    case constant1:
        statement sequence
        break;
    case constant2:
        statement sequence
        break;
    case constant3:
        statement sequence
        break;
    .
    .
    .
```

● False. The condition controlling an **if** must simply evaluate to either true or false.
● An **else** always associates with the nearest **if** in the same block that is not already associated with an **else**.
● An **if-else-if** ladder is a sequence of nested **if-else** statements.

```
      default:
          statement sequence
  }
```

The **switch** expression must evaluate to either a character or an integer value. (Floating-point expressions, for example, are not allowed.) Frequently, the expression controlling the **switch** is simply a variable. The **case** constants must be integer or character literals.

The **default** statement sequence is performed if no matches are found. The **default** is optional; if it is not present, no action takes place if all matches fail. When a match is found, the statements associated with that **case** are executed until the **break** is encountered or, in a concluding **case** or **default** statement, until the end of the **switch** is reached.

There are four important things to know about the **switch** statement:

● The **switch** differs from the **if** in that **switch** can test only for equality (that is, for matches between the **switch** expression and the **case** constants), whereas the **if** conditional expression can be of any type.

● No two **case** constants in the same **switch** can have identical values. Of course, a **switch** statement enclosed by an outer switch may have **case** constants that are the same.

● A **switch** statement is usually more efficient than nested **ifs**.

● The statement sequences associated with each **case** are *not* blocks. However, the entire **switch** statement *does* define a block. The importance of this will become apparent as you learn more about C++.

The following program demonstrates the **switch**. It asks for a number between 1 and 3, inclusive. It then displays a proverb linked to that number. Any other number causes an error message to be displayed.

```
/*
   A simple proverb generator that
   demonstrates the switch.
*/

#include <iostream>
using namespace std;
```

```
int main()
{
  int num;

  cout << "Enter a number from 1 to 3: ";
  cin >> num;

  switch(num) {        The value of num determines
    case 1:            the case sequence executed.
      cout << "A rolling stone gathers no moss.\n";
      break;
    case 2:
      cout << "A bird in hand is worth two in the bush.\n";
      break;
    case 3:
      cout << "A fool and his money are soon parted.\n";
      break;
    default:
      cout << "You must enter either 1, 2, or 3.\n";
  }

  return 0;
}
```

Here are two sample runs:

```
Enter a number from 1 to 3: 1
A rolling stone gathers no moss.

Enter a number from 1 to 3: 5
You must enter either 1, 2, or 3.
```

Technically, the **break** statement is optional, although most applications of the **switch** will use it. When encountered within the statement sequence of a **case**, the **break** statement causes program flow to exit from the entire **switch** statement and resume at the next statement outside the **switch**. However, if a **break** statement does not end the statement sequence associated with a **case**, then all the statements *at and below* the matching **case** will be executed until a **break** (or the end of the **switch**) is encountered. For example, study the following program carefully. Can you figure out what it will display on the screen?

```cpp
// A switch without break statements.

#include <iostream>
using namespace std;

int main()
{
  int i;

  for(i=0; i<5; i++) {
    switch(i) {
      case 0: cout << "less than 1\n";
      case 1: cout << "less than 2\n";
      case 2: cout << "less than 3\n";     ── No break statements here.
      case 3: cout << "less than 4\n";
      case 4: cout << "less than 5\n";
    }
    cout << '\n';
  }

  return 0;
}
```

This program displays the following output:

```
less than 1
less than 2
less than 3
less than 4
less than 5

less than 2
less than 3
less than 4
less than 5

less than 3
```

```
less than 4
less than 5

less than 4
less than 5

less than 5
```

As this program illustrates, execution will continue into the next **case** if no **break** statement is present.

You can have empty **cases**, as shown in this example:

```
switch(i) {
  case 1:
  case 2:◄─────────────────────  Empty case sequences.
  case 3:
    cout << "i is less than 4";
    break;
  case 4:
    cout << "i is 4";
    break;
```

In this fragment, if **i** has the value 1, 2, or 3, then the message

```
i is less than 4
```

is displayed. If it is 4, then

```
i is 4
```

is displayed. The "stacking" of **cases**, as shown in this example, is very common when several **cases** share common code.

Nested switch Statements

It is possible to have a **switch** as part of the statement sequence of an outer **switch**. Even if the **case** constants of the inner and outer **switch** contain common values, no conflicts will arise. For example, the following code fragment is perfectly acceptable:

```
switch(ch1) {
  case 'A': cout << "This A is part of outer switch";
```

```
switch(ch2) {          A nested switch.
  case 'A':
    cout << "This A is part of inner switch";
    break;
  case 'B': // ...
}
break;
case 'B': // ...
```

1-Minute Drill

● The expression controlling the **switch** must be of what type?

● When the **switch** expression matches a **case** constant, what happens?

● When a **case** sequence is not terminated by a **break**, what happens?

Ask the Expert

Question: Under what conditions should I use an if-else-if ladder rather than a switch when coding a multiway branch?

Answer: In general, use an **if-else-if** ladder when the conditions controlling the selection process do not rely upon a single value. For example, consider the following **if-else-if** sequence:

```
if(x < 10) // ...
else if(y > 0) // ...
else if(!done) // ...
```

This sequence cannot be recoded into a **switch** because all three conditions involve different variables—and differing types. What variable would control the **switch**? Also, you will need to use an **if-else-if** ladder when testing floating-point values or other objects that are not of types valid for use in a **switch** expression.

● The **switch** expression must be of type integer or character.
● When a matching **case** constant is found, the statement sequence associated with that **case** is executed.
● When a **case** sequence is not terminated by a **break**, execution falls through into the next **case**.

Help.cpp

Project 3-1: Start Building a C++ Help System

This project builds a simple help system that displays the syntax for the C++ control statements. The program displays a menu containing the control statements and then waits for you to choose one. After one is chosen, the syntax of the statement is displayed. In this first version of the program, help is available for only the **if** and **switch** statements. The other control statements are added by subsequent projects.

Step-by-Step

1. Create a file called **Help.cpp**.

2. The program begins by displaying the following menu:

```
Help on:
  1. if
  2. switch
Choose one:
```

To accomplish this, you will use the statement sequence shown here:

```
cout << "Help on:\n";
cout << "  1. if\n";
cout << "  2. switch\n";
cout << "Choose one: ";
```

3. Next, the program obtains the user's selection, as shown here:

```
cin >> choice;
```

4. Once the selection has been obtained, the program uses this **switch** statement to display the syntax for the selected statement:

```
switch(choice) {
  case '1':
    cout << "The if:\n\n";
    cout << "if(condition) statement;\n";
    cout << "else statement;\n";
    break;
  case '2':
    cout << "The switch:\n\n";
    cout << "switch(expression) {\n";
    cout << "  case constant:\n";
    cout << "    statement sequence\n";
```

```
      cout << "     break;\n";
      cout << "   // ...\n";
      cout << "}\n";
      break;
    default:
      cout << "Selection not found.\n";
}
```

Notice how the **default** clause catches invalid choices. For example, if the user enters 3, no **case** constants will match, causing the **default** sequence to execute.

5. Here is the entire **Help.cpp** program listing:

```
/*
   Project 3-1

   A simple help system.
*/

#include <iostream>
using namespace std;

int main() {
  char choice;

  cout << "Help on:\n";
  cout << "  1. if\n";
  cout << "  2. switch\n";
  cout << "Choose one: ";
  cin >> choice;

  cout << "\n";

  switch(choice) {
    case '1':
      cout << "The if:\n\n";
      cout << "if(condition) statement;\n";
      cout << "else statement;\n";
      break;
    case '2':
      cout << "The switch:\n\n";
      cout << "switch(expression) {\n";
      cout << "  case constant:\n";
      cout << "     statement sequence\n";
      cout << "     break;\n";
```

```
        cout << "  // ...\n";
        cout << "}\n";
        break;
    default:
        cout << "Selection not found.\n";
    }

    return 0;
}
```

Here is a sample run:

```
Help on:
  1. if
  2. switch
Choose one: 1

The if:

if(condition) statement;
else statement;
```

The for Loop

You have been using a simple form of the **for** loop since Module 1. You might be surprised at just how powerful and flexible the **for** loop is. Let's begin by reviewing the basics, starting with the most traditional forms of the **for**.

The general form of the **for** loop for repeating a single statement is

for(*initialization; expression; increment*) *statement;*

For repeating a block, the general form is

for(*initialization; expression; increment*)
{
  statement sequence
}

The *initialization* is usually an assignment statement that sets the initial value of the *loop control variable,* which acts as the counter that controls the loop.

The *expression* is a conditional expression that determines whether the loop will repeat. The *increment* defines the amount by which the loop control variable will change each time the loop is repeated. Notice that these three major sections of the loop must be separated by semicolons. The **for** loop will continue to execute as long as the conditional expression tests true. Once the condition becomes false, the loop will exit, and program execution will resume on the statement following the **for** block.

The following program uses a **for** loop to print the square roots of the numbers between 1 and 99. Notice that in this example, the loop control variable is called **num**.

```cpp
// Show square roots of 1 to 99.

#include <iostream>
#include <cmath>
using namespace std;

int main()
{
  int num;
  double sq_root;

  for(num=1; num < 100; num++) {
    sq_root = sqrt((double) num);
    cout << num << " " << sq_root << '\n';
  }

  return 0;
}
```

This program uses the standard function **sqrt( )**. As explained in Module 2, the **sqrt( )** function returns the square root of its argument. The argument must be of type **double**, and the function returns a value of type **double**. The header **<cmath>** is required.

The **for** loop can proceed in a positive or negative fashion, and it can increment the loop control variable by any amount. For example, the following program prints the numbers 50 to –50, in decrements of 10:

```cpp
// A negatively running for loop.
```

```
#include <iostream>
using namespace std;

int main()
{
  int i;

  for(i=50; i >= -50; i = i-10) cout << i << ' ';

  return 0;
}
```

A negatively running **for** loop.

Here is the output from the program:

```
50 40 30 20 10 0 -10 -20 -30 -40 -50
```

An important point about **for** loops is that the conditional expression is always tested at the top of the loop. This means that the code inside the loop may not be executed at all if the condition is false to begin with. Here is an example:

```
for(count=10; count < 5; count++)
  cout << count; // this statement will not execute
```

This loop will never execute, because its control variable, **count**, is greater than 5 when the loop is first entered. This makes the conditional expression, **count<5**, false from the outset; thus, not even one iteration of the loop will occur.

Some Variations on the for Loop

The **for** is one of the most versatile statements in the C++ language because it allows a wide range of variations. For example, multiple loop control variables can be used. Consider the following fragment of code:

```
for(x=0, y=10; x <= y; ++x, --y)
  cout << x << ' ' << y << '\n';
```

Multiple loop control variables.

Here, commas separate the two initialization statements and the two increment expressions. This is necessary in order for the compiler to understand that there

Ask the Expert

Question: Does C++ support mathematical functions other than sqrt( )?

Answer: Yes! In addition to **sqrt( )**, C++ supports an extensive set of mathematical library functions. For example, **sin( )**, **cos( )**, **tan( )**, **log( )**, **pow( )**, **ceil( )**, and **floor( )** are just a few. If mathematical programming is your interest, you will want to explore the C++ math functions. All C++ compilers support these functions, and their descriptions will be found in your compiler's documentation. They all require the header **<cmath>**.

are two initialization and two increment statements. In C++, the comma is an operator that essentially means "do this and this." Its most common use is in the **for** loop. You can have any number of initialization and increment statements, but in practice, more than two or three make the **for** loop unwieldy.

The condition controlling the loop may be any valid C++ expression. It does not need to involve the loop control variable. In the next example, the loop continues to execute until the **rand( )** function produces a value greater than 20,000.

```
/*
   Loop until a random number that is
   greater than 20,000.
*/

#include <iostream>
#include <cstdlib>
using namespace std;

int main()
{
  int i;
  int r;


  r = rand();

  for(i=0; r <= 20000; i++)
```

This conditional expression does not use the loop control variable.

```
   r = rand();

 cout << "Number is " << r <<
    ". It was generated on try " << i << ".";

 return 0;
}
```

Here is a sample run:

```
Number is 26500. It was generated on try 3.
```

Each time through the loop, a new random number is obtained by calling **rand( )**. When a value greater than 20,000 is generated, the loop condition becomes false, terminating the loop.

Missing Pieces

Another aspect of the **for** loop that is different in C++ than in many computer languages is that pieces of the loop definition need not be there. For example, if you want to write a loop that runs until the number 123 is typed in at the keyboard, it could look like this:

```
// A for loop with no increment.

#include <iostream>
using namespace std;

int main()
{
  int x;

  for(x=0; x != 123; ) {          No increment expression.
    cout << "Enter a number: ";
    cin >> x;
  }

  return 0;
}
```

Here, the increment portion of the **for** definition is blank. This means that each time the loop repeats, **x** is tested to see whether it equals 123, but no further action takes place. If, however, you type 123 at the keyboard, the loop condition becomes false and the loop exits. The **for** loop will not modify the loop control variable if no increment portion of the loop is present.

Another variation on the **for** is to move the initialization section outside of the loop, as shown in this fragment:

```
x = 0;

for( ; x<10; )
{
  cout << x << ' ';
  ++x;
}
```

x is initialized outside the loop.

Here, the initialization section has been left blank, and **x** is initialized before the loop is entered. Placing the initialization outside of the loop is generally done only when the initial value is derived through a complex process that does not lend itself to containment inside the **for** statement. Notice that in this example, the increment portion of the **for** is located inside the body of the loop.

The Infinite for Loop

You can create an *infinite loop* (a loop that never terminates) using this **for** construct:

```
for(;;)
{
  //...
}
```

This loop will run forever. Although there are some programming tasks, such as operating system command processors, that require an infinite loop, most "infinite loops" are really just loops with special termination requirements. Near the end of this module, you will see how to halt a loop of this type. (Hint: It's done using the **break** statement.)

Loops with No Body

In C++, the body associated with a **for** loop can be empty. This is because the *null statement* is syntactically valid. Bodiless loops are often useful. For example, the following program uses one to sum the numbers from 1 to 10:

```cpp
// The body of a for loop can be empty.

#include <iostream>
#include <cstdlib>
using namespace std;

int main()
{
  int i;
  int sum = 0;


  // sum the numbers from 1 through 10
  for(i=1; i <= 10; sum += i++) ;         This loop has no body.

  cout << "Sum is " << sum;

  return 0;
}
```

The output from the program is shown here:

```
Sum is 55
```

Notice that the summation process is handled entirely within the **for** statement and no body is needed. Pay special attention to the iteration expression:

```
sum += i++
```

Don't be intimidated by statements like this. They are common in professionally written C++ programs and are easy to understand if you break them down into their parts. In words, this statement says, "add to **sum** the value of **sum** plus i, then increment i." Thus, it is the same as this sequence of statements:

```
sum = sum + i;
i++;
```

Declaring Loop Control Variables Inside the for Loop

Often, the variable that controls a for loop is needed only for the purposes of the loop and is not used elsewhere. When this is the case, it is possible to declare the variable inside the initialization portion of the **for**. For example, the following program computes both the summation and the factorial of the numbers 1 through 5. It declares its loop control variable i inside the **for**:

```
// Declare loop control variable inside the for.

#include <iostream>
using namespace std;

int main() {
  int sum = 0;
  int fact = 1;

  // compute the factorial of the numbers through 5
  for(int i = 1; i <= 5; i++) {
    sum += i;  // i is known throughout the loop
    fact *= i;
  }

  // but, i is not known here.

  cout << "Sum is " << sum << "\n";
  cout << "Factorial is " << fact;

  return 0;
}
```

Here, **i** is declared inside the **for** loop.

Here is the output produced by the program:

```
Sum is 15
Factorial is 120
```

When you declare a variable inside a **for** loop, there is one important point to remember: the variable is known only within the **for** statement. Thus, in the language of programming, the *scope* of the variable is limited to the **for** loop. Outside the **for** loop, the variable will cease to exist. Therefore, in the preceding example, **i** is not accessible outside the **for** loop. If you need to use the loop control variable elsewhere in your program, you will not be able to declare it inside the **for** loop.

Note

Whether a variable declared within the initialization portion of a **for** loop is restricted to that loop or not has changed over time. Originally, the variable was available after the **for**, but this was changed during the C++ standardization process. Today, the ANSI/ISO Standard C++ restricts the variable to the scope of the **for** loop. Some compilers, however, do not. You will need to check this feature in the environment you are using.

Before moving on, you might want to experiment with your own variations on the **for** loop. As you will find, it is a fascinating loop.

1-Minute Drill

● Can portions of a **for** statement be empty?

● Show how to create an infinite loop using **for**.

● What is the scope of a variable declared within a **for** statement?

The while Loop

Another loop is the **while**. The general form of the **while** loop is

while(*expression*) *statement*;

where *statement* may be a single statement or a block of statements. The *expression* defines the condition that controls the loop, and it can be any valid expression. The statement is performed while the condition is true. When the condition becomes false, program control passes to the line immediately following the loop.

● Yes. All three parts of the **for**—initialization, condition, and iteration—can be empty.

● for(; ;)

● The scope of a variable declared within a **for** is limited to the loop. Outside the loop, it is unknown.

The next program illustrates the **while** in a short but sometimes fascinating program. Virtually all computers support an extended character set beyond that defined by ASCII. The extended characters, if they exist, often include special characters such as foreign language symbols and scientific notations. The ASCII characters use values that are less than 128. The extended character set begins at 128 and continues to 255. This program prints all characters between 32 (which is a space) and 255. When you run this program, you will most likely see some very interesting characters.

3

```
/*
   This program displays all printable characters,
   including the extended character set, if one exists.
*/

#include <iostream>
using namespace std;

int main()
{
  unsigned char ch;

  ch = 32;
  while(ch) {                      Use a while loop.
    cout << ch;
    ch++;
  }

  return 0;
}
```

Examine the loop expression in the preceding program. You might be wondering why only **ch** is used to control the **while**. Since **ch** is an unsigned character, it can only hold the values 0 through 255. When it holds the value 255 and is then incremented, its value will "wrap around" to zero. Therefore, the test for **ch** being zero serves as a convenient stopping condition.

As with the **for** loop, the **while** checks the conditional expression at the top of the loop, which means that the loop code may not execute at all. This eliminates the need for performing a separate test before the loop. The following program illustrates this characteristic of the **while** loop. It displays a line of periods. The number of periods displayed is equal to the value entered by the user. The program does not allow lines longer than 80 characters.

The test for a permissible number of periods is performed inside the loop's conditional expression, not outside of it.

```cpp
#include <iostream>
using namespace std;

int main()
{
  int len;

  cout << "Enter length (1 to 79): ";
  cin >> len;

  while(len>0 && len<80)  {
    cout << '.';
    len--;
  }

  return 0;
}
```

If **len** is out of range, then the **while** loop will not execute even once. Otherwise, the loop executes until **len** reaches 80.

There need not be any statements at all in the body of the **while** loop. Here is an example:

```cpp
while(rand() != 100) ;
```

This loop iterates until the random number generated by **rand( )** equals 100.

The do-while Loop

The last of C++'s loops is the **do-while**. Unlike the **for** and the **while** loops, in which the condition is tested at the top of the loop, the **do-while** loop checks its condition at the bottom of the loop. This means that a **do-while** loop will always execute at least once. The general form of the **do-while** loop is

```cpp
do {
    statements;
} while(condition);
```

Ask the Expert

Question: Given the flexibility inherent in all of C++'s loops, what criteria should I use when selecting a loop? That is, how do I choose the right loop for a specific job?

Answer: Use a **for** loop when performing a known number of iterations. Use the **do-while** when you need a loop that will always perform at least one iteration. The **while** is best used when the loop will repeat an unknown number of times.

Although the braces are not necessary when only one statement is present, they are often used to improve readability of the **do-while** construct, thus preventing confusion with the **while**. The **do-while** loop executes as long as the conditional expression is true.

The following program loops until the number 100 is entered:

```
#include <iostream>
using namespace std;

int main()
{
  int num;

  do {
    cout << "Enter a number (100 to stop): ";
    cin >> num;
  } while(num != 100);

  return 0;
}
```

A **do-while** loop always executes at least once.

Using a **do-while** loop, we can further improve the Magic Number program. This time, the program loops until you guess the number.

```
// Magic Number program: 3rd improvement.

#include <iostream>
#include <cstdlib>
using namespace std;
```

```
int main()
{
  int magic; // magic number
  int guess; // user's guess

  magic = rand(); // get a random number

  do {
    cout << "Enter your guess: ";
    cin >> guess;
    if(guess == magic) {
      cout << "** Right ** ";
      cout << magic << " is the magic number.\n";
    }
    else {
      cout << "...Sorry, you're wrong.";
      if(guess > magic)
          cout << " Your guess is too high.\n";
      else cout << " Your guess is too low.\n";
    }
  } while(guess != magic);

  return 0;
}
```

Here is a sample run:

```
Enter your guess: 10
...Sorry, you're wrong. Your guess is too low.
Enter your guess: 100
...Sorry, you're wrong. Your guess is too high.
Enter your guess: 50
...Sorry, you're wrong. Your guess is too high.
Enter your guess: 41
** Right ** 41 is the magic number.
```

One last point: Like the **for** and **while**, the body of the **do-while** loop can be empty, but this is seldom the case in practice.

1-Minute Drill

- What is the main difference between the **while** and the **do-while** loops?
- Can the body of a **while** loop be empty?

Help2.cpp

Project 3-2: Improve the C++ Help System

This project expands on the C++ help system that was created in Project 3-1. This version adds the syntax for the **for**, **while**, and **do-while** loops. It also checks the user's menu selection, looping until a valid response is entered. To do this, it uses a **do-while** loop. In general, using a **do-while** loop to handle menu selection is common because you will always want the loop to execute at least once.

Step-by-Step

1. Copy **Help.cpp** to a new file called **Help2.cpp**.

2. Change the portion of the program that displays the choices so that it uses the **do-while** loop shown here:

```
do {
  cout << "Help on:\n";
  cout << "  1. if\n";
  cout << "  2. switch\n";
  cout << "  3. for\n";
  cout << "  4. while\n";
  cout << "  5. do-while\n";
  cout << "Choose one: ";

  cin >> choice;

} while( choice < '1' || choice > '5');
```

- The **while** checks its condition at the top of the loop. The **do-while** checks its condition at the bottom of the loop. Thus, a **do-while** will always execute at least once.
- Yes, the body of a **while** loop (or any other C++ loop) can be empty.

After making this change, the program will loop, displaying the menu until the user enters a response that is between 1 and 5. You can see how useful the **do-while** loop is in this context.

3. Expand the **switch** statement to include the **for**, **while**, and **do-while** loops, as shown here:

```
switch(choice) {
  case '1':
    cout << "The if:\n\n";
    cout << "if(condition) statement;\n";
    cout << "else statement;\n";
    break;
  case '2':
    cout << "The switch:\n\n";
    cout << "switch(expression) {\n";
    cout << "  case constant:\n";
    cout << "    statement sequence\n";
    cout << "    break;\n";
    cout << "  // ...\n";
    cout << "}\n";
    break;
  case '3':
    cout << "The for:\n\n";
    cout << "for(init; condition; iteration)";
    cout << " statement;\n";
    break;
  case '4':
    cout << "The while:\n\n";
    cout << "while(condition) statement;\n";
    break;
  case '5':
    cout << "The do-while:\n\n";
    cout << "do {\n";
    cout << "  statement;\n";
    cout << "} while (condition);\n";
    break;
}
```

Notice that no **default** statement is present in this version of the **switch**. Since the menu loop ensures that a valid response will be entered, it is no longer necessary to include a **default** statement to handle an invalid choice.

4. Here is the entire **Help2.cpp** program listing:

```
/*
   Project 3-2

   An improved Help system that uses a
   a do-while to process a menu selection.
*/

#include <iostream>
using namespace std;

int main() {
  char choice;

  do {
    cout << "Help on:\n";
    cout << "  1. if\n";
    cout << "  2. switch\n";
    cout << "  3. for\n";
    cout << "  4. while\n";
    cout << "  5. do-while\n";
    cout << "Choose one: ";

    cin >> choice;

  } while( choice < '1' || choice > '5');

  cout << "\n\n";

  switch(choice) {
    case '1':
      cout << "The if:\n\n";
      cout << "if(condition) statement;\n";
      cout << "else statement;\n";
      break;
    case '2':
      cout << "The switch:\n\n";
      cout << "switch(expression) {\n";
      cout << "  case constant:\n";
      cout << "    statement sequence\n";
      cout << "    break;\n";
```

3

```
        cout << "  // ...\n";
        cout << "}\n";
        break;
    case '3':
      cout << "The for:\n\n";
      cout << "for(init; condition; iteration)";
      cout << " statement;\n";
      break;
    case '4':
      cout << "The while:\n\n";
      cout << "while(condition) statement;\n";
      break;
    case '5':
      cout << "The do-while:\n\n";
      cout << "do {\n";
      cout << "  statement;\n";
      cout << "} while (condition);\n";
      break;
  }

  return 0;
}
```

Ask the Expert

Question: Earlier you showed how a variable could be declared in the initialization portion of the for loop. Can variables be declared inside any other C++ control statement?

Answer: Yes. In C++, it is possible to declare a variable within the conditional expression of an **if** or **switch**, within the conditional expression of a **while** loop, or within the initialization portion of a **for** loop. A variable declared in one of these places has its scope limited to the block of code controlled by that statement.

You have already seen an example of declaring a variable within a **for** loop. Here is an example that declares a variable within an **if**:

3

```
if(int x = 20) {
  x = x - y;
  if(x > 10) y = 0;
}
```

The **if** declares **x** and assigns it the value 20. Since this is a true value, the target of the **if** executes. Because variables declared within a conditional statement have their scope limited to the block of code controlled by that statement, **x** is not known outside the **if**.

As mentioned in the discussion of the **for** loop, whether a variable declared within a control statement is known only to that statement or is available after that statement may vary between compilers. You should check the compiler that you are using before assuming a specific behavior in this regard. Of course, the ANSI/ISO C++ standard stipulates that the variable is known only within the statement in which it is declared.

Most programmers do not declare variables inside any control statement other than the **for**. In fact, the declaration of variables within the other statements is controversial, with some programmers suggesting that to do so is bad practice.

Using break to Exit a Loop

It is possible to force an immediate exit from a loop, bypassing the loop's conditional test, by using the **break** statement. When the **break** statement is encountered inside a loop, the loop is immediately terminated, and program control resumes at the next statement following the loop. Here is a simple example:

```
#include <iostream>
using namespace std;

int main()
{
  int t;

  // Loops from 0 to 9, not to 100!
```

```
for(t=0; t<100; t++) {
  if(t==10) break;   ◄────────  Break out of the for
  cout << t << ' ';              when t equals 10.
}

return 0;
}
```

The output from the program is shown here:

```
0 1 2 3 4 5 6 7 8 9
```

As the output illustrates, this program prints the numbers 0 through 9 on the screen before ending. It will not go to 100, because the **break** statement will cause it to terminate early.

When loops are nested (that is, when one loop encloses another), a **break** will cause an exit from only the innermost loop. Here is an example:

```
#include <iostream>
using namespace std;

int main()
{
  int t, count;

  for(t=0; t<10; t++) {
    count = 1;
    for(;;) {
      cout << count << ' ';
      count++;
      if(count==10) break;
    }
    cout << '\n';
  }

  return 0;
}
```

Here is the output produced by this program:

```
1 2 3 4 5 6 7 8 9
1 2 3 4 5 6 7 8 9
```

```
1 2 3 4 5 6 7 8 9
1 2 3 4 5 6 7 8 9
1 2 3 4 5 6 7 8 9
1 2 3 4 5 6 7 8 9
1 2 3 4 5 6 7 8 9
1 2 3 4 5 6 7 8 9
1 2 3 4 5 6 7 8 9
1 2 3 4 5 6 7 8 9
```

As you can see, this program prints the numbers 1 through 9 on the screen ten times. Each time the **break** is encountered in the inner **for** loop, control is passed back to the outer **for** loop. Notice that the inner **for** is an infinite loop that uses the **break** statement to terminate.

The **break** statement can be used with any loop statement. It is most appropriate when a special condition can cause immediate termination. One common use is to terminate infinite loops, as the foregoing example illustrates.

One other point: A **break** used in a **switch** statement will affect only that **switch**, and not any loop the **switch** happens to be in.

Using continue

It is possible to force an early iteration of a loop, bypassing the loop's normal control structure. This is accomplished using **continue**. The **continue** statement forces the next iteration of the loop to take place, skipping any code between itself and the conditional expression that controls the loop. For example, the following program prints the even numbers between 0 and 100:

```
#include <iostream>
using namespace std;

int main()
{
  int x;

  for(x=0; x<=100; x++) {
    if(x%2) continue;        ◄─────── Continue the loop early
    cout << x << ' ';                 when x is odd.
  }

  return 0;
}
```

Only even numbers are printed, because an odd number will cause the **continue** statement to execute, resulting in early iteration of the loop, bypassing the **cout** statement. Remember that the % operator produces the remainder of an integer division. Thus, when **x** is odd, the remainder is 1, which is true. When **x** is even, the remainder is 0, which is false.

In **while** and **do-while** loops, a **continue** statement will cause control to go directly to the conditional expression and then continue the looping process. In the case of the **for**, the increment part of the loop is performed, then the conditional expression is executed, and then the loop continues.

1-Minute Drill

● Within a loop, what happens when a **break** is executed?

● What does **continue** do?

● Assuming a loop that encloses a **switch**, does a **break** in the **switch** cause the loop to terminate?

Help3.cpp

Project 3-3: Finish the C++ Help System

This project puts the finishing touches on the C++ help system that was created by the previous projects. This version adds the syntax for **break**, **continue**, and **goto**. It also allows the user to request the syntax for more than one statement. It does this by adding an outer loop that runs until the user enters a **q** as a menu selection.

Step-by-Step

1. Copy **Help2.cpp** to a new file called **Help3.cpp**.

2. Surround all of the program code with an infinite **for** loop. Break out of this loop, using **break**, when a **q** is entered. Since this loop surrounds all of the program code, breaking out of this loop causes the program to terminate.

● Within a loop, **break** causes immediate termination of the loop. Execution resumes at the first line of code after the loop.
● The **continue** statement causes a loop to iterate immediately, bypassing any remaining code.
● No.

3. Change the menu loop, as shown here:

```
do {
  cout << "Help on:\n";
  cout << "  1. if\n";
  cout << "  2. switch\n";
  cout << "  3. for\n";
  cout << "  4. while\n";
  cout << "  5. do-while\n";
  cout << "  6. break\n";
  cout << "  7. continue\n";
  cout << "  8. goto\n";
  cout << "Choose one (q to quit): ";
  cin >> choice;
} while( choice < '1' || choice > '8' && choice != 'q');
```

Notice that this loop now includes the **break**, **continue**, and **goto** statements. It also accepts a **q** as a valid choice.

4. Expand the **switch** statement to include the **break**, **continue**, and **goto** statements, as shown here:

```
case '6':
  cout << "The break:\n\n";
  cout << "break;\n";
  break;
case '7':
  cout << "The continue:\n\n";
  cout << "continue;\n";
  break;
case '8':
  cout << "The goto:\n\n";
  cout << "goto label;\n";
  break;
```

5. Here is the entire **Help3.cpp** program listing:

```
/*
   Project 3-3

   The finished Help system that processes multiple requests.
*/

#include <iostream>
```

```
using namespace std;

int main() {
  char choice;

  for(;;) {
    do {
      cout << "Help on:\n";
      cout << "  1. if\n";
      cout << "  2. switch\n";
      cout << "  3. for\n";
      cout << "  4. while\n";
      cout << "  5. do-while\n";
      cout << "  6. break\n";
      cout << "  7. continue\n";
      cout << "  8. goto\n";
      cout << "Choose one (q to quit): ";
      cin >> choice;
    } while( choice < '1' || choice > '8' && choice != 'q');

    if(choice == 'q') break;

    cout << "\n\n";

    switch(choice) {
      case '1':
        cout << "The if:\n\n";
        cout << "if(condition) statement;\n";
        cout << "else statement;\n";
        break;
      case '2':
        cout << "The switch:\n\n";
        cout << "switch(expression) {\n";
        cout << "  case constant:\n";
        cout << "    statement sequence\n";
        cout << "    break;\n";
        cout << "  // ...\n";
        cout << "}\n";
        break;
      case '3':
        cout << "The for:\n\n";
        cout << "for(init; condition; iteration)";
        cout << " statement;\n";
        break;
```

```
        case '4':
          cout << "The while:\n\n";
          cout << "while(condition) statement;\n";
          break;
        case '5':
          cout << "The do-while:\n\n";
          cout << "do {\n";
          cout << "  statement;\n";
          cout << "} while (condition);\n";
          break;
        case '6':
          cout << "The break:\n\n";
          cout << "break;\n";
          break;
        case '7':
          cout << "The continue:\n\n";
          cout << "continue;\n";
          break;
        case '8':
          cout << "The goto:\n\n";
          cout << "goto label;\n";
          break;
      }
      cout << "\n";
  }

  return 0;
}
```

6. Here is a sample run:

```
Help on:
  1. if
  2. switch
  3. for
  4. while
  5. do-while
  6. break
  7. continue
  8. goto
Choose one (q to quit): 1

The if:
```

```
if(condition) statement;
else statement;

Help on:
  1. if
  2. switch
  3. for
  4. while
  5. do-while
  6. break
  7. continue
  8. goto
Choose one (q to quit): 6

The break:

break;

Help on:
  1. if
  2. switch
  3. for
  4. while
  5. do-while
  6. break
  7. continue
  8. goto
Choose one (q to quit): q
```

Nested Loops

As you have seen in some of the preceding examples, one loop can be nested inside of another. Nested loops are used to solve a wide variety of programming problems and are an essential part of programming. So, before leaving the topic of C++'s loop statements, let's look at one more nested loop example. The following program uses a nested **for** loop to find the factors of the numbers from 2 to 100:

```
/*
   Use nested loops to find factors of numbers
   between 2 and 100.
```

```
*/

#include <iostream>
using namespace std;

int main() {

  for(int i=2; i <= 100; i++) {
    cout << "Factors of " << i << ": ";

    for(int j = 2; j < i; j++)
      if((i%j) == 0) cout << j << " ";

    cout << "\n";
  }

  return 0;
}
```

Here is a portion of the output produced by the program:

```
Factors of 2:
Factors of 3:
Factors of 4: 2
Factors of 5:
Factors of 6: 2 3
Factors of 7:
Factors of 8: 2 4
Factors of 9: 3
Factors of 10: 2 5
Factors of 11:
Factors of 12: 2 3 4 6
Factors of 13:
Factors of 14: 2 7
Factors of 15: 3 5
Factors of 16: 2 4 8
Factors of 17:
Factors of 18: 2 3 6 9
Factors of 19:
Factors of 20: 2 4 5 10
```

In the program, the outer loop runs i from 2 through 100. The inner loop successively tests all numbers from 2 up to i, printing those that evenly divide i.

Using the goto Statement

The **goto** is C++'s unconditional jump statement. Thus, when encountered, program flow jumps to the location specified by the **goto**. The statement fell out of favor with programmers many years ago because it encouraged the creation of "spaghetti code." However, the **goto** is still occasionally—and sometimes effectively—used. This book will not make a judgment regarding its validity as a form of program control. It should be stated, however, that there are no programming situations that require the use of the **goto** statement; it is not needed to make the language complete. Rather, it is a convenience which, if used wisely, can be of benefit in certain programming situations. As such, the **goto** is not used in this book outside of this section. The chief concern most programmers have about the **goto** is its tendency to clutter a program and render it nearly unreadable. However, there are times when the use of the **goto** can clarify program flow rather than confuse it.

The **goto** requires a label for operation. A *label* is a valid C++ identifier followed by a colon. Furthermore, the label must be in the same function as the **goto** that uses it. For example, a loop from 1 to 100 could be written using a **goto** and a label, as shown here:

```
x = 1;
loop1:
  x++;
  if(x < 100) goto loop1;      Execution jumps to loop1.
```

One good use for the **goto** is to exit from a deeply nested routine. For example, consider the following code fragment:

```
for(...) {
  for(...) {
    while(...) {
      if(...) goto stop;
      .
      .
      .
    }
  }
}
stop:
  cout << "Error in program.\n";
```

Eliminating the **goto** would force a number of additional tests to be performed. A simple **break** statement would not work here, because it would only cause the program to exit from the innermost loop.

✓ Mastery Check

1. Write a program that reads characters from the keyboard until a $ is typed. Have the program count the number of periods. Report the total at the end of the program.

2. In the **switch**, can the code sequence from one **case** run into the next? Explain.

3. Show the general form of the **if-else-if** ladder.

4. Given

```
if(x < 10)
  if(y > 100) {
    if(!done) x = z;
    else y = z;
  }
else cout << "error"; // what if?
```

to what **if** does the last **else** associate?

5. Show the **for** statement for a loop that counts from 1000 to 0 by –2.

6. Is the following fragment valid?

```
for(int i = 0; i < num; i++)
  sum += i;

count = i;
```

7. Explain what **break** does.

☑️ *Mastery Check*

8. In the following fragment, after the **break** statement executes, what is displayed?

```
for(i = 0; i < 10; i++) {
  while(running) {
    if(x<y) break;
    // ...
  }
  cout << "after while\n";
}
cout << "After for\n";
```

9. What does the following fragment print?

```
for(int i = 0; i<10; i++) {
  cout << i << " ";
  if(!(i%2)) continue;
  cout << "\n";
}
```

10. The iteration expression in a **for** loop need not always alter the loop control variable by a fixed amount. Instead, the loop control variable can change in any arbitrary way. Using this concept, write a program that uses a **for** loop to generate and display the progression 1, 2, 4, 8, 16, 32, and so on.

11. The ASCII lowercase letters are separated from the uppercase letters by 32. Thus, to convert a lowercase letter to uppercase, subtract 32 from it. Use this information to write a program that reads characters from the keyboard. Have it convert all lowercase letters to uppercase, and all uppercase letters to lowercase, displaying the result. Make no changes to any other character. Have the program stop when the user enters a period. At the end, have the program display the number of case changes that have taken place.

12. What is C++'s unconditional jump statement?

Module 4

Arrays, Strings, and Pointers

The Goals of This Module

- Use one-dimensional arrays
- Use two-dimensional and multidimensional arrays
- Understand strings
- Read strings from the keyboard
- Explore the standard string functions
- Initialize arrays
- Employ arrays of strings
- Understand pointer fundamentals
- Apply the pointer operators
- Use pointers in expressions
- Relate pointers to arrays
- Understand multiple indirection

This module discusses arrays, strings, and pointers. Although these may seem to be three disconnected topics, they aren't. In C++ they are intertwined, and an understanding of one aids in the understanding of the others.

An *array* is a collection of variables of the same type that are referred to by a common name. Arrays may have from one to several dimensions, although the one-dimensional array is the most common. Arrays offer a convenient means of creating lists of related variables.

The array that you will probably use most often is the character array, because it is used to hold a character string. The C++ language does not define a built-in string data type. Instead, strings are implemented as arrays of characters. This approach to strings allows greater power and flexibility than are available in languages that use a distinct string type.

A *pointer* is an object that contains a memory address. Typically, a pointer is used to access the value of another object. Often this other object is an array. In fact, pointers and arrays are related to each other more than you might expect.

One-Dimensional Arrays

A one-dimensional array is a list of related variables. Such lists are common in programming. For example, you might use a one-dimensional array to store the account numbers of the active users on a network. Another array might store the current batting averages for a baseball team. When computing the average of a list of values, you will often use an array to hold the values. Arrays are fundamental to modern programming.

The general form of a one-dimensional array declaration is

type name[*size*];

Here, *type* declares the base type of the array. The base type determines the data type of each element that makes up the array. The number of elements the array can hold is specified by *size*. For example, the following declares an integer array named **sample** that is ten elements long:

```
int sample[10];
```

An individual element within an array is accessed through an index. An *index* describes the position of an element within an array. In C++, all arrays have zero as the index of their first element. Because **sample** has ten elements, it has index values of 0 through 9. You access an array element by indexing the array using the number of the element. To index an array, specify the number of the element you want, surrounded by square brackets. Thus, the first element in **sample** is **sample[0]**, and the last element is **sample[9]**. For example, the following program loads **sample** with the numbers 0 through 9:

```
#include <iostream>
using namespace std;

int main()
{
  int sample[10]; // this reserves 10 integer elements
  int t;

  // load the array
  for(t=0; t<10; ++t) sample[t] = t;

  // display the array
  for(t=0; t<10; ++t)
    cout << "This is sample[" << t << "]: " << sample[t] << "\n";

  return 0;
}
```

Notice how **sample** is indexed.

4

The output from this example is shown here:

```
This is sample[0]: 0
This is sample[1]: 1
This is sample[2]: 2
This is sample[3]: 3
This is sample[4]: 4
This is sample[5]: 5
This is sample[6]: 6
This is sample[7]: 7
This is sample[8]: 8
This is sample[9]: 9
```

In C++, all arrays consist of contiguous memory locations. (That is, all array elements reside next to each other in memory.) The lowest address corresponds to the first element, and the highest address corresponds to the last element. For example, after this fragment is run:

```
int nums[5];
int i;

for(i=0; i<5; i++) nums[i] = i;
```

nums looks like this:

nums[0]	nums[1]	nums[2]	nums[3]	nums[4]
0	1	2	3	4

Arrays are common in programming because they let you deal easily with sets of related variables. Here is an example. The following program creates an array of ten elements and assigns each element a value. It then computes the average of those values and finds the minimum and the maximum value.

```cpp
/*
   Compute the average and find the minimum
   and maximum of a set of values.
*/

#include <iostream>
using namespace std;

int main()
{
  int i, avg, min_val, max_val;
  int nums[10];

  nums[0] = 10;
  nums[1] = 18;
  nums[2] = 75;
  nums[3] = 0;
  nums[4] = 1;
  nums[5] = 56;
  nums[6] = 100;
  nums[7] = 12;
  nums[8] = -19;
  nums[9] = 88;

  // compute the average
  avg = 0;
  for(i=1; i<10; i++)
     avg += nums[i];          ◄——— Sum the values in **nums**.
```

```
avg /= 10;          Calculate the average.

cout << "Average is " << avg << '\n';

// find minimum and maximum values        Find the minimum and
min_val = max_val = nums[0];              maximum values in nums.
for(i=1; i<10; i++) {
  if(nums[i] < min_val) min_val = nums[i];
  if(nums[i] > max_val) max_val = nums[i];
}

cout << "Minimum value: " << min_val << '\n';
cout << "Maximum value: " <<  max_val << '\n';

return 0;
}
```

4

The output from the program is shown here:

```
Average is 33
Minimum value: -19
Maximum value: 100
```

Notice how the program cycles through the elements in the **nums** array. Storing the values in an array makes this process easy. As the program illustrates, the loop control variable of a **for** loop is used as an index. Loops such as this are very common when working with arrays.

There is an array restriction that you must be aware of. In C++, you cannot assign one array to another. For example, the following is illegal:

```
int a[10], b[10];

// ...

a = b; // error -- illegal
```

To transfer the contents of one array into another, you must assign each value individually, like this:

```
for(i=0; i < 10; i++) a[i] = b[i];
```

No Bounds Checking

C++ performs no bounds checking on arrays. This means that there is nothing that stops you from overrunning the end of an array. In other words, you can index an array of size *N* beyond *N* without generating any compile-time or runtime error messages, even though doing so will often cause catastrophic program failure. For example, the compiler will compile and run the following code without issuing any error messages even though the array **crash** is being overrun:

```
int crash[10], i;

for(i=0; i<100; i++) crash[i]=i;
```

In this case, the loop will iterate 100 times, even though **crash** is only ten elements long! This causes memory that is not part of **crash** to be overwritten.

    If an array overrun occurs during an assignment operation, memory that is being used for other purposes, such as holding other variables, might be overwritten. If an array overrun occurs when data is being read, then invalid data will corrupt the program. Either way, as the programmer, it is your job both to ensure that all arrays are large enough to hold what the program will put in them, and to provide bounds checking whenever necessary.

1-Minute Drill

● What is a one-dimensional array?

● The index of the first element in an array is always zero. True or false?

● Does C++ provide bounds checking on arrays?

Two-Dimensional Arrays

C++ allows multidimensional arrays. The simplest form of the multidimensional array is the two-dimensional array. A *two-dimensional array* is, in essence, a list

---

● A one-dimensional array is a list of related values.
● True. Zero is always the first index.
● No, C++ provides no bounds checking on arrays.

Ask the Expert

Question: Since overrunning an array can lead to catastrophic failures, why doesn't C++ provide bounds checking on array operations?

Answer: C++ was designed to allow professional programmers to create the fastest, most efficient code possible. Toward this end, very little runtime error checking is included, because it slows (often dramatically) the execution of a program. Instead, C++ expects you, the programmer, to be responsible enough to prevent array overruns in the first place, and to add appropriate error checking on your own as needed. Also, as you will learn later in this book, it is possible for you to define array types of your own that perform bounds checking if your program actually requires this feature.

4

of one-dimensional arrays. To declare a two-dimensional integer array **twoD** of size 10,20, you would write

```
int twoD[10][20];
```

Pay careful attention to the declaration. Unlike some other computer languages, which use commas to separate the array dimensions, C++ places each dimension in its own set of brackets. Similarly, to access an element, specify the indices within their own set of brackets. For example, for point 3,5 of array **twoD**, you would use **twoD[3][5]**.

In the next example, a two-dimensional array is loaded with the numbers 1 through 12.

```
#include <iostream>
using namespace std;

int main()
{
  int t,i, nums[3][4];

  for(t=0; t < 3; ++t) {
    for(i=0; i < 4; ++i) {
      nums[t][i] = (t*4)+i+1;         Indexing nums
      cout << nums[t][i] << ' ';       requires two indexes.
    }
```

```
    cout << '\n';
  }

  return 0;
}
```

In this example, **nums[0][0]** will have the value 1, **nums[0][1]** the value 2, **nums[0][2]** the value 3, and so on. The value of **nums[2][3]** will be 12. Conceptually, the array will look like that shown here:

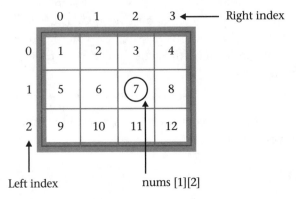

Two-dimensional arrays are stored in a row-column matrix, where the first index indicates the row and the second indicates the column. This means that when array elements are accessed in the order in which they are actually stored in memory, the right index changes faster than the left.

You should remember that storage for all array elements is determined at compile time. Also, the memory used to hold an array is required the entire time that the array is in existence. In the case of a two-dimensional array, you can use this formula to determine the number of bytes of memory that are needed:

bytes = number of rows × number of columns × number of bytes in type

Therefore, assuming four-byte integers, an integer array with dimensions 10,5 would have 10×5×4 (or 200) bytes allocated.

Multidimensional Arrays

C++ allows arrays with more than two dimensions. Here is the general form of a multidimensional array declaration:

type name[*size1*][*size2*]...[*sizeN*];

For example, the following declaration creates a 4×10×3–integer array:

```
int multidim[4][10][3];
```

Arrays of three or more dimensions are not often used, due to the amount of memory required to hold them. Remember, storage for all array elements is allocated during the entire lifetime of an array. When multidimensional arrays are used, large amounts of memory can be consumed. For example, a four-dimensional character array with dimensions 10,6,9,4 would require 10×6×9×4 (or 2,160) bytes. If each array dimension is increased by a factor of 10 each (that is, 100×60×90×40), then the memory required for the array increases to 21,600,000 bytes! As you can see, large multidimensional arrays may cause a shortage of memory for other parts of your program. Thus, a program with arrays of more than two or three dimensions may find itself quickly out of memory!

1-Minute Drill

- Each dimension in a multidimensional array is specified with its own set of brackets. True or false?

- Show how to declare a two-dimensional integer array called **list** with the dimensions 4×9.

- Given **list** from the preceding question, show how to access element 2, 3.

Bubble.cpp

Project 4-1: Sorting an Array

Because a one-dimensional array organizes data into an indexable linear list, it is the perfect data structure for sorting. In this project, you will learn a simple way to sort an array. As you may know, there are a number of different sorting algorithms. The quick sort, the shaker sort, and the shell sort are just three. However, the best known, simplest, and easiest to understand sorting algorithm is called the *bubble sort*. While the bubble sort is not very efficient—in fact, its performance is unacceptable for sorting large arrays—it may be used effectively for sorting small ones.

- True.
- `int list[4][9]`
- `list[2][3]`

Step-by-Step

1. Create a file called **Bubble.cpp**.

2. The bubble sort gets its name from the way it performs the sorting operation. It uses repeated comparison and, if necessary, exchange of adjacent elements in the array. In this process, small values move toward one end, and large ones toward the other end. The process is conceptually similar to bubbles finding their own level in a tank of water. The bubble sort operates by making several passes through the array, exchanging out-of-place elements when necessary. The number of passes required to ensure that the array is sorted is equal to one less than the number of elements in the array.

Here is the code that forms the core of the bubble sort. The array being sorted is called **nums**.

```
// This is the bubble sort.
for(a=1; a<size; a++)
  for(b=size-1; b>=a; b--) {
    if(nums[b-1] > nums[b]) { // if out of order
      // exchange elements
      t = nums[b-1];
      nums[b-1] = nums[b];
      nums[b] = t;
    }
  }
```

Notice that the sort relies on two **for** loops. The inner loop checks adjacent elements in the array, looking for out-of-order elements. When an out-of-order element pair is found, the two elements are exchanged. With each pass, the smallest element of those remaining moves into its proper location. The outer loop causes this process to repeat until the entire array has been sorted.

3. Here is the entire **Bubble.cpp** program:

```
/*
   Project 4-1
   Demonstrate the Bubble sort.
*/
#include <iostream>
#include <cstdlib>
using namespace std;
```

```
int main()
{
  int nums[10];
  int a, b, t;
  int size;

  size = 10; // number of elements to sort

  // give the array some random initial values
  for(t=0; t<size; t++) nums[t] = rand();

  // display original array
  cout << "Original array is:\n    ";
  for(t=0; t<size; t++) cout << nums[t] << ' ';
  cout << '\n';

  // This is the bubble sort.
  for(a=1; a<size; a++)
    for(b=size-1; b>=a; b--) {
      if(nums[b-1] > nums[b]) { // if out of order
        // exchange elements
        t = nums[b-1];
        nums[b-1] = nums[b];
        nums[b] = t;
      }
    }

  // display sorted array
  cout << "\nSorted array is:\n    ";
  for(t=0; t<size; t++) cout << nums[t] << ' ';

  return 0;
}
```

The output is shown here:

```
Original array is:
   41 18467 6334 26500 19169 15724 11478 29358 26962 24464

Sorted array is:
   41 6334 11478 15724 18467 19169 24464 26500 26962 29358
```

4. Although the bubble sort is good for small arrays, it is not efficient when used on larger ones. The best general-purpose sorting algorithm is the quick sort. The quick sort, however, relies on features of C++ that you have not yet learned. Also, the C++ standard library contains a function called **qsort( )** that implements a version of the quick sort, but to use it, you will also need to know more about C++.

Strings

By far the most common use for one-dimensional arrays is to create character strings. C++ supports two types of strings. The first, and most commonly used, is the *null-terminated string,* which is a null-terminated character array. (A null is zero.) Thus, a null-terminated string contains the characters that make up the string followed by a null. Null-terminated strings are widely used because they offer a high level of efficiency and give the programmer detailed control over string operations. When a C++ programmer uses the term *string,* he or she is usually referring to a null-terminated string. The second type of string defined by C++ is the **string** class, which is part of the C++ class library. Thus, **string** is not a built-in type. It provides an object-oriented approach to string handling but is not as widely used as the null-terminated string. Here, null-terminated strings are examined.

String Fundamentals

When declaring a character array that will hold a null-terminated string, you need to declare it one character longer than the largest string that it will hold. For example, if you want to declare an array **str** that could hold a 10-character string, here is what you would write:

```
char str[11];
```

Specifying the size as 11 makes room for the null at the end of the string.

As you learned earlier in this book, C++ allows you to define string constants. A string constant is a list of characters enclosed in double quotes. Here are some examples:

"hello there"   "I like C++"   "Mars"   ""

It is not necessary to manually add the null terminator onto the end of string constants; the C++ compiler does this for you automatically. Therefore, the string "Mars" will appear in memory like this:

M	a	r	s	0

The last string shown is "". This is called a *null string*. It contains only the null terminator and no other characters. Null strings are useful because they represent the empty string.

Reading a String from the Keyboard

The easiest way to read a string entered from the keyboard is to use a **char** array in a **cin** statement. For example, the following program reads a string entered by the user:

```
// Using cin to read a string from the keyboard.

#include <iostream>
using namespace std;

int main()
{
  char str[80];

  cout << "Enter a string: ";
  cin >> str; // read string from keyboard     ←——— Read a string using cin.
  cout << "Here is your string: ";
  cout << str;

  return 0;
}
```

Here is a sample run:

```
Enter a string: testing
Here is your string: testing
```

Although this program is technically correct, it will not always work the way that you expect. To see why, run the program and try entering the string "This is a test". Here is what you will see:

```
Enter a string: This is a test
Here is your string: This
```

When the program redisplays your string, it shows only the word "This", not the entire sentence. The reason for this is that the C++ I/O system stops reading a string when the first *whitespace* character is encountered. Whitespace characters include spaces, tabs, and newlines.

To solve the whitespace problem, you will need to use another of C++'s library functions, **gets( )**. The general form of a call to **gets( )** is

gets(*array-name*);

If you need your program to read a string, call **gets( )** with the name of the array, without any index, as its argument. Upon return from **gets( )**, the array will hold the string input from the keyboard. The **gets( )** function will continue to read characters until you enter a carriage return. The header used by **gets( )** is **<cstdio>**.

This version of the preceding program uses **gets( )** to allow the entry of strings containing spaces:

```
// Using gets() to read a string from the keyboard.

#include <iostream>
#include <cstdio>
using namespace std;

int main()
{
  char str[80];

  cout << "Enter a string: ";
  gets(str); // read a string using gets()
  cout << "Here is your string: ";
  cout << str;

  return 0;
}
```

Read a string using **gets( )**.

Here is a sample run:

```
Enter a string: This is a test
Here is your string: This is a test
```

Now, spaces are read and included in the string. One other point: Notice that in a **cout** statement, **str** can be used directly. In general, the name of a character array that holds a string can be used any place that a string constant can be used.

Keep in mind that neither **cin** nor **gets( )** performs any bounds checking on the array. Therefore, if the user enters a string longer than the size of the array, the array will be overwritten. Later, you will learn an alternative to **gets( )** that avoids this problem.

1-Minute Drill

- What is a null-terminated string?
- To hold a string that is 8 characters long, how long must the character array be?
- What function can be used to read a string containing spaces from the keyboard?

4

Some String Library Functions

C++ supports a wide range of string manipulation functions. The most common are

```
strcpy( )
strcat( )
strcmp( )
strlen( )
```

The string functions all use the same header, **<cstring>**. Let's take a look at these functions now.

strcpy

A call to **strcpy( )** takes this general form:

```
strcpy(to, from);
```

The **strcpy( )** function copies the contents of the string *from* into *to*. Remember, the array that forms *to* must be large enough to hold the string contained in *from*. If it isn't, the *to* array will be overrun, which will probably crash your program.

strcat

A call to **strcat( )** takes this form:

```
strcat(s1, s2);
```

- A null-terminated string is an array of characters that ends with a null.
- The array must be at least 9 characters long if it is to hold an 8-character string.
- The **gets( )** function can be used to read strings containing embedded spaces.

The **strcat( )** function appends *s2* to the end of *s1*; *s2* is unchanged. You must ensure that *s1* is large enough to hold its original contents and those of *s2*.

strcmp

A call to **strcmp( )** takes this general form:

strcmp(*s1*, *s2*);

The **strcmp( )** function compares two strings and returns 0 if they are equal. If *s1* is greater than *s2* lexicographically (that is, according to dictionary order), then a positive number is returned; if it is less than *s2*, a negative number is returned.

The key to using **strcmp( )** is to remember that it returns false when the strings match. Therefore, you will need to use the ! operator if you want something to occur when the strings are equal. For example, the condition controlling the following **if** statement is true when **str** is equal to "C++":

```
if(!strcmp(str, "C++") cout << "str is C++";
```

strlen

The general form of a call to **strlen( )** is

strlen(*s*);

where *s* is a string. The **strlen( )** function returns the length of the string pointed to by *s*.

A String Function Example

The following program illustrates the use of all four string functions:

```
// Demonstrate the string functions.
#include <iostream>
#include <cstdio>
#include <cstring>
using namespace std;

int main()
```

```
{
  char s1[80], s2[80];

  strcpy(s1, "C++");
  strcpy(s2, " is power programming.");

  cout << "lengths: " << strlen(s1);
  cout << ' ' << strlen(s2) << '\n';

  if(!strcmp(s1, s2))
     cout << "The strings are equal\n";
  else cout << "not equal\n";

  strcat(s1, s2);
  cout << s1 << '\n';

  strcpy(s2, s1);
  cout << s1 << " and " << s2 << "\n";

  if(!strcmp(s1, s2))
    cout << "s1 and s2 are now the same.\n";

  return 0;
}
```

4

Here is the output:

```
lengths: 3 22
not equal
C++ is power programming.
C++ is power programming. and C++ is power programming.
s1 and s2 are now the same.
```

Using the Null Terminator

The fact that strings are null-terminated can often be used to simplify various operations. For example, the following program converts a string to uppercase:

```
// Convert a string to uppercase.
#include <iostream>
#include <cstring>
#include <cctype>
using namespace std;
```

```
int main()
{
  char str[80];
  int i;

  strcpy(str, "this is a test");

  for(i=0; str[i]; i++) str[i] = toupper(str[i]);

  cout << str;

  return 0;
}
```

This loop stops when the null terminator is indexed.

The output from this program is shown here:

```
THIS IS A TEST
```

This program uses the library function **toupper( )**, which returns the uppercase equivalent of its character argument, to convert each character in the string. The **toupper( )** function uses the header **<cctype>**.

Notice that the test condition of the **for** loop is simply the array indexed by the control variable. The reason this works is that a true value is any non-zero value. Remember, all character values are non-zero, but the null terminating the string is zero. Therefore, the loop runs until it encounters the null terminator, which causes **str[i]** to become zero. Because the null terminator marks the end of the string, the loop stops precisely where it is supposed to. You will see many examples that use the null terminator in a similar fashion in professionally written C++ code.

1-Minute Drill

● What does the **strcat( )** function do?

● What does **strcmp( )** return when it compares two equivalent strings?

● Show how to obtain the length of a string called **mystr**.

● The **strcat( )** function concatenates (that is, joins) two strings.
● The **strcmp( )** function returns 0 when it compares two equivalent strings.
● strlen(mystr)

Ask the Expert

Question: Besides toupper( ), does C++ support other character-manipulation functions?

Answer: Yes. The C++ standard library contains several other character-manipulation functions. For example, the complement to **toupper( )** is **tolower( )**, which returns the lowercase equivalent of its character argument. You can determine the case of a letter by using **isupper( )**, which returns true if the letter is uppercase, and **islower( )**, which returns true if the letter is lowercase. Other character functions include **isalpha( )**, **isdigit( )**, **isspace( )**, and **ispunct( )**. These functions each take a character argument and determine the category of that argument. For example, **isalpha( )** returns true if its argument is a letter of the alphabet.

4

Array Initialization

C++ allows arrays to be initialized. The general form of array initialization is similar to that of other variables, as shown here:

type-specifier array_name[size] = {value-list};

The *value-list* is a comma-separated list of values that are type compatible with the base type of the array. The first value will be placed in the first position of the array, the second value in the second position, and so on. Notice that a semicolon follows the }.

In the following example, a ten-element integer array is initialized with the numbers 1 through 10.

```
int i[10] = {1, 2, 3, 4, 5, 6, 7, 8, 9, 10};
```

This means that i[0] will have the value 1, and i[9] will have the value 10.

Character arrays that will hold strings allow a shorthand initialization that takes this form:

char array_name[size] = "string";

For example, the following code fragment initializes **str** to the string "C++":

```
char str[4] = "C++";
```

This is the same as writing

```
char str[4] = {'C', '+', '+', '\0'};
```

Because strings in C++ must end with a null, you must make sure that the array you declare is long enough to include it. This is why **str** is four characters long in these examples, even though "C++" is only three. When a string constant is used, the compiler automatically supplies the null terminator.

Multidimensional arrays are initialized in the same way as one-dimensional arrays. For example, the following program initializes an array called **sqrs** with the numbers 1 through 10 and their squares:

```
int sqrs[10][2] = {
  1, 1,
  2, 4,
  3, 9,
  4, 16,
  5, 25,
  6, 36,
  7, 49,
  8, 64,
  9, 81,
  10, 100
};
```

Examine Figure 4-1 to see how the **sqrs** array appears in memory.

When initializing a multidimensional array, you may add braces around the initializers for each dimension. This is called *subaggregate grouping*. For example, here is another way to write the preceding declaration:

```
int sqrs[10][2] = {
  {1, 1},
  {2, 4},
  {3, 9},
  {4, 16},
  {5, 25},
  {6, 36},
```

```
  {7, 49},
  {8, 64},
  {9, 81},
  {10, 100}
};
```

When using subaggregate grouping, if you don't supply enough initializers for a given group, the remaining members will automatically be set to zero.

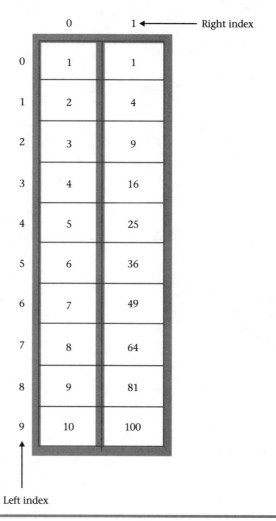

Figure 4-1   The initialized sqrs array

The following program uses the **sqrs** array to find the square of a number entered by the user. It first looks up the number in the array and then prints the corresponding square.

```cpp
#include <iostream>
using namespace std;

int main()
{
  int i, j;
  int sqrs[10][2] = {
    {1, 1},
    {2, 4},
    {3, 9},
    {4, 16},
    {5, 25},
    {6, 36},
    {7, 49},
    {8, 64},
    {9, 81},
    {10, 100}
  };

  cout << "Enter a number between 1 and 10: ";
  cin >> i;

  // look up i
  for(j=0; j<10; j++)
    if(sqrs[j][0]==i) break;
  cout << "The square of " << i << " is ";
  cout << sqrs[j][1];

  return 0;
}
```

Here is a sample run:

```
Enter a number between 1 and 10: 4
The square of 4 is 16
```

Unsized Array Initializations

When declaring an initialized array, it is possible to let C++ automatically determine the array's dimension. To do this, do not specify a size for the array. Instead, the compiler determines the size by counting the number of initializers and creating an array large enough to hold them. For example,

```
int nums[] = { 1, 2, 3, 4 };
```

creates an array called **nums** that is four elements long that contains the values 1, 2, 3, and 4. Because no explicit size is specified, an array such as **nums** is called an *unsized array*.

Unsized arrays are quite useful. For example, imagine that you are using array initialization to build a table of Internet addresses, as shown here:

```
char e1[16] = "www.osborne.com";
char e2[16] = "www.weather.com";
char e3[15] = "www.amazon.com";
```

As you might guess, it is very tedious to manually count the characters in each message to determine the correct array dimension. It is also error-prone because it is possible to miscount and incorrectly size the array. It is better to let the compiler size the arrays, as shown here:

```
char e1[] = "www.osborne.com";
char e2[] = "www.weather.com";
char e3[] = "www.amazon.com";
```

Besides being less tedious, the unsized array initialization method allows you to change any of the messages without fear of accidentally forgetting to resize the array.

Unsized array initializations are not restricted to one-dimensional arrays. For a multidimensional array, you must specify all but the leftmost dimension so that the array can be properly indexed. Using unsized array initializations, you can build tables of varying lengths, with the compiler automatically allocating enough storage for them. For example, here **sqrs** is declared as an unsized array:

```
int sqrs[][2] = {
  1, 1,
```

```
  2, 4,
  3, 9,
  4, 16,
  5, 25,
  6, 36,
  7, 49,
  8, 64,
  9, 81,
  10, 100
};
```

The advantage to this declaration over the sized version is that the table may be lengthened or shortened without changing the array dimensions.

Arrays of Strings

A special form of a two-dimensional array is an array of strings. It is not uncommon in programming to use an array of strings. The input processor to a database, for instance, may verify user commands against a string array of valid commands. To create an array of strings, a two-dimensional character array is used, with the size of the left index determining the number of strings and the size of the right index specifying the maximum length of each string. For example, the following declares an array of 30 strings, each having a maximum length of 80 characters.

```
char str_array[30][80];
```

Accessing an individual string is quite easy: you simply specify only the left index. For example, the following statement calls **gets( )** with the third string in **str_array**:

```
gets(str_array[2]);
```

To access an individual character within the third string, you will use a statement like this:

```
cout << str_array[2][3];
```

This displays the fourth character of the third string.

The following program demonstrates a string array by implementing a very simple computerized telephone directory. The two-dimensional array **numbers** holds pairs of names and numbers. To find a number, you enter the name. The number is displayed.

```
// A simple computerized telephone directory.
#include <iostream>
#include <cstdio>
using namespace std;

int main()
{
  int i;
  char str[80];
  char numbers[10][80] = {
    "Tom", "555-3322",
    "Mary", "555-8976",
    "Jon", "555-1037",
    "Rachel", "555-1400",
    "Sherry", "555-8873"
  };

  cout << "Enter name: ";
  cin >> str;

  for(i=0; i < 10; i += 2)
    if(!strcmp(str, numbers[i])) {
      cout << "Number is " << numbers[i+1] << "\n";
      break;
    }

  if(i == 10) cout << "Not found.\n";


  return 0;
}
```

This is an array of 10 strings, each capable of holding up to 79 characters.

4

Here is a sample run:

```
Enter name: Jon
Number is 555-1037
```

Notice how the **for** loop increments its loop control variable, **i**, by 2 each time through the loop. This is necessary because names and numbers alternate in the array.

1-Minute Drill

- Show how to initialize a four-element array of **int** to the values 1, 2, 3, and 4.

- How can this initialization be rewritten?
  ```
  char str[6] = {'H', 'e', 'l', 'l', 'o', '\0' };
  ```

- Rewrite the following as an unsized array:
  ```
  int nums[4] = {44, 55, 66, 77};
  ```

Pointers

The pointer is one of C++'s most powerful features. It is also one of its most troublesome. Despite their potential for misuse, pointers are a crucial part of C++ programming. For example, they allow C++ to support such things as linked lists and dynamic memory allocation. They also provide one means by which a function can alter the contents of an argument. However, these and other uses of pointers will be discussed in subsequent modules. In this module, you will learn the basics about pointers and see how to manipulate them.

In a few places in the following discussions, it is necessary to refer to the size of several of C++'s basic data types. For the sake of discussion, assume that characters are one byte in length, integers are four bytes long, **float**s are four bytes long, and **double**s have a length of eight bytes. Thus, we will be assuming a typical 32-bit environment.

What Are Pointers?

A *pointer* is an object that contains a memory address. Very often this address is the location of another object, such as a variable. For example, if **x** contains the address of **y**, then **x** is said to "point to" **y**.

- `int list[4] = { 1, 2, 3, 4 };`
- `char str[6] = "Hello";`
- `int nums[] = {44, 55, 66, 77};`

Pointer variables must be declared as such. The general form of a pointer variable declaration is

type *var-name;

Here, *type* is the pointer's base type. The *base type* determines what type of data the pointer will be pointing to. *var-name* is the name of the pointer variable. For example, to declare **ip** to be a pointer to an **int**, use this declaration:

```
int *ip;
```

Since the base type of **ip** is **int**, it can be used to point to **int** values.

Here, a **float** pointer is declared:

```
float *fp;
```

In this case, the base type of **fp** is **float**, which means that it can be used to point to a **float** value.

In general, in a declaration statement, preceding a variable name with an * causes that variable to become a pointer.

The Pointer Operators

There are two special operators that are used with pointers: * and **&**. The **&** is a unary operator that returns the memory address of its operand. (Recall that a unary operator requires only one operand.) For example,

```
ptr = &total;
```

puts into **ptr** the memory address of the variable **total**. This address is the location of **total** in the computer's internal memory. It has *nothing* to do with the *value* of **total**. The operation of **&** can be remembered as returning "the address of" the variable it precedes. Therefore, the preceding assignment statement could be verbalized as "**ptr** receives the address of **total**." To better understand this assignment, assume that the variable **total** is located at address 100. Then, after the assignment takes place, **ptr** has the value 100.

The second operator is *, and it is the complement of &. It is a unary operator that returns the value of the variable located at the address specified by its operand. Continuing with the same example, if **ptr** contains the memory address of the variable **total**, then

```
val = *ptr;
```

will place the value of **total** into **val**. For example, if **total** originally had the value 3,200, then **val** will have the value 3,200, because that is the value stored at location 100, the memory address that was assigned to **ptr**. The operation of * can be remembered as "at address." In this case, then, the statement could be read as "**val** receives the value at address **ptr**."

The following program executes the sequence of the operations just described:

```cpp
#include <iostream>
using namespace std;

int main()
{
  int total;
  int *ptr;
  int val;

  total = 3200; // assign 3,200 to total

  ptr = &total; // get address of total

  val = *ptr;   // get value at that address

  cout << "Total is: " << val << '\n';

  return 0;
}
```

It is unfortunate that the multiplication symbol and the "at address" symbol are the same. This fact sometimes confuses newcomers to the C++ language. These operators have no relationship to each other. Keep in mind that both & and * have a higher precedence than any of the arithmetic operators except the unary minus, with which they have equal precedence.

The act of using a pointer is often called *indirection* because you are accessing one variable indirectly through another variable.

1-Minute Drill

- What is a pointer?
- Show how to declare a **long int** pointer called **valPtr**.
- As they relate to pointers, what do the ***** and **&** operators do?

The Base Type of a Pointer Is Important

In the preceding discussion, you saw that it was possible to assign **val** the value of **total** indirectly through a pointer. At this point, you may have thought of this important question: How does C++ know how many bytes to copy into **val** from the address pointed to by **ptr**? Or, more generally, how does the compiler transfer the proper number of bytes for any assignment involving a pointer? The answer is that the base type of the pointer determines the type of data upon which the pointer operates. In this case, because **ptr** is an **int** pointer, four bytes of information are copied into **val** (assuming a 32-bit **int**) from the address pointed to by **ptr**. However, if **ptr** had been a **double** pointer, for example, then eight bytes would have been copied.

It is important to ensure that pointer variables always point to the correct type of data. For example, when you declare a pointer to be of type **int**, the compiler assumes that anything it points to will be an integer variable. If it doesn't point to an integer variable, then trouble is usually not far behind! For example, the following fragment is incorrect:

```
int *p;
double f;
// ...
p = &f; // ERROR
```

This fragment is invalid because you cannot assign a **double** pointer to an integer pointer. That is, **&f** generates a pointer to a **double**, but **p** is a pointer to an **int**. These two types are not compatible. (In fact, the compiler would flag an error at this point and not compile your program.)

- A pointer is an object that contains the memory address of another object.
- `long int *valPtr;`
- The ***** obtains the value stored at the address that it precedes. The **&** obtains the address of the object that it precedes.

Although two pointers must have compatible types in order for one to be assigned to another, you can override this restriction (at your own risk) using a cast. For example, the following fragment is now technically correct:

```
int *p ;
double f;
// ...
p = (int *) &f; // Now technically OK
```

The cast to **int** * causes the **double** pointer to be converted to an integer pointer. However, to use a cast for this purpose is questionable practice. The reason is that the base type of a pointer determines how the compiler treats the data it points to. In this case, even though **p** is actually pointing to a floating-point value, the compiler still "thinks" that **p** is pointing to an **int** (because **p** is an **int** pointer).

To better understand why using a cast to assign one type of pointer to another is not usually a good idea, consider the following short program:

```
// This program will not work right.
#include <iostream>
using namespace std;

int main()
{
  double x, y;
  int *p;

  x = 123.23;
  p = (int *) &x; // use cast to assign double * to int *

  y = *p;     // What will this do?  ◄── ┌─────────────────────────┐
  cout << y; // What will this print?    │ These statements won't  │
                                         │ yield the desired result.│
                                         └─────────────────────────┘
  return 0;
}
```

Here is the output produced by the program. (You might see a different value.)

```
1.37439e+009
```

This value is clearly not 123.23! Here is why. In the program, **p** (which is an integer pointer) has been assigned the address of **x** (which is a **double**). Thus, when **y** is assigned the value pointed to by **p**, **y** receives only four bytes of data (and not the eight required for a **double** value), because **p** is an integer pointer. Therefore, the **cout** statement displays not 123.23, but a garbage value instead.

Assigning Values Through a Pointer

You can use a pointer on the left-hand side of an assignment statement to assign a value to the location pointed to by the pointer. Assuming that **p** is an **int** pointer, this assigns the value 101 to the location pointed to by **p**.

```
*p = 101;
```

You can verbalize this assignment like this: "At the location pointed to by **p**, assign the value 101." To increment or decrement the value at the location pointed to by a pointer, you can use a statement like this:

```
(*p)++;
```

The parentheses are necessary because the * operator has lower precedence than does the ++ operator.

The following program demonstrates an assignment through a pointer:

```
#include <iostream>
using namespace std;

int main()
{
  int *p, num;

  p = &num;

  *p = 100;        ←———————  Assign num the value 100 through p.
  cout << num << ' ';
  (*p)++;          ←———————  Increment num through p.
  cout << num << ' ';
  (*p)--;          ←———————  Decrement num through p.
  cout << num << '\n';

  return 0;
}
```

The output from the program is shown here:

```
100 101 100
```

Pointer Expressions

Pointers can be used in most C++ expressions. However, some special rules apply. Remember also that you may need to surround some parts of a pointer expression with parentheses in order to ensure that the outcome is what you desire.

Pointer Arithmetic

There are only four arithmetic operators that can be used on pointers: ++, − −, +, and −. To understand what occurs in pointer arithmetic, let **p1** be an **int** pointer with a current value of 2,000 (that is, it contains the address 2,000). Assuming 32-bit integers, after the expression

```
p1++;
```

the contents of **p1** will be 2,004, not 2,001! The reason for this is that each time **p1** is incremented, it will point to the next **int**. The same is true of decrements. For example, again assuming that **p1** has the value 2000, the expression

```
p1--;
```

causes **p1** to have the value 1996.

Generalizing from the preceding example, the following rules apply to pointer arithmetic. Each time that a pointer is incremented, it will point to the memory location of the next element of its base type. Each time it is decremented, it will point to the location of the previous element of its base type. In the case of character pointers, an increment or decrement will appear as "normal" arithmetic because characters are one byte long. However, every other type of pointer will increase or decrease by the length of its base type.

You are not limited to only increment and decrement operations. You can also add or subtract integers to or from pointers. The expression

```
p1 = p1 + 9;
```

makes **p1** point to the ninth element of **p1**'s base type, beyond the one to which it is currently pointing.

Although you cannot add pointers, you can subtract one pointer from another (provided they are both of the same base type). The remainder will be the number of elements of the base type that separate the two pointers.

Other than addition and subtraction of a pointer and an integer, or the subtraction of two pointers, no other arithmetic operations can be performed on pointers. For example, you cannot add or subtract **float** or **double** values to or from pointers.

To graphically see the effects of pointer arithmetic, execute the next short program. It creates an **int** pointer (i) and a **double** pointer (f). It then adds the values 0 through 9 to these pointers and displays the results. Observe how each address changes, relative to its base type, each time the loop is repeated. (For most 32-bit compilers, **i** will increase by 4s and **f** will increase by 8s.) Notice that when using a pointer in a **cout** statement, its address is automatically displayed in the addressing format applicable to the CPU and environment.

4

```
#include <iostream>
using namespace std;

int main()
{
  int *i, j[10];
  double *f, g[10];
  int x;

  i = j;
  f = g;

  for(x=0; x<10; x++)
    cout << i+x << ' ' << f+x << '\n';

  return 0;
}
```

Display the addresses produced by adding **x** to each pointer.

Here is a sample run. (The precise values you see may differ from these.)

```
0012FE5C 09012FE84
0012FE60 0012FE8C
0012FE64 0012FE94
0012FE68 0012FE9C
0012FE6C 0012FEA4
0012FE70 0012FEAC
0012FE74 0012FEB4
0012FE78 0012FEBC
0012FE7C 0012FEC4
0012FE80 0012FECC
```

Pointer Comparisons

Pointers may be compared using the relational operators, such as **==**, **<**, and **>**. In general, for the outcome of a pointer comparison to be meaningful, the two pointers usually must have some relationship to each other. For example, both may point to elements within the same array. (You will see an example of this in Project 4-2.) There is, however, one other type of pointer comparison: any pointer can be compared to the null pointer, which is zero.

1-Minute Drill

● All pointer arithmetic is performed relative to the _____ _____ of the pointer.

● Assuming that type **double** is 8 bytes long, when a **double** pointer is incremented, by how much is its value increased?

● In general, two pointers can be meaningfully compared in what case?

Pointers and Arrays

In C++, there is a close relationship between pointers and arrays. In fact, frequently a pointer and an array are interchangeable. Consider this fragment:

```
char str[80];
char *p1;

p1 = str;
```

Here, **str** is an array of 80 characters and **p1** is a character pointer. However, it is the third line that is of interest. In this line, **p1** is assigned the address of the first element in the **str** array. (That is, after the assignment, **p1** will point to **str[0]**.) Here's why: In C++, using the name of an array without an index generates a pointer to the first element in the array. Thus, the assignment

---

● base type
● The pointer will be increased by 8.
● In general, pointer comparisons are valid only when both pointers point to the same object, such as an array.

```
p1 = str;
```

assigns the address of **str**[0] to **p1**. This is a crucial point to understand: When an unindexed array name is used in an expression, it yields a pointer to the first element in the array.

Since, after the assignment, **p1** points to the beginning of **str**, you can use **p1** to access elements in the array. For example, if you want to access the fifth element in **str**, you can use

```
str[4]
```

or

```
*(p1+4)
```

Both statements obtain the fifth element. Remember, array indices start at zero, so when **str** is indexed, a 4 is used to access the fifth element. A 4 is also added to the pointer **p1** to get the fifth element, because **p1** currently points to the first element of **str**.

The parentheses surrounding **p1+4** are necessary because the * operation has a higher priority than the + operation. Without them, the expression would first find the value pointed to by **p1** (the first location in the array) and then add 4 to it.

In effect, C++ allows two methods of accessing array elements: *pointer arithmetic* and *array indexing*. This is important because pointer arithmetic can sometimes be faster than array indexing—especially when you are accessing an array in strictly sequential order. Since speed is often a consideration in programming, the use of pointers to access array elements is very common in C++ programs. Also, you can sometimes write tighter code by using pointers instead of array indexing.

Here is an example that demonstrates the difference between using array indexing and pointer arithmetic to access the elements of an array. We will create two versions of a program that reverse the case of letters within a string. The first version uses array indexing. The second uses pointer arithmetic. The first version is shown here:

```
// Reverse case using array indexing.
#include <iostream>
#include <cctype>
```

```
using namespace std;

int main()
{
  int i;
  char str[80] = "This Is A Test";

  cout << "Original string: " << str << "\n";

  for(i = 0; str[i]; i++) {
    if(isupper(str[i]))
      str[i] = tolower(str[i]);
    else if(islower(str[i]))
      str[i] = toupper(str[i]);
  }

  cout << "Inverted-case string: " << str;

  return 0;
}
```

The output from the program is shown here:

```
Original string: This Is A Test
Inverted-case string: tHIS iS a tEST
```

Notice that the program uses the **isupper( )** and **islower( )** library functions
to determine the case of a letter. The **isupper( )** function returns true when its
argument is an uppercase letter; **islower( )** returns true when its argument is a
lowercase letter. Inside the **for** loop, **str** is indexed, and the case of each letter is
checked and changed. The loop iterates until the null terminating **str** is indexed.
Since a null is zero (false), the loop stops.

Here is the same program rewritten to use pointer arithmetic:

```
// Reverse case using pointer arithmetic.
#include <iostream>
#include <cctype>
using namespace std;

int main()
{
  char *p;
```

```
char str[80] = "This Is A Test";

cout << "Original string: " << str << "\n";

p = str; // assign p the address of the start of the array

while(*p) {
  if(isupper(*p))
    *p = tolower(*p);
  else if(islower(*p))        ◄────  Access str through a pointer.
    *p = toupper(*p);
  p++;
}

cout << "Inverted-case string: " << str;

return 0;
}
```

4

In this version, **p** is set to the start of **str**. Then, inside the **while** loop, the letter at **p** is checked and changed, and then **p** is incremented. The loop stops when **p** points to the null terminator that ends **str**.

Because of the way some C++ compilers generate code, these two programs may not be equivalent in performance. Generally, it takes more machine instructions to index an array than it does to perform arithmetic on a pointer. Consequently, in professionally written C++ code, it is common to see the pointer version used more frequently. However, as a beginning C++ programmer, feel free to use array indexing until you are comfortable with pointers.

Indexing a Pointer

As you have just seen, it is possible to access an array using pointer arithmetic. What you might find surprising is that the reverse is also true. In C++, it is possible to index a pointer as if it were an array. Here is an example. It is a third version of the case-changing program.

```
// Index a pointer as if it were an array.
#include <iostream>
#include <cctype>
```

```
using namespace std;

int main()
{
  char *p;
  int i;
  char str[80] = "This Is A Test";

  cout << "Original string: " << str << "\n";

  p = str; // assign p the address of the start of the array

  // now, index p
  for(i = 0; p[i]; i++) {
    if(isupper(p[i]))
      p[i] = tolower(p[i]);
    else if(islower(p[i]))       ◄──── Access p as if it were an array.
      p[i] = toupper(p[i]);
  }

  cout << "Inverted-case string: " << str;

  return 0;
}
```

The program creates a **char** pointer called **p** and then assigns to that pointer the address of the first element in **str**. Inside the **for** loop, **p** is indexed using the normal array indexing syntax. This is perfectly valid because in C++, the statement p[i] is functionally identical to *(**p+i**). This further illustrates the close relationship between pointers and arrays.

1-Minute Drill

● Can an array be accessed through a pointer?

● Can a pointer be indexed as if it were an array?

● An array name used by itself, with no index, yields what?

● Yes, an array can be accessed through a pointer.
● Yes, a pointer can be indexed as if it were an array.
● An array name used by itself, with no index, yields a pointer to the first element of the array.

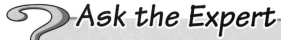

Ask the Expert

Question: Are pointers and arrays interchangeable?

Answer: As the preceding few pages have shown, pointers and arrays are strongly related and are interchangeable in many cases. For example, a pointer that points to the beginning of an array can access that array using either pointer arithmetic or array-style indexing. However, pointers and arrays are not completely interchangeable. For example, consider this fragment:

```
int nums[10];
int i;

for(i=0; i<10; i++) {
  *nums = i; // this is OK
  nums++; // ERROR -- cannot modify nums
}
```

Here, **nums** is an array of integers. As the comments describe, while it is perfectly acceptable to apply the * operator to **nums** (which is a pointer operation), it is illegal to modify **nums**' value. The reason for this is that **nums** is a constant that points to the beginning of an array. Thus, you cannot increment it. More generally, while an array name without an index does generate a pointer to the beginning of an array, it cannot be changed.

Although an array name generates a pointer constant, it can still take part in pointer-style expressions, as long as it is not modified. For example, the following is a valid statement that assigns **nums[3]** the value 100:

```
*(nums+3) = 100; // This is OK because nums is not changed
```

String Constants

You might be wondering how string constants, like the one in the fragment shown here, are handled by C++:

```
cout << strlen("Xanadu");
```

The answer is that when the compiler encounters a string constant, it stores it in the program's *string table* and generates a pointer to the string. Thus, "Xanadu" yields a pointer to its entry in the string table. Therefore, the following program is perfectly valid and prints the phrase **Pointers add power to C++.**:

```
#include <iostream>
using namespace std;

int main()
{
  char *ptr;

  ptr = "Pointers add power to C++.\n";

  cout << ptr;

  return 0;
}
```

ptr is assigned the address of this string constant.

In this program, the characters that make up a string constant are stored in the string table, and **ptr** is assigned a pointer to the string in that table.

Since a pointer into your program's string table is generated automatically whenever a string constant is used, you might be tempted to use this fact to modify the contents of the string table. However, this is usually not a good idea because many C++ compilers create optimized tables in which one string constant may be used at two or more different places in your program. Thus, changing a string may cause undesired side effects.

StrRev.cpp

Project 4-2: Reversing a String in Place

Earlier it was mentioned that comparing one pointer to another is meaningful only if the two pointers point to a common object, such as an array. Now that you understand how pointers and arrays relate, you can apply pointer comparisons to streamline some types of algorithms. In this project, you will see an example.

The program developed here reverses the contents of a string, in place. Thus, instead of copying the string back-to-front into another array, it reverses the contents of the string inside the array that holds it. The program uses two pointer variables to accomplish this. One initially points to the beginning of a string, and the other initially points to the last character in the string. A loop is set up that continues to run as long as the start pointer is less than the end pointer. Each time through the loop, the characters pointed to by the pointers are swapped and the pointers are advanced. When the start pointer is greater than or equal to the end pointer, the string has been reversed.

Step-by-Step

1. Create a file called **StrRev.cpp**.

2. Begin by adding these lines to the file:

```
/*
   Project 4-2
   Reverse a string in place.
*/
#include <iostream>
#include <cstring>
using namespace std;

int main()
{
  char str[] = "this is a test";
  char *start, *end;
  int len;
  char t;
```

The string to be reversed is contained in **str**. The pointers **start** and **end** will be used to access the string.

3. Add these lines, which display the original string, obtain the string's length, and set the initial values for the **start** and **end** pointers:

```
cout << "Original: " << str << "\n";

len = strlen(str);

start = str;
end = &str[len-1];
```

Notice that **end** points to the last character in the string, not the null terminator.

4. Add the code that reverses the string:

```
while(start < end) {
  // swap chars
  t = *start;
  *start = *end;
```

```
  *end = t;

  // advance pointers
  start++;
  end--;
}
```

The process works like this. As long as the **start** pointer points to a memory location that is less than the **end** pointer, the loop iterates. Inside the loop, the characters being pointed to by **start** and **end** are swapped. Then **start** is incremented and **end** is decremented. When **end** is greater than or equal to **start**, all of the characters in the string have been reversed. Since both **start** and **end** point into the same array, their comparison is meaningful.

5. Here is the complete **StrRev.cpp** program:

```
/*
   Project 4-2
   Reverse a string in place.
*/
#include <iostream>
#include <cstring>
using namespace std;

int main()
{
  char str[] = "this is a test";
  char *start, *end;
  int len;
  char t;

  cout << "Original: " << str << "\n";

  len = strlen(str);

  start = str;
  end = &str[len-1];

  while(start < end) {
    // swap chars
    t = *start;
    *start = *end;
    *end = t;

    // advance pointers
    start++;
```

```
      end--;
    }


    cout << "Reversed: " << str << "\n";
    return 0;
}
```

The output from the program is shown here:

```
Original: this is a test
Reversed: tset a si siht
```

Arrays of Pointers

Pointers can be arrayed like any other data type. For example, the declaration for an **int** pointer array of size 10 is

```
int *pi[10];
```

Here, **pi** is an array of ten integer pointers.

To assign the address of an **int** variable called **var** to the third element of the pointer array, you would write

```
int var;

pi[2] = &var;
```

Remember, **pi** is an array of **int** pointers. The only thing that the array elements can hold are the addresses of integer values—not the values themselves.

To find the value of **var**, you would write

```
*pi[2]
```

Like other arrays, arrays of pointers can be initialized. A common use for initialized pointer arrays is to hold pointers to strings. Here is an example that uses a two-dimensional array of character pointers to implement a small dictionary:

```
// Use a 2-D array of pointers to create a dictionary.

#include <iostream>
#include <cstring>
```

```
using namespace std;

int main() {

  char *dictionary[][2] = {
    "pencil", "A writing instrument.",
    "keyboard", "An input device.",
    "rifle", "A shoulder-fired firearm.",
    "airplane", "A fixed-wing aircraft.",
    "network", "An interconnected group of computers.",
    "", ""
  };
  char word[80];
  int i;

  cout << "Enter word: ";
  cin >> word;

  for(i = 0; *dictionary[i][0]; i++) {
    if(!strcmp(dictionary[i][0], word)) {
      cout << dictionary[i][1] << "\n";
      break;
    }
  }

  if(!*dictionary[i][0])
    cout << word << " not found.\n";

  return 0;
}
```

> This is a two-dimensional array of **char** pointers, which is used to point to pairs of strings.

> To find a definition, **word** is searched for in **dictionary**. If a match is found, the definition is displayed.

Here is a sample run:

```
Enter word: network
An interconnected group of computers.
```

When the array **dictionary** is created, it is initialized with a set of words and their meanings. Recall, C++ stores all string constants in the string table associated with your program, so the array need only store pointers to the strings. The program works by testing the word entered by the user against the strings stored in the dictionary. If a match is found, the meaning is displayed. If no match is found, an error message is printed.

Notice that **dictionary** ends with two null strings. These mark the end of the array. Recall that a null string contains only the terminating null character.

The **for** loop runs until the first character in a string is null. This condition is tested with this expression:

```
*dictionary[i][0]
```

The array indices specify a pointer to a string. The * obtains the character at that location. If this character is null, then the expression is false and the loop terminates. Otherwise, the expression is true and the loop continues.

The Null Pointer Convention

After a pointer is declared, but before it has been assigned, it will contain an arbitrary value. Should you try to use the pointer prior to giving it a value, you will probably crash your program. While there is no sure way to avoid using an uninitialized pointer, C++ programmers have adopted a procedure that helps prevent some errors. By convention, if a pointer contains the null (zero) value, it is assumed to point to nothing. Thus, if all unused pointers are given the null value and you avoid the use of a null pointer, you can avoid the accidental misuse of an uninitialized pointer. This is a good practice to follow.

Any type of pointer can be initialized to null when it is declared. For example, the following initializes **p** to null:

```
float *p = 0; // p is now a null pointer
```

To check for a null pointer, use an **if** statement, like one of these:

```
if(p) // succeeds if p is not null
```

```
if(!p) // succeeds if p is null
```

1-Minute Drill

● String constants used in a program are stored in a _____ _____.

● What does this declaration create? `float *fpa[18];`

● By convention, a pointer containing null is assumed to be unused. True or false?

● string table
● The declaration creates an array of 18 **float** pointers.
● True.

Multiple Indirection

A pointer to a pointer is a form of *multiple indirection,* or a chain of pointers. Consider Figure 4-2. As you can see, in the case of a normal pointer, the value of the pointer is the address of a value. In the case of a pointer to a pointer, the first pointer contains the address of the second pointer, which points to the location that contains the desired value.

Multiple indirection can be carried on to whatever extent desired, but there are few cases where more than a pointer to a pointer is needed, or, indeed, even wise to use. Excessive indirection is difficult to follow and prone to conceptual errors.

A variable that is a pointer to a pointer must be declared as such. This is done by placing an additional asterisk in front of its name. For example, this declaration tells the compiler that **balance** is a pointer to a pointer of type **int**:

```
int **balance;
```

It is important to understand that **balance** is not a pointer to an integer, but rather a pointer to an **int** pointer.

When a target value is indirectly pointed to by a pointer to a pointer, accessing that value requires that the asterisk operator be applied twice, as is shown in this short example:

```
#include <iostream>
using namespace std;

int main()
{
  int x, *p, **q;

  x = 10;

  p = &x;          ←———— Assign p address of x.

  q = &p;          ←———— Assign q the address of p.

  cout << **q; // prints the value of x
                            Access x's value through q.
  return 0;                 Notice that two * are required.
}
```

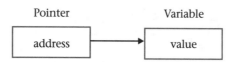

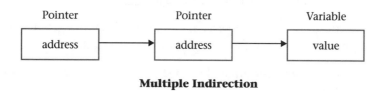

Figure 4-2   Single and multiple indirection

Here, **p** is declared as a pointer to an integer, and **q** as a pointer to a pointer to an integer. The **cout** statement will print the number 10 on the screen.

Ask the Expert

Question: Given the power of pointers, I can see that their misuse could easily cause extensive damage to a program. Do you have any tips on avoiding pointer errors?

Answer: First, make sure that pointer variables are initialized before using them. That is, make sure that a pointer actually points to something before you attempt to use it! Second, make sure that the type of the object to which a pointer points is the same as the base type of pointer. Third, don't perform operations through null pointers. Recall that a null pointer indicates that the pointer points nowhere. Finally, don't cast pointers "just to make your code compile." Usually, pointer mismatch errors indicate that you are thinking about something incorrectly. Casting one type of pointer into another is usually needed only in unusual circumstances.

4

☑️ *Mastery Check*

1. Show how to declare a **short int** array called **hightemps** that is 31 elements long.

2. In C++, all arrays begin indexing at _____.

3. Write a program that searches an array of ten integers for duplicate values. Have the program display each duplicate found.

4. What is a null-terminated string?

5. Write a program that prompts the user for two strings and then compares the strings for equality, but ignores case differences. Thus, "ok" and "OK" will compare as equal.

6. When using **strcat( )**, how large must the recipient array be?

7. In a multidimensional array, how is each index specified?

8. Show how to initialize an **int** array called **nums** with the values 5, 66, and 88.

9. What is the principal advantage of an unsized array declaration?

10. What is a pointer? What are the two pointer operators?

11. Can a pointer be indexed like an array? Can an array be accessed through a pointer?

12. Write a program that counts the uppercase letters in a string. Have it display the result.

13. What is it called when one pointer points to another pointer?

14. Of what significance is a null pointer in C++?

Module 5

Introducing Functions

The Goals of This Module

- Know the general form of a function
- Create functions
- Use function arguments
- Return values from functions
- Learn about scopes
- Understand local and global variables
- Pass pointers and arrays to a function
- Return pointers from a function
- Pass command-line arguments to main( )
- Learn about function prototypes
- Create recursive functions

This module begins an in-depth discussion of the function. Functions are the building blocks of C++, and a firm understanding of them is fundamental to becoming a successful C++ programmer. Here, you will learn how to create a function. You will also learn about passing arguments, returning values, local and global variables, function prototypes, and recursion.

Function Fundamentals

A *function* is a subroutine that contains one or more C++ statements and performs a specific task. Every program that you have written so far has used one function: **main( )**. They are called the building blocks of C++ because a program is a collection of functions. All of the "action" statements of a program are found within functions. Thus, a function contains the statements that you typically think of as being the executable part of a program.

Although very simple programs, such as many of those shown in this book, will have only a **main( )** function, most programs will contain several functions. In fact, a large, commercial program will define hundreds of functions.

The General Form of a Function

All C++ functions share a common form, which is shown here:

```
return-type name(parameter-list)
{
  //  body of function
}
```

Here, *return-type* specifies the type of data returned by the function. This can be any valid type, except an array. If the function does not return a value, its return type must be **void**. The name of the function is specified by *name*. This can be any legal identifier that is not already in use. The *parameter-list* is a sequence of type and identifier pairs separated by commas. Parameters are essentially variables that receive the value of the arguments passed to the function when it is called. If the function has no parameters, then the parameter list will be empty.

Braces surround the body of the function. The function body is composed of the C++ statements that define what the function does. The function terminates and returns to the calling code when the closing curly brace is reached.

Creating a Function

It is easy to create a function. Since all functions share the same general form, they are all similar in structure to the **main( )** functions that you have been using. Let's begin with a simple example that contains two functions: **main( )** and **myfunc( )**. Before running this program (or reading the description that follows), examine it closely and try to figure out exactly what it displays on the screen.

5

```cpp
// This program contains two functions: main() and myfunc().

#include <iostream>
using namespace std;

void myfunc(); // myfunc's prototype          This is the prototype
                                              for myfunc( ).

int main()
{
  cout << "In main()\n";

  myfunc(); // call myfunc()

  cout << "Back in main()\n";

  return 0;
}

// This is the function's definition.
void myfunc()
{                                             This is the function
  cout << "Inside myfunc()\n";                called myfunc( ).
}
```

The program works like this. First, **main( )** begins, and it executes the first **cout** statement. Next, **main( )** calls **myfunc( )**. Notice how this is achieved: the function's name is followed by parentheses. In this case, the function call is a statement and, therefore, must end with a semicolon. Next, **myfunc( )** executes its **cout** statement and then returns to **main( )** when the closing } is encountered. In **main( )**, execution resumes at the line of code immediately following the call to **myfunc( )**. Finally, **main( )** executes its second **cout** statement and then terminates. The output is shown here:

```
In main()
Inside myfunc()
Back in main()
```

The way **myfunc( )** is called and the way that it returns represent a specific instance of a process that applies to all functions. In general, to call a function, specify its name followed by parentheses. When a function is called, execution jumps to the function. Execution continues inside the function until its closing curly brace is encountered. When the function ends, program execution returns to the caller at the statement immediately following the function call.

Notice this statement in the preceding program:

```
void myfunc(); // myfunc's prototype
```

As the comment states, this is the *prototype* for **myfunc( )**. Although we will discuss prototypes in detail later, a few words are necessary now. A function prototype declares the function prior to its definition. The prototype allows the compiler to know the function's return type, as well as the number and type of any parameters that the function may have. The compiler needs to know this information prior to the first time the function is called. This is why the prototype occurs before **main( )**. The only function that does not require a prototype is **main( )**, since it is predefined by C++.

The keyword **void**, which precedes both the prototype for **myfunc( )** and its definition, formally states that **myfunc( )** does not return a value. In C++, functions that don't return values are declared as **void**.

Using Arguments

It is possible to pass one or more values to a function that you create. A value passed to a function is called an *argument*. Thus, arguments are a way to get information into a function.

When you create a function that takes one or more arguments, variables that will receive those arguments must also be declared. These variables are called the *parameters* of the function. Here is an example that defines a function called **box( )** that computes the volume of a box and displays the result. It has three parameters.

```
void box(int length, int width, int height)
{
  cout << "volume of box is " << length * width * height << "\n";
}
```

In general, each time **box( )** is called, it will compute the volume by multiplying the values passed to it in **length**, **width**, and **height**.

To call **box( )**, you must specify three arguments. For example:

```
box(7, 20, 4);
box(50, 3, 2);
box(8, 6, 9);
```

The values specified between the parentheses are arguments passed to **box( )**, and the value of each argument is copied into its matching parameter. Therefore, in the first call to **box( )**, 7 is copied into **length**, 20 is copied into **width**, and 4 is copied into **height**. In the second call, 50 is copied into **length**, 3 into **width**, and 2 into **height**. In the third call, 8 is copied into **length**, 6 into **width**, and 9 into **height**.

The following program demonstrates **box( )**:

```
// A simple program that demonstrates box().

#include <iostream>
using namespace std;

void box(int length, int width, int height); // box()'s prototype

int main()
{
  box(7, 20, 4); ◄─────────  Pass arguments to box( ).
  box(50, 3, 2);
  box(8, 6, 9);
```

5

```
   return 0;
}

// Compute the volume of a box.
void box(int length, int width, int height)
{
   cout << "volume of box is " << length * width * height << "\n";
}
```

> These parameters receive the values of the arguments passed to **box( )**.

The output from the program is shown here:

```
volume of box is 560
volume of box is 300
volume of box is 432
```

Tip

Remember the term *argument* refers to the value that is used to call a function. The variable that receives the value of an argument is called a *parameter*. In fact, functions that take arguments are called *parameterized functions*.

1-Minute Drill

- When a function is called, what happens to program execution?
- What is the difference between an argument and a parameter?
- If a function requires a parameter, where is it declared?

Using return

In the preceding examples, the function returned to its caller when its closing curly brace was encountered. While this is acceptable for many functions, it won't work for all. Often, you will want to control precisely how and when a function returns. To do this, you will use the **return** statement.

The **return** statement has two forms: one that returns a value, and one that does not. We will begin with the version of **return** that does not return a value.

- When a function is called, program execution jumps to the function. When the function returns, program execution returns to the caller at the statement immediately following the function call.
- An argument is a value passed to a function. A parameter is a variable that receives the value.
- A parameter is declared after a function's name, inside the parentheses.

If a function has a **void** return type (that is, if the function does not return a value), then it can use this form of **return**:

```
return;
```

When **return** is encountered, execution returns immediately to the caller. Any code remaining in the function is ignored. For example, consider this program:

```
// Using return.

#include <iostream>
using namespace std;

void f();

int main()
{
  cout << "Before call\n";

  f();

  cout << "After call\n";

  return 0;
}

// A void function that uses return.
void f()
{
  cout << "Inside f()\n";

  return; // return to caller  ←———— This causes an immediate
                                      return, bypassing the
                                      remaining cout statement.
  cout <<"This won't display.\n";
}
```

5

The output from the program is shown here:

```
Before call
Inside f()
After call
```

As the output shows, f( ) returns to **main**( ) as soon as the **return** statement is encountered. The second **cout** statement is never executed.

Here is a more practical example of **return**. The **power**( ) function shown in the next program displays the outcome of an integer raised to a positive integer power. If the exponent is negative, the **return** statement causes the function to terminate before any attempt is made to compute the result.

```
#include <iostream>
using namespace std;

void power(int base, int exp);

int main()
{
  power(10, 2);
  power(10, -2);

  return 0;
}

// Raise an integer to a positive power.
void power(int base, int exp)
{
  int i;

  if(exp < 0) return; /* Can't do negative exponents. */

  i = 1;

  for( ; exp; exp--) i = base * i;
  cout << "The answer is: " << i;
}
```

Return when **exp** is negative.

The output from the program is shown here:

```
The answer is: 100
```

When **exp** is negative (as it is in the second call), **power**( ) returns, bypassing the rest of the function.

A function may contain several **return** statements. As soon as one is encountered, the function returns. For example, this fragment is perfectly valid:

```
void f()
{
  // ...

  switch(c) {
    case 'a': return;
    case 'b': // ...
    case 'c': return;
  }
  if(count < 100) return;
  // ...
}
```

Be aware, however, that having too many **returns** can destructure a function and confuse its meaning. It is best to use multiple **returns** only when they help clarify a function.

Returning Values

A function can return a value to its caller. Thus, a return value is a way to get information out of a function. To return a value, use the second form of the **return** statement, shown here:

return *value*;

Here, *value* is the value being returned. This form of the **return** statement can be used only with functions that do not return **void**.

A function that returns a value must specify the type of that value. The return type must be compatible with the type of data used in the **return** statement. If it isn't, a compile-time error will result. A function can be declared to return any valid C++ data type, except that a function cannot return an array.

To illustrate the process of functions returning values, the **box( )** function can be rewritten as shown here. In this version, **box( )** returns the volume. Notice that the placement of the function on the right side of an assignment statement assigns the return value to a variable.

```
// Returning a value.

#include <iostream>
using namespace std;

int box(int length, int width, int height); // return the volume

int main()
{
  int answer;

  answer = box(10, 11, 3); // assign return value
  cout << "The volume is " << answer;

  return 0;
}

// This function returns a value.
int box(int length, int width, int height)
{
  return length * width * height ;
}
```

The return value from **box( )** is assigned to **answer**.

Return the volume.

Here is the output:

```
The volume is 330
```

In this example, **box( )** returns the value of **length * width * height** using the **return** statement. This value is then assigned to **answer**. That is, the value returned by the **return** statement becomes **box( )**'s value in the calling routine.

Since **box( )** now returns a value, it is not preceded by the keyword **void**. (Remember, **void** is only used when a function does *not* return a value.) Instead, **box( )** is declared as returning a value of type **int**. Notice that the return type of a function precedes its name in both its prototype and its definition.

Of course, **int** is not the only type of data a function can return. As stated earlier, a function can return any type of data except an array. For example, the following program reworks **box( )** so that it takes **double** parameters and returns a **double** value:

```
// Returning a double value.
```

```
#include <iostream>
using namespace std;

// use double data
double box(double length, double width, double height);

int main()
{
  double answer;

  answer = box(10.1, 11.2, 3.3); // assign return value
  cout << "The volume is " <<  answer;

  return 0;
}

// This version of box uses double data.
double box(double length, double width, double height)
{
  return length * width * height ;
}
```

Here is the output:

```
The volume is 373.296
```

One more point: If a non-**void** function returns because its closing curly brace is encountered, an undefined (that is, unknown) value is returned. Because of a quirk in the formal C++ syntax, a non-**void** function need not actually execute a **return** statement. This can happen if the end of the function is reached prior to a **return** statement being encountered. However, because the function is declared as returning a value, a value will still be returned—even though it is just a garbage value. Of course, good practice dictates that any non-**void** function that you create should return a value via an explicit **return** statement.

Using Functions in Expressions

In the preceding example, the value returned by **box( )** was assigned to a variable, and then the value of this variable was displayed via a **cout** statement. While not incorrect, these programs could be written more efficiently by using

5

the return value directly in the **cout** statement. For example, the **main( )** function in the preceding program can be written more efficiently like this:

```
int main()
{
  // use the return value of box( ) directly
  cout << "The volume is " <<  box(10.1, 11.2, 3.3);

  return 0;
}
```

> Use the return value of **box( )** directly in a **cout** statement.

When the **cout** statement executes, **box( )** is automatically called so that its return value can be obtained. This value is then output. There is no reason to first assign it to some variable.

In general, a non-**void** function can be used in any type of expression. When the expression is evaluated, the function is automatically called so that its return value can be obtained. For example, the following program sums the volume of three boxes and then displays the average volume:

```
// Use box() in an expression.

#include <iostream>
using namespace std;

// use double data
double box(double length, double width, double height);

int main()
{
  double sum;

  sum = box(10.1, 11.2, 3.3) + box(5.5, 6.6, 7.7) +
        box(4.0, 5.0, 8.0);

  cout << "The sum of the volumes is " <<  sum << "\n";
  cout << "The average volume is " << sum / 3.0 << "\n";

  return 0;
}

// This version of box uses double data.
double box(double length, double width, double height)
```

```
{
  return length * width * height ;
}
```

The output of this program is shown here:

```
The sum of the volumes is 812.806
The average volume is 270.935
```

1-Minute Drill

● Show the two forms of the **return** statement.

● Can a **void** function return a value?

● Can a function call be part of an expression?

Scope Rules

Up to this point, we have been using variables without formally discussing where they can be declared, how long they remain in existence, and what parts of a program have access to them. These attributes are determined by the *scope rules* defined by C++.

In general, the scope rules of a language govern the visibility and lifetime of an object. Although C++ defines a finely grained system of scopes, there are two basic ones: *local* and *global*. In both of these scopes, you can declare variables. In this section, you will see how variables declared in a local scope differ from variables declared in the global scope, and how each relates to the function.

Local Scope

A local scope is created by a block. (Recall that a block begins with an opening curly brace and ends with a closing curly brace.) Thus, each time you start a

---

● Here are the two forms of **return**:
return;
return *value*;

● No, **void** functions cannot return values.

● A call to a non-**void** function can be used in an expression. When this happens, the function is executed so that its return value can be obtained.

new block, you are creating a new scope. A variable can be declared within any block. A variable that is declared inside a block is called a *local variable*.

A local variable can be used only by statements located within the block in which it is declared. Stated another way, local variables are not known outside their own code blocks. Thus, statements defined outside a block cannot access an object defined within it. In essence, when you declare a local variable, you are localizing that variable and protecting it from unauthorized access and/or modification. Indeed, the scope rules provide the foundation for encapsulation.

One of the most important things to understand about local variables is that they exist only while the block of code in which they are declared is executing. A local variable is created when its declaration statement is encountered within its block, and destroyed when the block is left. Because a local variable is destroyed upon exit from its block, its value is lost.

The most common code block in which variables are declared is the function. Each function defines a block of code that begins with the function's opening curly brace and ends with its closing curly brace. A function's code and data are private to that function and cannot be accessed by any statement in any other function except through a call to that function. (It is not possible, for instance, to use a **goto** statement to jump into the middle of another function.) The body of a function is hidden from the rest of the program, and it can neither affect nor be affected by other parts of the program. Thus, the contents of one function are completely separate from the contents of another. Stated another way, the code and data that are defined within one function cannot interact with the code or data defined in another function, because the two functions have a different scope.

Because each function defines its own scope, the variables declared within one function have no effect on those declared in another—even if those variables share the same name. For example, consider the following program:

```
#include <iostream>
using namespace std;

void f1();

int main()
{
  int val = 10;

  cout << "val in main(): " << val << '\n';
```

This **val** is local to **main( )**.

```
  f1();
  cout << "val in main(): " << val << '\n';

  return 0;
}

void f1()
{
  int val = 88;  ◄───────────  This val is local to fl( ).

  cout << "val in f1(): " << val << "\n";
}
```

Here is the output:

5

```
val in main(): 10
val in f1(): 88
val in main(): 10
```

An integer called **val** is declared twice, once in **main( )** and once in **f1( )**. The **val** in **main( )** has no bearing on, or relationship to, the one in **f1( )**. The reason for this is that each **val** is known only to the function in which it is declared. As the output shows, even though the **val** declared in **f1( )** is set to 88, the content of **val** in **main( )** remains 10.

Because a local variable is created and destroyed with each entry and exit from the block in which it is declared, a local variable will not hold its value between activations of its block. This is especially important to remember in terms of a function call. When a function is called, its local variables are created. Upon its return, they are destroyed. This means that local variables cannot retain their values between calls.

If a local variable declaration includes an initializer, then the variable is initialized each time the block is entered. For example:

```
/*
   A local variable is initialized each
   time its block is entered.
*/

#include <iostream>
using namespace std;
```

```
void f();

int main()
{

  for(int i=0; i < 3; i++) f();

  return 0;
}

// num is initialized each time f() is called.
void f()
{
  int num = 99;          num is set to 99 each
                         time f( ) is called.

  cout << num << "\n";

  num++; // this has no lasting effect
}
```

The output shown here confirms that **num** is initialized each time **f( )** is called:

```
99
99
99
```

A local variable that is not initialized will have an unknown value until it is assigned one.

Local Variables Can Be Declared Within Any Block

It is common practice to declare all variables needed within a function at the beginning of that function's code block. This is done mainly so that anyone reading the code can easily determine what variables are used. However, the beginning of the function's block is not the only place where local variables can be declared. A local variable can be declared anywhere, within any block of code. A variable declared within a block is local to that block. This means that the variable does not exist until the block is entered and is destroyed when the block is exited. Furthermore, no code outside that block—including other code in the function—can access that variable. To understand this, try the following program:

```
// Variables can be local to a block.

#include <iostream>
using namespace std;

int main() {
  int x = 19; // x is known to all code.

  if(x == 19) {
    int y = 20;  ◄─────────────  y is local to the if block.

    cout << "x + y is " << x + y << "\n";
  }

  //  y = 100; // Error!  y not known here.

  return 0;
}
```

5

The variable **x** is declared at the start of **main( )**'s scope and is accessible to all subsequent code within **main( )**. Within the **if** block, **y** is declared. Since a block defines a scope, **y** is visible only to other code within its block. This is why outside of its block, the line

```
y = 100;
```

is commented out. If you remove the leading comment symbol, a compile-time error will occur, because **y** is not visible outside of its block. Within the **if** block, **x** can be used because code within a block has access to variables declared by an enclosing block.

Although local variables are typically declared at the beginning of their block, they need not be. A local variable can be declared anywhere within a block as long as it is declared before it is used. For example, this is a perfectly valid program:

```
#include <iostream>
using namespace std;

int main()
{
  cout << "Enter a number: ";
```

```
    int a; // declare one variable
    cin >> a;

    cout << "Enter a second number: ";
    int b; // declare another variable
    cin >> b;

    cout << "Product: " << a*b << '\n';

    return 0;
}
```

Here, **a** and **b** are declared as needed.

In this example, **a** and **b** are not declared until just before they are needed. Frankly, most programmers declare local variables at the beginning of the function that uses them, but this is a stylistic issue.

Name Hiding

When a local variable declared in an inner block has the same name as a variable declared in an outer block, the variable declared in the inner block *hides* the one in the outer block. For example:

```
#include <iostream>
using namespace std;

int main()
{
  int i;
  int j;

  i = 10;
  j = 100;

  if(j > 0) {
    int i; // this i is separate from outer i

    i = j / 2;
    cout << "inner i: " << i << '\n';
  }

  cout << "outer i: " << i << '\n';

  return 0;
}
```

This **i** hides the outer **i**.

The output from this program is shown here:

```
inner i: 50
outer i: 10
```

The i declared within the if block hides the outer i. Changes that take place on the inner i have no effect on the outer i. Furthermore, outside of the if block, the inner i is unknown and the outer i comes back into view.

Function Parameters

The parameters to a function are within the scope of the function. Thus, they are local to the function. Except for receiving the values of the arguments, parameters behave like any other local variables.

Global Scope

Since local variables are known only within the function in which they are declared, a question may have occurred to you: How do you create a variable that can be shared by more than one function? The answer is to declare the variable in the global scope. The *global scope* is the declarative region that is outside of all functions. Declaring a variable in the global scope creates a *global variable*.

Ask the Expert

Question   What does the keyword auto do? I have heard that it is used to declare local variables. Is this right?

Answer   The C++ language contains the keyword **auto**, which can be used to declare local variables. However, since all local variables are, by default, assumed to be **auto**, it is virtually never used. Thus, you will not see it used in any of the examples in this book. However, if you choose to use it, place it immediately before the variable's type, as shown here:

```
auto char ch;
```

Again, **auto** is optional and not used elsewhere in this book.

5

Global variables are known throughout the entire program. They can be used by any piece of code, and they maintain their values during the entire execution of the program. Therefore, their scope extends to the entire program. You can create global variables by declaring them outside of any function. Because they are global, they can be accessed by any expression, regardless of which function contains the expression.

The following program demonstrates the use of a global variable. The variable **count** has been declared outside of all functions. Its declaration is before the **main( )** function. However, it could have been placed anywhere, as long as it was not in a function. Remember, though, that since you must declare a variable before you use it, it is best to declare global variables at the top of the program.

```
// Use a global variable.

#include <iostream>
using namespace std;

void func1();
void func2();
                        count is global.
int count; // This is a global variable.

int main()
{
  int i; // This is a local variable

  for(i=0; i<10; i++) {
    count = i * 2;          This refers to the global count.
    func1();
  }

  return 0;
}                This also refers to
                the global count.
void func1()
{
  cout << "count: " << count; // access global count
  cout << '\n'; // output a newline
  func2();
}
```

```
void func2()                    This count is local to func2( ).
{
  int count; // this is a local variable

    for(count=0; count<3; count++) cout << '.';        This refers to the
}                                                      local count.
```

The output from the program is shown here:

```
count: 0
...count: 2
...count: 4
...count: 6
...count: 8
...count: 10
...count: 12
...count: 14
...count: 16
...count: 18
...
```

Looking closely at this program, it should be clear that both **main( )** and **func1( )** use the global variable **count**. In **func2( )**, however, a local variable called **count** is declared. When **func2( )** uses **count**, it is referring to its local variable, not the global one. It is important to understand that if a global variable and a local variable have the same name, all references to that variable name inside the function in which the local variable is declared will refer to the local variable and have no effect on the global variable. Thus, a local variable hides a global variable of the same name.

Global variables are initialized at program startup. If a global variable declaration includes an initializer, then the variable is initialized to that value. If a global variable does not include an initializer, then its value is set to zero.

Storage for global variables is in a fixed region of memory set aside for this purpose by your program. Global variables are helpful when the same data is used by several functions in your program, or when a variable must hold its value throughout the duration of the program. You should avoid using unnecessary global variables, however, for three reasons:

● They take up memory the entire time your program is executing, not just when they are needed.

- Using a global variable where a local variable will do makes a function less general, because it relies on something that must be defined outside itself.

- Using a large number of global variables can lead to program errors because of unknown, and unwanted, side effects. A major problem in developing large programs is the accidental modification of a variable's value due to its use elsewhere in a program. This can happen in C++ if you use too many global variables in your programs.

1-Minute Drill

- What are the main differences between local and global variables?

- Can a local variable be declared anywhere within a block?

- Does a local variable hold its value between calls to the function in which it is declared?

Passing Pointers and Arrays to Functions

The preceding examples have used simple values, such as **int** or **double**, as arguments. However, there will be times when you will want to use pointers and arrays as arguments. While passing these types of arguments is straightforward, some special issues need to be addressed.

- A local variable is known only within the block in which it is declared. It is created upon entry into its block and destroyed when the block is left. A global variable is declared outside all functions. It can be used by all functions and exists during the entire lifetime of the program.
- Yes, a local variable can be declared anywhere within a block as long as it is declared before it is used.
- No, local variables are destroyed when the function in which they are declared returns.

Passing a Pointer

To pass a pointer as an argument, you must declare the parameter as a pointer
type. Here is an example:

```
// Pass a pointer to a function.

#include <iostream>
using namespace std;                        f( ) takes an int * pointer
                                            as a parameter.
void f(int *j); // f() declares a pointer parameter

int main()
{
  int i;
  int *p;

  p = &i; // p now points to i

  f(p); // pass a pointer                   f( ) is called with a
                                            pointer to an integer.
  cout << i;  // i is now 100

  return 0;
}

// f() receives a pointer to an int.
void f(int *j)
{
  *j = 100; // var pointed to by j is assigned 100
}
```

5

Study this program carefully. As you can see, f( ) takes one parameter: an
int pointer. Inside **main( )**, p is assigned the address of i. Next, f( ) is called
with **p** as an argument. When the pointer parameter **j** receives **p**, it then also
points to **i** within **main( )**. Thus, the assignment

```
*j = 100;
```

causes i to be given the value 100. For the general case, f( ) assigns 100 to whatever address it is called with.

In the preceding example, it is not actually necessary to use the pointer variable p. Instead, you can simply precede i with an & when f( ) is called. This causes the address of i to be passed to f( ). The revised program is shown here:

```
// Pass a pointer to a function.

#include <iostream>
using namespace std;

void f(int *j);

int main()
{
  int i;

  f(&i);             No need for p. The address
                     of i is passed directly.

  cout << i;

  return 0;
}

void f(int *j)
{
  *j = 100; // var pointed to by j is assigned 100
}
```

It is crucial that you understand one thing about passing pointers to functions: when you perform an operation within the function that uses the pointer, you are operating on the variable that is pointed to by that pointer. Thus, the function will be able to change the value of the object pointed to by the parameter.

Passing an Array

When an array is an argument to a function, the address of the first element of the array is passed, not a copy of the entire array. (Recall that an array name without any index is a pointer to the first element in the array.) This means that the parameter declaration must be of a compatible type. There are three ways to declare a parameter that is to receive an array pointer. First, it can be declared as an array of the same type and size as that used to call the function, as shown here:

```cpp
#include <iostream>
using namespace std;

void display(int num[10]);

int main()
{
  int t[10], i;

  for(i=0; i < 10; ++i) t[i]=i;

  display(t); // pass array t to a function

  return 0;
}

// Print some numbers.
void display(int num[10])          Parameter declared
{                                  as a sized array.
  int i;

  for(i=0; i < 10; i++) cout << num[i] << ' ';
}
```

Even though the parameter **num** is declared to be an integer array of ten elements, the C++ compiler will automatically convert it to an **int** pointer. This is necessary because no parameter can actually receive an entire array. Since only a pointer to the array will be passed, a pointer parameter must be there to receive it.

A second way to declare an array parameter is to specify it as an unsized array, as shown here:

```cpp
void display(int num[])          Parameter declared as an unsized array.
{
  int i;

  for(i=0; i < 10; i++) cout << num[i] << ' ';
}
```

Here, **num** is declared to be an integer array of unknown size. Since C++ provides no array boundary checks, the actual size of the array is irrelevant to the parameter (but not to the program, of course). This method of declaration is also automatically transformed into an **int** pointer by the compiler.

The final way that **num** can be declared is as a pointer. This is the method most commonly used in professionally written C++ programs. Here is an example:

```
void display(int *num)  ◄───────────┐
{                         ┌──────────────────────┐
    int i;                │ Parameter declared   │
                          │ as a pointer.        │
                          └──────────────────────┘
    for(i=0; i < 10; i++) cout << num[i] << ' ';
}
```

The reason it is possible to declare **num** as a pointer is that any pointer can be indexed using [ ], as if it were an array. Recognize that all three methods of declaring an array parameter yield the same result: a pointer.

It is important to remember that when an array is used as a function argument, its address is passed to a function. This means that the code inside the function will be operating on, and potentially altering, the actual contents of the array used to call the function. For example, in the following program examine the function **cube( )**, which converts the value of each element in an array into its cube. To call **cube( )**, pass the address of the array as the first argument and the size of the array as the second.

```
// Change the contents of an array using a function.

#include <iostream>
using namespace std;

void cube(int *n, int num);

int main()
{
    int i, nums[10];

    for(i=0; i < 10; i++) nums[i] = i+1;
```

```
   cout << "Original contents: ";
   for(i=0; i < 10; i++) cout << nums[i] << ' ';
   cout << '\n';
```

> Pass address of **nums** to **cube( )**.

```
   cube(nums, 10); // compute cubes

   cout << "Altered contents: ";
   for(i=0; i<10; i++) cout << nums[i] << ' ';

   return 0;
}

// Cube the elements in an array.
void cube(int *n, int num)
{
   while(num) {
      *n = *n * *n * *n;
      num--;
      n++;
   }
}
```

> This changes the value of the array element pointed to by **n**.

5

Here is the output produced by this program:

```
Original contents: 1 2 3 4 5 6 7 8 9 10
Altered contents: 1 8 27 64 125 216 343 512 729 1000
```

As you can see, after the call to **cube( )**, the contents of array **nums** in **main( )** will be cubes of its original values. That is, the values of the elements of **nums** have been modified by the statements within **cube( )**, because **n** points to **nums**.

Passing Strings

Because a string is simply a character array that is null-terminated, when you pass a string to a function, only a pointer to the beginning of the string is actually passed. This is a pointer of type **char ***. For example, consider the following program. It defines the function **strInvertCase( )**, which inverts the case of the letters within a string.

```
// Pass a string to a function.

#include <iostream>
#include <cstring>
#include <cctype>
using namespace std;

void strInvertCase(char *str);

int main()
{
  char str[80];

  strcpy(str, "This Is A Test");

  strInvertCase(str);

  cout << str; // display modified string

  return 0;
}

// Invert the case of the letters within a string.
void strInvertCase(char *str)
{
  while(*str) {

    // invert case
    if(isupper(*str)) *str = tolower(*str);
    else if(islower(*str)) *str = toupper(*str);

    str++; // move on to next char
  }
}
```

Here is the output:

```
tHIS iS a tEST
```

1-Minute Drill

- Show how to declare a **void** function called **count** that has one **long int** pointer parameter called **ptr**.

- When a pointer is passed to a function, can the function alter the contents of the object pointed to by the pointer?

- Can an array be passed to a function? Explain.

Returning Pointers

Functions can return pointers. Pointers are returned like any other data type and pose no special problem. However, because the pointer is one of C++'s more confusing features, a short discussion of pointer return types is warranted.

To return a pointer, a function must declare its return type to be a pointer. For example, here the return type of f( ) is declared to be an **int** pointer:

```
int *f();
```

If a function's return type is a pointer, then the value used in its **return** statement must also be a pointer. (As with all functions, the return value must be compatible with the return type.)

The following program demonstrates the use of a pointer return type. The function **get_substr( )** searches a string for a substring. It returns a pointer to the first matching substring. If no match is found, a null pointer is returned. For example, if the string is "I like C++" and the search string is "like", then the function returns a pointer to the *l* in "like".

- void count(long int *ptr)
- Yes, the object being pointed to can be changed by code inside the function.
- Arrays cannot be passed to a function. Instead, a pointer to an array is passed. Thus, changes made to the array inside the function affect the array used as an argument.

5

```
// Return a pointer.

#include <iostream>
using namespace std;

char *get_substr(char *sub, char *str);

int main()
{
  char *substr;

  substr = get_substr("three", "one two three four");

  cout << "substring found: " << substr;

  return 0;
}

// Return pointer to substring or null if not found.
char *get_substr(char *sub, char *str)
{
  int t;
  char *p, *p2, *start;

  for(t=0; str[t]; t++) {
    p = &str[t]; // reset pointers
    start = p;
    p2 = sub;
    while(*p2 && *p2==*p) { // check for substring
      p++;
      p2++;
    }

    /* If at end of p2 (i.e., substring), then
       a match has been found. */
    if(!*p2)
      return start; // return pointer to beginning of substring
  }
  return 0; // no match found
}
```

get_substr( ) returns a **char** pointer.

Here is the output produced by the program:

```
substring found: three four
```

The main( ) Function

As you know, the **main( )** function is special because it is the first function called when your program executes. It signifies the beginning of your program. Unlike some programming languages that always begin execution at the "top" of the program, C++ begins every program with a call to the **main( )** function, no matter where that function is located in the program. (However, it is common for **main( )** to be the first function in your program so that it can be easily found.)

There can be only one **main( )** in a program. If you try to include more than one, your program will not know where to begin execution. Actually, most compilers will catch this type of error and report it. As mentioned earlier, since **main( )** is predefined by C++, it does not require a prototype.

5

argc and argv: Arguments to main( )

Sometimes you will want to pass information into a program when you run it. This is generally accomplished by passing *command-line arguments* to **main( )**. A command-line argument is the information that follows the program's name on the command line of the operating system. (In Windows, the Run command also uses a command line.) For example, you might compile C++ programs from the command line by typing something like this:

cl *prog-name*

where *prog-name* is the program you want compiled. The name of the program is passed into the C++ compiler as a command-line argument.

C++ defines two built-in, but optional, parameters to **main( )**. They are **argc** and **argv**, and they receive the command-line arguments. These are the only parameters defined by C++ for **main( )**. However, other arguments may be supported in your specific operating environment, so you will want to check your compiler's documentation. Let's now look at **argc** and **argv** more closely.

Note

Technically, the names of the command-line parameters are arbitrary—you can use any names you like. However, **argc** and **argv** have been used by convention for several years, and it is best that you use these names so that anyone reading your program can quickly identify them as the command-line parameters.

The **argc** parameter is an integer that holds the number of arguments on the command line. It will always be at least 1, because the name of the program qualifies as the first argument.

The **argv** parameter is a pointer to an array of character pointers. Each pointer in the **argv** array points to a string containing a command-line argument. The program's name is pointed to by **argv[0]**; **argv[1]** will point to the first argument, **argv[2]** to the second argument, and so on. All command-line arguments are passed to the program as strings, so numeric arguments will have to be converted by your program into their proper internal format.

It is important that you declare **argv** properly. The most common method is

```
char *argv[];
```

You can access the individual arguments by indexing **argv**. The following program demonstrates how to access the command-line arguments. It displays all of the command-line arguments that are present when it is executed.

```cpp
// Display command-line arguments.

#include <iostream>
using namespace std;

int main(int argc, char *argv[])
{

  for(int i = 0; i < argc; i++) {
    cout << argv[i] << "\n";
  }

  return 0;
}
```

For example, if the program is called ComLine, then executing it like this:

```
C>ComLine one two three
```

causes the following output:

```
ComLine
one
two
three
```

    C++ does not stipulate the exact nature of a command-line argument, because host environments (operating systems) vary considerably on this point. However, the most common convention is as follows: each command-line argument must be separated by spaces or tabs. Often commas, semicolons, and the like are not valid argument separators. For example,

```
one, two, and three
```

is made up of four strings, while

```
one,two,and three
```

has two strings—the comma is not a legal separator.

    If you need to pass a command-line argument that does, in fact, contain spaces, then you must place it between quotes. For example, this will be treated as a single command-line argument:

```
"this is one argument"
```

Keep in mind that the examples provided here apply to a wide variety of environments, but not necessarily to yours.

    Usually, you will use **argc** and **argv** to get initial options or values (such as a filename) into your program. In C++, you can have as many command-line arguments as the operating system will allow. Using command-line arguments will give your program a professional appearance and facilitate the program's use in batch files.

5

Passing Numeric Command-Line Arguments

When you pass numeric data as a command-line argument to a program, that data will be received in string form. Your program will need to convert it into the binary, internal format using one of the standard library functions supported by C++. Three of the most commonly used functions for this purpose are shown here:

atof( )   Converts a string to a **double** and returns the result.

atol( )   Converts a string to a **long int** and returns the result.

atoi( )   Converts a string to an **int** and returns the result.

Each is called with a string containing a numeric value as an argument. Each uses the header **<cstdlib>**.

The following program demonstrates the conversion of a numeric command-line argument into its binary equivalent. It computes the sum of the two numbers that follow its name on the command line. The program uses the **atof( )** function to convert its numeric argument into its internal representation.

```
/* This program displays the sum of the two numeric
   command line arguments.
*/

#include <iostream>
#include <cstdlib>
using namespace std;

int main(int argc, char *argv[])
{

  double a, b;

  if(argc!=3) {
    cout << "Usage: add num num\n";
    return 1;
  }

  a = atof(argv[1]); // convert first command-line arg
  b = atof(argv[2]); // convert second comnand-line arg

  cout << a + b;
```

Use **atof( )** to convert command-line numeric strings into **double**s.

```
    return 0;
}
```

To add two numbers, use this type of command line (assuming the program is called *add*):

```
C>add 100.2 231
```

 1-Minute Drill

● What are the two parameters to **main( )** usually called? Explain what each contains.

● What is always the first command-line argument?

● A numeric command-line argument is passed as string. True or false?

5

Function Prototypes

Function prototypes were discussed briefly at the beginning of this module. Now it is time to explain them more fully. In C++, all functions must be declared before they are used. Typically, this is accomplished by use of a function prototype. Prototypes specify three things about a function:

● Its return type

● The type of its parameters

● The number of its parameters

Prototypes allow the compiler to perform three important operations:

● They tell the compiler what type of code to generate when a function is called. Different return types must be handled differently by the compiler.

● The two parameters to **main( )** are usually called **argc** and **argv**. **argc** specifies the number of command-line arguments present. **argv** is a pointer to an array of strings that contains the arguments.
● The first command-line argument is always the name of the program, itself.
● True.

● They allow C++ to find and report any illegal type conversions between the type of arguments used to call a function and the type definition of its parameters.

● They allow the compiler to detect differences between the number of arguments used to call a function and the number of parameters in the function.

The general form of a function prototype is shown here. It is the same as a function definition, except that no body is present.

type func-name(type parm_name1, type parm_name2,...,
type parm_nameN);

The use of parameter names in a prototype is optional. However, their use does let the compiler identify any type mismatches by name when an error occurs, so it is a good idea to include them.

To better understand the usefulness of function prototypes, consider the following program. If you try to compile it, an error message will be issued, because the program attempts to call **sqr_it( )** with an integer argument instead of the integer pointer required. (There is no automatic conversion from integer to pointer.)

```
/* This program uses a function prototype to
   enforce strong type checking.
*/

void sqr_it(int *i); // prototype

int main()
{
  int x;

  x = 10;
  sqr_it(x); // Error! Type mismatch!

  return 0;
}

void sqr_it(int *i)
{
  *i = *i * *i;
}
```

Prototype prevents parameter type mismatches. Here, **sqr_it( )** is expecting a pointer but is called with an integer.

It is possible for a function definition to also serve as its prototype if the definition occurs prior to the function's first use in the program. For example, this is a valid program:

```
// Use a function's definition as its prototype.

#include <iostream>
using namespace std;

// Determine if a number is even.
bool isEven(int num) {
  if(!(num %2)) return true; // num is even
  return false;
}

int main()
{
  if(isEven(4)) cout << "4 is even\n";
  if(isEven(3)) cout << "this won't display";

  return 0;
}
```

Because **isEven( )** is defined before it is used, its definition also serves as its prototype.

5

Here, the function **isEven( )** is defined before it is used in **main( )**. Thus, its definition can also serve as its prototype, and no separate prototype is needed.

In general, it is usually easier and better to simply declare a prototype for each function used by a program rather than trying to make sure that each function is defined before it is used. This is especially true for large programs in which it is hard to keep track of which functions use what other functions. Furthermore, it is possible to have two functions that call each other. In this case, prototypes must be used.

Headers Contain Prototypes

Earlier in this book, you were introduced to the standard C++ headers. You have learned that these headers contain information needed by your programs. While this partial explanation is true, it does not tell the whole story. C++'s headers contain the prototypes for the functions in the standard library. (They also contain various values and definitions used by those functions.) Like functions that you write, the standard library functions must be prototyped before they are used. For this reason, any program that uses a library function must also include the header containing the prototype of that function.

To find out which header a library function requires, look in your compiler's library documentation. Along with a description of each function, you will find the name of the header that must be included in order to use that function.

1-Minute Drill

- What is a function prototype? What is the purpose of a prototype?
- Aside from **main( )**, must all functions be prototyped?
- When you use a standard library function, why must you include its header?

Recursion

The last topic that we will examine in this module is *recursion*. Sometimes called *circular definition*, recursion is the process of defining something in terms of itself. As it relates to programming, recursion is the process of a function calling itself. A function that calls itself is said to be *recursive*.

The classic example of recursion is the function **factr( )**, which computes the factorial of an integer. The factorial of a number N is the product of all the whole numbers between 1 and N. For example, 3 factorial is 1×2×3, or 6. Both **factr( )** and its iterative equivalent are shown here:

```
// Demonstrate recursion.

#include <iostream>
using namespace std;

int factr(int n);
int fact(int n);

int main()
{
  // use recursive version
  cout << "4 factorial is " << factr(4);
```

- A prototype declares a function's name, return type, and parameters. A prototype tells the compiler how to generate code when the function is called and ensures that it is called correctly.
- Yes, all functions except for **main( )** must be prototyped.
- In addition to other things, a header includes the prototype for the library function.

```
  cout << '\n';

  // use iterative version
  cout << "4 factorial is " << fact(4);
  cout << '\n';

  return 0;
}

// Recursive version.
int factr(int n)
{
  int answer;

  if(n==1) return(1);
  answer = factr(n-1)*n;          Execute a recursive call to factr( ).
  return(answer);
}

// Iterative version.
int fact(int n)
{
  int t, answer;

  answer = 1;
  for(t=1; t<=n; t++) answer = answer*(t);
  return(answer);
}
```

5

The operation of the nonrecursive version of **fact( )** should be clear. It uses a loop starting at 1 and progressively multiplies each number by the moving product.

The operation of the recursive **factr( )** is a little more complex. When **factr( )** is called with an argument of 1, the function returns 1; otherwise, it returns the product of **factr(n–1)*n**. To evaluate this expression, **factr( )** is called with **n–1**. This happens until **n** equals 1 and the calls to the function begin returning. For example, when the factorial of 2 is calculated, the first call to **factr( )** will cause a second call to be made with the argument of 1. This call will return 1, which is then multiplied by 2 (the original **n** value). The answer is then 2. You might find it interesting to insert **cout** statements into **factr( )** that will show at what level each call is, and what the intermediate answers are.

When a function calls itself, new local variables and parameters are allocated storage (usually on the system stack), and the function code is executed with these new variables from the start. A recursive call does not make a new copy of the function; only the arguments are new. As each recursive call returns, the old local variables and parameters are removed from the stack, and execution resumes at the point of the function call inside the function. Recursive functions could be said to "telescope" out and back.

Keep in mind that most recursive routines do not significantly reduce code size. Also, the recursive versions of most routines may execute a bit more slowly than their iterative equivalents, due to the added overhead of the additional function calls. Too many recursive calls to a function may cause a stack overrun. Because storage for function parameters and local variables is on the stack, and each new call creates a new copy of these variables, it is possible that the stack will be exhausted. If this occurs, other data may be destroyed as well. However, you probably will not have to worry about any of this unless a recursive function runs wild.

The main advantage of recursive functions is that they can be used to create versions of several algorithms that are clearer and simpler than those produced with their iterative relatives. For example, the Quicksort sorting algorithm is quite difficult to implement in an iterative way. Also, some problems, especially those related to artificial intelligence, seem to lend themselves to recursive solutions.

When writing a recursive function, you must include a conditional statement, such as an **if**, somewhere to force the function to return without execution of the recursive call. If you don't provide the conditional statement, then once you call the function, it will never return. This is a very common error. When developing programs with recursive functions, use **cout** statements liberally so that you can watch what is going on, and abort execution if you see that you have made a mistake.

Here is another example of a recursive function, called **reverse( )**. It prints its string argument backwards on the screen.

```
// Print a string backwards using recursion.

#include <iostream>
using namespace std;

void reverse(char *s);
```

```
int main()
{
  char str[] = "this is a test";

  reverse(str);

  return 0;
}

// Print string backwards.
void reverse(char *s)
{
  if(*s)
    reverse(s+1);
  else
    return;

  cout << *s;
}
```

The **reverse( )** function first checks to see if it is passed a pointer to the null terminating the string. If not, then **reverse( )** calls itself with a pointer to the next character in the string. When the null terminator is finally found, the calls begin unraveling, and the characters are displayed in reverse order.

One last point: Recursion is often difficult for beginners. Don't be discouraged if it seems a bit confusing right now. Over time, you will grow more accustomed to it.

QSDemo.cpp

Project 5-1: The Quicksort

In Module 4, you were shown a simple sorting method called the bubble sort. It was mentioned at the time that substantially better sorts exist. Here you will develop a version of one of the best: the Quicksort. The Quicksort, invented and named by C.A.R. Hoare, is the best general-purpose sorting algorithm currently available. The reason it could not be shown in Module 4 is that the best implementations of the Quicksort rely on recursion. The version we will develop sorts a character array, but the logic can be adapted to sort any type of object.

The Quicksort is built on the idea of partitions. The general procedure is to select a value, called the *comparand,* and then to partition the array into two sections. All elements greater than or equal to the partition value are put on one side, and those less than the value are put on the other. This process is then repeated for each remaining section until the array is sorted. For example, given the array **fedacb** and using the value **d** as the comparand, the first pass of the Quicksort would rearrange the array as follows:

Initial   f e d a c b
Pass1   b c a d e f

This process is then repeated for each section—that is, **bca** and **def**. As you can see, the process is essentially recursive in nature and, indeed, the cleanest implementation of Quicksort is as a recursive function.

You can select the comparand value in two ways. You can either choose it at random, or you can select it by averaging a small set of values taken from the array. For optimal sorting, you should select a value that is precisely in the middle of the range of values. However, this is not easy to do for most sets of data. In the worst case, the value chosen is at one extremity. Even in this case, however, Quicksort still performs correctly. The version of Quicksort that we will develop selects the middle element of the array as the comparand.

One other thing: The C++ library contains a function called **qsort( )** which also performs a Quicksort. You might find it interesting to compare it to the version shown here.

Step-By-Step

1. Create a file called **QSDemo.cpp**.

2. The Quicksort will be implemented by a pair of functions. The first, called **quicksort( )**, provides a convenient interface for the user and sets up a call to the actual sorting function called **qs( )**. First, create the **quicksort( )** function, as shown here:

```
// Set up a call to the actual sorting function.
void quicksort(char *items, int len)
{
  qs(items, 0, len-1);
}
```

Here, **items** points to the array to be sorted, and **len** specifies the number of elements in the array. As shown in the next step, **qs( )** requires an initial partition, which **quicksort( )** supplies. The advantage of using **quicksort( )** is that it can be called with just a pointer to the array to be sorted and the number of elements in the array. It then provides the beginning and ending indices of the region to be sorted.

3. Add the actual Quicksort function, called **qs( )**, shown here:

```
// A recursive version of Quicksort for sorting characters.
void qs(char *items, int left, int right)
{
  int i, j;
  char x, y;

  i = left; j = right;
  x = items[( left+right) / 2 ];

  do {
    while((items[i] < x) && (i < right)) i++;
    while((x < items[j]) && (j > left)) j--;

    if(i <= j) {
      y = items[i];
      items[i] = items[j];
      items[j] = y;
      i++; j--;
    }
  } while(i <= j);

  if(left < j) qs(items, left, j);
  if(i < right) qs(items, i, right);
}
```

This function must be called with the indices of the region to be sorted.
The left parameter must contain the beginning (left boundary) of the
partition. The right parameter must contain the ending (right boundary)
of the partition. When first called, the partition represents the entire array.
Each recursive call progressively sorts a smaller partition.

4. To use the Quicksort, simply call **quicksort( )** with the name of the array
to be sorted and its length. After the call returns, the array will be sorted.
Remember, this version works only for character arrays, but you can adapt
the logic to sort any type of arrays you want.

Here is a program that demonstrates the Quicksort:

```
/*
  Project 5-1
  A version of the Quicksort for sorting characters.
```

```
*/

#include <iostream>
#include <cstring>

using namespace std;

void quicksort(char *items, int len);

void qs(char *items, int left, int right);

int main() {

  char str[] = "jfmckldoelazlkper";
  int i;

  cout << "Original order: " << str << "\n";

  quicksort(str, strlen(str));

  cout << "Sorted order: " << str << "\n";

  return 0;

}

// Set up a call to the actual sorting function.
void quicksort(char *items, int len)
{
  qs(items, 0, len-1);
}

// A recursive version of Quicksort for sorting characters.
void qs(char *items, int left, int right)
{
  int i, j;
  char x, y;

  i = left; j = right;
  x = items[( left+right) / 2 ];

  do {
    while((items[i] < x) && (i < right)) i++;
    while((x < items[j]) && (j > left)) j--;

    if(i <= j) {
```

```
      y = items[i];
      items[i] = items[j];
      items[j] = y;
      i++; j--;
    }
  } while(i <= j);

  if(left < j) qs(items, left, j);
  if(i < right) qs(items, i, right);
}
```

The output from the program is shown here:

```
Original order: jfmckldoelazlkper
Sorted order: acdeefjkklllmoprz
```

Ask the Expert

Question   I have heard of something called the "default-to-int" rule. What is it and does it apply to C++?

Answer   In the original C language, and for early versions of C++, if no type specifier was present in a declaration, **int** was assumed. For example, in old-style code, the following function would be valid and would return an **int** result:

```
f() { // default to int return type
{
  int x;
  // ...
  return x;
}
```

Here, the type returned by f( ) is **int** by default, since no other return type is specified. However, the "default-to-int" rule (also called the "implicit int" rule) is not supported by modern versions of C++. Although most compilers will continue to support the "default-to-int" rule for the sake of backward compatibility, you should explicitly specify the return type of every function that you write. Since older code frequently made use of the default integer return type, this change is also something to keep in mind when converting legacy code.

☑ *Mastery Check*

1. Show the general form of a function.

2. Create a function called **hypot( )** that computes the length of the hypotenuse of a right triangle given the lengths of the two opposing sides. Demonstrate its use in a program. For this problem, you will need to use the **sqrt( )** standard library function, which returns the square root of its argument. It has this prototype:

   double sqrt(double *val*);

   It uses the header **<cmath>**.

3. Can a function return a pointer? Can a function return an array?

4. Create your own version of the standard library function **strlen( )**. Call your version **mystrlen( )**, and demonstrate its use in a program.

5. Does a local variable maintain its value between calls to the function in which it is declared?

6. Give one benefit of global variables. Give one disadvantage.

7. Create a function called **byThrees( )** that returns a series of numbers, with each value 3 greater than the preceding one. Have the series start at 0. Thus, the first five numbers returned by **byThrees( )** are 0, 3, 6, 9, and 12. Create another function called **reset( )** that causes **byThrees( )** to start the series over again from 0. Demonstrate your functions in a program. Hint: You will need to use a global variable.

8. Write a program that requires a password that is specified on the command line. Your program doesn't have to actually do anything except report whether the password was entered correctly or incorrectly.

9. A prototype prevents a function from being called with the improper number of arguments. True or false?

10. Write a recursive function that prints the number 1 through 10. Demonstrate its use in a program.

Module 6

A Closer Look at Functions

The Goals of This Module

- Understand how arguments are passed to functions
- Examine the reference
- Pass references to functions
- Return references
- Use independent references
- Overload functions
- Use default function arguments
- Avoid ambiguity when overloading functions

This module continues our examination of the function. It discusses three of C++'s most important function-related topics: references, function overloading, and default arguments. These features vastly expand the capabilities of a function. A reference is an implicit pointer. Function overloading is the quality that allows one function to be implemented two or more different ways, each performing a separate task. Function overloading is one way that C++ supports polymorphism. Using a default argument, it is possible to specify a value for a parameter that will be automatically used when no corresponding argument is specified.

We will begin with an explanation of the two ways that arguments can be passed to functions, and the implications of both methods. An understanding of argument passing is needed in order to understand the reference.

Two Approaches to Argument Passing

In general, there are two ways that a computer language can pass an argument to a subroutine. The first is *call-by-value*. This method copies the *value* of an argument into the parameter of the subroutine. Therefore, changes made to the parameters of the subroutine have no effect on the arguments used to call it.

Call-by-reference is the second way a subroutine can be passed arguments. In this method, the *address* of an argument (not its value) is copied into the parameter. Inside the subroutine, this address is used to access the actual argument specified in the call. This means that changes made to the parameter *will affect* the argument used to call the subroutine.

How C++ Passes Arguments

By default, C++ uses *call-by-value* for passing arguments. This means that the code inside a function cannot alter the arguments used to call the function. In this book, all of the programs up to this point have used the call-by-value method. For example, consider the **reciprocal( )** function in this program:

```
// Changing a call-by-value parameter does not affect the
// argument.

#include <iostream>
using namespace std;
```

```
double reciprocal(double x);

int main()
{
  double t = 10.0;

  cout << "Reciprocal of 10.0 is " << reciprocal(t) << "\n";

  cout << "Value of t is still: " << t << "\n";

  return 0;
}

// Return the reciprocal of a value.
double reciprocal(double x)
{
  x = 1 / x; // create reciprocal ◄────  This does not change the
                                         value of t inside main( ).
  return x;
}
```

The output from the program is shown here:

```
Reciprocal of 10.0 is 0.1
Value of t is still: 10
```

As the output shows, when the assignment

```
x = 1/x;
```

takes place inside **reciprocal( )**, the only thing modified is the local variable **x**. The variable **t** used as an argument will still have the value 10 and is unaffected by the operations inside the function.

Using a Pointer to Create a Call-by-Reference

Even though C++'s default parameter-passing convention is call-by-value, it is possible to manually create a call-by-reference by passing the address of an argument (that is, a pointer) to a function. It is then possible to change the value of the argument outside of the function. You saw an example of this in the preceding module when the passing of pointers was discussed. As you know, pointers are passed to functions just like any other values. Of course, it is necessary to declare the parameters as pointer types.

To see how passing a pointer allows you to manually create a call-by-reference, consider a function called **swap( )** that exchanges the values of the two variables pointed to by its arguments. Here is one way to implement it:

```
// Exchange the values of the variables pointed to by x and y.
void swap(int *x, int *y)
{
  int temp;

  temp = *x; // save the value at addressx
  *x = *y;   // put y into x
  *y = temp; // put x into y
}
```

Exchange the values of the variables pointed to by **x** and **y**.

The **swap( )** function declares two pointer parameters, **x** and **y**. It uses these parameters to exchange the values of the variables pointed to by the arguments passed to the function. Remember, *x and *y refer to the variables pointed to by **x** and **y**. Thus, the statement

```
*x = *y;
```

puts the value of the object pointed to by **y** into the object pointed to by **x**. Consequently, when the function terminates, the contents of the variables used to call the function will be swapped.

Since **swap( )** expects to receive two pointers, you must remember to call **swap( )** with the *addresses* of the variables you want to exchange. The correct method is shown in this program:

```
// Demonstrate the pointer version of swap().

#include <iostream>
using namespace std;

// Declare swap() using pointers.
void swap(int *x, int *y);

int main()
{
  int i, j;

  i = 10;
  j = 20;
```

```
   cout << "Initial values of i and j: ";
   cout << i << ' ' << j << '\n';

   swap(&j, &i); // call swap() with addresses of i and j
```

Call **swap( )** with the addresses of the variables that you want to exchange.

```
   cout << "Swapped values of i and j: ";
   cout << i << ' ' << j << '\n';

   return 0;
}
```

Exchange the values of the variables pointed to by **x** and **y** using explicit pointer operations.

```
// Exchange values pointed to by x and y.
void swap(int *x, int *y)
{
  int temp;

  temp = *x; // save the value at x
  *x = *y;   // put value at y into the variable at x
  *y = temp; // put value at x into the variable at y
}
```

6

In **main( )**, the variable **i** is assigned the value 10, and **j**, the value 20. Then **swap( )** is called with the addresses of **i** and **j**. The unary operator **&** is used to produce the addresses of the variables. Therefore, the addresses of **i** and **j**, not their values, are passed into **swap( )**. When **swap( )** returns, **i** and **j** will have their values exchanged, as the following output shows:

```
Initial values of i and j: 10 20
Swapped values of i and j: 20 10
```

1-Minute Drill

● Explain call-by-value.

● Explain call-by-reference.

● What parameter-passing mechanism does C++ use by default?

● Call-by-value copies the value of the argument into the parameter of the subroutine.
● Call-by-reference copies the address of the argument into the parameter of the subroutine.
● By default, C++ uses call-by-value.

Reference Parameters

While it is possible to achieve a call-by-reference manually by using the pointer operators, this approach is rather clumsy. First, it compels you to perform all operations through pointers. Second, it requires that you remember to pass the addresses (rather than the values) of the arguments when calling the function. Fortunately, in C++, it is possible to tell the compiler to automatically use call-by-reference rather than call-by-value for one or more parameters of a particular function. You can accomplish this with a *reference parameter*. When you use a reference parameter, the address (not the value) of an argument is automatically passed to the function. Within the function, operations on the reference parameter are automatically dereferenced, so there is no need to use the pointer operators.

A reference parameter is declared by preceding the parameter name in the function's declaration with an **&**. Operations performed on a reference parameter affect the argument used to call the function, not the reference parameter itself.

To understand reference parameters, let's begin with a simple example. In the following, the function f( ) takes one reference parameter of type **int**:

```
// Using a reference parameter.

#include <iostream>
using namespace std;

void f(int &i); // here, i is a reference parameter

int main()
{
  int val = 1;

  cout << "Old value for val: " << val << '\n';

  f(val); // pass address of val to f()

  cout << "New value for val: " << val << '\n';

  return 0;
}

void f(int &i)
{
  i = 10; // this modifies calling argument
}
```

Declare a reference parameter.

Assign a value to the variable referred to by **i**.

This program displays the following output:

```
Old value for val: 1
New value for val: 10
```

Pay special attention to the definition of f( ), shown here:

```
void f(int &i)
{
  i = 10; // this modifies calling argument
}
```

Notice the declaration of **i**. It is preceded by an **&**, which causes it to become a reference parameter. (This declaration is also used in the function's prototype.) Inside the function, the following statement

```
i = 10;
```

does *not* cause **i** to be given the value 10. Instead, it causes the variable *referenced* by **i** (in this case, **val**) to be assigned the value 10. Notice that this statement does not use the * pointer operator. When you use a reference parameter, the C++ compiler automatically knows that it is an address and dereferences it for you. In fact, using the * would be an error.

Since **i** has been declared as a reference parameter, the compiler will automatically pass **f( )** the *address* of any argument it is called with. Thus, in **main( )**, the statement

```
f(val);  // pass address of val to f()
```

passes the address of **val** (not its value) to **f( )**. There is no need to precede **val** with the **&** operator. (Doing so would be an error.) Since **f( )** receives the address of **val** in the form of a reference, it can modify the value of **val**.

To illustrate reference parameters in actual use—and to fully demonstrate their benefits—the **swap( )** function is rewritten using references in the following program. Look carefully at how **swap( )** is declared and called.

```
// Use reference parameters to create the swap() function.

#include <iostream>
using namespace std;
```

6

```
// Declare swap() using reference parameters.
void swap(int &x, int &y);

int main()
{
  int i, j;

  i = 10;
  j = 20;

  cout << "Initial values of i and j: ";
  cout << i << ' ' << j << '\n';

  swap(j, i);

  cout << "Swapped values of i and j: ";
  cout << i << ' ' << j << '\n';

  return 0;
}

/* Here, swap() is defined as using call-by-reference,
   not call-by-value. Thus, it can exchange the two
   arguments it is called with.
*/
void swap(int &x, int &y)
{
  int temp;

  // use references to exchange the values of the arguments
  temp = x;
  x = y;
  y = temp;
}
```

Here, the addresses of **i** and **j** are automatically passed to **swap( )**.

Now, the exchange takes place automatically through the references.

The output is the same as the previous version. Again, notice that by making x and y reference parameters, there is no need to use the * operator when exchanging values. Remember, the compiler automatically generates the addresses of the arguments used to call **swap( )** and automatically dereferences x and y.

Let's review. When you create a reference parameter, that parameter automatically refers to (that is, implicitly points to) the argument used to call the function. Further, there is no need to apply the **&** operator to an argument. Also, inside the function, the reference parameter is used directly; the * operator is not used. All operations involving the reference parameter automatically refer to the argument used in the call to the function. Finally, when you assign a value to a reference parameter, you are actually assigning that value to the variable to which the reference is pointing. In the case of a function parameter, this will be the variable used in the call to the function.

One last point: The C language does not support references. Thus, the only way to create a call-by-reference in C is to use pointers, as shown earlier in the first version of **swap( )**. When converting C code to C++, you will want to convert these types of parameters to references, where feasible.

Ask the Expert

6

Question   In some C++ code, I have seen a declaration style in which the **&** is associated with the type name as shown here:

```
int& i;
```

rather than the variable name, like this:

```
int &i;
```

Is there a difference?

Answer   The short answer is no, there is no difference between the two declarations. For example, here is another way to write the prototype to **swap( )**:

```
void swap(int& x, int& y);
```

As you can see, the **&** is immediately adjacent to **int** and not to **x**. Furthermore, some programmers also specify pointers by associating the * with the type rather the variable, as shown here:

```
float* p;
```

These types of declarations reflect the desire by some programmers for C++ to contain a separate reference or pointer type. However, the trouble with associating the **&** or * with the type rather than the variable is that, according to the formal C++ syntax, neither the **&** nor the * is distributive over a list of variables, and this can lead to confusing declarations. For example, the following declaration creates one, *not two*, **int** pointers:

```
int* a, b;
```

Here, **b** is declared as an integer (not an integer pointer) because, as specified by the C++ syntax, when used in a declaration, an * or an & is linked to the individual variable that it precedes, not to the type that it follows.

It is important to understand that as far as the C++ compiler is concerned, it doesn't matter whether you write **int *p** or **int* p**. Thus, if you prefer to associate the * or & with the type rather than the variable, feel free to do so. However, to avoid confusion, this book will continue to associate the * and the & with the variable name that each modifies, rather than with the type name.

1-Minute Drill

● How is a reference parameter declared?

● When calling a function that uses a reference parameter, must you precede the argument with a **&**?

● Inside a function that receives a reference parameter, do operations on that parameter need to be preceded with a * or **&**?

Returning References

A function can return a reference. In C++ programming, there are several uses for reference return values. You will see some of these later in this book. However, reference return values have other important applications, which you can use now.

● A reference parameter is declared by preceding the parameter name with an **&**.
● No, the argument is automatically passed by reference when a reference parameter is used.
● No, the parameter is operated upon normally. However, changes made to the parameter affect the calling argument.

When a function returns a reference, it returns an implicit pointer to its return value. This gives rise to a rather startling possibility: the function can be used on the left side of an assignment statement! For example, consider this simple program:

```
// Returning a reference.

#include <iostream>
using namespace std;

double &f(); // return a reference.    ◄──    Here, f( ) returns a
                                              reference to a double.
double val = 100.0;

int main()
{
  double x;

  cout << f() << '\n'; // display val's value

  x = f(); // assign value of val to x
  cout << x << '\n'; // display x's value

  f() = 99.1; // change val's value
  cout << f() << '\n'; // display val's new value
                                    This returns a reference to
  return 0;                         the global variable val.
}

// This function returns a reference to a double.
double &f()
{
  return val; // return reference to val  ◄──
}
```

The output of this program is shown here:

```
100
100
99.1
```

Let's examine this program closely. At the beginning, f( ) is declared as returning a reference to a **double**, and the global variable **val** is initialized to 100. In **main( )**, the following statement displays the original value of **val**:

```
cout << f() << '\n'; // display val's value
```

When f( ) is called, it returns a reference to **val** using this **return** statement:

```
return val; // return reference to val
```

This statement automatically returns a reference to **val** rather than **val**'s value. This reference is then used by the **cout** statement to display **val**'s value.

In the line

```
x = f(); // assign value of val to x
```

the reference to **val** returned by f( ) assigns the value of **val** to **x**.

The most interesting line in the program is shown here:

```
f() = 99.1; // change val's value
```

This statement causes the value of **val** to be changed to 99.1. Here is why: since f( ) returns a reference to **val**, this reference becomes the target of the assignment statement. Thus, the value of 99.1 is assigned to **val** indirectly, through the reference to it returned by f( ).

Here is another sample program that uses a reference return type:

```
// Return a reference to an array element.

#include <iostream>
using namespace std;

double &change_it(int i); // return a reference

double vals[] = { 1.1, 2.2, 3.3, 4.4, 5.5 };

int main()
{
  int i;

  cout << "Here are the original values: ";
  for(i=0; i < 5; i++)
    cout << vals[i] << ' ';
```

```
   cout << '\n';

   change_it(1) = 5298.23; // change 2nd element
   change_it(3) = -98.8; // change 4th element

   cout << "Here are the changed values: ";
   for(i=0; i < 5; i++)
     cout << vals[i] << ' ';
   cout << '\n';

   return 0;
}

double &change_it(int i)
{
   return vals[i]; // return a reference to the ith element
}
```

This program changes the values of the second and fourth elements in the **vals** array. The program displays the following output:

```
Here are the original values: 1.1 2.2 3.3 4.4 5.5
Here are the changed values: 1.1 5298.23 3.3 -98.8 5.5
```

Let's see how this is accomplished.

The **change_it( )** function is declared as returning a reference to a **double**. Specifically, it returns a reference to the element of **vals** that is specified by its parameter **i**. The reference returned by **change_it( )** is then used in **main( )** to assign a value to that element.

When returning a reference, be careful that the object being referred to does not go out of scope. For example, consider this function:

```
// Error, cannot return reference to local var.
int &f()
{
   int i = 10;

   return i;  ←——————— Error! i will go out-of-scope
}                         when f( ) returns.
```

In **f( )**, the local variable **i** will go out of scope when the function returns. Therefore, the reference to **i** returned by **f( )** will be undefined. Actually, some compilers will not compile **f( )** as written for precisely this reason. However, this type of problem can be created indirectly, so be careful which object you return a reference to.

Independent References

Even though the reference is included in C++ primarily for supporting call-by-reference parameter passing and for use as a function return type, it is possible to declare a stand-alone reference variable. This is called an *independent reference*. It must be stated at the outset, however, that non-parameter reference variables are seldom used, because they tend to confuse and destructure your program. With these reservations in mind, we will take a short look at them here.

An independent reference must point to some object. Thus, an independent reference must be initialized when it is declared. Generally, this means that it will be assigned the address of a previously declared variable. Once this is done, the name of the reference variable can be used anywhere that the variable it refers to can be used. In fact, there is virtually no distinction between the two. For example, consider the program shown here:

```
// Use an independent reference.

#include <iostream>
using namespace std;

int main()
{
  int j, k;
  int &i = j; // independent reference

  j = 10;

  cout << j << " " << i; // outputs 10 10

  k = 121;
  i = k; // copies k's value into j, not k's address

  cout << "\n" << j;  // outputs 121

  return 0;
}
```

An independent reference.

This program displays the following output:

```
10 10
121
```

The address pointed to by a reference variable is fixed; it cannot be changed. Thus, when the statement

```
i = k;
```

is evaluated, it is **k**'s value that is copied into **j** (referred to by **i**), not its address.

As stated earlier, it is generally not a good idea to use independent references, because they are not necessary and they tend to garble your code. Having two names for the same variable is an inherently confusing situation.

A Few Restrictions When Using References

There are some restrictions that apply to reference variables:

● You cannot reference a reference variable.

● You cannot create arrays of references.

● You cannot create a pointer to a reference. That is, you cannot apply the & operator to a reference.

1-Minute Drill

● Can a function return a reference?

● What is an independent reference?

● Can you create a reference to a reference?

● Yes, a function can return a reference.
● An independent reference is essentially another name for some object.
● No, you cannot create a reference to a reference.

Function Overloading

In this section, you will learn about one of C++'s most exciting features: function overloading. In C++, two or more functions can share the same name as long as their parameter declarations are different. In this situation, the functions that share the same name are said to be *overloaded*, and the process is referred to as *function overloading*. Function overloading is one way that C++ achieves polymorphism.

In general, to overload a function, simply declare different versions of it. The compiler takes care of the rest. You must observe one important restriction: the type and/or number of the parameters of each overloaded function must differ. It is not sufficient for two functions to differ only in their return types. They must differ in the types or number of their parameters. (Return types do not provide sufficient information in all cases for C++ to decide which function to use.) Of course, overloaded functions *may* differ in their return types, too. When an overloaded function is called, the version of the function whose parameters match the arguments is executed.

Let's begin with a short sample program:

```
// Overload a function three times.

#include <iostream>
using namespace std;

void f(int i);        // integer parameter
void f(int i, int j); // two integer parameters
void f(double k);     // one double parameter

int main()
{
  f(10);       // call f(int)

  f(10, 20); // call f(int, int)

  f(12.23);  // call f(double)

  return 0;
}
```

A separate prototype is needed for each version of an overloaded function.

```
void f(int i)  ◄───────────────────────┐
{                                       │
  cout << "In f(int), i is " << i << '\n';
}
                              ┌─────────────────────────┐
void f(int i, int j) ◄────────│ Here are the three different │
{                             │ implementations of f( ).     │
  cout << "In f(int, int), i is " << i;
  cout << ", j is " << j << '\n';
}

void f(double k) ◄──────────────────────┘
{
  cout << "In f(double), k is " << k << '\n';
}
```

This program produces the following output:

```
In f(int), i is 10
In f(int, int), i is 10, j is 20
In f(double), k is 12.23
```

As you can see, f( ) is overloaded three times. The first version takes one integer parameter, the second version requires two integer parameters, and the third version has one **double** parameter. Because the parameter list for each version is different, the compiler is able to call the correct version of each function based on the type of the arguments specified at the time of the call.

To understand the value of function overloading, consider a function called **neg( )** that returns the negation of its arguments. For example, when called with the value –10, **neg( )** returns 10. When called with 9, it returns –9. Without function overloading, if you wanted to create negation functions for data of type **int**, **double**, and **long**, you would need three different functions, each with a different name, such as **ineg( )**, **lneg( )**, and **fneg( )**. However, through the use of function overloading, you can use one name, such as **neg( )**, to refer to all functions that return the negation of their argument. Thus, overloading supports the polymorphic concept of "one interface, multiple methods." The following program demonstrates this:

```
// Create various version of the neg() function.

#include <iostream>
```

6

```
using namespace std;

int neg(int n);         // neg() for int.
double neg(double n);   // neg() for double.
long neg(long n);       // neg() for long.


int main()
{

  cout << "neg(-10): " << neg(-10) << "\n";
  cout << "neg(9L): " << neg(9L) << "\n";
  cout << "neg(11.23): " << neg(11.23) << "\n";

  return 0;
}

// neg()for int.
int neg(int n)
{
  return -n;
}

// neg()for double.
double neg(double n)
{
  return -n;
}

// neg()for long.
long neg(long n)
{
  return -n;
}
```

The output is shown here:

```
neg(-10): 10
neg(9L): -9
neg(11.23): -11.23
```

This program creates three similar but different functions called **neg**, each of which returns the absolute value of its argument. The compiler knows which function to use in each given situation because of the type of the argument.

The value of overloading is that it allows related sets of functions to be accessed using a common name. Thus, the name **neg** represents the *general action* that is being performed. It is left to the compiler to choose the right *specific* version for a particular circumstance. You, the programmer, need only remember the general action being performed. Therefore, through the application of polymorphism, three things to remember have been reduced to one. Although this example is fairly simple, if you expand the concept, you can see how overloading can help you manage greater complexity.

Another advantage to function overloading is that it is possible to define slightly different versions of the same function that are specialized for the type of data upon which they operate. For example, consider a function called **min( )** that determines the minimum of two values. It is possible to create versions of **min( )** that behave differently for different data types. When comparing two integers, **min( )** returns the smallest integer. When two characters are compared, **min( )** could return the letter that is first in alphabetical order, ignoring case differences. In the ASCII sequence, uppercase characters are represented by values that are 32 less than the lowercase letters. Thus, ignoring case would be useful when alphabetizing. When comparing two pointers, it is possible to have **min( )** compare the values pointed to by the pointers and return the pointer to the smallest value. Here is a program that implements these versions of **min( )**:

6

```cpp
// Create various versions of min().

#include <iostream>
using namespace std;

int min(int a, int b);      // min() for ints
char min(char a, char b);   // min() for chars
int * min(int *a, int *b);  // min() for int pointers

int main()
{
  int i=10, j=22;

  cout << "min('X', 'a'): " << min('X', 'a') << "\n";
  cout << "min(9, 3): " << min(9, 3) << "\n";
  cout << "*min(&i, &j): " << *min(&i, &i) << "\n";

  return 0;
}
```

```
// min() for ints.  Return the smallest value.
int min(int a, int b)
{
  if(a < b) return a;
  else return b;
}
```

Each version of **min( )** can be specialized. This version returns the smallest **int** value.

```
// min() for chars -- ignore case.
char min(char a, char b)
{
  if(tolower(a) < tolower(b)) return a;
  else return b;
}
```

This version of **min( )** ignores case.

```
/*
   min() for int pointers.
   Compare values and return pointer to smallest value.
*/
int * min(int *a, int *b)
{
  if(*a < *b) return a;
  else return b;
}
```

This version of **min( )** returns a pointer to the smallest value.

Here is the output produced by the program:

```
min('X', 'a'): a
min(9, 3): 3
*min(&i, &j): 10
```

When you overload a function, each version of that function can perform any activity you desire. That is, there is no rule stating that overloaded functions must relate to one another. However, from a stylistic point of view, function overloading implies a relationship. Thus, while you can use the same name to overload unrelated functions, you should not. For example, you could use the name **sqr( )** to create functions that return the *square* of an **int** and the *square root* of a **double**. These two operations are fundamentally different, however, and applying function overloading in this manner defeats its original purpose. (In fact, programming in this manner is considered to be extremely bad style!) In practice, you should overload only closely related operations.

Automatic Type Conversions and Overloading

As you will recall from Module 2, C++ provides certain automatic type conversions. These conversions also apply to parameters of overloaded functions. For example, consider the following:

```
/*
    Automatic type conversions can affect
    overloaded function resolution.
*/

#include <iostream>
using namespace std;

void f(int x);

void f(double x);

int main() {
  int i = 10;
  double d = 10.1;
  short s = 99;
  float r = 11.5F;

  f(i); // calls f(int)
  f(d); // calls f(double)

  f(s); // calls f(int) -- type conversion
  f(r); // calls f(double) -- type conversion

  return 0;
}

void f(int x) {
  cout << "Inside f(int): " << x << "\n";
}

void f(double x) {
  cout << "Inside f(double): " << x << "\n";
}
```

Automatic type conversions occur here.

6

The output from the program is shown here:

```
Inside f(int): 10
Inside f(double): 10.1
Inside f(int): 99
Inside f(double): 11.5
```

In this example, only two versions of **f( )** are defined: one that has an **int** parameter and one that has a **double** parameter. However, it is possible to pass **f( )** a **short** or **float** value. In the case of **short**, C++ automatically converts it to **int**. Thus, **f(int)** is invoked. In the case of **float**, the value is converted to **double** and **f(double)** is called.

It is important to understand, however, that the automatic conversions apply only if there is no direct match between a parameter and an argument. For example, here is the preceding program with the addition of a version of **f( )** that specifies a **short** parameter:

```
// Now, add f(short).

#include <iostream>
using namespace std;

void f(int x);
void f(short x);          f(short) has
void f(double x);         been added.

int main() {
  int i = 10;
  double d = 10.1;
  short s = 99;
  float r = 11.5F;

  f(i); // calls f(int)
  f(d); // calls f(double)

  f(s); // now calls f(short)      Now, no type conversion occurs
                                   because f(short) is available.

  f(r); // calls f(double) -- type conversion

  return 0;
```

```
}

void f(int x) {
  cout << "Inside f(int): " << x << "\n";
}

void f(short x) {
  cout << "Inside f(short): " << x << "\n";
}

void f(double x) {
  cout << "Inside f(double): " << x << "\n";
}
```

Now when the program is run, the following output is produced:

```
Inside f(int): 10
Inside f(double): 10.1
Inside f(short): 99
Inside f(double): 11.5
```

6

In this version, since there is a version of f( ) that takes a **short** argument, when f( ) is called with a **short** value, f(**short**) is invoked and the automatic conversion to **int** does not occur.

1-Minute Drill

- When a function is overloaded, what condition must be met?
- Why should overloaded functions perform related actions?
- Does the return type of a function participate in overload resolution?

- Overloaded functions share the same name, but their parameter declarations are different.
- Overloaded functions should perform related actions because function overloading implies a relationship between functions.
- No, the return types of overloaded functions can differ, but it does not affect overload resolution.

Project 6-1: Create Overloaded Output Functions

In this project, you will create a collection of overloaded functions that output various data types to the screen. Although using **cout** statements is quite convenient, such a collection of output functions offers an alternative that might appeal to some programmers. In fact, both Java and C# use output functions rather than output operators. By creating overloaded output functions, you can use either method and have the best of both worlds. Furthermore, you can tailor your output functions to meet your specific needs. For example, you can make the Boolean values display "true" or "false" rather than 1 and 0.

You will be creating two sets of functions called **println( )** and **print( )**. The **println( )** function displays its argument followed by a newline. The **print( )** function will display its argument, but does not append a newline. For example,

```
print(1);
println('X');
print("Function overloading is powerful. ");
print(18.22);
```

displays

```
1X
Function overloading is powerful. 18.22
```

In this project, **print( )** and **println( )** will be overloaded for data of type **bool**, **char**, **int**, **long**, **char ***, and **double**, but you can add other types on your own.

Step-by-Step

1. Create a file called **Print.cpp**.

2. Begin the project with these lines:

```
/*
   Project 6-1

   Create overloaded print() and println() functions
   that display various types of data.
*/
```

```
include <iostream>
using namespace std;
```

3. Add the prototypes for the **print( )** and **println( )** functions, as shown here:

```
// These output a newline.
void println(bool b);
void println(int i);
void println(long i);
void println(char ch);
void println(char *str);
void println(double d);

// These functions do not output a newline.
void print(bool b);
void print(int i);
void print(long i);
void print(char ch);
void print(char *str);
void print(double d);
```

6

4. Implement the **println( )** functions, as shown here:

```
// Here are the println() functions.
void println(bool b)
{
  if(b) cout << "true\n";
  else cout << "false\n";
}

void println(int i)
{
  cout << i << "\n";
}

void println(long i)
{
  cout << i << "\n";
}

void println(char ch)
{
```

```
   cout << ch << "\n";
}

void println(char *str)
{
   cout << str << "\n";
}

void println(double d)
{
   cout << d << "\n";
}
```

Notice that each function appends a newline character to the output. Also notice that **println(bool)** displays either "true" or "false" when a Boolean value is output. This illustrates how you can easily customize output to meet your own needs and tastes.

5. Implement the **print( )** functions, as shown next:

```
// Here are the print() functions.
void print(bool b)
{
   if(b) cout << "true";
   else cout << "false";
}

void print(int i)
{
   cout << i;
}

void print(long i)
{
   cout << i;
}

void print(char ch)
{
   cout << ch;
}

void print(char *str)
{
```

```
    cout << str;
}

void print(double d)
{
  cout << d;
}
```

These functions are the same as their **println( )** counterparts except that they do not output a newline. Thus, subsequent output appears on the same line.

6. Here is the complete **Print.cpp** program:

```
/*
   Project 6-1

   Create overloaded print() and println() functions
   that display various types of data.
*/

#include <iostream>
using namespace std;

// These output a newline.
void println(bool b);
void println(int i);
void println(long i);
void println(char ch);
void println(char *str);
void println(double d);

// These functions do not output a newline.
void print(bool b);
void print(int i);
void print(long i);
void print(char ch);
void print(char *str);
void print(double d);

int main()
{
  println(true);
  println(10);
  println("This is a test");
```

```
  println('x');
  println(99L);
  println(123.23);

  print("Here are some values: ");
  print(false);
  print(' ');
  print(88);
  print(' ');
  print(100000L);
  print(' ');
  print(100.01);

  println(" Done!");

  return 0;
}

// Here are the println() functions.
void println(bool b)
{
  if(b) cout << "true\n";
  else cout << "false\n";
}

void println(int i)
{
  cout << i << "\n";
}

void println(long i)
{
  cout << i << "\n";
}

void println(char ch)
{
  cout << ch << "\n";
}

void println(char *str)
{
  cout << str << "\n";
}

void println(double d)
```

```
{
  cout << d << "\n";
}

// Here are the print() functions.
void print(bool b)
{
  if(b) cout << "true";
  else cout << "false";
}

void print(int i)
{
  cout << i;
}

void print(long i)
{
  cout << i;
}

void print(char ch)
{
  cout << ch;
}

void print(char *str)
{
  cout << str;
}

void print(double d)
{
  cout << d;
}
```

The output from the program is shown here:

```
true
10
This is a test
x
99
123.23
Here are some values: false 88 100000 100.01 Done!
```

Default Function Arguments

The next function-related feature to be discussed is the *default argument*. In C++, you can give a parameter a default value that is automatically used when no argument corresponding to that parameter is specified in a call to a function. Default arguments can be used to simplify calls to complex functions. Also, they can sometimes be used as a "shorthand" form of function overloading.

A default argument is specified in a manner syntactically similar to a variable initialization. Consider the following example, which declares **myfunc( )** as taking two **int** arguments. The first defaults to 0. The second defaults to 100.

```
void myfunc(int x = 0, int y = 100);
```

Now **myfunc( )** can be called by one of the three methods shown here:

```
myfunc(1, 2); // pass explicit values

myfunc(10);    // pass x a value, let y default

myfunc();      // let both x and y default
```

The first call passes the value 1 to **x** and 2 to **y**. The second gives **x** the value 10 and allows **y** to default to 100. Finally, the third call causes both **x** and **y** to default. The following program demonstrates this process:

```
// Demonstrate default arguments.

#include <iostream>
using namespace std;

void myfunc(int x = 0, int y = 100);   ◀——— myfunc( ) specifies
                                             default arguments for
int main()                                   both parameters.
{
  myfunc(1, 2);

  myfunc(10);

  myfunc();

  return 0;
```

```
}

void myfunc(int x, int y)
{
  cout << "x: " << x << ", y: " << y << "\n";
}
```

The output shown here confirms the use of the default arguments:

```
x: 1, y: 2
x: 10, y: 100
x: 0, y: 100
```

When creating a function that has default argument values, the default values must be specified only once, and this must happen the first time the function is declared within the file. In the preceding example, the default argument was specified in **myfunc( )**'s prototype. If you try to specify new (or even the same) default values in **myfunc( )**'s definition, the compiler will display an error message and will not compile your program.

Even though default arguments cannot be redefined within a program, you can specify different default arguments for each version of an overloaded function; that is, different versions of the overloaded function can have different default arguments.

It is important to understand that all parameters that take default values must appear to the right of those that do not. For example, the following prototype is invalid:

```
// Wrong!
void f(int a = 1, int b);
```

Once you've begun defining parameters that take default values, you cannot specify a nondefaulting parameter. That is, a declaration like the following is also wrong and will not compile:

```
int myfunc(float f, char *str, int i=10, int j); // Wrong!
```

Since **i** has been given a default value, **j** must be given one, too.

One reason that default arguments are included in C++ is that they enable the programmer to manage greater complexity. To handle the widest variety of situations, quite frequently a function will contain more parameters than are

6

required for its most common usage. Thus, when the default arguments apply, you need to remember and specify only the arguments that are meaningful to the exact situation, not all those needed for the most general case.

Default Arguments Versus Overloading

One application of default arguments is as a shorthand form of function overloading. To see why this is the case, imagine that you want to create two customized versions of the standard **strcat( )** function. One version will operate like **strcat( )** and concatenate the entire contents of one string to the end of another. The other version will take a third argument that specifies the number of characters to concatenate. That is, this second version will concatenate only a specified number of characters from one string to the end of another. Thus, assuming that you call your customized functions **mystrcat( )**, they will have the following prototypes:

```
void mystrcat(char *s1, char *s2, int len);
void mystrcat(char *s1, char *s2);
```

The first version will copy **len** characters from **s2** to the end of **s1**. The second version will copy the entire string pointed to by **s2** onto the end of the string pointed to by **s1** and will operate like **strcat( )**.

While it would not be wrong to implement two versions of **mystrcat( )** to create the two versions that you desire, there is an easier way. Using a default argument, you can create only one version of **mystrcat( )** that performs both operations. The following program demonstrates this:

```
// A customized version of strcat().

#include <iostream>
#include <cstring>
using namespace std;                          Here, len defaults to zero.

void mystrcat(char *s1, char *s2, int len = 0);

int main()
{
  char str1[80] = "This is a test";
  char str2[80] = "0123456789";
```

```
  mystrcat(str1, str2, 5); // concatenate 5 chars
  cout << str1 << '\n';

  strcpy(str1, "this is a test"); // reset str1

  mystrcat(str1, str2); // concatenate entire string
  cout << str1 << '\n';

  return 0;
}
```

> Here, **len** is specified, and only 5 characters are copied.

> Here, **len** defaults to zero and the entire string is concatenated.

```
// A custom version of strcat().
void mystrcat(char *s1, char *s2, int len)
{
  // find end of s1
  while(*s1) s1++;

  if(len==0) len = strlen(s2);

  while(*s2 && len) {
    *s1 = *s2; // copy chars
    s1++;
    s2++;
    len--;
  }

  *s1 = '\0'; // null terminate s1
}
```

The output from the program is shown here:

```
This is a test01234
this is a test0123456789
```

As the program illustrates, **mystrcat( )** concatenates up to **len** characters from the string pointed to by **s2** onto the end of the string pointed to by **s1**. However, if **len** is zero, as it will be when it is allowed to default, **mystrcat( )** concatenates the entire string pointed to by **s2** onto **s1**. (Thus, when **len** is zero, the function operates like the standard **strcat( )** function.) By using a default argument for **len**, it is possible to combine both operations into one function. As this example illustrates, default arguments sometimes provide a shorthand form of function overloading.

Using Default Arguments Correctly

Although default arguments are a powerful tool when used correctly, they can also be misused. The point of default arguments is to allow a function to perform its job in an efficient, easy-to-use manner while still allowing considerable flexibility. Toward this end, all default arguments should reflect the way a function is generally used, or a reasonable alternate usage. When there is no single value that is normally associated with a parameter, then there is no reason to declare a default argument. In fact, declaring default arguments when there is insufficient basis for doing so destructures your code, because they are liable to mislead and confuse anyone reading your program. Finally, a default argument should cause no harm. That is, the accidental use of a default argument should not have irreversible, negative consequences. For example, forgetting to specify an argument should not cause an important data file to be erased!

1-Minute Drill

● Show how to declare a **void** function called **count( )** that takes two **int** parameters called **a** and **b**, and give each a default value of 0.

● Can default arguments be declared in both a function's prototype and its definition?

● Is this declaration correct? If not, why not?
```
int f(int x=10, double b);
```

Function Overloading and Ambiguity

Before concluding this module, it is necessary to discuss a type of error unique to C++: *ambiguity*. It is possible to create a situation in which the compiler is unable to choose between two (or more) correctly overloaded functions. When

---

● `void count(int a=0, int b=0);`
● No, the default arguments must be declared in the first declaration of the function, which is usually its prototype.
● No, a nondefaulting parameter cannot follow one with a default argument.

this happens, the situation is said to be *ambiguous*. Ambiguous statements are errors, and programs containing ambiguity will not compile.

By far the main cause of ambiguity involves C++'s automatic type conversions. C++ automatically attempts to convert the type of the arguments used to call a function into the type of the parameters defined by the function. Here is an example:

```
int myfunc(double d);
// ...
cout << myfunc('c');  // not an error, conversion applied
```

As the comment indicates, this is not an error, because C++ automatically converts the character **c** into its **double** equivalent. Actually, in C++, very few type conversions of this sort are disallowed. While automatic type conversions are convenient, they are also a prime cause of ambiguity. Consider the following program:

```
// Overloading ambiguity.

#include <iostream>
using namespace std;

float myfunc(float i);
double myfunc(double i);

int main()
{
  // unambiguous, calls myfunc(double)
  cout << myfunc(10.1) << " ";

  // ambiguous
  cout << myfunc(10); // Error!   ◄──────  Which version of
                                           myfunc( ) should
                                           this use?

  return 0;
}

float myfunc(float i)
{
  return i;
}

double myfunc(double i)
{
  return -i;
}
```

6

Here, **myfunc( )** is overloaded so that it can take arguments of either type **float** or type **double**. In the unambiguous line, **myfunc(double)** is called because, unless explicitly specified as **float**, all floating-point constants in C++ are automatically of type **double**. However, when **myfunc( )** is called using the integer 10, ambiguity is introduced because the compiler has no way of knowing whether it should be converted to a **float** or to a **double**. Both are valid conversions. This confusion causes an error message to be displayed and prevents the program from compiling.

The central issue illustrated by the preceding example is that it is not the overloading of **myfunc( )** relative to **double** and **float** that causes the ambiguity. Rather, the confusion is caused by the specific call to **myfunc( )** using an indeterminate type of argument. Put differently, it is not the overloading of **myfunc( )** that is in error, but the specific invocation.

Here is another example of ambiguity caused by the automatic type conversions in C++:

```
// Another example of overloading ambiguity.

#include <iostream>
using namespace std;

char myfunc(unsigned char ch);
char myfunc(char ch);

int main()
{
  cout << myfunc('c');  // this calls myfunc(char)
  cout << myfunc(88) << " "; // Error, ambiguous! ◄─────┐

  return 0;                          ┌──────────────────────┐
}                                    │ Should 88 be converted to │
                                     │ **char** or **unsigned char**? │
char myfunc(unsigned char ch)        └──────────────────────┘
{
  return ch-1;
}

char myfunc(char ch)
{
  return ch+1;
}
```

In C++, **unsigned char** and **char** are *not* inherently ambiguous. (They are different types.) However, when **myfunc( )** is called with the integer 88, the compiler does not know which function to call. That is, should 88 be converted into a **char** or **unsigned char**? Both are valid conversions.

Another way you can cause ambiguity is by using default arguments in an overloaded function. To see how, examine this program:

```
// More function overloading ambiguity.

#include <iostream>
using namespace std;

int myfunc(int i);
int myfunc(int i, int j=1);

int main()
{
  cout << myfunc(4, 5) << " "; // unambiguous
  cout << myfunc(10); // Error, ambiguous!

  return 0;
}

int myfunc(int i)
{
  return i;
}

int myfunc(int i, int j)
{
  return i*j;
}
```

Here, is **j** defaulting or is the single-parameter version of **myfunc( )** being invoked?

In the first call to **myfunc( )**, two arguments are specified; therefore, no ambiguity is introduced, and **myfunc(int i, int j)** is called. However, the second call to **myfunc( )** results in ambiguity, because the compiler does not know whether to call the version of **myfunc( )** that takes one argument, or to apply the default to the version that takes two arguments.

As you continue to write your own C++ programs, be prepared to encounter ambiguity errors. Unfortunately, until you become more experienced, you will find that they are fairly easy to create.

✓ Mastery Check

1. What are the two ways that an argument can be passed to a subroutine?

2. In C++, what is a reference? How is a reference parameter created?

3. Given this fragment,

```
int f(char &c, int *i);
// ...
char ch = 'x';
int i = 10;
```

show how to call f( ) with the **ch** and **i**.

4. Create a **void** function called **round( )** that rounds the value of its **double** argument to the nearest whole value. Have **round( )** use a reference parameter and return the rounded result in this parameter. Demonstrate **round( )** in a program. To solve this problem, you will need to use the **modf( )** standard library function, which is shown here:

   double modf(double *num*, double **i*);

The **modf( )** function decomposes *num* into its integer and fractional parts. It returns the fractional portion and places the integer part in the variable pointed to by *i*. It requires the header **<cmath>**.

5. Modify the reference version of **swap( )** so that in addition to exchanging the values of its arguments, it returns a reference to the smaller of its two arguments. Call this function **min_swap( )**.

6. Why can't a function return a reference to a local variable?

7. How must the parameter lists of two overloaded functions differ?

☑ Mastery Check

8. In Project 6-1, you created a collection of **print( )** and **println( )** functions. To these functions, add a second parameter that specifies an indentation level. For example, when **print( )** is called like this,

```
print("test", 18);
```

output will indent 18 spaces and then will display the string "test". Have the indentation parameter default to 0 so that when it is not present, no indentation occurs.

9. Given this prototype,

```
bool myfunc(char ch, int a=10, int b=20);
```

show the ways that **myfunc( )** can be called.

10. Briefly explain how function overloading can introduce ambiguity.

6

Module 7

More Data Types and Operators

The Goals of This Module

- Use const and volatile
- Learn the storage class specifiers
- Work with static variables.
- Enhance performance with register variables
- Create enumerations and typedefs
- Learn the bitwise operators
- Apply the shift operators
- Use the ? and comma operator
- Utilize compound assignments
- Learn operator precedence

This module returns to the topics of data types and operators. In addition to the data types that you have been using so far, C++ supports several others. Some of these consist of modifiers added to the types you already know about. Other data types include enumerations and **typedefs**. C++ also provides several additional operators that greatly expand the range of programming tasks to which C++ can be applied. These operators include the bitwise, shift, ?, and **sizeof** operators.

The const and volatile Qualifiers

C++ has two types of qualifiers that affect the ways in which variables can be accessed or modified. These modifiers are **const** and **volatile**. Formally called the *cv-qualifiers,* they precede the base type when a variable is declared.

const

A variable declared with the **const** modifier cannot have its value changed during the execution of your program. Thus, a **const** "variable" isn't really variable! You can give a variable declared as **const** an initial value, however. For example,

```
const int max_users = 9;
```

creates an **int** variable called **max_users** that contains the value 9. This variable can be used in expressions like any other variable, but its value cannot be modified by your program.

A common use of **const** is to create a *named constant.* Often programs require the same value for many different purposes. For example, a program might have several different arrays that are all the same size. In this case, you can specify the size of the arrays using a **const** variable. The advantage to this approach is that if the size needs to be changed at a later date, you need change only the value of the **const** variable and then recompile the program. You don't need to change the size in each array declaration. This approach avoids errors and is easier, too. The following example illustrates this application of **const**:

```
#include <iostream>
using namespace std;

const int num_employees = 100;
```
This creates a named constant called **num_employees** that has the value 100.

```
int main()
{
  int empNums[num_employees];
  double salary[num_employees];
  char *names[num_employees];
```
num_employees is used here to specify the size of the arrays.

```
  // ...
}
```

In this example, if you need to use a new size for the arrays, you need change only the declaration of **num_employees** and then recompile the program. All three arrays will then automatically be resized.

Another important use of **const** is to prevent an object from being modified through a pointer. For example, you might want to prevent a function from changing the value of the object pointed to by a parameter. To do this, declare a pointer parameter as **const**. This prevents the object pointed to by the parameter from being modified by a function. That is, when a pointer parameter is preceded by **const**, no statement in the function can modify the variable pointed to by that parameter. For example, the **negate( )** function in the following program returns the negation of the value pointed to by its parameter. The use of **const** in the parameter declaration prevents the code inside the function from modifying the value pointed to by the parameter.

```
// Use a const pointer parameter.

#include <iostream>
using namespace std;

int negate(const int *val);

int main()
{
```

7

```
  int result;
  int v = 10;

  result = negate(&v);

  cout << v << " negated is " << result;
  cout << "\n";

  return 0;
}

int negate(const int *val)
{
  return - *val;
}
```

This specifies **val** as a **const** pointer.

Since **val** is declared as being a **const** pointer, the function can make no changes to the value pointed to by **val**. Since **negate( )** does not attempt to change **val**, the program compiles and runs correctly. However, if **negate( )** were written as shown in the next example, a compile-time error would result.

```
// This won't work!
int negate(const int *val)
{
  *val = - *val; // Error, can't change
  return *val;
}
```

In this case, the program attempts to alter the value of the variable pointed to by **val**, which is prevented because **val** is declared as **const**.

The **const** modifier can also be used on reference parameters to prevent a function from modifying the object referenced by a parameter. For example, the following version of **negate( )** is incorrect because it attempts to modify the variable referred to by **val**:

```
// This won't work either!
int negate(const int &val)
{
  val = -val; // Error, can't change
  return val;
}
```

volatile

The **volatile** modifier tells the compiler that a variable's value may be changed in ways not explicitly specified by the program. For example, the address of a global variable might be passed to an interrupt-driven clock routine that updates the variable with each tick of the clock. In this situation, the contents of the variable are altered without the use of any explicit assignment statement in the program. The reason the external alteration of a variable may be important is that a C++ compiler is permitted to automatically optimize certain expressions, on the assumption that the content of a variable is unchanged if it does not occur on the left side of an assignment statement. However, if factors beyond program control change the value of a variable, then problems can occur. To prevent such problems, you must declare such variables **volatile**, as shown here:

```
volatile int current_users;
```

Because it is declared as **volatile**, the value of **current_users** will be obtained each time it is referenced.

1-Minute Drill

- Can the value of a **const** variable be changed by the program?
- If a variable has its value changed by events outside the program, how should that variable be declared?

Storage Class Specifiers

There are five *storage class* specifiers supported by C++. They are

    auto
    extern
    register
    static
    mutable

- No, a **const** variable cannot have its value changed by the program.
- If a variable has its value changed by events outside the program, it must be declared as **volatile**.

These are used to tell the compiler how a variable should be stored. The storage specifier precedes the rest of the variable declaration.

The **mutable** specifier applies only to **class** objects, which are discussed later in this book. Each of the other specifiers is examined here.

auto

The **auto** specifier declares a local variable. However, it is rarely (if ever) used, because local variables are **auto** by default. It is extremely rare to see this keyword used in a program. It is a holdover from the C language.

extern

All the programs that you have worked with so far have been quite small. However, in reality, computer programs tend to be much larger. As a program file grows, the compilation time eventually becomes long enough to be annoying. When this happens, you should break your program into two or more separate files. Then, changes to one file will not require that the entire program be recompiled. Instead, you can simply recompile the file that changed, and link the existing object code for the other files. The multiple file approach can yield a substantial time savings with large projects. The **extern** keyword helps support this approach. Let's see how.

In programs that consist of two or more files, each file must know the names and types of the global variables used by the program. However, you cannot simply declare copies of the global variables in each file. The reason is that your program can only have one copy of each global variable. Therefore, if you try to declare the global variables needed by your program in each file, an error will occur when the linker tries to link the files. It will find the duplicated global variables and will not link your program. The solution to this dilemma is to declare all of the global variables in one file and use **extern** declarations in the others, as shown in Figure 7-1.

File One declares **x**, **y**, and **ch**. In File Two, the global variable list is copied from File One, and the **extern** specifier is added to the declarations. The **extern** specifier allows a variable to be made known to a module, but does not actually create that variable. In other words, **extern** lets the compiler know what the types and names are for these global variables without actually creating storage for them again. When the linker links the two modules together, all references to the external variables are resolved.

```
File One                   File Two
int x, y;                  extern int x, y;
char ch;                   extern char ch;

int main()                 void func22()
{                          {
   // ...                     x = y/10;
}                          }

void func1()               void func23()
{                          {
  x = 123;                   y = 10;
}                          }
```

Figure 7-1   Using global variables in separately compiled modules

7

   While we haven't yet worried about the distinction between the declaration and the definition of a variable, it is important here. A *declaration* declares the name and type of a variable. A *definition* causes storage to be allocated for the variable. In most cases, variable declarations are also definitions. However, by preceding a variable name with the **extern** specifier, you can declare a variable without defining it.

The extern Linkage Specification

A variation on **extern** provides a *linkage specification,* which is an instruction to the compiler about how a function is to be handled by the linker. By default, functions are linked as C++ functions, but a linkage specification lets you link a function for a different type of language. The general form of a linkage specifier is shown here:

   extern *"language" function-prototype*

where *language* denotes the desired language. For example, this specifies that
myCfunc( ) will have C linkage:

```
extern "C" void myCfunc();
```

All C++ compilers support both C and C++ linkage. Some may also allow
linkage specifiers for FORTRAN, Pascal, or BASIC. (You will need to check the
documentation for your compiler.) You can specify more than one function
at a time using this form of the linkage specification:

```
extern "language" {
    prototypes
}
```

For most programming tasks, you won't need to use a linkage specification.

static Variables

Variables of type **static** are permanent variables within their own function or
file. They differ from global variables because they are not known outside their
function or file. Because **static** affects local variables differently than it does
global ones, local and global variables will be examined separately.

static Local Variables

When the **static** modifier is applied to a local variable, permanent storage for
the variable is allocated in much the same way that it is for a global variable.
This allows a **static** variable to maintain its value between function calls. (That
is, its value is not lost when the function returns, unlike the value of a normal
local variable.) The key difference between a **static** local variable and a global
variable is that the **static** local variable is known only to the block in which it
is declared.

To declare a **static** variable, precede its type with the word **static**. For example,
this statement declares **count** as a **static** variable:

```
static int count;
```

A **static** variable may be given an initial value. For example, this statement
gives **count** an initial value of 200:

```
static int count = 200;
```

Local **static** variables are initialized only once, when program execution begins, not each time the block in which they are declared is entered.

The **static** local variable is important to functions that must preserve a value between calls. If **static** variables were not available, then global variables would have to be used—opening the door to possible side effects.

To see an example of a **static** variable, try this program. It keeps a running average of the numbers entered by the user.

```
// Compute a running average of numbers entered by the user.

#include <iostream>
using namespace std;

int running_avg(int i);

int main()
{
  int num;

  do {
    cout << "Enter numbers (-1 to quit): ";
    cin >> num;
    if(num != -1)
      cout << "Running average is: " << running_avg(num);
    cout << '\n';
  } while(num > -1);

  return 0;
}

int running_avg(int i)
{
  static int sum = 0, count = 0;

  sum = sum + i;

  count++;

  return sum / count;
}
```

> Because **sum** and **count** are **static**, they will retain their values between calls to **running_avg( )**.

Here, the local variables **sum** and **count** are both declared as **static** and initialized to 0. Remember, for **static** variables the initialization only occurs once—not each time the function is entered. The program uses **running_avg( )** to compute and report the current average of the numbers entered by the user. Because both **sum** and **count** are **static**, they will maintain their values between calls, causing the program to work properly. To prove to yourself that the **static** modifier is necessary, try removing it and running the program. As you can see, the program no longer works correctly, because the running total is lost each time **running_avg( )** returns.

static Global Variables

When the **static** specifier is applied to a global variable, it tells the compiler to create a global variable that is known only to the file in which the **static** global variable is declared. This means that even though the variable is global, other functions in other files have no knowledge of it and cannot alter its contents. Thus, it is not subject to side effects. Therefore, for the few situations where a local **static** variable cannot do the job, you can create a small file that contains only the functions that need the global **static** variable, separately compile that file, and use it without fear of side effects.

For an example of global **static** variables, we will rework the running average program from the preceding section. In this version, the program is broken into the two files shown here. The function **reset( )**, which resets the average, is also added.

```cpp
// ---------------------- First File ----------------------

#include <iostream>
using namespace std;

int running_avg(int i);
void reset();

int main()
{
  int num;

  do {
    cout << "Enter numbers (-1 to quit, -2 to reset): ";
    cin >> num;
    if(num == -2) {
      reset();
      continue;
    }
```

```
   if(num != -1)
     cout << "Running average is: " << running_avg(num);
   cout << '\n';
 } while(num != -1);

 return 0;
}

// --------------------- Second File ---------------------

static int sum = 0, count = 0;
```

> These are known only in the file in which they are declared.

```
int running_avg(int i)
{
  sum = sum + i;

  count++;

  return sum / count;
}

void reset()
{
  sum = 0;
  count = 0;
}
```

7

Here, **sum** and **count** are now global **static** variables that are restricted to the second file. Thus, they can be accessed by both **running_avg( )** and **reset( )** in the second file, but not elsewhere. This allows them to be reset by a call to **reset( )** so that a second set of numbers can be averaged. (When you run the program, you can reset the average by entering –2.) However, no functions outside the second file can access those variables. For example, if you try to access either **sum** or **count** from the first file, you will receive an error message.

To review: The name of a local **static** variable is known only to the function or block of code in which it is declared, and the name of a global **static** variable is known only to the file in which it resides. In essence, the **static** modifier allows variables to exist that are known to the scopes that need them, thereby controlling and limiting the possibility of side effects. Variables of type **static** enable you, the programmer, to hide portions of your program from other portions. This can be a tremendous advantage when you are trying to manage a very large and complex program.

Ask the Expert

Question: I have heard that some C++ programmers do not use static global variables. Is this true?

Answer: Although **static** global variables are still valid and widely used in C++ code, the C++ Standard discourages their use. Instead, it recommends another method of controlling access to global variables that involves the use of namespaces, which are described later in this book. However, **static** global variables are widely used by C programmers because C does not support namespaces. For this reason, you will continue to see **static** global variables for a long time to come.

register Variables

Perhaps the most frequently used storage class specifier is **register**. The **register** modifier tells the compiler to store a variable in such a way that it can be accessed as quickly as possible. Typically, this means storing the variable either in a register of the CPU or in cache memory. As you probably know, accessing the registers of the CPU (or cache memory) is fundamentally faster than accessing the main memory of the computer. Thus, a variable stored in a register will be accessed much more quickly than if that variable had been stored in RAM. Because the speed by which variables can be accessed has a profound effect on the overall speed of your programs, the careful use of **register** is an important programming technique.

Technically, **register** is only a request to the compiler, which the compiler is free to ignore. The reason for this is easy to understand: there are a finite number of registers (or fast-access memory), and these may differ from environment to environment. Thus, if the compiler runs out of fast-access memory, it simply stores the variable normally. Generally, this causes no harm, but of course the **register** advantage is lost. You can usually count on at least two variables being optimized for speed.

Since only a limited number of variables can actually be granted the fastest access, it is important to choose carefully those to which you apply the **register** modifier. (Only by choosing the right variables can you gain the greatest increase in performance.) In general, the more often a variable is accessed, the more benefit there will be to optimizing it as a **register** variable. For this reason, variables that control or are accessed within loops are good candidates for the **register** specifier.

Here is an example that uses **register** variables to improve the performance of the **summation( )** function, which computes the summation of the values in an array. This example assumes that only two variables will actually be optimized for speed.

```
// Demonstrate register.

#include <iostream>
using namespace std;

int summation(int nums[], int n);

int main()
{
  int vals[] = { 1, 2, 3, 4, 5 };
  int result;

  result = summation(vals, 5);

  cout << "Summation is " << result << "\n";

  return 0;
}

// Return summation of an array of ints.
int summation(int nums[], int n)
{
  register int i;  ─────────────┐
  register int sum = 0;  ───────┤  These variables are optimized for speed.

  for(i = 0; i < n; i++)
    sum = sum + nums[i];

  return sum;
}
```

7

Here, the variable **i**, which controls the **for** loop, and **sum**, which is accessed inside the loop, are specified as **register**. Since they are both used within the loop, both benefit from being optimized for fast access. This example assumed that only two variables could actually be optimized for speed, so **n** and **nums** were not specified as **register** because they are not accessed as often as **i** and **sum** within the loop. However, in environments in which more than two variables can be optimized, they too could be specified as **register** to further improve performance.

Ask the Expert

Question: When I tried adding the register specifier to a program, I saw no change in performance. Why not?

Answer: Because of advances in compiler technology, most compilers today will automatically optimize your code. Thus, in many cases, adding the **register** specifier to a declaration might not result in any performance increase because that variable is already optimized. However, in some cases, using **register** is still beneficial because it lets you tell the compiler which variables you think are the most important to optimize. This can be valuable for functions that use a large number of variables, all of which cannot be optimized. Thus, **register** still fulfills an important role despite advances in compiler design.

1-Minute Drill

● A **static** local variable _____ its value between function calls.

● You use **extern** to declare a variable without defining that variable. True or false?

● What specifier requests that the compiler optimize a variable for speed?

Enumerations

In C++, you can define a list of named integer constants. Such a list is called an *enumeration*. These constants can then be used anywhere that an integer can. Enumerations are defined using the keyword **enum** and have this general format:

enum *type-name* { *value-list* } *variable-list*;

Here, *type-name* is the type name of the enumeration. The *value-list* is a comma-separated list of names that represent the values of the enumeration.

● preserves
● True.
● The **register** specifier requests that the compiler optimize a variable for speed.

The *variable-list* is optional because variables may be declared later using the enumeration type name.

The following fragment defines an enumeration called **transport** and two variables of type **transport** called **t1** and **t2**:

```
enum transport { car, truck, airplane, train, boat } t1, t2;
```

Once you have defined an enumeration, you can declare additional variables of its type using its name. For example, this statement declares one variable, called **how**, of enumeration **transport**:

```
transport how;
```

The statement can also be written like this:

```
enum transport how;
```

However, the use of **enum** here is redundant. In C (which also supports enumerations), this second form was required, so you may see it used in some programs.

Assuming the preceding declarations, the following gives **how** the value **airplane**:

```
how = airplane;
```

The key point to understand about an enumeration is that each of the symbols stands for an integer value. As such, they can be used in any integer expression. Unless initialized otherwise, the value of the first enumeration symbol is 0, the value of the second symbol is 1, and so forth. Therefore,

```
cout << car << ' ' << train;
```

displays **0 3**.

Although enumerated constants are automatically converted to integers, integers are not automatically converted into enumerated constants. For example, the following statement is incorrect:

```
how = 1; // Error
```

7

This statement causes a compile-time error because there is no automatic conversion from integer to **transport**. You can fix the preceding statement by using a cast, as shown here:

```
how = (transport) 1; // now OK, but probably poor style
```

This causes **how** to contain the value **truck**, because it is the **transport** constant associated with the value 1. As the comment suggests, although this statement is now correct, it would be considered to be poor style except in unusual circumstances.

It is possible to specify the value of one or more of the enumerated constants by using an initializer. This is done by following the symbol with an equal sign and an integer value. When an initializer is used, each symbol that appears after it, is assigned a value 1 greater than the previous initialization value. For example, the following statement assigns the value of 10 to **airplane**:

```
enum transport { car, truck, airplane = 10, train, boat };
```

Now, the values of these symbols are as follows:

car	0
truck	1
airplane	10
train	11
boat	12

One common, but erroneous, assumption sometimes made about enumerations is that the symbols can be input and output as a string. This is not the case. For example, the following code fragment will not perform as desired:

```
// This will not print "train" on the screen.
how = train;
cout << how;
```

Remember, the symbol **train** is simply a name for an integer; it is not a string. Thus, the preceding code will display the numeric value of **train**, not the string "train". Actually, to create code that inputs and outputs enumeration symbols as strings is quite tedious. For example, the following code is needed in order to display, in words, the kind of transportation that **how** contains:

```
switch(how) {
  case car:
    cout << "Automobile";
    break;
  case truck:
    cout << "Truck";
    break;
  case airplane:
    cout << "Airplane";
    break;
  case train:
    cout << "Train";
    break;
  case boat:
    cout << "Boat";
    break;
}
```

Sometimes it is possible to declare an array of strings and use the enumeration value as an index in order to translate the value into its corresponding string. For example, the following program prints the names of three types of transportation:

```
// Demonstrate an enumeration.

#include <iostream>
using namespace std;

enum transport { car, truck, airplane, train, boat };

char name[][20] = {
  "Automobile",
  "Truck",
  "Airplane",
  "Train",
  "Boat"
};

int main()
{
  transport how;

  how = car;
  cout << name[how] << '\n';
```

Use an enumeration value to index an array.

```
  how = airplane;
  cout << name[how] << '\n';

  how = train;
  cout << name[how] << '\n';

  return 0;
}
```

The output is shown here:

```
Automobile
Airplane
Train
```

The approach used by this program to convert an enumeration value into a string can be applied to any type of enumeration as long as that enumeration does not contain initializers. To properly index the array of strings, the enumerated constants must begin at zero and be in strictly ascending order, each precisely one greater than the previous.

Given the fact that enumeration values must be converted manually to their human-readable string values, they find their greatest use in routines that do not make such conversions. It is common to see an enumeration used to define a compiler's symbol table, for example.

typedef

C++ allows you to define new data type names with the **typedef** keyword. When you use **typedef**, you are not actually creating a new data type, but rather defining a new name for an existing type. This process can help make machine-dependent programs more portable; only the **typedef** statements have to be changed. It also helps you self-document your code by allowing descriptive names for the standard data types. The general form of the **typedef** statement is

   typedef *type name*;

where *type* is any valid data type, and *name* is the new name for this type. The new name you define is in addition to, not a replacement for, the existing type name.

For example, you could create a new name for **float** using

```
typedef float balance;
```

This statement would tell the compiler to recognize **balance** as another name for **float**. Next, you could create a **float** variable using **balance**:

```
balance over_due;
```

Here, **over_due** is a floating-point variable of type **balance**, which is another name for **float**.

1-Minute Drill

- An enumeration is a list of named _____ constants.
- Enumerated values begin with what integer value?
- Show how to declare **BigInt** to be another name for **long int**.

7

Bitwise Operators

Since C++ is designed to allow full access to the computer's hardware, it gives you the ability to operate directly upon the bits within a byte or word. Toward this end, C++ contains the bitwise operators. *Bitwise operations* refer to the testing, setting, or shifting of the actual bits in a byte or word, which correspond to C++'s character and integer types. Bitwise operations cannot be used on **bool**, **float**, **double**, **long double**, **void**, or other more complex data types. Bitwise operations are important in a wide variety of systems-level programming in which status information from a device must be interrogated or constructed. Table 7-1 lists the bitwise operators. Each operator is examined in turn.

- integer
- Enumerated values begin with the value 0.
- typedef long int BigInt;

Operator	Action
&	AND
|	OR
^	Exclusive OR (XOR)
~	One's complement (NOT)
>>	Shift right
<<	Shift left

Table 7-1 The Bitwise Operators

AND, OR, XOR, and NOT

The bitwise AND, OR, and one's complement (NOT) are governed by the same truth table as their logical equivalents, except that they work on a bit-by-bit level. The exclusive OR (XOR) operates according to the following truth table:

p	q	p ^ q
0	0	0
1	0	1
1	1	0
0	1	1

As the table indicates, the outcome of an XOR is true only if exactly one of the operands is true; it is false otherwise.

In terms of its most common usage, you can think of the bitwise AND as a way to turn bits off. That is, any bit that is 0 in either operand will cause the corresponding bit in the outcome to be set to 0. For example:

```
      1 1 0 1  0 0 1 1
      1 0 1 0  1 0 1 0
   &  -------------------
      1 0 0 0  0 0 1 0
```

The following program demonstrates the & by turning any lowercase letter into uppercase by resetting the sixth bit to 0. As the ASCII character set is defined, the lowercase letters are the same as the uppercase ones except that the lowercase ones are greater in value by exactly 32. Therefore, to transform a lowercase letter to uppercase, just turn off the sixth bit, as this program illustrates:

```
// Uppercase letters using bitwise AND.

#include <iostream>
using namespace std;

int main()
{
  char ch;

  for(int i = 0 ; i < 10; i++)  {
    ch = 'a' + i;
    cout << ch;

    // This statement turns off the 6th bit.
    ch = ch & 223; // ch is now uppercase

    cout << ch << " ";
  }

  cout << "\n";

  return 0;
}
```

Use the bitwise AND
to turn off bit 6.

The output from this program is shown here:

```
aA bB cC dD eE fF gG hH iI jJ
```

The value 223 used in the AND statement is the decimal representation of 1101
1111. Thus, the AND operation leaves all bits in **ch** unchanged except for the
sixth one, which is set to zero.

The AND operator is also useful when you want to determine whether a bit
is on or off. For example, this statement checks to see if bit 4 in **status** is set:

```
if(status & 8) cout << "bit 4 is on";
```

The reason 8 is used is that in binary it is represented as 0000 1000. That is,
the number 8 translated into binary has only the fourth bit set. Therefore, the **if**
statement can succeed only when bit 4 of **status** is also on. An interesting use of
this feature is the **show_binary( )** function, shown next. It displays, in binary

format, the bit pattern of its argument. You will use **show_binary( )** later in this module to examine the effects of other bitwise operations.

```cpp
// Display the bits within a byte.
void show_binary(unsigned int u)
{
  int t;

  for(t=128; t > 0; t = t/2)
    if(u & t) cout << "1 ";
    else cout << "0 ";

  cout << "\n";
}
```

The **show_binary( )** function works by successively testing each bit in the low-order byte of **u**, using the bitwise AND, to determine if it is on or off. If the bit is on, the digit 1 is displayed; otherwise, 0 is displayed.

The bitwise OR, as the reverse of AND, can be used to turn bits on. Any bit that is set to 1 in either operand will cause the corresponding bit in the variable to be set to 1. For example,

```
    1 1 0 1  0 0 1 1
    1 0 1 0  1 0 1 0
|   --------------------
    1 1 1 1  1 0 1 1
```

You can make use of the OR to change the uppercasing program used earlier into a lowercasing program, as shown here:

```cpp
// Lowercase letters using bitwise OR.

#include <iostream>
using namespace std;

int main()
{
  char ch;

  for(int i = 0 ; i < 10; i++)  {
    ch = 'A' + i;
```

```
   cout << ch;

   // This statement turns on the 6th bit.
   ch = ch | 32; // ch is now lowercase
```
Use the bitwise OR
to turn on bit 6.

```
   cout << ch << " ";
  }

  cout << "\n";

  return 0;
}
```

The output is shown here:

```
Aa Bb Cc Dd Ee Ff Gg Hh Ii Jj
```

When the sixth bit is set, each uppercase letter is transformed into its lowercase equivalent.

An exclusive OR, usually abbreviated XOR, will set a bit on only if the bits being compared are different, as illustrated here:

```
    0 1 1 1 1 1 1 1
    1 0 1 1 1 0 0 1
^   -----------------------
    1 1 0 0 0 1 1 0
```

The XOR operator has an interesting property that makes it a simple way to encode a message. When some value X is XORed with another value Y, and then when that result is XORed with Y again, X is produced. That is, given the sequence

```
R1 = X ^ Y;
R2 = R1 ^ Y;
```

then R2 is the same value as X. Thus, the outcome of a sequence of two XORs using the same value produces the original value. You can use this principle to create a simple cipher program in which some integer is the key that is used to both encode and decode a message by XORing the characters in that message.

To encode, the XOR operation is applied the first time, yielding the ciphertext. To decode, the XOR is applied a second time, yielding the plaintext. Here is a simple example that uses this approach to encode and decode a short message:

```cpp
// Use XOR to encode and decode a message.

#include <iostream>
using namespace std;

int main()
{
  char msg[] = "This is a test";
  char key = 88;

  cout << "Original message: " << msg << "\n";

  for(int i = 0 ; i < strlen(msg); i++)
    msg[i] = msg[i] ^ key;            ← This constructs the
                                        encoded string.
  cout << "Encoded message: " << msg << "\n";

  for(int i = 0 ; i < strlen(msg); i++)    This constructs a
    msg[i] = msg[i] ^ key;          ←   decoded string.

  cout << "Decoded message: " << msg << "\n";

  return 0;
}
```

Here is the output:

```
Original message: This is a test
Encoded message: 01+x1+x9x,=+,
Decoded message: This is a test
```

As the output proves, the result of two XORs using the same key produces the decoded message.

The unary 1's complement (NOT) operator reverses the state of all the bits of the operand. For example, if some integer called **A** has the bit pattern 1001 0110, then ~A produces a result with the bit pattern 0110 1001. The following program demonstrates the NOT operator by displaying a number and its complement in binary, using the **show_binary( )** function developed earlier:

```
#include <iostream>
using namespace std;

void show_binary(unsigned int u);

int main()
{
  unsigned u;

  cout << "Enter a number between 0 and 255: ";
  cin >> u;

  cout << "Here's the number in binary: ";
  show_binary(u);

  cout << "Here's the complement of the number: ";
  show_binary(~u);

  return 0;
}

// Display the bits within a byte.
void show_binary(unsigned int u)
{
  int t;

  for(t=128; t>0; t = t/2)
    if(u & t) cout << "1 ";
    else cout << "0 ";

  cout << "\n";
}
```

Here is a sample run produced by the program:

```
Enter a number between 0 and 255: 99
Here's the number in binary: 0 1 1 0 0 0 1 1
Here's the complement of the number: 1 0 0 1 1 1 0 0
```

In general, &, |, ^, and ~ apply their operations directly to each bit in a value individually. For this reason, bitwise operations are not usually used in conditional statements the way the relational and logical operators are. For example, if x equals 7, then x && 8 evaluates to true, whereas x & 8 evaluates to false.

The Shift Operators

The shift operators, >> and <<, move all bits in a variable to the right or left as specified. The general form of the right-shift operator is

variable >> *num-bits*

and the left-shift operator is

variable << *num-bits*

The value of *num-bits* determines how many bit places the bits are shifted. Each left-shift causes all bits within the specified variable to be shifted left one position and a zero bit to be brought in on the right. Each right-shift shifts all bits to the right one position and brings in a zero on the left. However, if the variable is a signed integer containing a negative value, then each right-shift brings in a 1 on the left, which preserves the sign bit. Remember, a shift is not a rotation. That is, the bits shifted off of one end do not come back around to the other.

The shift operators work only with integral types, such as **int**, **char**, **long int**, or **short int**. They cannot be applied to floating-point values, for example.

Bit shift operations can be very useful for decoding input from external devices such as D/A converters and for reading status information. The bitwise shift operators can also be used to perform very fast multiplication and division of integers. A shift left will effectively multiply a number by 2, and a shift right will divide it by 2.

The following program illustrates the effects of the shift operators:

```
// Example of bitshifting.

#include <iostream>
using namespace std;

void show_binary(unsigned int u);

int main()
{
  int i=1, t;

  // shift left
  for(t=0; t < 8; t++) {
    show_binary(i);
```

```
   i = i << 1;
 }

 cout << "\n";

 // shift right
 for(t=0; t < 8; t++) {
   i = i >> 1;
   show_binary(i);
 }

 return 0;
}

// Display the bits within a byte.
void show_binary(unsigned int u)
{
  int t;

  for(t=128; t>0; t=t/2)
    if(u & t) cout << "1 ";
    else cout << "0 ";

  cout << "\n";
}
```

| Left-shift **i** one position. |

| Right-shift **i** one position. |

This program produces the following output:

```
0 0 0 0 0 0 0 1
0 0 0 0 0 0 1 0
0 0 0 0 0 1 0 0
0 0 0 0 1 0 0 0
0 0 0 1 0 0 0 0
0 0 1 0 0 0 0 0
0 1 0 0 0 0 0 0
1 0 0 0 0 0 0 0

1 0 0 0 0 0 0 0
0 1 0 0 0 0 0 0
0 0 1 0 0 0 0 0
0 0 0 1 0 0 0 0
0 0 0 0 1 0 0 0
0 0 0 0 0 1 0 0
0 0 0 0 0 0 1 0
0 0 0 0 0 0 0 1
```

1-Minute Drill

● What are the bitwise operators for AND, OR, NOT, and XOR?

● A bitwise operator works on a bit-by-bit basis. True or false?

● Given an integer called **x**, show how to left-shift **x** two places.

rotate.cpp

Project 7-1: Create Bitwise Rotation Functions

Although C++ provides two shift operators, it does not define a rotate operator. A *rotate* is similar to a shift except that the bit shifted off one end is inserted onto the other end. Thus, bits are not lost, just moved. There are both left and right rotations. For example, 1010 0000 rotated left one place is 0100 0001. The same value rotated right one place is 0101 0000. In each case, the bit shifted out is inserted onto the other end. Although the lack of rotation operators may seem to be a flaw in C++'s otherwise exemplary complement of bitwise operators, it really isn't, because you can easily create a left- and right-rotate by using the other bitwise operators.

This project creates two functions: **rrotate( )** and **lrotate( )**, which rotate a byte in the right or left direction. Each function takes two parameters. The first is the value to be rotated. The second is the number of places to rotate. Each function returns the result. This project involves several bit manipulations and shows the bitwise operators in action.

Step-by-Step

1. Create a file called **rotate.cpp**.

2. Add the **lrotate( )** function shown here. It performs a left-rotate.

```
// Left-rotate a byte n places.
unsigned char lrotate(unsigned char val, int n)
{
  unsigned int t;

  t = val;

  for(int i=0; i < n; i++) {
```

● The bitwise operators are **&**, |, ~, and ^.
● True.
● x << 2

```
    t = t << 1;

    /* If a bit shifts out, it will be in bit 8
       of the integer t. If this is the case,
       put that bit on the right side. */
    if(t & 256)
      t = t | 1; // put a 1 on the right end
  }

  return t; // return the lower 8 bits.
}
```

Here is how **lrotate( )** works. The function is passed the value to rotate in **val**, and the number of places to rotate is passed in **n**. The function assigns **val** to **t**, which is an **unsigned int**. Transferring the value to an **unsigned int** is necessary because it allows bits shifted off the left side to be recovered. Here's why. Because an **unsigned int** is larger than a byte, when a bit is shifted off the left side of a byte value, it simply moves to bit 8 of the integer value. The value of this bit can then be copied into bit 0 of the byte value, thus performing a rotation.

The actual rotation is performed as follows: A loop is established that performs the required number of rotations, one at a time. Inside the loop, the value of **t** is left-shifted one place. This causes a 0 to be brought in on the right. However, if the value of bit 8 of the result (which is the bit shifted out of the byte value) is a 1, then bit 0 is set to 1. Otherwise, bit 0 remains 0.

The eighth bit is tested using the statement

```
if(t & 256)
```

The value 256 is the decimal value in which only bit 8 is set. Thus, **t & 256** will be true only when **t** has the value 1 in bit 8.

After the rotation has been completed, **t** is returned. Since **lrotate( )** is declared to return an **unsigned char** value, only the lower 8 bits of **t** are returned.

3. Add the **rrotate( )** function shown next. It performs a right rotate.

```
// Right-rotate a byte n places.
unsigned char rrotate(unsigned char val, int n)
{
```

```
unsigned int t;

t = val;

// First, move the value 8 bits higher.
t = t << 8;

for(int i=0; i < n; i++) {
  t = t >> 1;

  /* If a bit shifts out, it will be in bit 7
     of the integer t. If this is the case,
     put that bit on the left side. */
  if(t & 128)
    t = t | 32768; // put a 1 on left end
}

/* Finally, move the result back to the
   lower 8 bits of t. */
t = t >> 8;

return t;
}
```

The right-rotate is slightly more complicated than the left-rotate because the value passed in **val** must be shifted into the second byte of **t** so that bits being shifted off the right side can be caught. Once the rotation is complete, the value must be shifted back into the low-order byte of **t** so that the value can be returned. Because the bit being shifted out moves to bit 7, the following statement checks whether that value is a 1:

```
if(t & 128)
```

The decimal value 128 has only bit 7 set. If it is set, then **t** is ORed with 32768, which is the decimal value in which bit 15 is set, and bits 14 through 0 are cleared. This causes bit 15 of **t** to be set and the other bits to remain unchanged.

4. Here is an entire program that demonstrates **lrotate( )** and **rrotate( )**. It uses the **show_binary( )** function to display the results of each rotation.

```
/*
  Project 7-1

  Left and right rotate functions for byte values.
```

```
*/

#include <iostream>
using namespace std;

unsigned char rrotate(unsigned char val, int n);
unsigned char lrotate(unsigned char val, int n);
void show_binary(unsigned int u);

int main()
{
  char ch = 'T';

  cout << "Original value in binary:\n";
  show_binary(ch);

  cout << "Rotating right 8 times:\n";
  for(int i=0; i < 8; i++) {
    ch = rrotate(ch, 1);
    show_binary(ch);
  }

  cout << "Rotating left 8 times:\n";
  for(int i=0; i < 8; i++) {
    ch = lrotate(ch, 1);
    show_binary(ch);
  }

  return 0;
}

// Left-rotate a byte n places.
unsigned char lrotate(unsigned char val, int n)
{
  unsigned int t;

  t = val;

  for(int i=0; i < n; i++) {
    t = t << 1;

    /* If a bit shifts out, it will be in bit 8
       of the integer t. If this is the case,
       put that bit on the right side. */
```

7

```
      if(t & 256)
        t = t | 1; // put a 1 on the right end
    }

  return t; // return the lower 8 bits.
}

// Right-rotate a byte n places.
unsigned char rrotate(unsigned char val, int n)
{
  unsigned int t;

  t = val;

  // First, move the value 8 bits higher.
  t = t << 8;

  for(int i=0; i < n; i++) {
    t = t >> 1;

    /* If a bit shifts out, it will be in bit 7
       of the integer t. If this is the case,
       put that bit on the left side. */
    if(t & 128)
      t = t | 32768; // put a 1 on left end
  }

  /* Finally, move the result back to the
     lower 8 bits of t. */
  t = t >> 8;

  return t;
}

// Display the bits within a byte.
void show_binary(unsigned int u)
{
  int t;

  for(t=128; t>0; t = t/2)
    if(u & t) cout << "1 ";
    else cout << "0 ";

  cout << "\n";
}
```

5. The output from the program is shown here:

```
Original value in binary:
0 1 0 1 0 1 0 0
Rotating right 8 times:
0 0 1 0 1 0 1 0
0 0 0 1 0 1 0 1
1 0 0 0 1 0 1 0
0 1 0 0 0 1 0 1
1 0 1 0 0 0 1 0
0 1 0 1 0 0 0 1
1 0 1 0 1 0 0 0
0 1 0 1 0 1 0 0
Rotating left 8 times:
1 0 1 0 1 0 0 0
0 1 0 1 0 0 0 1
1 0 1 0 0 0 1 0
0 1 0 0 0 1 0 1
1 0 0 0 1 0 1 0
0 0 0 1 0 1 0 1
0 0 1 0 1 0 1 0
0 1 0 1 0 1 0 0
```

The ? Operator

One of C++'s most fascinating operators is the ?. The ? operator is often used to replace **if-else** statements of this general form:

```
if (condition)
    var = expression1;
else
    var = expression2;
```

Here, the value assigned to *var* depends upon the outcome of the condition controlling the **if**.

The ? is called a *ternary operator* because it requires three operands. It takes the general form

```
Exp1 ? Exp2 : Exp3;
```

where *Exp1*, *Exp2*, and *Exp3* are expressions. Notice the use and placement of the colon.

The value of a ? expression is determined like this: *Exp1* is evaluated. If it is true, then *Exp2* is evaluated and becomes the value of the entire ? expression. If *Exp1* is false, then *Exp3* is evaluated, and its value becomes the value of the expression. Consider this example, which assigns **absval** the absolute value of **val**:

```
absval = val < 0 ? -val : val; // get absolute value of val
```

Here, **absval** will be assigned the value of **val** if **val** is zero or greater. If **val** is negative, then **absval** will be assigned the negative of that value (which yields a positive value). The same code written using an **if-else** statement would look like this:

```
if(val < 0) absval  = -val;
else absval = val;
```

Here is another example of the ? operator. This program divides two numbers, but will not allow a division by zero.

```
/* This program uses the ? operator to prevent
   a division by zero. */

#include <iostream>
using namespace std;

int div_zero();

int main()
{
  int i, j, result;

  cout << "Enter dividend and divisor: ";
  cin >> i >> j;

  // This statement prevents a divide by zero error.
  result = j ? i/j : div_zero();

  cout << "Result: " << result;

  return 0;
}

int div_zero()
{
```

Use the **?** to prevent a divide-by-zero error.

```
    cout << "Cannot divide by zero.\n";
    return 0;
}
```

Here, if **j** is non-zero, then **i** is divided by **j**, and the outcome is assigned to **result**. Otherwise, the **div_zero( )** error handler is called, and zero is assigned to **result**.

The Comma Operator

Another interesting C++ operator is the comma. You have seen some examples of the comma operator in the **for** loop, where it has been used to allow multiple initialization or increment statements. However, the comma can be used as a part of any expression. It strings together several expressions. The value of a comma-separated list of expressions is the value of the right-most expression. The values of the other expressions will be discarded. This means that the expression on the right side will become the value of the total comma-separated expression. For example,

```
var = (count=19, incr=10, count+1);
```

first assigns **count** the value 19, assigns **incr** the value 10, then adds 1 to **count**, and finally assigns **var** the value produced by the entire comma expression, which is 20. The parentheses are necessary because the comma operator has a lower precedence than the assignment operator.

To actually see the effects of the comma operator, try running the following program:

```
#include <iostream>
using namespace std;

int main()
{
  int i, j;

  j = 10;

  i = (j++, j+100, 999+j);
```

The comma means "do this and this and this."

7

```
cout << i;

return 0;
}
```

This program prints "1010" on the screen. Here is why: **j** starts with the value 10. **j** is then incremented to 11. Next, **j** is added to 100. Finally, **j** (still containing 11) is added to 999, which yields the result 1010.

Essentially, the comma's effect is to cause a sequence of operations to be performed. When it is used on the right side of an assignment statement, the value assigned is the value of the last expression in the comma-separated list. You can, in some ways, think of the comma operator as having the same meaning that the word "and" has in English when used in the phrase "do this and this and this."

1-Minute Drill

● Given this expression:

```
x = 10 > 11 ? 1 : 0;
```

what is the value of **x** after the expression evaluates?

● The **?** operator is called a ternary operator because it has _____ operands.

● What does the comma do?

Multiple Assignments

C++ allows a convenient method of assigning many variables the same value: using multiple assignments in a single statement. For example, this fragment assigns **count**, **incr**, and **index** the value 10:

```
count = incr = index = 10;
```

In professionally written programs, you will often see variables assigned a common value using this format.

● The value of **x** will be 0.
● three
● The comma causes a sequence of operations to be performed.

Compound Assignment

C++ has a special compound-assignment operator that simplifies the coding of a certain type of assignment statement. For example,

```
x = x+10;
```

can be rewritten using a compound assignment operator, as shown next:

```
x += 10;
```

The operator pair **+=** tells the compiler to assign to **x** the value of **x** plus 10. Compound assignment operators exist for all the binary operators in C++ (that is, those that require two operands). Their general form is

var op = expression;

Here is another example:

```
x = x-100;
```

is the same as

```
x -= 100;
```

Because it saves you some typing, compound assignment is also sometimes referred to as *shorthand assignment*. You will see shorthand notation used widely in professionally written C++ programs, so you should become familiar with it.

Using sizeof

Sometimes it is helpful to know the size, in bytes, of a type of data. Since the sizes of C++'s built-in types can differ between computing environments, knowing the size of a variable in advance, in all situations, is not possible. To solve this problem, C++ includes the **sizeof** compile-time operator, which has these general forms:

sizeof (*type*)
sizeof *var-name*

7

The first version returns the size of the specified data type, and the second returns the size of the specified variable. As you can see, if you want to know the size of a data type, such as **int**, you must enclose the type name in parentheses. If you want to know the size of a variable, no parentheses are needed, although you can use them if you desire.

To see how **sizeof** works, try the following short program. For many 32-bit environments, it displays the values 1, 4, 4, and 8.

```
// Demonstrate sizeof.

#include <iostream>
using namespace std;

int main()
{
  char ch;
  int i;

  cout << sizeof ch << ' '; // size of char
  cout << sizeof i << ' ';   // size of int
  cout << sizeof (float) << ' '; // size of float
  cout << sizeof (double) << ' '; // size of double

  return 0;
}
```

You can apply **sizeof** to any data type. For example, when it is applied to an array, it returns the number of bytes used by the array. Consider this fragment:

```
int nums[4];

cout << sizeof nums;
```

Assuming 4-byte integers, this fragment displays the value 16 (that is, 4 bytes times 4 elements).

As mentioned earlier, **sizeof** is a compile-time operator. All information necessary for computing the size of a variable or data type is known during compilation. The **sizeof** operator primarily helps you to generate portable code that depends upon the size of the C++ data types. Remember, since the sizes of types in C++ are defined by the implementation, it is bad style to make assumptions about their sizes in code that you write.

1-Minute Drill

- Show how to assign the variables **t1**, **t2**, and **t3** the value 10 using one assignment statement.
- How can

```
x = x + 100
```

be rewritten?

- The **sizeof** operator returns the size of a variable or type in _____.

Precedence Summary

Table 7-2 lists the precedence, from highest to lowest, of all C++ operators. Most operators associate from left to right. The unary operators, the assignment operators, and the ? operator associate from right to left. Note that the table includes a few operators that you have not yet learned about, many of which are used in object-oriented programming.

Precedence	Operators
Highest	( ) [ ] -> :: .
	! ~ ++ -- - * & sizeof new delete typeid _type-casts_
	.* ->*
	* / %
	+ -
	<< >>
	< <= > >=
	== !=
	&
	^
	|
	&&
	||
	?:
	= += -= *= /= %= >>= <<= &= ^= |=
Lowest	,

Table 7-2   Precedence of the C++ Operators

- `t1 = t2 = t3 = 10;`
- `x += 100;`
- bytes

☑ *Mastery Check*

1. Show how to declare an **int** variable called **test** that can't be changed by the program. Give it an initial value of 100.

2. The **volatile** specifier tells the compiler that a variable might be changed by forces outside the program. True or false?

3. In a multifile project, what specifier do you use to tell one file about a global variable declared in another file?

4. What is the most important attribute of a **static** local variable?

5. Write a program that contains a function called **counter( )**, which simply counts how many times it is called. Have it return the current count.

6. Given this fragment, which variable would most benefit from being specified as **register**?

```
int myfunc()
{
  int x;
  int y;
  int z;

  z = 10;
  y = 0;

  for(x=z; x < 15; x++)
    y += x;

  return y;
}
```

7. How does **&** differ from **&&**?

8. What does this statement do?

```
x *= 10;
```

☑ *Mastery Check*

9. Using the **rrotate( )** and **lrotate( )** functions from Project 7-1, it is possible to encode and decode a string. To code the string, left-rotate each letter by some amount that is specified by a key. To decode, right-rotate each character by the same amount. Use a key that consists of a string of characters. There are many ways to compute the number of rotations from the key. Be creative. The solution shown in Appendix A is only one of many.

10. On your own, expand **show_binary( )** so that it shows all bits within an **unsigned int** rather than just the first eight.

7

Module 8

Classes and Objects

The Goals of This Module

- Know the general form of a class
- Create classes and objects
- Add member functions to a class
- Use constructors and destructors
- Parameterize constructors
- Create inline functions
- Use arrays of objects
- Initialize arrays of objects
- Apply pointers to objects

U p to this point, you have been writing programs that did not use any of C++'s object-oriented capabilities. Thus, the programs in the preceding modules reflected structured programming, not object-oriented programming. To write object-oriented programs, you will need to use classes. The class is C++'s basic unit of encapsulation. Classes are used to create objects. Classes and objects are so fundamental to C++ that much of the remainder of this book is devoted to them in one way or another.

Class Fundamentals

Let's begin by reviewing the terms *class* and *object*. A *class* is a template that defines the form of an *object*. A class specifies both code and data. C++ uses a class specification to construct objects. Objects are *instances* of a class. Thus, a class is essentially a set of plans that specify how to build an object. It is important to be clear on one issue: a class is a logical abstraction. It is not until an object of that class has been created that a physical representation of that class exists in memory.

When you define a class, you declare the data that it contains and the code that operates on that data. While very simple classes might contain only code or only data, most real-world classes contain both. Data is contained in *instance variables* defined by the class, and code is contained in functions. The code and data that constitute a class are called *members* of the class.

The General Form of a Class

A class is created by use of the keyword **class**. The general form of a simple **class** declaration is

```
class class-name {
    private data and functions
public:
    public data and functions
} object-list;
```

Here *class-name* specifies the name of the class. This name becomes a new type name that can be used to create objects of the class. You can also create objects of the class by specifying them immediately after the class declaration in *object-list*, but this is optional. Once a class has been declared, objects can be created where needed.

A class can contain private as well as public members. By default, all items defined in a class are private. This means that they can be accessed only by other members of their class, and not by any other part of your program. This is one way encapsulation is achieved—you can tightly control access to certain items of data by keeping them private.

To make parts of a class public (that is, accessible to other parts of your program), you must declare them after the **public** keyword. All variables or functions defined after the **public** specifier are accessible by other parts of your program. Typically, your program will access the private members of a class through its public functions. Notice that the **public** keyword is followed by a colon.

Although there is no syntactic rule that enforces it, a well-designed class should define one and only one logical entity. For example, a class that stores names and telephone numbers will not normally also store information about the stock market, average rainfall, sunspot cycles, or other unrelated information. The point here is that a well-designed class groups logically connected information. Putting unrelated information into the same class will quickly destructure your code!

Let's review: In C++, a **class** creates a new data type that can be used to create objects. Specifically, a class creates a logical framework that defines a relationship between its members. When you declare a variable of a class, you are creating an object. An object has physical existence and is a specific instance of a class. That is, an object occupies memory space, but a type definition does not.

8

Defining a Class

To illustrate classes, we will be evolving a class that encapsulates information about vehicles, such as cars, vans, and trucks. This class is called **Vehicle**, and it will store three items of information about a vehicle: the number of passengers that it can carry, its fuel capacity, and its average fuel consumption (in miles per gallon).

The first version of **Vehicle** is shown here. It defines three instance variables: **passengers**, **fuelcap**, and **mpg**. Notice that **Vehicle** does not contain any functions. Thus, it is currently a data-only class. (Subsequent sections will add functions to it.)

```
class Vehicle {
public:
  int passengers; // number of passengers
```

```
   int fuelcap;     // fuel capacity in gallons
   int mpg;         // fuel consumption in miles per gallon
};
```

The instance variables defined by **Vehicle** illustrate the way that instance variables are declared in general. The general form for declaring an instance variable is shown here:

type var-name;

Here, *type* specifies the type of variable, and *var-name* is the variable's name. Thus, you declare an instance variable in the same way that you declare other variables. For **Vehicle**, the variables are preceded by the **public** access specifier. As explained, this allows them to be accessed by code outside of **Vehicle**.

A **class** definition creates a new data type. In this case, the new data type is called **Vehicle**. You will use this name to declare objects of type **Vehicle**. Remember that a **class** declaration is only a type description; it does not create an actual object. Thus, the preceding code does not cause any objects of type **Vehicle** to come into existence.

To actually create a **Vehicle** object, simply use a declaration statement, such as the following:

```
Vehicle minivan; // create a Vehicle object called minivan
```

After this statement executes, **minivan** will be an instance of **Vehicle**. Thus, it will have "physical" reality.

Each time you create an instance of a class, you are creating an object that contains its own copy of each instance variable defined by the class. Thus, every **Vehicle** object will contain its own copies of the instance variables **passengers**, **fuelcap**, and **mpg**. To access these variables, you will use the *dot* (.) operator. The dot operator links the name of an object with the name of a member. The general form of the dot operator is shown here:

object.member

Thus, the object is specified on the left, and the member is put on the right. For example, to assign the **fuelcap** variable of **minivan** the value 16, use the following statement:

```
minivan.fuelcap = 16;
```

In general, you can use the dot operator to access instance variables and call functions.

Here is a complete program that uses the **Vehicle** class:

```
// A program that uses the Vehicle class.

#include <iostream>
using namespace std;

// Declare the Vehicle class.
class Vehicle {            Declare the Vehicle class.
public:
  int passengers; // number of passengers
  int fuelcap;    // fuel capacity in gallons
  int mpg;        // fuel consumption in miles per gallon
};
                                    Create an instance of
                                    Vehicle called minivan.
int main() {
  Vehicle minivan; // create a Vehicle object
  int range;

  // Assign values to fields in minivan.
  minivan.passengers = 7;
  minivan.fuelcap = 16;      Notice the use of the dot
  minivan.mpg = 21;          operator to access a member.

  // Compute the range assuming a full tank of gas.
  range = minivan.fuelcap * minivan.mpg;

  cout << "Minivan can carry " << minivan.passengers <<
          " with a range of " << range << "\n";

  return 0;
}
```

Let's look closely at this program. The **main( )** function creates an instance of **Vehicle** called **minivan**. Then the code within **main( )** accesses the instance variables associated with **minivan**, assigning them values and then using those values. The code inside **main( )** can access the members of **Vehicle** because they are declared **public**. If they had not been specified as **public**, their access would have been limited to the **Vehicle** class, and **main( )** would not have been able to use them.

When you run the program, you will see the following output:

```
Minivan can carry 7 with a range of 336
```

Before moving on, let's review a fundamental principle: each object has its own copies of the instance variables defined by its class. Thus, the contents of the variables in one object can differ from the contents of the variables in another. There is no connection between the two objects except for the fact that they are both objects of the same type. For example, if you have two **Vehicle** objects, each has its own copy of **passengers**, **fuelcap**, and **mpg**, and the contents of these can differ between the two objects. The following program demonstrates this fact:

```cpp
// This program creates two Vehicle objects.

#include <iostream>
using namespace std;

// Declare the Vehicle class.
class Vehicle {
public:
  int passengers; // number of passengers
  int fuelcap;    // fuel capacity in gallons
  int mpg;        // fuel consumption in miles per gallon
};

int main() {
  Vehicle minivan; // create a Vehicle object
  Vehicle sportscar; // create another object

  int range1, range2;

  // Assign values to fields in minivan.
  minivan.passengers = 7;
  minivan.fuelcap = 16;
  minivan.mpg = 21;

  // Assign values to fields in sportscar.
  sportscar.passengers = 2;
  sportscar.fuelcap = 14;
  sportscar.mpg = 12;

  // Compute the ranges assuming a full tank of gas.
```

minivan and **sportscar** each have their own copies of **Vehicle**'s instance variables.

```
range1 = minivan.fuelcap * minivan.mpg;
range2 = sportscar.fuelcap * sportscar.mpg;

cout << "Minivan can carry " <<  minivan.passengers <<
        " with a range of " << range1 << "\n";

cout << "Sportscar can carry " <<  sportscar.passengers <<
        " with a range of " << range2 << "\n";

return 0;
}
```

The output produced by this program is shown here:

```
Minivan can carry 7 with a range of 336
Sportscar can carry 2 with a range of 168
```

As you can see, **minivan**'s data is completely separate from the data contained in **sportscar**. Figure 8-1 depicts this situation.

1-Minute Drill

- A class can contain what two things?
- What operator is used to access the members of a class through an object?
- Each object has its own copies of the class' _____.

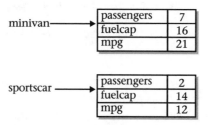

minivan ──▶	passengers	7
	fuelcap	16
	mpg	21

sportscar ──▶	passengers	2
	fuelcap	14
	mpg	12

Figure 8-1   One object's instance variables are separate from another's.

- A class can contain code and data.
- The dot operator is used to access the members of a class through an object.
- Instance variables

8

Adding Functions to a Class

So far, **Vehicle** contains only data, but no functions. Although data-only classes are perfectly valid, most classes will have function members. In general, member functions manipulate the data defined by the class and, in many cases, provide access to that data. Typically, other parts of your program will interact with a class through its functions.

To illustrate member functions, we will add one to the **Vehicle** class. Recall that **main( )** in the preceding examples computed the range of a vehicle by multiplying its fuel consumption rate by its fuel capacity. While technically correct, this is not the best way to handle this computation. The calculation of a vehicle's range is something that is best handled by the **Vehicle** class itself. The reason for this conclusion is easy to understand: The range of a vehicle is dependent upon the capacity of the fuel tank and the rate of fuel consumption, and both of these quantities are encapsulated by **Vehicle**. By adding a function to **Vehicle** that computes the range, you are enhancing its object-oriented structure.

To add a function to **Vehicle**, specify its prototype within **Vehicle**'s declaration. For example, the following version of **Vehicle** specifies a member function called **range( )**, which returns the range of the vehicle:

```
// Declare the Vehicle class.
class Vehicle {
public:
  int passengers; // number of passengers
  int fuelcap;    // fuel capacity in gallons
  int mpg;        // fuel consumption in miles per gallon

  int range();    // compute and return the range
};
```

Declare the **range( )** member function.

Because a member function, such as **range( )**, is prototyped within the class definition, it need not be prototyped elsewhere.

To implement a member function, you must tell the compiler to which class the function belongs by qualifying the function's name with its class name. For example, here is one way to code the **range( )** function:

```
// Implement the range member function.
int Vehicle::range() {
  return mpg * fuelcap;
}
```

Notice the :: that separates the class name **Vehicle** from the function name **range( )**. The :: is called the *scope resolution operator*. It links a class name with a member name in order to tell the compiler what class the member belongs to. In this case, it links **range( )** to the **Vehicle** class. In other words, :: states that this **range( )** is in **Vehicle**'s scope. Several different classes can use the same function names. The compiler knows which function belongs to which class because of the scope resolution operator and the class name.

The body of **range( )** consists solely of this line:

```
return mpg * fuelcap;
```

This statement returns the range of the vehicle by multiplying **fuelcap** by **mpg**. Since each object of type **Vehicle** has its own copy of **fuelcap** and **mpg**, when **range( )** is called, the range computation uses the calling object's copies of those variables.

Inside **range( )** the instance variables **fuelcap** and **mpg** are referred to directly, without preceding them with an object name or the dot operator. When a member function uses an instance variable that is defined by its class, it does so directly, without explicit reference to an object and without use of the dot operator. This is easy to understand if you think about it. A member function is always invoked relative to some object of its class. Once this invocation has occurred, the object is known. Thus, within a member function, there is no need to specify the object a second time. This means that **fuelcap** and **mpg** inside **range( )** implicitly refer to the copies of those variables found in the object that invokes **range( )**. Of course, code outside **Vehicle** must refer to **fuelcap** and **mpg** through an object and by using the dot operator.

A member function must be called relative to a specific object. There are two ways that this can happen. First, a member function can be called by code that is outside its class. In this case, you must use the object's name and the dot operator. For example, this calls **range( )** on **minivan**:

```
range = minivan.range();
```

The invocation **minivan.range( )** causes **range( )** to operate on **minivan**'s copy of the instance variables. Thus, it returns the range for **minivan**.

The second way a member function can be called is from within another member function of the same class. When one member function calls another member function of the same class, it can do so directly, without using the dot operator. In this case, the compiler already knows which object is being operated upon. It is only when a member function is called by code that does not belong to the class that the object name and the dot operator must be used.

The program shown here puts together all the pieces and missing details, and illustrates the **range( )** function:

```
// A program that uses the Vehicle class.

#include <iostream>
using namespace std;

// Declare the Vehicle class.
class Vehicle {
public:
  int passengers; // number of passengers
  int fuelcap;    // fuel capacity in gallons
  int mpg;        // fuel consumption in miles per gallon

  int range();    // compute and return the range    ◄─── Declare range( ).
};

// Implement the range member function.
int Vehicle::range() {  ◄──────────────  Implement range( ).
  return mpg * fuelcap;
}

int main() {
  Vehicle minivan; // create a Vehicle object
  Vehicle sportscar; // create another object

  int range1, range2;

  // Assign values to fields in minivan.
  minivan.passengers = 7;
  minivan.fuelcap = 16;
  minivan.mpg = 21;

  // Assign values to fields in sportscar.
  sportscar.passengers = 2;
  sportscar.fuelcap = 14;
  sportscar.mpg = 12;

  // Compute the ranges assuming a full tank of gas.
  range1 = minivan.range();  ◄───────────  Call range( ) on
  range2 = sportscar.range();               Vehicle objects.
```

```
cout << "Minivan can carry " <<  minivan.passengers <<
        " with a range of " << range1 << "\n";

cout << "Sportscar can carry " <<  sportscar.passengers <<
        " with a range of " << range2 << "\n";

return 0;
}
```

This program displays the following output:

```
Minivan can carry 7 with a range of 336
Sportscar can carry 2 with a range of 168
```

1-Minute Drill

- What is the **::** operator called?

- What does **::** do?

- If a member function is called from outside its class, it must be called through an object using the dot operator. True or false?

8

ielpClass.cpp

Project 8-1: Creating a Help Class

If one were to try to summarize the essence of the class in one sentence, it might be this: A class encapsulates functionality. Of course, sometimes the trick is knowing where one "functionality" ends and another begins. As a general rule, you will want your classes to be the building blocks of your larger application. To do this, each class must represent a single functional unit that performs clearly delineated actions. Thus, you will want your classes to be as small as possible—but no smaller! That is, classes that contain extraneous functionality confuse and destructure code, but classes that contain too little functionality are fragmented. What is the balance? It is at this point that the *science* of programming becomes the *art* of programming. Fortunately, most programmers find that this balancing act becomes easier with experience.

To begin gaining that experience, you will convert the help system from Project 3-3 in Module 3 into a Help class. Let's examine why this is a good idea. First, the help system defines one logical unit. It simply displays the syntax

---

- The **::** is the scope resolution operator.
- The **::** links a class to a member.
- True. From outside a class, a member function must be called on an object using the dot operator.

for the C++ control statements. Thus, its functionality is compact and well defined. Second, putting help in a class is an esthetically pleasing approach. Whenever you want to offer the help system to a user, simply instantiate a help-system object. Finally, because help is encapsulated, it can be upgraded or changed without causing unwanted side effects in the programs that use it.

Step-by-Step

1. Create a new file called **HelpClass.cpp**. To save you some typing, you might want to copy the file from Project 3-3, **Help3.cpp**, into **HelpClass.cpp**.

2. To convert the help system into a class, you must first determine precisely what constitutes the help system. For example, in **Help3.cpp**, there is code to display a menu, input the user's choice, check for a valid response, and display information about the item selected. The program also loops until q is pressed. If you think about it, it is clear that the menu, the check for a valid response, and the display of the information are integral to the help system. How user input is obtained, and whether repeated requests should be processed, are not. Thus, you will create a class that displays the help information, the help menu, and checks for a valid selection. These functions will be called **helpon( )**, **showmenu( )**, and **isvalid( )**, respectively.

3. Declare the **Help** class, as shown here:

```
// A class that encapsulates a help system.
class Help {
public:
  void helpon(char what);
  void showmenu();
  bool isvalid(char ch);
};
```

Notice that this is a function-only class; no instance variables are needed. As explained, data-only and code-only classes are perfectly valid. (Question 9 in the Mastery Check adds an instance variable to the **Help** class.)

4. Create the **helpon( )** function, as shown here:

```
// Display help information.
void Help::helpon(char what) {
  switch(what) {
    case '1':
      cout << "The if:\n\n";
      cout << "if(condition) statement;\n";
      cout << "else statement;\n";
```

```
      break;
    case '2':
      cout << "The switch:\n\n";
      cout << "switch(expression) {\n";
      cout << "  case constant:\n";
      cout << "    statement sequence\n";
      cout << "    break;\n";
      cout << "  // ...\n";
      cout << "}\n";
      break;
    case '3':
      cout << "The for:\n\n";
      cout << "for(init; condition; iteration)";
      cout << " statement;\n";
      break;
    case '4':
      cout << "The while:\n\n";
      cout << "while(condition) statement;\n";
      break;
    case '5':
      cout << "The do-while:\n\n";
      cout << "do {\n";
      cout << "  statement;\n";
      cout << "} while (condition);\n";
      break;
    case '6':
      cout << "The break:\n\n";
      cout << "break;\n";
      break;
    case '7':
      cout << "The continue:\n\n";
      cout << "continue;\n";
      break;
    case '8':
      cout << "The goto:\n\n";
      cout << "goto label;\n";
      break;
  }
  cout << "\n";
}
```

5. Create the **showmenu( )** function:

```
// Show the help menu.
void Help::showmenu() {
  cout << "Help on:\n";
```

```
    cout << "  1. if\n";
    cout << "  2. switch\n";
    cout << "  3. for\n";
    cout << "  4. while\n";
    cout << "  5. do-while\n";
    cout << "  6. break\n";
    cout << "  7. continue\n";
    cout << "  8. goto\n";
    cout << "Choose one (q to quit): ";
}
```

6. Create the **isvalid( )** function, shown here:

```
// Return true if a selection is valid.
bool Help::isvalid(char ch) {
  if(ch < '1' || ch > '8' && ch != 'q')
    return false;
  else
    return true;
}
```

7. Rewrite the **main( )** function from Project 3-3 so that it uses the new **Help** class. The entire listing for **HelpClass.cpp** is shown here:

```
/*
   Project 8-1

   Convert the Help system from Project 3-3 into
   a Help class.
*/

#include <iostream>
using namespace std;

// A class that encapsulates a help system.
class Help {
public:
  void helpon(char what);
  void showmenu();
  bool isvalid(char ch);
};

// Display help information.
void Help::helpon(char what) {
  switch(what) {
```

```
      case '1':
        cout << "The if:\n\n";
        cout << "if(condition) statement;\n";
        cout << "else statement;\n";
        break;
      case '2':
        cout << "The switch:\n\n";
        cout << "switch(expression) {\n";
        cout << "  case constant:\n";
        cout << "    statement sequence\n";
        cout << "    break;\n";
        cout << "  // ...\n";
        cout << "}\n";
        break;
      case '3':
        cout << "The for:\n\n";
        cout << "for(init; condition; iteration)";
        cout << " statement;\n";
        break;
      case '4':
        cout << "The while:\n\n";
        cout << "while(condition) statement;\n";
        break;
      case '5':
        cout << "The do-while:\n\n";
        cout << "do {\n";
        cout << "  statement;\n";
        cout << "} while (condition);\n";
        break;
      case '6':
        cout << "The break:\n\n";
        cout << "break;\n";
        break;
      case '7':
        cout << "The continue:\n\n";
        cout << "continue;\n";
        break;
      case '8':
        cout << "The goto:\n\n";
        cout << "goto label;\n";
        break;
    }
    cout << "\n";
}

// Show the help menu.
```

```
void Help::showmenu() {
  cout << "Help on:\n";
  cout << "  1. if\n";
  cout << "  2. switch\n";
  cout << "  3. for\n";
  cout << "  4. while\n";
  cout << "  5. do-while\n";
  cout << "  6. break\n";
  cout << "  7. continue\n";
  cout << "  8. goto\n";
  cout << "Choose one (q to quit): ";
}

// Return true if a selection is valid.
bool Help::isvalid(char ch) {
  if(ch < '1' || ch > '8' && ch != 'q')
    return false;
  else
    return true;
}

int main()
{
  char choice;
  Help hlpob; // create an instance of the Help class.

  // Use the Help object to display information.
  for(;;) {
    do {
      hlpob.showmenu();
      cin >> choice;
    } while(!hlpob.isvalid(choice));

    if(choice == 'q') break;
    cout << "\n";

    hlpob.helpon(choice);
  }

  return 0;
}
```

When you try the program, you will find that it is functionally the same as in Module 3. The advantage to this approach is that you now have a help system component that can be reused whenever it is needed.

Constructors and Destructors

In the preceding examples, the instance variables of each **Vehicle** object had to be set manually by use of a sequence of statements, such as:

```
minivan.passengers = 7;
minivan.fuelcap = 16;
minivan.mpg = 21;
```

An approach like this would never be used in professionally written C++ code. Aside from being error prone (you might forget to set one of the fields), there is simply a better way to accomplish this task: the constructor.

A *constructor* initializes an object when it is created. It has the same name as its class and is syntactically similar to a function. However, constructors have no explicit return type. The general form of constructor is shown here:

```
class-name( ) {
  // constructor code
}
```

Typically, you will use a constructor to give initial values to the instance variables defined by the class, or to perform any other startup procedures required to create a fully formed object.

The complement of the constructor is the *destructor*. In many circumstances, an object will need to perform some action or series of actions when it is destroyed. Local objects are created when their block is entered, and destroyed when the block is left. Global objects are destroyed when the program terminates. There are many reasons why a destructor may be needed. For example, an object may need to deallocate memory that it had previously allocated, or an open file may need to be closed. In C++, it is the destructor that handles these types of operations. The destructor has the same name as the constructor, but is preceded by a ~. Like constructors, destructors do not have return types.

Here is a simple example that uses a constructor and a destructor:

```
// A simple constructor and destructor.

#include <iostream>
using namespace std;

class MyClass {
public:
```

8

```
  int x;

  // Declare constructor and destructor.
  MyClass();  // constructor
  ~MyClass(); // destructor
};
```

Declare constructor and destructor for **MyClass**.

```
// Implement MyClass constructor.
MyClass::MyClass() {
  x = 10;
}

// Implement MyClass destructor.
MyClass::~MyClass() {
  cout << "Destructing...\n";
}

int main() {
  MyClass ob1;
  MyClass ob2;

  cout << ob1.x << " " << ob2.x << "\n";

  return 0;
}
```

The output from the program is shown here:

```
10 10
Destructing...
Destructing...
```

In this example, the constructor for **MyClass** is

```
// Implement MyClass constructor.
MyClass::MyClass() {
  x = 10;
}
```

Notice that the constructor is specified under **public**. This is because the constructor will be called from code defined outside of its class. This constructor assigns the instance variable **x** of **MyClass** the value 10. This constructor is called when an object is created. For example, in the line

```
MyClass ob1;
```

the constructor **MyClass( )** is called on the **ob1** object, giving **ob1.x** the value 10. The same is true for **ob2**. After construction, **ob2.x** also has the value 10.

The destructor for **MyClass** is shown next:

```
// Implement MyClass constructor.
MyClass::~MyClass() {
  cout << "Destructing...\n";
}
```

This destructor simply displays a message, but in real programs, the destructor would be used to release one or more resources (such as a file handle or memory) used by the class.

1-Minute Drill

● What is a constructor and when is it executed?

● Does a constructor have a return type?

● When is a destructor called?

Parameterized Constructors

In the preceding example, a parameterless constructor was used. While this is fine for some situations, most often you will need a constructor that has one or more parameters. Parameters are added to a constructor in the same way that they are added to a function: just declare them inside the parentheses after the constructor's name. For example, here is a parameterized constructor for **MyClass**:

```
Myclass::MyClass(int i) {
  x = i;
}
```

To pass an argument to the constructor, you must associate the value or values being passed with an object when it is being declared. C++ provides two ways to do this. The first method is illustrated here:

```
MyClass ob1 = MyClass(101);
```

● A constructor is a function that is executed when an object of its class is instantiated. A constructor is used to initialize the object being created.

● No, a constructor does not have a return type.

● A destructor is called when an object is destroyed.

This declaration creates a **MyClass** object called **ob1** and passes the value 101 to it. However, this form is seldom used (in this context), because the second method is shorter and more to the point. In the second method, the argument or arguments must follow the object's name and be enclosed between parentheses. For example, this statement accomplishes the same thing as the previous declaration:

```
MyClass ob1(101);
```

This is the most common way that parameterized objects are declared. Using this method, the general form of passing arguments to a constructor is

class-type var(arg-list);

Here, *arg-list* is a comma-separated list of arguments that are passed to the constructor.

Note

Technically, there is a small difference between the two initialization forms, which you will learn about later in this book. However, this difference does not affect the programs in this module, or most programs that you will write.

Here is a complete program that demonstrates the **MyClass** parameterized constructor:

```
// A parameterized constructor.

#include <iostream>
using namespace std;

class MyClass {
public:
  int x;

  // Declare constructor and destructor.
  MyClass(int i);  // constructor ◄─────────  Add a parameter
  ~MyClass(); // destructor                    to MyClass( ).
};

// Implement a parameterized constructor.
MyClass::MyClass(int i) {
    x = i;
}
```

```
// Implement MyClass destructor.
MyClass::~MyClass() {
  cout << "Destructing object whose x value is " <<
          x  <<" \n";
}

int main() {
  MyClass t1(5);
  MyClass t2(19);

  cout << t1.x << " " << t2.x << "\n";

  return 0;
}
```

Pass arguments to
MyClass constructor.

The output from this program is shown here:

```
5 19
Destructing object whose x value is 19
Destructing object whose x value is 5
```

In this version of the program, the **MyClass( )** constructor defines one
parameter called **i**, which is used to initialize the instance variable, **x**. Thus,
when the line

```
MyClass ob1(5);
```

executes, the value 5 is passed to **i**, which is then assigned to **x**.

Unlike constructors, destructors cannot have parameters. The reason for
this is easy to understand: there is no means by which to pass arguments to
an object that is being destroyed. Although the situation is rare, if your object
needs access to some runtime-defined data when its destructor is called, you
will need to create a specific variable for this purpose. Then, just prior to the
object's destruction, you will need to access that variable.

Adding a Constructor to the Vehicle Class

We can improve the **Vehicle** class by adding a constructor that automatically
initializes the **passengers**, **fuelcap**, and **mpg** fields when an object is constructed.
Pay special attention to how **Vehicle** objects are created.

```
// Add a constructor to the vehicle class.

#include <iostream>
```

```
using namespace std;

// Declare the Vehicle class.
class Vehicle {
public:
  int passengers; // number of passengers
  int fuelcap;    // fuel capacity in gallons
  int mpg;        // fuel consumption in miles per gallon

  // This is a constructor for Vehicle.
  Vehicle(int p, int f, int m);

  int range();    // compute and return the range
};

// Implement the Vehicle constructor.
Vehicle::Vehicle(int p, int f, int m) {
  passengers = p;
  fuelcap = f;
  mpg = m;
}

// Implement the range member function.
int Vehicle::range() {
  return mpg * fuelcap;
}

int main() {
  // Pass values to Vehicle constructor.
  Vehicle minivan(7, 16, 21);
  Vehicle sportscar(2, 14, 12);

  int range1, range2;

  // Compute the ranges assuming a full tank of gas.
  range1 = minivan.range();
  range2 = sportscar.range();

  cout << "Minivan can carry " << minivan.passengers <<
          " with a range of " << range1 << "\n";

  cout << "Sportscar can carry " << sportscar.passengers <<
          " with a range of " << range2 << "\n";

  return 0;
}
```

Vehicle's constructor initializes **passengers**, **fuelcap**, and **mpg**.

Pass the vehicle information to **Vehicle** using its constructor.

Both **minivan** and **sportscar** were initialized by the **Vehicle( )** constructor when they were created. Each object is initialized as specified in the parameters to its constructor. For example, in the line

```
Vehicle minivan(7, 16, 21);
```

the values 7, 16, and 21 are passed to the **Vehicle( )** constructor when **new** creates the object. Therefore, **minivan**'s copy of **passengers**, **fuelcap**, and **mpg** will contain the values 7, 16, and 21, respectively. Thus, the output from this program is the same as the previous version.

An Initialization Alternative

If a constructor takes only one parameter, then you can use an alternative method to initialize it. Consider the following program:

```
// An alternate initialization method.

#include <iostream>
using namespace std;

class MyClass {
public:
  int x;

  // Declare constructor and destructor.
  MyClass(int i);  // constructor
  ~MyClass(); // destructor
};

// Implement a parameterized constructor.
MyClass::MyClass(int i) {
    x = i;
}

// Implement MyClass destructor.
MyClass::~MyClass() {
  cout << "Destructing object whose x value is " <<
        x  <<" \n";
}
```

8

```
int main() {
  MyClass ob = 5;   // calls MyClass(5)
```

An alternative syntax for initializing an object.

```
  cout << ob.x << "\n";

  return 0;
}
```

Here, the constructor for **MyClass** takes one parameter. Pay special attention to how **ob** is declared in **main( )**. It uses this declaration:

```
MyClass ob = 5;
```

In this form of initialization, 5 is automatically passed to the **i** parameter in the **MyClass( )** constructor. That is, the declaration statement is handled by the compiler as if it were written like this:

```
MyClass ob = MyClass(5);
```

In general, any time that you have a constructor that requires only one argument, you can use either *ob(x)* or *ob = x* to initialize an object. The reason is that whenever you create a constructor that takes one argument, you are also implicitly creating a conversion from the type of that argument to the type of the class.

Remember that the alternative shown here applies only to constructors that have exactly one parameter.

1-Minute Drill

- Assuming a class called **Test**, show how to declare a constructor that takes one **int** parameter called **count**.

- How can this statement be rewritten?

```
Test ob = Test(10);
```

- How else can the declaration in the second question be rewritten?

- `Test::Test(int count) { ...`
- `Test ob(10);`
- `Test ob = 10;`

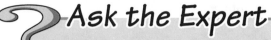

Ask the Expert

Question: Can one class be declared within another? That is, can classes be nested?

Answer: Yes, it is possible to define one class within another. Doing so creates a *nested class*. Since a **class** declaration does, in fact, define a scope, a nested class is valid only within the scope of the enclosing class. Frankly, because of the richness and flexibility of C++'s other features, such as inheritance, discussed later in this book, the need to create a nested class is virtually nonexistent.

Inline Functions

Before we continue exploring the class, a small but important digression is in order. Although it does not pertain specifically to object-oriented programming, one very useful feature of C++, called an *inline function,* is frequently used in class definitions. An inline function is a function that is expanded inline at the point at which it is invoked, instead of actually being called. There are two ways to create an inline function. The first is to use the **inline** modifier. For example, to create an inline function called **f** that returns an **int** and takes no parameters, you declare it like this:

```
inline int f()
{
  // ...
}
```

The **inline** modifier precedes all other aspects of a function's declaration.

The reason for **inline** functions is efficiency. Every time a function is called, a series of instructions must be executed, both to set up the function call, including pushing any arguments onto the stack, and to return from the function. In some cases, many CPU cycles are used to perform these procedures. However, when a function is expanded inline, no such overhead exists, and the overall speed of your program will increase. Even so, in cases where the inline function is large, the overall size of your program will also increase. For this reason, the best inline functions are those that are small. Most large functions should be left as normal functions.

8

The following program demonstrates **inline**:

```
// Demonstrate inline.

#include <iostream>
using namespace std;

class cl {
  int i; // private by default
public:
  int get_i();
  void put_i(int j);
} ;

inline int cl::get_i()
{
  return i;
}

inline void cl::put_i(int j)
{
  i = j;
}

int main()
{
  cl s;

  s.put_i(10);
  cout << s.get_i();

  return 0;
}
```

get_i( ) and **put_i( )** are expanded inline.

It is important to understand that technically, **inline** is a *request*, not a *command*, that the compiler generate inline code. There are various situations that might prevent the compiler from complying with the request. Here are some examples:

● Some compilers will not generate inline code if a function contains a loop, a **switch**, or a **goto**.

● Often, you cannot have inline recursive functions.

● Inline functions that contain **static** variables are frequently disallowed.

Remember: Inline restrictions are implementation-dependent, so you must check your compiler's documentation to find out about any restrictions that may apply in your situation.

Creating Inline Functions Inside a Class

Another way to create an inline function is by defining the code to a member function *inside* a class definition. Any function that is defined inside a class definition is automatically made into an inline function. It is not necessary to precede its declaration with the keyword **inline**. For example, the preceding program can be rewritten as shown here:

```
#include <iostream>
using namespace std;

class cl {
  int i; // private by default
public:
  // Automatic inline functions.
  int get_i() { return i; }            Define get_i( ) and
  void put_i(int j) { i = j; }         put_i( ) inside their class.
} ;

int main()
{
  cl s;

  s.put_i(10);
  cout << s.get_i();

  return 0;
}
```

Notice the way the function code is arranged. For very short functions, this arrangement reflects common C++ style. However, you could write them as shown here:

```
class cl {
  int i; // private by default
public:
  // inline functions
  int get_i()
  {
```

```
      return i;
  }

  void put_i(int j)
  {
      i = j;
  }
};
```

Short functions, like those illustrated in this example, are usually defined inside the class declaration. In-class, inline functions are quite common when working with classes because frequently a public function provides access to a private variable. Such functions are called *accessor functions*. Part of successful object-oriented programming is controlling access to data through member functions. Because most C++ programmers define accessor functions and other short member functions inside their classes, this convention will be followed by the rest of the C++ examples in this book. It is an approach that you should use, too.

Here is the **Vehicle** class recoded so that its constructor, destructor, and **range( )** function are defined inside the class. Also, the **passengers**, **fuelcap**, and **mpg** fields have been made private, and accessor functions have been added to get their values.

```
// Defines constructor, destructor, and range() function in-line.

#include <iostream>
using namespace std;
                                                ┌─────────────────┐
                                                │ Make these      │
// Declare the Vehicle class.                   │ variables private.│
class Vehicle {                                 └─────────────────┘
  // These are now private.
  int passengers; // number of passengers
  int fuelcap;    // fuel capacity in gallons
  int mpg;        // fuel consumption in miles per gallon
public:
  // This is a constructor for Vehicle.
  Vehicle(int p, int f, int m) {
    passengers = p;
    fuelcap = f;
    mpg = m;
  }
```

```
// Compute and return the range.
  int range() { return mpg * fuelcap; }

  // Accessor functions.
  int get_passengers() { return passengers; }
  int get_fuelcap() { return fuelcap; }
  int get_mpg() { return mpg; }
};

int main() {
  // Pass values to Vehicle constructor.
  Vehicle minivan(7, 16, 21);
  Vehicle sportscar(2, 14, 12);

  int range1, range2;

  // Compute the ranges assuming a full tank of gas.
  range1 = minivan.range();
  range2 = sportscar.range();

  cout << "Minivan can carry " << minivan.get_passengers() <<
          " with a range of " << range1 << "\n";

  cout << "Sportscar can carry " << sportscar.get_passengers() <<
          " with a range of " << range2 << "\n";

  return 0;
}
```

> Define functions inline and access private variables through accessor functions.

Because the member variables of **Vehicle** are now private, the accessor function **get_passengers( )** must be used inside **main( )** to obtain the number of passengers that a vehicle can hold.

1-Minute Drill

● What does **inline** do?

● Can an inline function be declared inside a **class** declaration?

● What is an accessor function?

● **inline** causes a function's code to be expanded inline rather than called.
● Yes, an inline function can be declared within a **class**.
● An accessor function is a short function that gets or sets the value of a private instance variable.

8

Project 8-2: Creating a Queue Class

As you may know, a *data structure* is a means of organizing data. The simplest data structure is the *array,* which is a linear list that supports random access to its elements. Arrays are often used as the underpinning for more sophisticated data structures, such as stacks and queues. A *stack* is a list in which elements can be accessed in first-in, last-out (FILO) order only. A *queue* is a list in which elements can be accessed in first-in, first-out (FIFO) order only. Thus, a stack is like a stack of plates on a table; the first down is the last to be used. A queue is like a line at a bank; the first in line is the first served.

What makes data structures such as stacks and queues interesting is that they combine storage for information with the functions that access that information. Thus, stacks and queues are *data engines* in which storage and retrieval is provided by the data structure itself, and not manually by your program. Such a combination is, obviously, an excellent choice for a class, and in this project, you will create a simple queue class.

In general, queues support two basic operations: put and get. Each put operation places a new element on the end of the queue. Each get operation retrieves the next element from the front of the queue. Queue operations are consumptive. Once an element has been retrieved, it cannot be retrieved again. The queue can also become full if there is no space available to store an item, and it can become empty if all of the elements have been removed.

One last point: there are two basic types of queues, circular and non-circular. A circular queue reuses locations in the underlying array when elements are removed. A non-circular queue does not and eventually becomes exhausted. For the sake of simplicity, this example creates a non-circular queue, but with a little thought and effort, you can easily transform it into a circular queue.

Step-by-Step

1. Create a file called **Queue.cpp**.

2. Although there are other ways to support a queue, the method we will use is based upon an array. That is, an array will provide the storage for the items put into the queue. This array will be accessed through two indices. The *put* index determines where the next element of data will be stored. The *get* index indicates at what location the next element of data will be obtained. Keep in mind that the get operation is consumptive, and it is not possible to retrieve the same element twice. Although the queue that we will be creating stores characters, the same logic can be used to store any type of object. Begin creating the **Queue** class with these lines:

```
const int maxQsize = 100;

class Queue {
```

```
char q[maxQsize]; // this array holds the queue
int size; // the maximum number of elements that the queue can store
int putloc, getloc; // the put and get indices
```

The **const** variable **maxQsize** defines the size of the largest queue that can be created. The actual size of the queue is stored in the **size** field.

3. The constructor for the **Queue** class creates a queue of a given size. Here is the **Queue** constructor:

```
public:

// Construct a queue of a specific length.
Queue(int len) {
  // Queue must be less than max and positive.
  if(len > maxQsize) len = maxQsize;
  else if(len <= 0) len = 1;

  size = len;
  putloc = getloc = 0;
}
```

If the requested queue size is greater than **maxQsize**, then the maximum size queue is created. If the requested queue size is zero or less, a queue of length 1 is created. The size of the queue is stored in the **size** field. The put and get indices are initially set to zero.

4. The **put( )** function, which stores elements, is shown next:

```
// Put a character into the queue.
void put(char ch) {
  if(putloc == size) {
    cout << " -- Queue is full.\n";
    return;
  }

  putloc++;
  q[putloc] = ch;
}
```

The function begins by checking for a queue-full condition. If **putloc** is equal to the size of the queue, then there is no more room in which to store elements. Otherwise, **putloc** is incremented, and the new element is stored at that location. Thus, **putloc** is always the index of the last element stored.

8

5. To retrieve elements, use the **get( )** function, shown next:

```
// Get a character from the queue.
char get() {
  if(getloc == putloc) {
    cout << " -- Queue is empty.\n";
    return 0;
  }

  getloc++;
  return q[getloc];
}
```

Notice first the check for queue-empty. If **getloc** and **putloc** both index the same element, then the queue is assumed to be empty. This is why **getloc** and **putloc** were both initialized to zero by the **Queue** constructor. Next, **getloc** is incremented and the next element is returned. Thus, **getloc** always indicates the location of the last element retrieved.

6. Here is the entire **Queue.cpp** program:

```
/*
   Project 8-2

   A queue class for characters.
*/
#include <iostream>
using namespace std;

const int maxQsize = 100;

class Queue {
  char q[maxQsize]; // this array holds the queue
  int size; // the maximum number of elements that the queue can store
  int putloc, getloc; // the put and get indices
public:

  // Construct a queue of a specific length.
  Queue(int len) {
    // Queue must be less than max and positive.
    if(len > maxQsize) len = maxQsize;
    else if(len <= 0) len = 1;

    size = len;
    putloc = getloc = 0;
  }

  // Put a character into the queue.
```

```
    void put(char ch) {
      if(putloc == size) {
        cout << " -- Queue is full.\n";
        return;
      }

      putloc++;
      q[putloc] = ch;
    }

    // Get a character from the queue.
    char get() {
      if(getloc == putloc) {
        cout << " -- Queue is empty.\n";
        return 0;
      }

      getloc++;
      return q[getloc];
    }
};

// Demonstrate the Queue class.
int main() {
  Queue bigQ(100);
  Queue smallQ(4);
  char ch;
  int i;

  cout << "Using bigQ to store the alphabet.\n";
  // put some numbers into bigQ
  for(i=0; i < 26; i++)
    bigQ.put('A' + i);

  // retrieve and display elements from bigQ
  cout << "Contents of bigQ: ";
  for(i=0; i < 26; i++) {
    ch = bigQ.get();
    if(ch != 0) cout << ch;
  }

  cout << "\n\n";


  cout << "Using smallQ to generate errors.\n";

  // Now, use smallQ to generate some errors
  for(i=0; i < 5; i++) {
    cout << "Attempting to store " <<
                (char) ('Z' - i);
```

8

```
    smallQ.put('Z' - i);

    cout << "\n";
  }
  cout << "\n";

  // more errors on smallQ
  cout << "Contents of smallQ: ";
  for(i=0; i < 5; i++) {
    ch = smallQ.get();

    if(ch != 0) cout << ch;
  }

  cout << "\n";
}
```

7. The output produced by the program is shown here:

```
Using bigQ to store the alphabet.
Contents of bigQ: ABCDEFGHIJKLMNOPQRSTUVWXYZ

Using smallQ to generate errors.
Attempting to store Z
Attempting to store Y
Attempting to store X
Attempting to store W
Attempting to store V -- Queue is full.


Contents of smallQ: ZYXW -- Queue is empty.
```

8. On your own, try modifying **Queue** so that it stores other types of objects. For example, have it store **int**s or **double**s.

Arrays of Objects

You can create arrays of objects in the same way that you create arrays of any other data type. For example, the following program creates an array of **MyClass** objects. The objects that comprise the elements of the array are accessed using the normal array-indexing syntax.

```
// Create an array of objects.

#include <iostream>
```

```
using namespace std;

class MyClass {
  int x;
public:
  void set_x(int i) { x = i; }
  int get_x() { return x; }
};

int main()
{
  MyClass obs[4];         ◄──────────  Create an array of objects.
  int i;

  for(i=0; i < 4; i++)
    obs[i].set_x(i);

  for(i=0; i < 4; i++)
    cout << "obs[" << i << "].get_x(): " <<
            obs[i].get_x() << "\n";

  return 0;
}
```

This program produces the following output:

```
obs[0].get_x(): 0
obs[1].get_x(): 1
obs[2].get_x(): 2
obs[3].get_x(): 3
```

Initializing Object Arrays

If a class includes a parameterized constructor, an array of objects can be initialized. For example, here **MyClass** is a parameterized class, and **obs** is an initialized array of objects of that class.

```
// Initialize an array of objects.

#include <iostream>
using namespace std;

class MyClass {
  int x;
public:
```

```
  MyClass(int i) { x = i; }
  int get_x() { return x; }
};

int main()
{
  MyClass obs[4] = { -1, -2, -3, -4 };
  int i;

  for(i=0; i < 4; i++)
    cout << "obs[" << i << "].get_x(): " <<
            obs[i].get_x() << "\n";

  return 0;
}
```

One way to initialize an array of objects.

In this example, the values –1 through –4 are passed to the **MyClass** constructor function. This program displays the following output:

```
obs[0].get_x(): -1
obs[1].get_x(): -2
obs[2].get_x(): -3
obs[3].get_x(): -4
```

Actually, the syntax shown in the initialization list is shorthand for this longer form:

```
MyClass obs[4] = { MyClass(-1), MyClass (-2),
                   MyClass (-3), MyClass (-4) };
```

Another way to initialize the array.

As explained earlier, when a constructor takes only one argument, there is an implicit conversion from the type of that argument to the type of the class. The longer form simply calls the constructor directly.

When initializing an array of objects whose constructor takes more than one argument, you must use the longer form of initialization. For example:

```
#include <iostream>
using namespace std;

class MyClass {
  int x, y;
```

```
public:
  MyClass(int i, int j) { x = i; y = j; }
  int get_x() { return x; }
  int get_y() { return y; }
};

int main()
{
  MyClass obs[4][2] = {
    MyClass(1, 2), MyClass(3, 4),
    MyClass(5, 6), MyClass(7, 8),
    MyClass(9, 10), MyClass(11, 12),
    MyClass(13, 14), MyClass(15, 16)
  };

  int i;

  for(i=0; i < 4; i++) {
    cout << obs[i][0].get_x() << ' ';
    cout << obs[i][0].get_y() << "\n";
    cout << obs[i][1].get_x() << ' ';
    cout << obs[i][1].get_y() << "\n";
  }

  return 0;
}
```

> The long initialization form must be used when two or more arguments are required by the object's constructor.

In this example, **MyClass'** constructor takes two arguments. In **main( )**, the array **obs** is declared and initialized using direct calls to **MyClass'** constructor. When initializing arrays you can always use the long form of initialization, even if the object takes only one argument. It's just that the short form is more convenient when only one argument is required. The program displays the following output:

```
1 2
3 4
5 6
7 8
9 10
11 12
13 14
15 16
```

Pointers to Objects

You can access an object either directly (as has been the case in all preceding examples), or by using a pointer to that object. To access a specific element of an object when using a pointer to the object, you must use the *arrow operator*: –>. It is formed by using the minus sign followed by a greater-than sign.

To declare an object pointer, you use the same declaration syntax that you would use to declare a pointer for any other type of data. The next program creates a simple class called **P_example**, defines an object of that class called **ob**, and defines a pointer to an object of type **P_example** called **p**. It then illustrates how to access **ob** directly, and how to use a pointer to access it indirectly.

```cpp
// A simple example using an object pointer.

#include <iostream>
using namespace std;

class P_example {
  int num;
public:
  void set_num(int val) { num = val; }
  void show_num(){ cout << num << "\n"; }
};

int main()
{
  P_example ob, *p; // declare an object and pointer to it

  ob.set_num(1); // call functions directly on ob
  ob.show_num();
```
Pointers to objects are used like other types of pointers.
```cpp
  p = &ob; // assign p the address of ob
  p->set_num(20); // call functions through a pointer to ob
  p->show_num();
```
Notice the use of the arrow operator.
```cpp
  return 0;
}
```

Notice that the address of **ob** is obtained using the **&** (address of) operator in the same way that the address is obtained for any type of variable.

As you know, when a pointer is incremented or decremented, it is increased or decreased in such a way that it will always point to the next element of its base type. The same thing occurs when a pointer to an object is incremented or decremented: the next object is pointed to. To illustrate this, the preceding program has been modified here so that **ob** is a two-element array of type **P_example**. Notice how **p** is incremented and decremented to access the two elements in the array.

```
// Incrementing and decrementing an object pointer.

#include <iostream>
using namespace std;

class P_example {
  int num;
public:
  void set_num(int val) { num = val; }
  void show_num(){ cout << num << "\n"; }
};

int main()
{
  P_example ob[2], *p;

  ob[0].set_num(10);   // access objects directly
  ob[1].set_num(20);

  p = &ob[0];  // obtain pointer to first element
  p->show_num(); // show value of ob[0] using pointer

  p++;  // advance to next object
  p->show_num(); // show value of ob[1] using pointer

  p--;  // retreat to previous object
  p->show_num(); // again show value of ob[0]

  return 0;
}
```

The output from this program is **10, 20, 10**.

As you will see later in this book, object pointers play a pivotal role in one of C++'s most important concepts: polymorphism.

1-Minute Drill

● Can an array of objects be given initial values?

● Given a pointer to an object, what operator is used to access a member?

Object References

Objects can be referenced in the same way as any other data type. No special restrictions or instructions apply.

● Yes, an array of objects can be given initial values.
● When accessing a member through a pointer, use the arrow operator.

✓ Mastery Check

1. What is the difference between a class and an object?

2. What keyword is used to declare a class?

3. What does each object have its own copy of?

4. Show how to declare a class called **Test** that contains two private **int** variables called **count** and **max**.

5. What name does a constructor have? What name does a destructor have?

6. Given this class declaration:

```
class Sample {
  int i;
public:
  Sample(int x) { i = x }
  // ...
};
```

show how to declare a **Sample** object that initializes **i** to the value 10.

7. When a member function is declared within a class declaration, what optimization automatically takes place?

8. Create a class called **Triangle** that stores the length of the base and height of a right triangle in two private instance variables. Include a constructor that sets these values. Define two functions. The first is **hypot( )**, which returns the length of the hypotenuse. The second is **area( )**, which returns the area of the triangle.

9. Expand the **Help** class so that it stores an integer ID number that identifies each user of the class. Display the ID when a help object is destroyed. Return the ID when the function **getID( )** is called.

8

Module 9

A Closer Look at Classes

The Goals of This Module

- Overload constructors
- Assign objects
- Pass objects to functions
- Return objects from functions
- Create copy constructors
- Use friend functions
- Examine the structure and union
- Understand this
- Learn operator overloading fundamentals
- Overload binary operators
- Overload unary operators
- Overload operators using nonmember functions

This module continues the discussion of the class begun in Module 8. It examines a number of class-related topics, including overloading constructors, passing objects to functions, and returning objects. It also describes a special type of constructor, called the *copy constructor,* which is used when a copy of an object is needed. Next, friend functions are described, followed by structures and unions, and the **this** keyword. The module concludes with a discussion of operator overloading, one of C++'s most exciting features.

Overloading Constructors

Although they perform a unique service, constructors are not much different from other types of functions, and they too can be overloaded. To overload a class' constructor, simply declare the various forms it will take. For example, the following program defines three constructors:

```
// Overload the constructor.

#include <iostream>
using namespace std;

class Sample {
public:
  int x;
  int y;

  // Overload the default constructor.
  Sample() { x = y = 0; }

  // Constructor with one parameter.
  Sample(int i) { x = y = i; }          Overload the Sample constructor.

  // Constructor with two parameters.
  Sample(int i, int j) { x = i; y = j; }
};

int main() {
  Sample t;          // invoke default constructor
  Sample t1(5);      // use Sample(int)
  Sample t2(9, 10);  // use Sample(int, int)
```

```
    cout << "t.x: " << t.x << ", t.y: " << t.y << "\n";
    cout << "t1.x: " << t1.x << ", t1.y: " << t1.y << "\n";
    cout << "t2.x: " << t2.x << ", t2.y: " << t2.y << "\n";

    return 0;
}
```

The output is shown here:

```
t.x: 0, t.y: 0
t1.x: 5, t1.y: 5
t2.x: 9, t2.y: 10
```

This program creates three constructors. The first is a parameterless constructor, which initializes both **x** and **y** to zero. This constructor becomes the default constructor, replacing the default constructor supplied automatically by C++. The second takes one parameter, assigning its value to both **x** and **y**. The third constructor takes two parameters, initializing **x** and **y** individually.

Overloaded constructors are beneficial for several reasons. First, they add flexibility to the classes that you create, allowing an object to be constructed in a variety of ways. Second, they offer convenience to the user of your class by allowing an object to be constructed in the most natural way for the given task. Third, by defining both a default constructor and a parameterized constructor, you allow both initialized and uninitialized objects to be created.

Assigning Objects

If both objects are of the same type (that is, both are objects of the same class), then one object can be assigned to another. It is not sufficient for the two classes to simply be physically similar—their type names must be the same. By default, when one object is assigned to another, a bitwise copy of the first object's data is assigned to the second. Thus, after the assignment, the two objects will be identical, but separate. The following program demonstrates object assignment:

```
// Demonstrate object assignment.

#include <iostream>
using namespace std;
```

```
class Test {
  int a, b;
public:
  void setab(int i, int j) { a = i, b = j; }
  void showab() {
    cout << "a is " << a << '\n';
    cout << "b is " << b << '\n';
  }
};

int main()
{
  Test ob1, ob2;

  ob1.setab(10, 20);
  ob2.setab(0, 0);
  cout << "ob1 before assignment: \n";
  ob1.showab();
  cout << "ob2 before assignment: \n";
  ob2.showab();
  cout << '\n';

  ob2 = ob1; // assign ob1 to ob2        ◄────────── Assign one object to another.

  cout << "ob1 after assignment: \n";
  ob1.showab();
  cout << "ob2 after assignment: \n";
  ob2.showab();
  cout << '\n';

  ob1.setab(-1, -1); // change ob1

  cout << "ob1 after changing ob1: \n";
  ob1.showab();
  cout << "ob2 after changing ob1: \n";
  ob2.showab();

  return 0;
}
```

This program displays the following output:

```
ob1 before assignment:
a is 10
```

```
b is 20
ob2 before assignment:
a is 0
b is 0

ob1 after assignment:
a is 10
b is 20
ob2 after assignment:
a is 10
b is 20

ob1 after changing ob1:
a is -1
b is -1
ob2 after changing ob1:
a is 10
b is 20
```

As the program shows, the assignment of one object to another creates two objects that contain the same values. The two objects are otherwise still completely separate. Thus, a subsequent modification of one object's data has no effect on that of the other. However, you will need to watch for side effects, which may still occur. For example, if an object A contains a pointer to some other object B, then when a copy of A is made, the copy will also contain a field that points to B. Thus, changing B will affect both objects. In situations like this, you may need to bypass the default bitwise copy by defining a custom assignment operator for the class, as explained later in this module.

Passing Objects to Functions

An object can be passed to a function in the same way as any other data type. Objects are passed to functions using the normal C++ call-by-value parameter-passing convention. This means that a *copy* of the object, not the actual object itself, is passed to the function. Therefore, changes made to the object inside the function do not affect the object used as the argument to the function. The following program illustrates this point:

```
// Pass an object to a function.
```

9

```
#include <iostream>
using namespace std;

class MyClass {
  int val;
public:
  MyClass(int i) {
    val = i;
  }

  int getval() { return val; }
  void setval(int i) { val = i; }
};

void display(MyClass ob)          ◄──────  display( ) takes a MyClass
{                                           object as a parameter.
  cout << ob.getval() << '\n';
}

void change(MyClass ob)
{
  ob.setval(100); // no effect on argument

  cout << "Value of ob inside change(): ";
  display(ob);
}

int main()
{
  MyClass a(10);

  cout << "Value of a before calling change(): ";
  display(a);          ◄────────  Pass a MyClass object to display( ).

  change(a);
  cout << "Value of a after calling change(): ";
  display(a);

  return 0;
}
```

The output is shown here:

```
Value of a before calling change(): 10
Value of ob inside change(): 100
Value of a after calling change(): 10
```

As the output shows, changing the value of **ob** inside **change( )** has no effect on a inside **main( )**.

Constructors, Destructors, and Passing Objects

Although passing simple objects as arguments to functions is a straightforward procedure, some rather unexpected events occur that relate to constructors and destructors. To understand why, consider this short program:

```cpp
// Constructors, destructors, and passing objects.

#include <iostream>
using namespace std;

class MyClass {
  int val;
public:
  MyClass(int i) {
    val = i;
    cout << "Inside constructor\n";
  }

  ~MyClass() { cout << "Destructing\n"; }
  int getval() { return val; }
};

void display(MyClass ob)
{
  cout << ob.getval() << '\n';
}

int main()
{
  MyClass a(10);

  cout << "Before calling display().\n";
  display(a);
  cout << "After display() returns.\n";

  return 0;
}
```

9

This program produces the following unexpected output:

```
Inside constructor
Before calling display().
10
Destructing
After display() returns.
Destructing  ◄─────────────  Notice the second "Destructing" message.
```

As you can see, there is one call to the constructor (which occurs when **a** is created), but there are *two* calls to the destructor. Let's see why this is the case.

When an object is passed to a function, a copy of that object is made. (And this copy becomes the parameter in the function.) This means that a new object comes into existence. When the function terminates, the copy of the argument (that is, the parameter) is destroyed. This raises two fundamental questions: First, is the object's constructor called when the copy is made? Second, is the object's destructor called when the copy is destroyed? The answers may, at first, surprise you.

When a copy of an argument is made during a function call, the normal constructor is *not* called. Instead, the object's *copy constructor* is called. A copy constructor defines how a copy of an object is made. (Later in this module you will see how to create a copy constructor.) However, if a class does not explicitly define a copy constructor, then C++ provides one by default. The default copy constructor creates a *bitwise* (that is, identical) copy of the object. The reason a bitwise copy is made is easy to understand if you think about it. Since a normal constructor is used to initialize some aspect of an object, it must not be called to make a copy of an already existing object. Such a call would alter the contents of the object. When passing an object to a function, you want to use the current state of the object, not its initial state.

However, when the function terminates and the copy of the object used as an argument is destroyed, the destructor function *is* called. This is necessary because the object has gone out of scope. This is why the preceding program had two calls to the destructor. The first was when the parameter to **display( )** went out of scope. The second is when **a** inside **main( )** was destroyed when the program ended.

To summarize: When a copy of an object is created to be used as an argument to a function, the normal constructor is not called. Instead, the default copy constructor makes a bit-by-bit identical copy. However, when the copy is destroyed (usually by going out of scope when the function returns), the destructor is called.

Passing Objects by Reference

Another way that you can pass an object to a function is by reference. In this case, a reference to the object is passed, and the function operates directly on the object used as an argument. Thus, changes made to the parameter *will* affect the argument, and passing an object by reference is not applicable to all situations. However, in the cases in which it is, two benefits result. First, because only an address to the object is being passed rather than the entire object, passing an object by reference can be much faster and more efficient than passing an object by value. Second, when an object is passed by reference, no new object comes into existence, so no time is wasted constructing or destructing a temporary object.

Here is an example that illustrates passing an object by reference:

```
// Constructors, destructors, and passing objects.

#include <iostream>
using namespace std;

class MyClass {
  int val;
public:
  MyClass(int i) {
    val = i;
    cout << "Inside constructor\n";
  }

  ~MyClass() { cout << "Destructing\n"; }
  int getval() { return val; }
  void setval(int i) { val = i; }
};

void display(MyClass &ob)          Here, the **MyClass** object is
{                                  passed by reference.
  cout << ob.getval() << '\n';
}
```

9

```
void change(MyClass &ob)
{
  ob.setval(100);
}

int main()
{
  MyClass a(10);

  cout << "Before calling display().\n";
  display(a);
  cout << "After display() returns.\n";

  change(a);
  cout << "After calling change().\n";
  display(a);

  return 0;
}
```

The output is

```
Inside constructor
Before calling display().
10
After display() returns.
After calling change().
100
Destructing
```

In this program, both **display( )** and **change( )** use reference parameters. Thus, the address of the argument, not a copy of the argument, is passed, and the functions operate directly on the argument. For example, when **change( )** is called, **a** is passed by reference. Thus, changes made to the parameter **ob** in **change( )** affect **a** in **main( )**. Also, notice that only one call to the constructor and one call to the destructor is made. This is because only one object, **a**, is created and destroyed. No temporary objects are needed by the program.

A Potential Problem When Passing Objects

Even when objects are passed to functions by means of the normal call-by-value parameter-passing mechanism, which, in theory, protects and insulates the calling argument, it is still possible for a side effect to occur that may affect, or even damage, the object used as an argument. For example, if an object allocates some system resource (such as memory) when it is created and frees that resource when it is destroyed, then its local copy inside the function will free that same resource when its destructor is called. This is a problem because the original object is still using this resource. This situation usually results in the original object being damaged.

One solution to this problem is to pass an object by reference, as shown in the preceding section. In this case, no copy of the object is made, and thus, no object is destroyed when the function returns. As explained, passing objects by reference can also speed up function calls, because only the address of the object is being passed. However, passing an object by reference may not be applicable to all cases. Fortunately, a more general solution is available: you can create your own version of the copy constructor. Doing so lets you define precisely how a copy of an object is made, allowing you to avoid the type of problems just described. However, before examining the copy constructor, let's look at another, related situation that can also benefit from a copy constructor.

Returning Objects

Just as objects can be passed to functions, functions can return objects. To return an object, first declare the function as returning a class type. Second, return an object of that type using the normal **return** statement. The following program has a member function called **mkBigger( )**. It returns an object that gives **val** a value twice as large as the invoking object.

9

```
// Returning objects.

#include <iostream>
using namespace std;

class MyClass {
  int val;
public:
  // Normal constructor.
  MyClass(int i) {
    val = i;
    cout << "Inside constructor\n";
```

```
    }

    ~MyClass() {
        cout << "Destructing\n";
    }

    int getval() { return val; }

    // Return an object.
    MyClass mkBigger() {              ◄──────  mkBigger( ) returns a MyClass object.
        MyClass o(val * 2);

        return o;
    }
};

void display(MyClass ob)
{
    cout << ob.getval() << '\n';
}

int main()
{
    cout << "Before constructing a.\n";
    MyClass a(10);
    cout << "After constructing a.\n\n";

    cout << "Before call to display().\n";
    display(a);
    cout << "After display() returns.\n\n";

    cout << "Before call to mkBigger().\n";
    a = a.mkBigger();
    cout << "After mkBigger() returns.\n\n";

    cout << "Before second call to display().\n";
    display(a);
    cout << "After display() returns.\n\n";

    return 0;
}
```

The following output is produced:

```
Before constructing a.
Inside constructor
After constructing a.

Before call to display().
10
Destructing
After display() returns.

Before call to mkBigger().
Inside constructor
Destructing
Destructing ←──────────────  Notice the second "Destructing" message.
After mkBigger() returns.

Before second call to display().
20
Destructing
After display() returns.

Destructing
```

In this example, **mkBigger( )** creates a local object called **o** that has a **val** value twice that of the invoking object. This object is then returned by the function and assigned to **a** inside **main( )**. Then **o** is destroyed, causing the first "Destructing" message to be displayed. But what explains the second call to the destructor?

When an object is returned by a function, a temporary object is automatically created, which holds the return value. It is this object that is actually returned by the function. After the value has been returned, this object is destroyed. This is why the output shows a second "Destructing" message just before the message "After mkBigger( ) returns." This is the temporary object being destroyed.

As was the case when passing an object to a function, there is a potential problem when returning an object from a function. The destruction of this temporary object may cause unexpected side effects in some situations. For example, if the object returned by the function has a destructor that releases a resource (such as memory or a file handle), that resource will be freed even though the object that is assigned the return value is still using it. The solution to this type of problem involves the use of a copy constructor, which is described next.

9

One last point: It is possible for a function to return an object by reference, but you need to be careful that the object being referenced does not go out of scope when the function is terminated.

1-Minute Drill

● Constructors cannot be overloaded. True or false?

● When an object is passed by value to a function, a copy is made. Is this copy destroyed when the function returns?

● When an object is returned by a function, a temporary object is created that contains the return value. True or false?

Creating and Using a Copy Constructor

As earlier examples have shown, when an object is passed to or returned from a function, a copy of the object is made. By default, the copy is a bitwise clone of the original object. This default behavior is often acceptable, but in cases where it is not, you can control precisely how a copy of an object is made by explicitly defining a copy constructor for the class. A copy constructor is a special type of overloaded constructor that is automatically invoked when a copy of an object is required.

To begin, let's review why you might need to explicitly define a copy constructor. When an object is passed to a function, a bitwise (that is, exact) copy of that object is made and given to the function parameter that receives the object. However, there are cases in which this identical copy is not desirable. For example, if the object uses a resource, such as an open file, then the copy will use the *same* resource as does the original object. Therefore, if the copy makes a change to that resource, it will be changed for the original object, too! Furthermore, when the function terminates, the copy will be destroyed, thus causing its destructor to be called. This may also have undesired effects on the original object.

● False, constructors can be overloaded.
● Yes, the copy of the argument is destroyed when the function returns.
● True, the return value of a function is a temporary object.

A similar situation occurs when an object is returned by a function. The compiler will generate a temporary object that holds a copy of the value returned by the function. (This is done automatically and is beyond your control.) This temporary object goes out of scope once the value is returned to the calling routine, causing the temporary object's destructor to be called. However, if the destructor destroys something needed by the calling routine, trouble will follow.

At the core of these problems is the creation of a bitwise copy of the object. To prevent them, you need to define precisely what occurs when a copy of an object is made so that you can avoid undesired side effects. The way you accomplish this is by creating a copy constructor.

Before we explore the use of the copy constructor, it is important for you to understand that C++ defines two distinct types of situations in which the value of one object is given to another. The first situation is assignment. The second situation is initialization, which can occur three ways:

- When one object explicitly initializes another, such as in a declaration
- When a copy of an object is made to be passed to a function
- When a temporary object is generated (most commonly, as a return value)

The copy constructor applies only to initializations. The copy constructor does not apply to assignments.

The most common form of copy constructor is shown here:

```
classname (const classname &obj) {
  // body of constructor
}
```

Here, *obj* is a reference to an object that is being used to initialize another object. For example, assuming a class called **MyClass**, and **y** as an object of type **MyClass**, then the following statements would invoke the **MyClass** copy constructor:

```
MyClass x = y; // y explicitly initializing x
func1(y);      // y passed as a parameter
y = func2();   // y receiving a returned object
```

In the first two cases, a reference to **y** would be passed to the copy constructor. In the third, a reference to the object returned by **func2( )** would be passed to the copy constructor. Thus, when an object is passed as a parameter, returned by a function, or used in an initialization, the copy constructor is called to duplicate the object.

Remember, the copy constructor is not called when one object is assigned to another. For example, the following sequence will not invoke the copy constructor:

```
MyClass x;
MyClass y;

x = y; // copy constructor not used here.
```

Again, assignments are handled by the assignment operator, not the copy constructor.

The following program demonstrates a copy constructor:

```
/* Copy constructor invoked when passing an object
   to a function. */

#include <iostream>
using namespace std;

class MyClass {
  int val;
  int copynumber;
public:
  // Normal constructor.
  MyClass(int i) {
    val = i;
    copynumber = 0;
    cout << "Inside normal constructor\n";
  }

  // Copy constructor
  MyClass(const MyClass &o) {        ◄────  This is the MyClass copy constructor.
    val = o.val;
    copynumber = o.copynumber + 1;
    cout << "Inside copy constructor.\n";
  }

  ~MyClass() {
    if(copynumber == 0)
```

```
             cout << "Destructing original.\n";
         else
             cout << "Destructing copy " <<
                     copynumber << "\n";
     }

   int getval() { return val; }
};

void display(MyClass ob)
{
   cout << ob.getval() << '\n';
}

int main()
{
   MyClass a(10);

   display(a);
```

The copy constructor is called when **a** is passed to **display( )**.

```
   return 0;
}
```

This program displays the following output:

```
Inside normal constructor
Inside copy constructor.
10
Destructing copy 1
Destructing original.
```

Here is what occurs when the program is run: When **a** is created inside **main( )**, the value of its **copynumber** is set to 0 by the normal constructor. Next, **a** is passed to **ob** of **display( )**. When this occurs, the copy constructor is called, and a copy of **a** is created. In the process, the copy constructor increments the value of **copynumber**. When **display( )** returns, **ob** goes out of scope. This causes its destructor to be called. Finally, when **main( )** returns, **a** goes out of scope.

You might want to try experimenting with the preceding program a bit. For example, create a function that returns a **MyClass** object, and observe when the copy constructor is called.

1-Minute Drill

● When the default copy constructor is used, how is a copy of an object made?

● A copy constructor is called when one object is assigned to another. True or false?

● Why might you need to explicitly define a copy constructor for a class?

Friend Functions

In general, only other members of a class have access to the private members of the class. However, it is possible to allow a nonmember function access to the private members of a class by declaring it as a *friend* of the class. To make a function a friend of a class, you include its prototype in the **public** section of the class declaration and precede it with the **friend** keyword. For example, in this fragment, **frnd( )** is declared to be a friend of the class **MyClass**:

```
class MyClass {
  // ...
public:
  friend void frnd(MyClass ob);
  // ...
};
```

As you can see, the keyword **friend** precedes the rest of the prototype. A function can be a friend of more than one class.

Here is a short example that uses a friend function to determine if the private fields of **MyClass** have a common denominator:

```
// Demonstrate a friend function.

#include <iostream>
using namespace std;

class MyClass {
```

● The default copy constructor makes a bitwise (that is, identical) copy.
● False, a copy constructor is not called when one object is assigned to another.
● You will need to explicitly define a copy constructor when a copy of an object must not be identical to the original, perhaps to prevent the original object from being harmed.

```
   int a, b;
public:
   MyClass(int i, int j) { a=i; b=j; }
   friend int comDenom(MyClass x); // a friend function
};

// Notice that comDenom() is a not a member function of any class.
int comDenom(MyClass x)
{
   /* Because comDenom() is a friend of MyClass, it can
      directly access a and b. */
   int max = x.a < x.b ? x.a : x.b;

   for(int i=2; i <= max; i++)
     if((x.a%i)==0 && (x.b%i)==0) return i;

   return 0;
}

int main()
{
   MyClass n(18, 111);

   if(comDenom(n))
     cout << "Common denominator is " <<
             comDenom(n) << "\n";
   else
     cout << "No common denominator.\n";

   return 0;
}
```

> **comDenom( )** is a friend of **MyClass**.

> **comDenom( )** is called normally without the use of an object or the dot operator.

9

In this example, the **comDenom( )** function is not a member of **MyClass**. However, it still has full access to the private members of **MyClass**. Specifically, it can access **x.a** and **x.b**. Notice also that **comDenom( )** is called normally—that is, not in conjunction with an object and the dot operator. Since it is not a member function, it does not need to be qualified with an object's name. (In fact, it *cannot* be qualified with an object.) Typically, a friend function is passed one or more objects of the class for which it is a friend, as is the case with **comDenom( )**.

While there is nothing gained by making **comDenom( )** a friend rather than a member function of **MyClass**, there are some circumstances in which friend functions are quite valuable. First, friends can be useful for overloading certain types of operators, as described later in this module. Second, friend functions simplify the creation of some types of I/O functions, as described in Module 11.

The third reason that friend functions may be desirable is that, in some cases, two or more classes can contain members that are interrelated relative to other parts of your program. For example, imagine two different classes called **Cube** and **Cylinder** that define the characteristics of a cube and cylinder, of which one of these characteristics is the color of the object. To enable the color of a cube and cylinder to be easily compared, you can define a friend function that compares the color component of each object, returning true if the colors match and false if they differ. The following program illustrates this concept:

```
// Friend functions can be shared by two or more classes.

#include <iostream>
using namespace std;

class Cylinder; // a forward declaration

enum colors { red, green, yellow };

class Cube {
  colors color;                                    sameColor( ) is a friend of Cube.
public:
  Cube(colors c) { color = c; }
  friend bool sameColor(Cube x, Cylinder y);
  // ...
};

class Cylinder {
  colors color;
public:
  Cylinder(colors c) { color= c; }
  friend bool sameColor(Cube x, Cylinder y);       sameColor( ) is also a
  // ...                                            friend of Cylinder.
};

bool sameColor(Cube x, Cylinder y)
{
  if(x.color == y.color) return true;
  else return false;
}
```

```
int main()
{
  Cube cube1(red);
  Cube cube2(green);
  Cylinder cyl(green);


  if(sameColor(cube1, cyl))
    cout << "cube1 and cyl are the same color.\n";
  else
    cout << "cube1 and cyl are different colors.\n";

  if(sameColor(cube2, cyl))
    cout << "cube2 and cyl are the same color.\n";
  else
    cout << "cube2 and cyl are different colors.\n";

  return 0;
}
```

The output produced by this program is shown here:

```
cube1 and cyl are different colors.
cube2 and cyl are the same color.
```

9

Notice that this program uses a *forward declaration* (also called a *forward reference*) for the class **Cylinder**. This is necessary because the declaration of **sameColor( )** inside **Cube** refers to **Cylinder** before it is declared. To create a forward declaration to a class, simply use the form shown in this program.

A friend of one class can be a member of another. For example, here is the preceding program rewritten so that **sameColor( )** is a member of **Cube**. Notice the use of the scope resolution operator when declaring **sameColor( )** to be a friend of **Cylinder**.

```
/* A function can be a member of one class and
   a friend of another. */

#include <iostream>
using namespace std;

class Cylinder; // a forward declaration
```

```
enum colors { red, green, yellow };

class Cube {
 colors color;
public:
   Cube(colors c) { color= c; }
   bool sameColor(Cylinder y);
   // ...
};

class Cylinder {
 colors color;
public:
   Cylinder(colors c) { color = c; }
   friend bool Cube::sameColor(Cube x, Cylinder y);
   // ...
};

bool Cube::sameColor(Cylinder y) {
   if(color == y.color) return true;
   else return false;
}

int main()
{
   Cube cube1(red);
   Cube cube2(green);
   Cylinder cyl(green);

   if(cube1.sameColor(cyl))
     cout << "cube1 and cyl are the same color.\n";
   else
     cout << "cube1 and cyl are different colors.\n";

   if(cube2.sameColor(cyl))
     cout << "cube2 and cyl are the same color.\n";
   else
     cout << "cube2 and cyl are different colors.\n";

   return 0;
}
```

sameColor( ) is now a member of **Cube**.

Cube::sameColor( ) is a friend of **Cylinder**.

Since **sameColor( )** is a member of **Cube**, it can access the **color** variable of objects of type **Cube** directly. Thus, only objects of type **Cylinder** need to be passed to **sameColor( )**.

1-Minute Drill

● What is a friend function? What keyword declares one?

● Is a friend function called on an object using the dot operator?

● Can a friend of one class be a member of another?

Structures and Unions

In addition to the keyword **class**, C++ gives you two other ways to create a class type. First, you can create a *structure*. Second, you can create a *union*. Each is examined here.

Structures

Structures are inherited from the C language and are declared using the keyword **struct**. A **struct** is syntactically similar to a **class**, and both create a class type. In the C language, a **struct** can contain only data members, but this limitation does not apply to C++. In C++, the **struct** is essentially just an alternative way to specify a class. In fact, in C++ the only difference between a **class** and a **struct** is that by default all members are public in a **struct** and private in a **class**. In all other respects, structures and classes are equivalent.

Here is an example of a structure:

9

```
#include <iostream>
using namespace std;

struct Test {
  int get_i() { return i; } // these are public
  void put_i(int j) { i = j; } // by default        Structure members
private:                                             are public by default.
  int i;
};
```

● A friend function is a nonmember function that has access to the private members of the class for which it is a friend. A friend is declared using **friend**.

● No, a friend function is called like a normal, nonmember function.

● Yes, a friend of one class can be a member of another.

```
int main()
{
  Test s;

  s.put_i(10);
  cout << s.get_i();

  return 0;
}
```

This simple program defines a structure type called **Test**, in which **get_i( )** and **put_i( )** are public and **i** is private. Notice the use of the keyword **private** to specify the private elements of the structure.

The following program shows an equivalent program that uses a **class** instead of a **struct**:

```
#include <iostream>
using namespace std;

class Test {
  int i; // private by default
public:
  int get_i() { return i; }
  void put_i(int j) { i = j; }
};

int main()
{
  Test s;

  s.put_i(10);
  cout << s.get_i();

  return 0;
}
```

For the most part, C++ programmers will use a **class** to define the form of an object that contains member functions and will use a **struct** in its more traditional role to create objects that contain only data members. Sometimes the acronym "POD" is used to describe a structure that does not contain member functions. It stands for "plain old data."

Unions

A *union* is a memory location that is shared by two or more different variables. A union is created using the keyword **union**, and its declaration is similar to that of a structure, as shown in this example:

```
union utype {
  short int i;
  char ch;
} ;
```

Ask the Expert

Question: Since **struct** and **class** are so similar, why does C++ have both?

Answer: On the surface, there is seeming redundancy in the fact that both structures and classes have virtually identical capabilities. Many newcomers to C++ wonder why this apparent duplication exists. In fact, it is not uncommon to hear the suggestion that either the keyword **class** or **struct** is unnecessary.

The answer to this line of reasoning is rooted in the desire to keep C++ compatible with C. As C++ is currently defined, a standard C structure is also a completely valid C++ structure. In C, which has no concept of public or private structure members, all structure members are public by default. This is why members of C++ structures are public (rather than private) by default. Since the **class** keyword is expressly designed to support encapsulation, it makes sense that its members are private by default. Thus, to avoid incompatibility with C on this issue, the structure default could not be altered, so a new keyword was added. However, in the long term, there is a more important reason for the separation of structures and classes. Because **class** is an entity syntactically separate from **struct**, the definition of a class is free to evolve in ways that may not be syntactically compatible with C-like structures. Since the two are separated, the future direction of C++ will not be encumbered by concerns of compatibility with C-like structures.

9

This defines a **union** in which a **short int** value and a **char** value share the same location. Be clear on one point: It is *not possible* to have this union hold *both* an integer and a character *at the same time*, because **i** and **ch** overlay each other. Instead, your program can treat the information in the union as an integer or as a character at any time. Thus, a union gives you two or more ways to view the same piece of data.

You can declare a union variable by placing its name at the end of the **union** declaration, or by using a separate declaration statement. For example, to declare a union variable called **u_var** of type **utype**, you would write

```
utype u_var;
```

In **u_var**, both the short integer **i** and the character **ch** share the same memory location. (Of course, **i** occupies two bytes and **ch** uses only one.) Figure 9-1 shows how **i** and **ch** both share the same address.

As far as C++ is concerned, a union is essentially a class in which all elements are stored in the same location. In fact, a union defines a class type. A union can contain constructor and destructor functions as well as member functions. Because the union is inherited from C, its members are public, not private, by default.

Here is a program that uses a union to display the characters that comprise the low- and high-order bytes of a short integer (assuming short integers are two bytes):

```cpp
// Demonstrate a union.

#include <iostream>
using namespace std;

union u_type {
  u_type(short int a) { i = a; };
  u_type(char x, char y) { ch[0] = x; ch[1] = y; }

  void showchars(){
    cout << ch[0] << " ";
    cout << ch[1] << "\n";
  }
```

```
  short int i;
  char ch[2];
};

int main()
{
  u_type u(1000);
  u_type u2('X', 'Y');

  cout << "u as integer: ";
  cout << u.i << "\n";
  cout << "u as chars: ";
  u.showchars();

  cout << "u2 as integer: ";
  cout << u2.i << "\n";
  cout << "u2 as chars: ";
  u2.showchars();

  return 0;
}
```

> Union data members share the same memory.

> The data in a **u_type** object can be viewed as a short integer or as two characters.

The output is shown here:

```
u as integer: 1000
u as chars: è
u2 as integer: 22872
u2 as chars: X Y
```

As the output shows, using the **u_type** union, it is possible to view the same data two different ways.

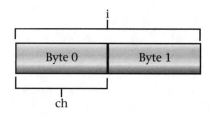

Figure 9-1   How i and ch of u_var both share the same address

Like the structure, the C++ union is derived from its C forerunner. However, in C, unions can include only data members; functions and constructors are not allowed. In C++, the union has the expanded capabilities of the class. But just because C++ gives unions greater power and flexibility does not mean that you have to use it. Often unions contain only data. However, in cases where you can encapsulate a union along with the routines that manipulate it, you will be adding considerable structure to your program by doing so.

There are several restrictions that must be observed when you use C++ unions. Most of these have to do with features of C++ that will be discussed later in this book, but they are mentioned here for completeness. First, a **union** cannot inherit a class. Further, a **union** cannot be a base class. A **union** cannot have virtual member functions. No **static** variables can be members of a **union**. A reference member cannot be used. A **union** cannot have as a member any object that overloads the = operator. Finally, no object can be a member of a **union** if the object has an explicit constructor or destructor.

Anonymous Unions

There is a special type of **union** in C++ called an *anonymous union*. An anonymous union does not include a type name, and no variables of the union can be declared. Instead, an anonymous union tells the compiler that its member variables are to share the same location. However, the variables themselves are referred to directly, without the normal dot operator syntax. For example, consider this program:

```
// Demonstrate an anonymous union.

#include <iostream>
#include <cstring>
using namespace std;

int main()
{
  // define anonymous union
  union {                          ← This is an anonymous union.
    long l;
    double d;
    char s[4];
  } ;

  // now, reference union elements directly
```

```
    l = 100000;
    cout << l << " ";
    d = 123.2342;
    cout << d << " ";
    strcpy(s, "hi");
    cout << s;

    return 0;
}
```

The elements of an anonymous union are referred to directly.

As you can see, the elements of the union are referenced as if they had been declared as normal local variables. In fact, relative to your program, that is exactly how you will use them. Further, even though they are defined within a **union** declaration, they are at the same scope level as any other local variable within the same block. This implies that the names of the members of an anonymous union must not conflict with other identifiers known within the same scope.

All restrictions involving **union**s apply to anonymous ones, with these additions. First, the only elements contained within an anonymous union must be data. No member functions are allowed. Anonymous unions cannot contain **private** or **protected** elements. (The **protected** specifier is discussed in Module 10.) Finally, global anonymous unions must be specified as **static**.

The this Keyword

Before moving on to operator overloading, it is necessary to describe another C++ keyword: **this**. Each time a member function is invoked, it is automatically passed a pointer, called **this**, to the object on which it is called. The **this** pointer is an *implicit* parameter to all member functions. Therefore, inside a member function, **this** can be used to refer to the invoking object.

As you know, a member function can directly access the private data of its class. For example, given this class:

```
class Test {
  int i;
  void f() { ... };
  // ...
};
```

9

inside f( ), the following statement can be used to assign **i** the value 10:

```
i = 10;
```

In actuality, the preceding statement is shorthand for this one:

```
this->i = 10;
```

To see how the **this** pointer works, examine the following short program:

```
// Use the "this" pointer.

#include <iostream>
using namespace std;

class Test {
  int i;
public:
  void load_i(int val) {
    this->i = val;        <--------------  Same as i = val;
  }
  int get_i() {
    return this->i;       <--------------  Same as return i;
  }
} ;

int main()
{
  Test o;

  o.load_i(100);
  cout << o.get_i();

  return 0;
}
```

This program displays the number **100**. This example is, of course, trivial, and no one would actually use the **this** pointer in this way. Soon, however, you will see why the **this** pointer is important to C++ programming.

One other point: Friend functions do not have a **this** pointer, because friends are not members of a class. Only member functions have a **this** pointer.

1-Minute Drill

● Can a **struct** contain member functions?

● What is the defining characteristic of a **union**?

● To what does **this** refer?

Operator Overloading

The remainder of this module explores one of C++'s most exciting and powerful features: *operator overloading*. In C++, operators can be overloaded relative to class types that you create. The principal advantage to overloading operators is that it allows you to seamlessly integrate new data types into your programming environment.

When you overload an operator, you define the meaning of an operator for a particular class. For example, a class that defines a linked list might use the + operator to add an object to the list. A class that implements a stack might use the + to push an object onto the stack. Another class might use the + operator in an entirely different way. When an operator is overloaded, none of its original meaning is lost. It is simply that a new operation, relative to a specific class, is defined. Therefore, overloading the + to handle a linked list, for example, does not cause its meaning relative to integers (that is, addition) to be changed.

Operator overloading is closely related to function overloading. To overload an operator, you must define what the operation means relative to the class to which it is applied. To do this, you create an **operator** function. The general form of an **operator** function is

```
type classname::operator#(arg-list)
{
  // operations
}
```

Here, the operator that you are overloading is substituted for the #, and *type* is the type of value returned by the specified operation. Although it can be of any

9

● Yes, a **struct** can contain member functions.
● The data members of a **union** all share the same memory.
● **this** is a pointer to the object on which a member function was called.

type you choose, the return value is often of the same type as the class for which the operator is being overloaded. This correlation facilitates the use of the overloaded operator in compound expressions. The specific nature of *arg-list* is determined by several factors, described in the sections that follow.

Operator functions can be either members or nonmembers of a class. Nonmember operator functions are often friend functions of the class, however. Although similar, there are some differences between the way a member operator function is overloaded and the way a nonmember operator function is overloaded. Each approach is described here.

Note

Because C++ defines many operators, the topic of operator overloading is quite large, and it is not possible to describe every aspect of it in this book. For a comprehensive description of operator overloading, refer to my book *C++: The Complete Reference,* Osborne/McGraw-Hill.

Operator Overloading Using Member Functions

To begin our examination of member operator functions, let's start with a simple example. The following program creates a class called **ThreeD**, which maintains the coordinates of an object in three-dimensional space. This program overloads the + and the = operators relative to the **ThreeD** class. Examine it closely.

```
// Define + and = for the ThreeD class.

#include <iostream>
using namespace std;

class ThreeD {
  int x, y, z; // 3-D coordinates
public:
  ThreeD() { x = y = z = 0; }
  ThreeD(int i, int j, int k) { x = i; y = j; z = k; }

  ThreeD operator+(ThreeD op2); // op1 is implied
  ThreeD operator=(ThreeD op2); // op1 is implied

  void show() ;
```

```
};

// Overload +.
ThreeD ThreeD::operator+(ThreeD op2)          ◄——— Overload + for ThreeD.
{
  ThreeD temp;

  temp.x = x + op2.x; // These are integer additions
  temp.y = y + op2.y; // and the + retains its original
  temp.z = z + op2.z; // meaning relative to them.
  return temp;   ◄————    Return a new object. Leave
}                         arguments unchanged.

// Overload assignment.
ThreeD ThreeD::operator=(ThreeD op2)          ◄——— Overload = for ThreeD.
{
  x = op2.x; // These are integer assignments
  y = op2.y; // and the = retains its original
  z = op2.z; // meaning relative to them.
  return *this;  ◄————    Return the modified object.
}

// Show X, Y, Z coordinates.
void ThreeD::show()
{
  cout << x << ", ";
  cout << y << ", ";
  cout << z << "\n";
}

int main()
{
  ThreeD a(1, 2, 3), b(10, 10, 10), c;

  cout << "Original value of a: ";
  a.show();
  cout << "Original value of b: ";
  b.show();

  cout << "\n";

  c = a + b; // add a and b together
  cout << "Value of c after c = a + b: ";
```

9

```
    c.show();

    cout << "\n";

    c = a + b + c; // add a, b and c together
    cout << "Value of c after c = a + b + c: ";
    c.show();

    cout << "\n";

    c = b = a;  // demonstrate multiple assignment
    cout << "Value of c after c = b = a: ";
    c.show();
    cout << "Value of b after c = b = a: ";
    b.show();

    return 0;
}
```

This program produces the following output:

```
Original value of a: 1, 2, 3
Original value of b: 10, 10, 10

Value of c after c = a + b: 11, 12, 13

Value of c after c = a + b + c: 22, 24, 26

Value of c after c = b = a: 1, 2, 3
Value of b after c = b = a: 1, 2, 3
```

As you examined the program, you may have been surprised to see that both operator functions have only one parameter each, even though they overload binary operations. The reason for this apparent contradiction is that when a binary operator is overloaded using a member function, only one argument is explicitly passed to it. The other argument is implicitly passed using the **this** pointer. Thus, in the line

```
temp.x = x + op2.x;
```

the x refers to **this–>x**, which is the x associated with the object that invokes the operator function. In all cases, it is the object on the left side of an operation that causes the call to the operator function. The object on the right side is passed to the function.

In general, when you use a member function, no parameters are used when overloading a unary operator, and only one parameter is required when overloading a binary operator. (You cannot overload the ternary ? operator.) In either case, the object that invokes the operator function is implicitly passed via the **this** pointer.

To understand how operator overloading works, let's examine the preceding program carefully, beginning with the overloaded operator +. When two objects of type **ThreeD** are operated on by the + operator, the magnitudes of their respective coordinates are added together, as shown in **operator+( )**. Notice, however, that this function does not modify the value of either operand. Instead, an object of type **ThreeD**, which contains the result of the operation, is returned by the function. To understand why the + operation does not change the contents of either object, think about the standard arithmetic + operation as applied like this: 10 + 12. The outcome of this operation is 22, but neither 10 nor 12 is changed by it. Although there is no rule that prevents an overloaded + operator from altering the value of one of its operands, it is best for the actions of an overloaded operator to be consistent with its original meaning.

Notice that **operator+( )** returns an object of type **ThreeD**. Although the function could have returned any valid C++ type, the fact that it returns a **ThreeD** object allows the + operator to be used in compound expressions, such as **a+b+c**. Here, **a+b** generates a result that is of type **ThreeD**. This value can then be added to **c**. Had any other type of value been generated by **a+b**, such an expression would not work.

In contrast with the + operator, the assignment operator does, indeed, cause one of its arguments to be modified. (This is, after all, the very essence of assignment.) Since the **operator=( )** function is called by the object that occurs on the left side of the assignment, it is this object that is modified by the assignment operation. Most often, the return value of an overloaded assignment operator is the object on the left, after the assignment has been made. (This is in keeping with the traditional action of the = operator.) For example, to allow statements like

```
a = b = c = d;
```

it is necessary for **operator=( )** to return the object pointed to by **this**, which will be the object that occurs on the left side of the assignment statement. This allows a chain of assignments to be made. The assignment operation is one of the most important uses of the **this** pointer.

9

In the preceding program, it was not actually necessary to overload the = because the default assignment operator provided by C++ is adequate for the **ThreeD** class. (As explained earlier in this module, the default assignment operation is a bitwise copy.) The = was overloaded simply to show the proper procedure. In general, you need to overload the = only when the default bitwise copy cannot be used. Because the default = operator is sufficient for **ThreeD**, subsequent examples in this module will not overload it.

Order Matters

When overloading binary operators, remember that in many cases, the order of the operands does make a difference. For example, although A + B is commutative, A – B is not. (That is, A – B is not the same as B – A!) Therefore, when implementing overloaded versions of the noncommutative operators, you must remember which operand is on the left and which is on the right. For example, here is how to overload the minus for the **ThreeD** class:

```
// Overload subtraction.
ThreeD ThreeD::operator-(ThreeD op2)
{
  ThreeD temp;

  temp.x = x - op2.x;
  temp.y = y - op2.y;
  temp.z = z - op2.z;
  return temp;
}
```

Remember, it is the operand on the left that invokes the operator function. The operand on the right is passed explicitly.

Using Member Functions to Overload Unary Operators

You can also overload unary operators, such as ++, − −, or the unary − or +. As stated earlier, when a unary operator is overloaded by means of a member function, no object is explicitly passed to the operator function. Instead, the operation is performed on the object that generates the call to the function through the implicitly passed **this** pointer. For example, here is a program that defines the increment operation for objects of type **ThreeD**:

```
// Overload the ++ unary operator.

#include <iostream>
using namespace std;

class ThreeD {
  int x, y, z; // 3-D coordinates
public:
  ThreeD() { x = y = z = 0; }
  ThreeD(int i, int j, int k) {x = i; y = j; z = k; }

  ThreeD operator++(); // prefix version of ++

  void show() ;
} ;

// Overload the prefix version of ++.
ThreeD ThreeD::operator++()          Overload ++ for ThreeD.
{
  x++; // increment x, y, and z
  y++;
  z++;
  return *this;          Return the incremented object.
}

// Show X, Y, Z coordinates.
void ThreeD::show()
{
  cout << x << ", ";
  cout << y << ", ";
  cout << z << "\n";
}

int main()
{
  ThreeD a(1, 2, 3);

  cout << "Original value of a: ";
  a.show();
```

9

```
  ++a;  // increment a
  cout << "Value after ++a: ";
  a.show();

  return 0;
}
```

The output is shown here:

```
Original value of a: 1, 2, 3
Value after ++a: 2, 3, 4
```

As the output verifies, **operator++( )** increments each coordinate in the object and returns the modified object. Again, this is in keeping with the traditional meaning of the **++** operator.

As you know, the **++** and **– –** have both a prefix and a postfix form. For example, both

```
++x;
```

and

```
x++;
```

are valid uses of the increment operator. As the comments in the preceding program state, the **operator++( )** function defines the prefix form of **++** relative to the **ThreeD** class. However, it is possible to overload the postfix form as well. The prototype for the postfix form of the **++** operator relative to the **ThreeD** class is shown here:

```
ThreeD operator++(int notused);
```

The parameter **notused** is not used by the function and should be ignored. This parameter is simply a way for the compiler to distinguish between the prefix and postfix forms of the increment operator. (The postfix decrement uses the same approach.)

Here is one way to implement a postfix version of **++** relative to the **ThreeD** class:

```
// Overload the postfix version of ++.
ThreeD ThreeD::operator++(int notused)
```
◄——— Notice the **notused** parameter.

```
{
  ThreeD temp = *this; // save original value

  x++;  // increment x, y, and z
  y++;
  z++;
  return temp; // return original value
}
```

Notice that this function saves the current state of the operand using the statement

```
ThreeD temp = *this;
```

and then returns **temp**. Keep in mind that the normal meaning of a postfix increment is to first obtain the value of the operand, and then to increment the operand. Therefore, it is necessary to save the current state of the operand and return its original value, before it is incremented, rather than its modified value.

The following program implements both forms of the **++** operator:

```
// Demonstrate prefix and postfix ++.

#include <iostream>
using namespace std;

class ThreeD {
  int x, y, z; // 3-D coordinates
public:
  ThreeD() { x = y = z = 0; }
  ThreeD(int i, int j, int k) {x = i; y = j; z = k; }

  ThreeD operator++(); // prefix version of ++
  ThreeD operator++(int notused); // postfix version of ++

  void show() ;
};

// Overload the prefix version of ++.
ThreeD ThreeD::operator++()
{
  x++;  // increment x, y, and z
  y++;
  z++;
  return *this; // return altered value
```

9

```
}

// Overload the postfix version of ++.
ThreeD ThreeD::operator++(int notused)
{
  ThreeD temp = *this; // save original value

  x++; // increment x, y, and z
  y++;
  z++;
  return temp; // return original value
}

// Show X, Y, Z coordinates.
void ThreeD::show( )
{
  cout << x << ", ";
  cout << y << ", ";
  cout << z << "\n";
}

int main()
{
  ThreeD a(1, 2, 3);
  ThreeD b;

  cout << "Original value of a: ";
  a.show();

  cout << "\n";

  ++a; // prefix increment          Calls prefix increment function.
  cout << "Value after ++a: ";
  a.show();

  a++; // postfix increment          Calls postfix increment function.
  cout << "Value after a++: ";
  a.show();

  cout << "\n";

  b = ++a; // b receives a's value after increment
```

```
    cout << "Value of a after b = ++a: ";
    a.show();
    cout << "Value of b after b = ++a: ";
    b.show();

    cout << "\n";

    b = a++; // b receives a's value prior to increment
    cout << "Value of a after b = a++: ";
    a.show();
    cout << "Value of b after b = a++: ";
    b.show();

    return 0;
}
```

The output from the program is shown here:

```
Original value of a: 1, 2, 3

Value after ++a: 2, 3, 4
Value after a++: 3, 4, 5

Value of a after b = ++a: 4, 5, 6
Value of b after b = ++a: 4, 5, 6

Value of a after b = a++: 5, 6, 7
Value of b after b = a++: 4, 5, 6
```

9

Remember that if the **++** precedes its operand, the **operator++( )** is called. If it follows its operand, the **operator++(int notused)** function is called. This same approach is also used to overload the prefix and postfix decrement operator relative to any class. You might want to try defining the decrement operator relative to **ThreeD** as an exercise.

As a point of interest, early versions of C++ did not distinguish between the prefix and postfix forms of the increment or decrement operators. For these old versions, the prefix form of the operator function was called for both uses of the operator. When working on older C++ code, be aware of this possibility.

1-Minute Drill

● Operators must be overloaded relative to a class. True or false?

● How many parameters does a member operator function have for a binary operator?

● For a binary member operator function, the left operand is passed via _____.

Nonmember Operator Functions

You can overload an operator for a class by using a nonmember function, which is often a friend of the class. As you learned earlier, friend functions do not have a **this** pointer. Therefore, when a friend is used to overload an operator, both operands are passed explicitly when a binary operator is overloaded, and one operand is passed explicitly when a unary operator is overloaded. The only operators that cannot be overloaded using friend functions are =, ( ), [ ], and –>.

The following program uses a friend instead of a member function to overload the + operation for the **ThreeD** class:

```
// Use friend operator functions.

#include <iostream>
using namespace std;

class ThreeD {
  int x, y, z; // 3-D coordinates
public:
  ThreeD() { x = y = z = 0; }
  ThreeD(int i, int j, int k) { x = i; y = j; z = k; }

  friend ThreeD operator+(ThreeD op1, ThreeD op2);

  void show() ;
} ;

// The + is now a friend function.
ThreeD operator+(ThreeD op1, ThreeD op2)
```

Here, **operator+( )** is a friend of **ThreeD**. Notice that two parameters are required.

● True, an operator must be overloaded relative to a class.
● A binary member operator function has one parameter, which receives the right operand.
● For a binary member operator function, the left operand is passed via **this**.

```
{
  ThreeD temp;

  temp.x = op1.x + op2.x;
  temp.y = op1.y + op2.y;
  temp.z = op1.z+ op2.z;
  return temp;
}

// Show X, Y, Z coordinates.
void ThreeD::show()
{
  cout << x << ", ";
  cout << y << ", ";
  cout << z << "\n";
}

int main()
{
  ThreeD a(1, 2, 3), b(10, 10, 10), c;

  cout << "Original value of a: ";
  a.show();
  cout << "Original value of b: ";
  b.show();

  cout << "\n";

  c = a + b; // add a and b together
  cout << "Value of c after c = a + b: ";
  c.show();

  cout << "\n";

  c = a + b + c; // add a, b and c together
  cout << "Value of c after c = a + b + c: ";
  c.show();

  cout << "\n";

  c = b = a;  // demonstrate multiple assignment
  cout << "Value of c after c = b = a: ";
  c.show();
  cout << "Value of b after c = b = a: ";
```

```
  b.show();

  return 0;
}
```

The output is shown here:

```
Original value of a: 1, 2, 3
Original value of b: 10, 10, 10

Value of c after c = a + b: 11, 12, 13

Value of c after c = a + b + c: 22, 24, 26

Value of c after c = b = a: 1, 2, 3
Value of b after c = b = a: 1, 2, 3
```

As you can see by looking at **operator+( )**, now both operands are passed to it. The left operand is passed in **op1**, and the right operand in **op2**.

In many cases, there is no benefit to using a friend function instead of a member function when overloading an operator. However, there is one situation in which a friend function is quite useful: when you want an object of a built-in type to occur on the left side of a binary operation. To understand why, consider the following. As you know, a pointer to the object that invokes a member operator function is passed in **this**. In the case of a binary operator, it is the object on the left that invokes the function. This is fine, provided that the object on the left defines the specified operation. For example, assuming some object called **T**, which has assignment and integer addition defined for it, then this is a perfectly valid statement:

```
T = T + 10; // will work
```

Since the object **T** is on the left side of the + operator, it invokes its overloaded operator function, which (presumably) is capable of adding an integer value to some element of **T**. However, this statement won't work:

```
T = 10 + T; // won't work
```

The problem with this statement is that the object on the left of the + operator is an integer, a built-in type for which no operation involving an integer and an object of T's type is defined.

The solution to the preceding problem is to overload the + using two friend functions. In this case, the operator function is explicitly passed both arguments and is invoked like any other overloaded function, based upon the types of its arguments. One version of the + operator function handles *object + integer*, and the other handles *integer + object*. Overloading the + (or any other binary operator) using friend functions allows a built-in type to occur on the left or right side of the operator. The following program illustrates this technique. It defines two versions of **operator+( )** to objects of type **ThreeD**. Both add an integer value to each of **ThreeD**'s instance variables. The integer can be on either the left or right side of the operator.

```
// Overload for integer + object and object + integer.

#include <iostream>
using namespace std;

class ThreeD {
  int x, y, z; // 3-D coordinates
public:
  ThreeD() { x = y = z = 0; }
  ThreeD(int i, int j, int k) { x = i; y = j; z = k; }

  friend ThreeD operator+(ThreeD op1, int op2);
  friend ThreeD operator+(int op1, ThreeD op2);

  void show() ;
} ;
```

These allow ob + int and int + ob.

9

```
// This allows ThreeD + int
ThreeD operator+(ThreeD op1, int op2)
{
  ThreeD temp;

  temp.x = op1.x + op2;
  temp.y = op1.y + op2;
  temp.z = op1.z + op2;
  return temp;
}

// This allows int + ThreeD
ThreeD operator+(int op1, ThreeD op2)
{
  ThreeD temp;
```

```
  temp.x = op2.x + op1;
  temp.y = op2.y + op1;
  temp.z = op2.z + op1;
  return temp;
}

// Show X, Y, Z coordinates.
void ThreeD::show()
{
  cout << x << ", ";
  cout << y << ", ";
  cout << z << "\n";
}

int main()
{
  ThreeD a(1, 2, 3), b;

  cout << "Original value of a: ";
  a.show();

  cout << "\n";

  b = a + 10; // object + integer
  cout << "Value of b after b = a + 10: ";
  b.show();

  cout << "\n";

  b = 10 + a; // integer + object
  cout << "Value of b after b = 10 + a: ";
  b.show();

  return 0;
}
```

Here, the built-in type occurs on the left side of an addition.

The output is shown here:

```
Original value of a: 1, 2, 3

Value of b after b = a + 10: 11, 12, 13

Value of b after b = 10 + a: 11, 12, 13
```

Because the **operator+( )** function is overloaded twice, it can accommodate the two ways in which an integer and an object of type **ThreeD** can occur in the addition operation.

Using a Friend to Overload a Unary Operator

You can also overload a unary operator by using a friend function. However, if you are overloading the **++** or **− −**, you must pass the operand to the function as a reference parameter. Since a reference parameter is an implicit pointer to the argument, changes to the parameter *will* affect the argument. Using a reference parameter allows the function to increment or decrement the object used as an operand.

When a friend is used for overloading the increment or decrement operators, the prefix form takes one parameter (which is the operand). The postfix form takes two parameters. The second parameter is an integer, which is not used.

Here is the way to overload both forms of a friend **operator++( )** function for the **ThreeD** class:

```
/* Overload prefix ++ using a friend function.
   This requires the use of a reference parameter. */
ThreeD operator++(ThreeD &op1)
{
  op1.x++;
  op1.y++;
  op1.z++;
  return op1;
}

/* Overload postfix ++ using a friend function.
   This requires the use of a reference parameter. */
ThreeD operator++(ThreeD &op1, int notused)
{
  ThreeD temp = op1;

  op1.x++;
  op1.y++;
  op1.z++;
  return temp;
}
```

9

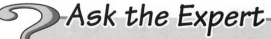

Ask the Expert

Question: Are there any special issues to consider when overloading the relational operators?

Answer: Overloading a relational operator, such as == or <, is a straightforward process. However, there is one small issue. As you know, an overloaded operator function often returns an object of the class for which it is overloaded. However, an overloaded relational operator typically returns **true** or **false**. This is in keeping with the normal usage of relational operators and allows the overloaded relational operators to be used in conditional expressions. The same rationale applies when overloading the logical operators.

To show you how an overloaded relational operator can be implemented, the following function overloads == relative to the ThreeD class:

```cpp
// Overload ==.
bool ThreeD::operator==(ThreeD op2)
{
  if((x == op2.x) && (y == op2.y) && (z == op2.z))
    return true;
  else
    return false;
}
```

Once **operator==( )** has been implemented, the following fragment is perfectly valid:

```cpp
ThreeD a(1, 1, 1), b(2, 2, 2);
// ...
if(a == b) cout << "a equals b\n";
else cout << "a does not equal b\n";
```

1-Minute Drill

● How many parameters does a nonmember binary operator function have?

● When using a nonmember operator function to overload the **++** operator, how must the operand be passed?

● One advantage to using friend operator functions is that it allows a built-in type (such as **int**) to be used as the left operand. True or false?

Operator Overloading Tips and Restrictions

The action of an overloaded operator as applied to the class for which it is defined need not bear any relationship to that operator's default usage, as applied to C++'s built-in types. For example, the **<<** and **>>** operators, as applied to **cout** and **cin**, have little in common with the same operators applied to integer types. However, for the purposes of the structure and readability of your code, an overloaded operator should reflect, when possible, the spirit of the operator's original use. For example, the **+** relative to **ThreeD** is conceptually similar to the **+** relative to integer types. There would be little benefit in defining the **+** operator relative to some class in such a way that it acts more the way you would expect the **||** operator, for instance, to perform. The central concept here is that although you can give an overloaded operator any meaning you like, for clarity it is best when its new meaning is related to its original meaning.

There are some restrictions to overloading operators. First, you cannot alter the precedence of any operator. Second, you cannot alter the number of operands required by the operator, although your operator function could choose to ignore an operand. Finally, except for the function call operator, operator functions cannot have default arguments.

Nearly all of the C++ operators can be overloaded. This includes specialized operators, such as the array indexing operator [ ], the function call operator ( ), and the **−>** operator. The only operators that you cannot overload are shown here:

. :: .* ?

The .* is a special-purpose operator whose use is beyond the scope of this book.

● A nonmember binary operator function has two parameters.
● When using a nonmember operator function to overload **++** operator, the operand must be passed by reference.
● True, using friend operator functions allows a built-in type (such as **int**) to be used as the left operand.

9

Project 9-1: Creating a Set Class

Operator overloading helps you create classes that can be fully integrated into the C++ programming environment. Consider this point: by defining the necessary operators, you enable a class type to be used in a program in just the same way as you would use a built-in type. You can act on objects of that class through operators and use objects of that class in expressions. To illustrate the creation and integration of a new class into the C++ environment, this project creates a class called **Set** that defines a set type.

Before we begin, it is important to understand precisely what we mean by a set. For the purposes of this project, a set is a collection of unique elements. That is, no two elements in any given set can be the same. The ordering of a set's members is irrelevant. Thus, the set

{ A, B, C }

is the same as the set

{ A, C, B }

A set can also be empty.

Sets support a number of operations. The ones that we will implement are

● Adding an element to a set

● Removing an element from a set

● Set union

● Set difference

Adding an element to a set and removing an element from a set are self-explanatory operations. The other two warrant some explanation.

The *union* of two sets is a set that contains all of the elements from both sets. (Of course, no duplicate elements are allowed.) We will use the + operator to perform a set union.

The *difference* between two sets is a set that contains those elements in the first set that are not part of the second set. We will use the – operator to perform a set difference. For example, given two sets S1 and S2, this statement removes the elements of S2 from S1, putting the result in S3:

S3 = S1 – S2

If S1 and S2 are the same, then S3 will be the null set.

The **Set** class will also include a function called **isMember( )**, which determines if a specified element is a member of a given set.

Of course, there are several other operations that can be performed on sets. Some are developed in the Mastery Check. Others you might find fun to try adding on your own.

For the sake of simplicity, the **Set** class stores sets of characters, but the same basic principles could be used to create a **Set** class capable of storing other types of elements.

Step-by-Step

1. Create a new file called **Set.cpp**.

2. Begin creating **Set** by specifying its class declaration, as shown here:

```cpp
const int MaxSize = 100;

class Set {
  int len; // number of members
  char members[MaxSize]; // this array holds the set

  /* The find() function is private because it
     is not used outside the Set class. */
  int Set::find(char ch); // find an element

public:

  // Construct a null set.
  Set() { len = 0; }

  // Return the number of elements in the set.
  int getLength() { return len; }

  void showset(); // display the set
  bool isMember(char ch);  // check for membership

  Set operator +(char ch); // add an element
  Set operator -(char ch); // remove an element

  Set operator +(Set ob2); // set union
  Set operator -(Set ob2); // set difference
};
```

9

Each set is stored in a **char** array referred to by **members**. The number of members actually in the set is stored in **len**. The maximum size of a set is **MaxSize**, which is set to 100. (You can increase this value if you work with larger sets.)

The **Set** constructor creates a *null set,* which is a set with no members. There is no need to create any other constructors, or to define an explicit copy constructor for the **Set** class, because the default bitwise copy is sufficient. The **getLength( )** function returns the value of **len**, which is the number of elements currently in the set.

3. Begin defining the member functions, starting with the private function **find( )**, as shown here:

```
/* Return the index of the element
   specified by ch, or -1 if not found. */
int Set::find(char ch) {
  int i;

  for(i=0; i < len; i++)
    if(members[i] == ch) return i;

  return -1;
}
```

This function determines if the element passed in **ch** is a member of the set. It returns the index of the element if it is found and –1 if the element is not part of the set. This function is private because it is not used outside the **Set** class. As explained earlier in this book, member functions can be private to their class. A private member function can be called only by other member functions in the class.

4. Add the **showset( )** function, as shown here:

```
// Show the set.
void Set::showset() {
  cout << "{ ";
  for(int i=0; i<len; i++)
    cout << members[i] << " ";

  cout << "}\n";
}
```

This function displays the contents of a set.

5. Add the **isMember( )** function, shown here, which determines if a character is a member of a set:

```
/* Return true if ch is a member of the set.
   Return false otherwise. */
bool Set::isMember(char ch) {
  if(find(ch) != -1) return true;
  return false;
}
```

This function calls **find( )** to determine if **ch** is a member of the invoking set. If it is, **isMember( )** returns **true**. Otherwise, it returns **false**.

6. Begin adding the set operators, beginning with set addition. To do this, overload + for objects of type **Set**, as shown here. This version adds an element to a set.

```
// Add a unique element to a set.
Set Set::operator +(char ch) {
  Set newset;

  if(len == MaxSize) {
    cout << "Set is full.\n";
    return *this; // return existing set
  }

  newset = *this; // duplicate the existing set

  // see if element already exists
  if(find(ch) == -1) { // if not found, then add
    // add new element to new set
    newset.members[newset.len] = ch;
    newset.len++;
  }
  return newset; // return updated set
}
```

9

This function bears some close examination. First, a new set is created, which will hold the contents of the original set plus the character specified by **ch**. Before the character in **ch** is added, a check is made to see if there is enough room in the set to hold another character. If there is room for the new element, the original set is assigned to **newset**. Next, the **find( )** function is called to determine if **ch** is already part of the set. If it is not, then **ch** is added and **len** is updated. In either case, **newset** is returned. Thus, the original set is untouched by this operation.

7. Overload **–** so that it removes an element from the set, as shown here:

```
// Remove an element from the set.
Set Set::operator -(char ch) {
  Set newset;
  int i = find(ch); // i will be -1 if element not found

  // copy and compress the remaining elements
  for(int j=0; j < len; j++)
    if(j != i) newset = newset + members[j];

  return newset;
}
```

This function starts by creating a new null set. Then, **find( )** is called to determine the index of **ch** within the original set. Recall that **find( )** returns –1 if **ch** is not a member. Next, the elements of the original set are added to the new set, except for the element whose index matches that returned by **find( )**. Thus, the resulting set contains all of the elements of the original set except for **ch**. If **ch** was not part of the original set to begin with, then the two sets are equivalent.

8. Overload the **+** and **–** again, as shown here. These versions implement set union and set difference.

```
// Set union.
Set Set::operator +(Set ob2) {
  Set newset = *this; // copy the first set

  // Add unique elements from second set.
  for(int i=0; i < ob2.len; i++)
    newset = newset + ob2.members[i];

  return newset; // return updated set
}

// Set difference.
Set Set::operator -(Set ob2) {
```

```
  Set newset = *this; // copy the first set

  // Subtract elements from second set.
  for(int i=0; i < ob2.len; i++)
    newset = newset - ob2.members[i];

  return newset; // return updated set
}
```

As you can see, these functions utilize the previously defined versions of the + and – operators to help perform their operations. In the case of set union, a new set is created that contains the elements of the first set. Then, the elements of the second set are added. Because the + operation only adds an element if it is not already part of the set, the resulting set is the union (without duplication) of the two sets. The set difference operator subtracts matching elements.

9. Here is the complete code for the **Set** class along with a **main( )** function that demonstrates it:

```
/*
   Project 9-1

   A set class for characters.
*/
#include <iostream>
using namespace std;

const int MaxSize = 100;

class Set {
  int len; // number of members
  char members[MaxSize]; // this array holds the set

  /* The find() function is private because it
     is not used outside the Set class. */
  int Set::find(char ch); // find an element

public:

  // Construct a null set.
  Set() { len = 0; }
```

9

```
  // Return the number of elements in the set.
  int getLength() { return len; }

  void showset(); // display the set
  bool isMember(char ch);  // check for membership

  Set operator +(char ch); // add an element
  Set operator -(char ch); // remove an element

  Set operator +(Set ob2); // set union
  Set operator -(Set ob2); // set difference
};

/* Return the index of the element
   specified by ch, or -1 if not found. */
int Set::find(char ch) {
  int i;

  for(i=0; i < len; i++)
    if(members[i] == ch) return i;

  return -1;
}

// Show the set.
void Set::showset() {
  cout << "{ ";
  for(int i=0; i<len; i++)
    cout << members[i] << " ";

  cout << "}\n";
}

/* Return true if ch is a member of the set.
   Return false otherwise. */
bool Set::isMember(char ch) {
  if(find(ch) != -1) return true;
  return false;
}

// Add a unique element to a set.
Set Set::operator +(char ch) {
  Set newset;
```

```
  if(len == MaxSize) {
    cout << "Set is full.\n";
    return *this; // return existing set
  }

  newset = *this; // duplicate the existing set

  // see if element already exists
  if(find(ch) == -1) { // if not found, then add
    // add new element to new set
    newset.members[newset.len] = ch;
    newset.len++;
  }
  return newset; // return updated set
}

// Remove an element from the set.
Set Set::operator -(char ch) {
  Set newset;
  int i = find(ch); // i will be -1 if element not found

  // copy and compress the remaining elements
  for(int j=0; j < len; j++)
    if(j != i) newset = newset + members[j];

  return newset;
}

// Set union.
Set Set::operator +(Set ob2) {
  Set newset = *this; // copy the first set

  // Add unique elements from second set.
  for(int i=0; i < ob2.len; i++)
    newset = newset + ob2.members[i];

  return newset; // return updated set
}

// Set difference.
Set Set::operator -(Set ob2) {
  Set newset = *this; // copy the first set

  // Subtract elements from second set.
```

9

```
  for(int i=0; i < ob2.len; i++)
    newset = newset - ob2.members[i];

  return newset; // return updated set
}

// Demonstrate the Set class.
int main() {
  // construct 10-element empty Set
  Set s1;
  Set s2;
  Set s3;

  s1 = s1 + 'A';
  s1 = s1 + 'B';
  s1 = s1 + 'C';

  cout << "s1 after adding A B C: ";
  s1.showset();

  cout << "\n";

  cout << "Testing for membership using isMember().\n";
  if(s1.isMember('B'))
    cout << "B is a member of s1.\n";
  else
    cout << "B is not a member of s1.\n";

  if(s1.isMember('T'))
    cout << "T is a member of s1.\n";
  else
    cout << "T is not a member of s1.\n";

  cout << "\n";

  s1 = s1 - 'B';
  cout << "s1 after s1 = s1 - 'B': ";
  s1.showset();

  s1 = s1 - 'A';
  cout << "s1 after s1 = s1 - 'A': ";
  s1.showset();

  s1 = s1 - 'C';
  cout << "s1 after a1 = s1 - 'C': ";
```

```
s1.showset();

cout << "\n";

s1 = s1 + 'A';
s1 = s1 + 'B';
s1 = s1 + 'C';
cout << "s1 after adding A B C: ";
s1.showset();

cout << "\n";

s2 = s2 + 'A';
s2 = s2 + 'X';
s2 = s2 + 'W';

cout << "s2 after adding A X W: ";
s2.showset();

cout << "\n";

s3 = s1 + s2;
cout << "s3 after s3 = s1 + s2: ";
s3.showset();

s3 = s3 - s1;
cout << "s3 after s3 - s1: ";
s3.showset();

cout << "\n";

cout << "s2 after s2 = s2 - s2: ";
s2 = s2 - s2;  // clear s2
s2.showset();

cout << "\n";

s2 = s2 + 'C'; // add ABC in reverse order
s2 = s2 + 'B';
s2 = s2 + 'A';

cout << "s2 after adding C B A: ";
s2.showset();

return 0;
}
```

9

The output from this program is shown here:

```
s1 after adding A B C: { A B C }

Testing for membership using isMember().
B is a member of s1.
T is not a member of s1.

s1 after s1 = s1 - 'B': { A C }
s1 after s1 = s1 - 'A': { C }
s1 after a1 = s1 - 'C': { }

s1 after adding A B C: { A B C }

s2 after adding A X W: { A X W }

s3 after s3 = s1 + s2: { A B C X W }
s3 after s3 - s1: { X W }

s2 after s2 = s2 - s2: { }

s2 after adding C B A: { C B A }
```

✓ *Mastery Check*

1. What is a copy constructor and when is it called? Show the general form of a copy constructor.

2. Explain what happens when an object is returned by a function. Specifically, when is its destructor called?

3. Given this class:

```
class T {
  int i, j;
public:
  int sum() {
    return i + j;
  }
};
```

show how to rewrite **sum( )** so that it uses **this**.

4. What is a structure? What is a union?

5. Inside a member function, to what does *****this** refer?

6. What is a **friend** function?

7. Show the general form used for overloading a binary member operator function.

8. To allow operations involving a class type and a built-in type, what must you do?

9. Can the **?** be overloaded? Can you change the precedence of an operator?

10. For the **Set** class developed in Project 9-1, define **<** and **>** such that they determine if one set is a subset or a superset of another set. Have **<** return **true** if the left set is a subset of the set on the right, and **false** otherwise. Have **>** return **true** if the left set is a superset of the set on the right, and **false** otherwise.

11. For the **Set** class, define the **&** so that it yields the intersection of two sets.

12. On your own, try adding other **Set** operators. For example, try defining **|** so that it yields the *symmetric difference* between two sets. The symmetric difference consists of those elements that the two sets do not have in common.

9

Module 10

Inheritance, Virtual Functions, and Polymorphism

The Goals of This Module

- Learn inheritance fundamentals
- Understand how base classes are inherited by derived classes
- Use protected access
- Call base class constructors
- Create a multilevel class hierarchy
- Understand base class pointers to derived class objects
- Create virtual functions
- Use pure virtual functions and abstract classes
- Apply polymorphism

This module discusses three features of C++ that directly relate to object-oriented programming: inheritance, virtual functions, and polymorphism. Inheritance is the feature that allows one class to inherit the characteristics of another. Using inheritance, you can create a general class that defines traits common to a set of related items. This class can then be inherited by other, more specific classes, each adding those things that are unique to it. Built on the foundation of inheritance is the virtual function. The virtual function supports polymorphism, the "one interface, multiple methods" philosophy of object-oriented programming.

Inheritance Basics

In the language of C++, a class that is inherited is called a *base class*. The class that does the inheriting is called a *derived class*. Therefore, a derived class is a specialized version of a base class. A derived class inherits all of the members defined by the base class and adds its own, unique elements.

C++ implements inheritance by allowing one class to incorporate another class into its declaration. This is done by specifying a base class when a derived class is declared. Let's begin with a short example that illustrates several of the key features of inheritance. The following program creates a base class called **TwoDShape** that stores the width and height of a two-dimensional object, and a derived class called **Triangle**. Pay close attention to the way that **Triangle** is declared.

```
// A simple class hierarchy.

#include <iostream>
#include <cstring>
using namespace std;

// A class for two-dimensional objects.
class TwoDShape {
public:
  double width;
  double height;

  void showDim() {
    cout << "Width and height are " <<
```

```
              width << " and " << height << "\n";
  }
};

// Triangle is derived from TwoDShape.
class Triangle : public TwoDShape {        ◄────────
public:
  char style[20];

  double area() {
    return width * height / 2;             ◄────────
  }

  void showStyle() {
    cout << "Triangle is " << style << "\n";
  }
};

int main() {
  Triangle t1;
  Triangle t2;

  t1.width = 4.0;◄────────
  t1.height = 4.0;
  strcpy(t1.style, "isosceles");

  t2.width = 8.0;
  t2.height = 12.0;
  strcpy(t2.style, "right");

  cout << "Info for t1:\n";
  t1.showStyle();
  t1.showDim();
  cout << "Area is " << t1.area() << "\n";

  cout << "\n";
  cout << "Info for t2:\n";
  t2.showStyle();
  t2.showDim();
  cout << "Area is " << t2.area() << "\n";

  return 0;
}
```

Triangle inherits **TwoDShape**. Notice the syntax.

Triangle can refer to the members of **TwoDShape** as if they were part of **Triangle**.

All members of **Triangle** are available to **Triangle** objects, even those inherited from **TwoDShape**.

10

The output from this program is shown here:

```
Info for t1:
Triangle is isosceles
Width and height are 4 and 4
Area is 8

Info for t2:
Triangle is right
Width and height are 8 and 12
Area is 48
```

Here, **TwoDShape** defines the attributes of a "generic" two-dimensional shape, such as a square, rectangle, triangle, and so on. The **Triangle** class creates a specific type of **TwoDShape**, in this case, a triangle. The **Triangle** class includes all of **TwoDShape** and adds the field **style**, the function **area( )**, and the function **showStyle( )**. A description of the type of triangle is stored in **style**, **area( )** computes and returns the area of the triangle, and **showStyle( )** displays the triangle style.

The following line shows how **Triangle** inherits **TwoDShape**:

```
class Triangle : public TwoDShape {
```

Here, **TwoDShape** is a base class that is inherited by **Triangle**, which is a derived class. As this example shows, the syntax for inheriting a class is remarkably simple and easy-to-use.

Because **Triangle** includes all of the members of its base class, **TwoDShape**, it can access **width** and **height** inside **area( )**. Also, inside **main( )**, objects **t1** and **t2** can refer to **width** and **height** directly, as if they were part of **Triangle**. Figure 10-1 depicts conceptually how **TwoDShape** is incorporated into **Triangle**.

One other point: Even though **TwoDShape** is a base for **Triangle**, it is also a completely independent, stand-alone class. Being a base class for a derived class does not mean that the base class cannot be used by itself.

The general form for inheritance is shown here:

```
class derived-class : access base-class {
    // body of derived class
}
```

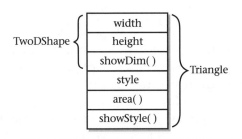

Figure 10-1 A conceptual depiction of the Triangle **class**

Here, *access* is optional. However, if present, it must be **public**, **private**, or **protected**. You will learn more about these options later in this module. For now, all inherited classes will use **public**. Using **public** means that all the public members of the base class will also be public members of the derived class.

A major advantage of inheritance is that once you have created a base class that defines the attributes common to a set of objects, it can be used to create any number of more specific derived classes. Each derived class can precisely tailor its own classification. For example, here is another class derived from **TwoDShape** that encapsulates rectangles:

```
// A derived class of TwoDShape for rectangles.
class Rectangle : public TwoDShape {
public:
  bool isSquare() {
    if(width == height) return true;
    return false;
  }

  double area() {
    return width * height;
  }
};
```

The **Rectangle** class includes **TwoDShape** and adds the functions **isSquare( )**, which determines if the rectangle is square, and **area( )**, which computes the area of a rectangle.

10

Member Access and Inheritance

As you learned in Module 8, members of a class are often declared as private to prevent their unauthorized use or tampering. Inheriting a class *does not* overrule the private access restriction. Thus, even though a derived class includes all of the members of its base class, it cannot access those members of the base class that are private. For example, if **width** and **height** are made private in **TwoDShape**, as shown here, then **Triangle** will not be able to access them.

```
// Access to private members is not granted to derived classes.

class TwoDShape {
  // these are now private
  double width;  ←——————————  width and height are now private.
  double height;
public:
  void showDim() {
    cout << "Width and height are " <<
            width << " and " << height << "\n";
  }
};

// Triangle is derived from TwoDShape.
class Triangle : public TwoDShape {
public:
  char style[20];

  double area() {
    return width * height / 2; // Error! Can't access. ←——┐
  }                            Can't access private members of a base class.
  void showStyle() {
    cout << "Triangle is " << style << "\n";
  }
};
```

The **Triangle** class will not compile because the reference to **width** and **height** inside the **area( )** function causes an access violation. Since **width** and **height** are now private, they are accessible only by other members of their own class. Derived classes have no access to them.

At first, you might think that it is a serious restriction that derived classes do not have access to the private members of base classes, because it would prevent the use of private members in many situations. Fortunately, this is not the case, because C++ provides various solutions. One is to use **protected** members, which is described in the next section. A second is to use public functions to provide access to private data. As you have seen in the preceding modules, C++ programmers typically grant access to the private members of a class through functions. Functions that provide access to private data are called *accessor functions*. Here is a rewrite of the **TwoDShape** class that adds accessor functions for **width** and **height**:

```cpp
// Access private data through accessor functions.

#include <iostream>
#include <cstring>
using namespace std;

// A class for two-dimensional objects.
class TwoDShape {
  // these are private
  double width;
  double height;
public:

  void showDim() {
    cout << "Width and height are " <<
            width << " and " << height << "\n";
  }

  // accessor functions
  double getWidth() { return width; }
  double getHeight() { return height; }
  void setWidth(double w) { width = w; }
  void setHeight(double h) { height = h; }
};

// Triangle is derived from TwoDShape.
class Triangle : public TwoDShape {
public:
  char style[20];

  double area() {
    return getWidth() * getHeight() / 2;
  }

  void showStyle() {
    cout << "Triangle is " << style << "\n";
```

The accessor functions for **width** and **height**

Use the accessor functions to obtain the width and height.

10

```
  }
};

int main() {
  Triangle t1;
  Triangle t2;

  t1.setWidth(4.0);
  t1.setHeight(4.0);
  strcpy(t1.style, "isosceles");

  t2.setWidth(8.0);
  t2.setHeight(12.0);
  strcpy(t2.style, "right");

  cout << "Info for t1:\n";
  t1.showStyle();
  t1.showDim();
  cout << "Area is " << t1.area() << "\n";

  cout << "\n";
  cout << "Info for t2:\n";
  t2.showStyle();
  t2.showDim();
  cout << "Area is " << t2.area() << "\n";

  return 0;
}
```

Ask the Expert

Question: I have heard the terms *superclass* and *subclass* used in discussions of Java programming. Do these terms have meaning in C++?

Answer: What Java calls a superclass, C++ calls a base class. What Java calls a subclass, C++ calls a derived class. You will commonly hear both sets of terms applied to a class of either language, but this book will continue to use the standard C++ terms. By the way, C# also uses the base class, derived class terminology.

1-Minute Drill

- How is a base class inherited by a derived class?
- Does a derived class include the members of its base class?
- Does a derived class have access to the private members of its base class?

Base Class Access Control

As explained, when one class inherits another, the members of the base class become members of the derived class. However, the accessibility of the base class members inside the derived class is determined by the access specifier used when inheriting the base class. The base class access specifier must be **public**, **private**, or **protected**. If the access specifier is not used, then it is **private** by default if the derived class is a **class**. If the derived class is a **struct**, then **public** is the default. Let's examine the ramifications of using **public** or **private** access. (The **protected** specifier is described in the next section.)

When a base class is inherited as **public**, all public members of the base class become public members of the derived class. In all cases, the private elements of the base class remain private to that class and are not accessible by members of the derived class. For example, in the following program, the public members of **B** become public members of **D**. Thus, they are accessible by other parts of the program.

```
// Demonstrate public inheritance.

#include <iostream>
using namespace std;

class B {
  int i, j;
public:
  void set(int a, int b) { i = a; j = b; }
  void show() { cout << i << " " << j << "\n"; }
};
```

10

- A base class is specified after the derived class' name, separated by a colon.
- Yes, a derived class includes the members of its base class.
- No, a derived class does not have access to the private members of its base class.

```
class D : public B {                    Here, B is inherited as public.
  int k;
public:
  D(int x) { k = x; }
  void showk() { cout << k << "\n"; }

  // i = 10; // Error! i is private to B and access is not allowed.
};
                                 Can't access i because it is private to B.
int main()
{
  D ob(3);

  ob.set(1, 2); // access member of base class
  ob.show();    // access member of base class

  ob.showk();   // uses member of derived class

  return 0;
}
```

Since set( ) and show( ) are **public** in B, they can be called on an object of type D from within **main( )**. Because i and j are specified as **private**, they remain private to B. This is why the line

```
// i = 10; // Error! i is private to B and access is not allowed.
```

is commented-out. **D** cannot access a private member of **B**.

The opposite of public inheritance is private inheritance. When the base class is inherited as **private**, then all public members of the base class become private members of the derived class. For example, the program shown next will not compile, because both **set( )** and **show( )** are now private members of **D**, and thus cannot be called from **main( )**.

```
// Use private inheritance. This program won't compile.

#include <iostream>
using namespace std;

class B {
  int i, j;
public:
  void set(int a, int b) { i = a; j = b; }
```

```
  void show() { cout << i << " " << j << "\n"; }
};

// Public elements of B become private in D.
class D : private B {  ←──────────┐
  int k;                           │ Now, inherit B as private.
public:
  D(int x) { k = x; }
  void showk() { cout << k << "\n"; }
};

int main()                              ┌─ Now, set( ) and show( ) are
{                                       │  inaccessible through D.
  D ob(3);

  ob.set(1, 2); // Error, can't access set()
  ob.show();    // Error, can't access show()

  return 0;
}
```

To review: when a base class is inherited as **private**, public members of the base class become private members of the derived class. This means that they are still accessible by members of the derived class, but cannot be accessed by other parts of your program.

Using protected Members

As you know, a private member of a base class is not accessible by a derived class. This would seem to imply that if you wanted a derived class to have access to some member in the base class, it would need to be public. Of course, making the member public also makes it available to all other code, which may not be desirable. Fortunately, this implication is wrong because C++ allows you to create a *protected member*. A protected member is public within a class hierarchy, but private outside that hierarchy.

A protected member is created by using the **protected** access modifier. When a member of a class is declared as **protected**, that member is, with one important exception, private. The exception occurs when a protected member is inherited. In this case, the protected member of the base class *is* accessible by

10

the derived class. Therefore, by using **protected**, you can create class members that are private to their class but that can still be inherited and accessed by a derived class. The **protected** specifier can also be used with structures.

Consider this sample program:

```
// Demonstrate protected members.

#include <iostream>
using namespace std;

class B {
protected:
  int i, j; // private to B, but accessible to D
public:
  void set(int a, int b) { i = a; j = b; }
  void show() { cout << i << " " << j << "\n"; }
};

class D : public B {
  int k;
public:
  // D may access B's i and j
  void setk() { k = i*j; }

  void showk() { cout << k << "\n"; }
};

int main()
{
  D ob;

  ob.set(2, 3); // OK, set() is public in B
  ob.show();    // OK, show() is public B

  ob.setk();
  ob.showk();

  return 0;
}
```

> Here, **i** and **j** are **protected**.

> **D** can access **i** and **j** because they are protected, not private.

Here, because **B** is inherited by **D** as public and because **i** and **j** are declared as protected, **D**'s function **setk( )** can access them. If **i** and **j** were declared as private by **B**, then **D** would not have access to them, and the program would not compile.

Ask the Expert

Question: Can you review public, protected, **and** private?

Answer: When a class member is declared as **public**, it can be accessed by any other part of a program. When a member is declared as **private**, it can be accessed only by members of its class. Further, derived classes do not have access to private base class members. When a member is declared as **protected**, it can be accessed only by members of its class and by its derived classes. Thus, **protected** allows a member to be inherited, but to remain private within a class hierarchy.

When a base class is inherited by use of **public**, its public members become public members of the derived class, and its protected members become protected members of the derived class. When a base class is inherited by use of **protected**, its public and protected members become protected members of the derived class. When a base class is inherited by use of **private**, its public and protected members become private members of the derived class. In all cases, private members of a base class remain private to that base class.

When a base class is inherited as public, protected members of the base class become protected members of the derived class. When a base class is inherited as private, protected members of the base class become private members of the derived class.

The **protected** access specifier may occur anywhere in a class declaration, although typically it occurs after the (default) private members are declared and before the public members. Thus, the most common full form of a class declaration is

```
class class-name{
    // private members by default
protected:
    // protected members
public:
    // public members
};
```

Of course, the protected category is optional.

In addition to specifying protected status for members of a class, the keyword **protected** can also act as an access specifier when a base class is inherited. When

10

a base class is inherited as protected, all public and protected members of the base class become protected members of the derived class. For example, in the preceding example, if **D** inherited **B**, as shown here:

```
class D : protected B {
```

then all members of **B** would become protected members of **D**.

1-Minute Drill

- When a base class is inherited as private, public members of the base class become private members of the derived class. True or false?

- Can a private member of a base class be made public through inheritance?

- To make a member accessible within a hierarchy, but private otherwise, what access specifier do you use?

Constructors and Inheritance

In a hierarchy, it is possible for both base classes and derived classes to have their own constructors. This raises an important question: what constructor is responsible for building an object of the derived class, the one in the base class, the one in the derived class, or both? The answer is this: the constructor for the base class constructs the base class portion of the object, and the constructor for the derived class constructs the derived class part. This makes sense because the base class has no knowledge of or access to any element in a derived class. Thus, their construction must be separate. The preceding examples have relied upon the default constructors created automatically by C++, so this was not an issue. However, in practice, most classes will have constructors. Here you will see how to handle this situation.

When only the derived class defines a constructor, the process is straightforward: simply construct the derived class object. The base class portion of the object is constructed automatically using its default constructor.

- True, when a base class is inherited as private, public members of the base class become private members of the derived class.
- No, a private member is always private to its class.
- To make a member accessible within a hierarchy, but otherwise private, use the **protected** access specifier.

For example, here is a reworked version of **Triangle** that defines a constructor. It also makes **style** private since it is now set by the constructor.

```
// Add a constructor to Triangle.

#include <iostream>
#include <cstring>
using namespace std;

// A class for two-dimensional objects.
class TwoDShape {
  // these are private
  double width;
  double height;
public:
  void showDim() {
    cout << "Width and height are " <<
            width << " and " << height << "\n";
  }

  // accessor functions
  double getWidth() { return width; }
  double getHeight() { return height; }
  void setWidth(double w) { width = w; }
  void setHeight(double h) { height = h; }
};

// Triangle is derived from TwoDShape.
class Triangle : public TwoDShape {
  char style[20]; // now private
public:

  // Constructor for Triangle.
  Triangle(char *str, double w, double h) {
    // Initialize the base class portion.
    setWidth(w);
    setHeight(h);

    // Initialize the derived class portion.
    strcpy(style, str);
  }

  double area() {
    return getWidth() * getHeight() / 2;
```

Initialize the **TwoDShape** portion of **Triangle**.

Initialize **style**, which is specific to **Triangle**.

10

```
  }

  void showStyle() {
    cout << "Triangle is " << style << "\n";
  }
};

int main() {
  Triangle t1("isosceles", 4.0, 4.0);
  Triangle t2("right", 8.0, 12.0);

  cout << "Info for t1:\n";
  t1.showStyle();
  t1.showDim();
  cout << "Area is " << t1.area() << "\n";

  cout << "\n";
  cout << "Info for t2:\n";
  t2.showStyle();
  t2.showDim();
  cout << "Area is " << t2.area() << "\n";

  return 0;
}
```

Here, **Triangle**'s constructor initializes the members of **TwoDShape** that it inherits along with its own **style** field.

When both the base class and the derived class define constructors, the process is a bit more complicated, because both the base class and derived class constructors must be executed.

Calling Base Class Constructors

When a base class has a constructor, the derived class must explicitly call it to initialize the base class portion of the object. A derived class can call a constructor defined by its base class by using an expanded form of the derived class' constructor declaration. The general form of this expanded declaration is shown here:

derived-constructor(arg-list) : *base-cons(arg-list)*;
{
   body of derived constructor
}

Here, *base-cons* is the name of the base class inherited by the derived class. Notice that a colon separates the constructor declaration of the derived class from the base class constructor. (If a class inherits more than one base class, then the base class constructors are separated from each other by commas.)

The following program shows how to pass arguments to a base class constructor. It defines a constructor for **TwoDShape** that initializes the **width** and **height** properties.

```cpp
// Add a constructor to TwoDShape.

#include <iostream>
#include <cstring>
using namespace std;

// A class for two-dimensional objects.
class TwoDShape {
  // these are private
  double width;
  double height;
public:

  // Constructor for TwoDShape.
  TwoDShape(double w, double h) {
    width = w;
    height = h;
  }

  void showDim() {
    cout << "Width and height are " <<
            width << " and " << height << "\n";
  }

  // accessor functions
  double getWidth() { return width; }
  double getHeight() { return height; }
  void setWidth(double w) { width = w; }
  void setHeight(double h) { height = h; }
};

// Triangle is derived from TwoDShape.
class Triangle : public TwoDShape {
  char style[20]; // now private
public:
```

10

```
// Constructor for Triangle.
Triangle(char *str, double w,
         double h) : TwoDShape(w, h) {
  strcpy(style, str);
}
```

Call the **TwoDShape** constructor.

```
  double area() {
    return getWidth() * getHeight() / 2;
  }

  void showStyle() {
    cout << "Triangle is " << style << "\n";
  }
};

int main() {
  Triangle t1("isosceles", 4.0, 4.0);
  Triangle t2("right", 8.0, 12.0);

  cout << "Info for t1:\n";
  t1.showStyle();
  t1.showDim();
  cout << "Area is " << t1.area() << "\n";

  cout << "\n";
  cout << "Info for t2:\n";
  t2.showStyle();
  t2.showDim();
  cout << "Area is " << t2.area() << "\n";

  return 0;
}
```

Here, **Triangle( )** calls **TwoDShape** with the parameters **w** and **h**, which initializes **width** and **height** using these values. **Triangle** no longer initializes these values itself. It need only initialize the value unique to it: **style**. This leaves **TwoDShape** free to construct its subobject in any manner that it so chooses. Furthermore, **TwoDShape** can add functionality about which existing derived classes have no knowledge, thus preventing existing code from breaking.

Any form of constructor defined by the base class can be called by the derived class' constructor. The constructor executed will be the one that matches the arguments. For example, here are expanded versions of both **TwoDShape** and **Triangle** that include additional constructors:

```
// Add a constructor to TwoDShape.

#include <iostream>
#include <cstring>
using namespace std;

// A class for two-dimensional objects.
class TwoDShape {
  // these are private
  double width;
  double height;
public:

  // Default constructor.
  TwoDShape() {
    width = height = 0.0;
  }

  // Constructor for TwoDShape.
  TwoDShape(double w, double h) {
    width = w;
    height = h;
  }

  // Construct object with equal width and height.
  TwoDShape(double x) {
    width = height = x;
  }

  void showDim() {
    cout << "Width and height are " <<
            width << " and " << height << "\n";
  }

  // accessor functions
  double getWidth() { return width; }
  double getHeight() { return height; }
  void setWidth(double w) { width = w; }
  void setHeight(double h) { height = h; }
};

// Triangle is derived from TwoDShape.
class Triangle : public TwoDShape {
  char style[20]; // now private
public:
```

Various **TwoDShape** constructors

10

```
/* A default constructor. This automatically invokes
   the default constructor of TwoDShape. */
Triangle() {
  strcpy(style, "unknown");
}

// Constructor with three parameters.
Triangle(char *str, double w,
         double h) : TwoDShape(w, h) {
  strcpy(style, str);
}

// Construct an isosceles triangle.
Triangle(double x) : TwoDShape(x) {
  strcpy(style, "isosceles");
}

double area() {
  return getWidth() * getHeight() / 2;
}

void showStyle() {
  cout << "Triangle is " << style << "\n";
}
};

int main() {
  Triangle t1;
  Triangle t2("right", 8.0, 12.0);
  Triangle t3(4.0);

  t1 = t2;

  cout << "Info for t1: \n";
  t1.showStyle();
  t1.showDim();
  cout << "Area is " << t1.area() << "\n";

  cout << "\n";

  cout << "Info for t2: \n";
  t2.showStyle();
  t2.showDim();
  cout << "Area is " << t2.area() << "\n";
```

Various **Triangle** constructors

```
  cout << "\n";

  cout << "Info for t3: \n";
  t3.showStyle();
  t3.showDim();
  cout << "Area is " << t3.area() << "\n";

  cout << "\n";

  return 0;
}
```

Here is the output from this version:

```
Info for t1:
Triangle is right
Width and height are 8 and 12
Area is 48

Info for t2:
Triangle is right
Width and height are 8 and 12
Area is 48

Info for t3:
Triangle is isosceles
Width and height are 4 and 4
Area is 8
```

1-Minute Drill

- How does a derived class execute its base class' constructor?

- Can parameters be passed to a base class constructor?

- What constructor is responsible for initializing the base class portion of a derived object, the one defined by the derived class or the one defined by the base class?

- A derived class specifies a base class constructor clause with its constructor.
- Yes, parameters can be passed to a base class constructor.
- The constructor responsible for initializing the base class portion of a derived object is the one defined by the base class.

TruckDemo.cpp

Project 10-1: Extending the Vehicle Class

This project creates a subclass of the **Vehicle** class first developed in Module 8. As you should recall, **Vehicle** encapsulates information about vehicles, including the number of passengers they can carry, their fuel capacity, and their fuel consumption rate. We can use the **Vehicle** class as a starting point from which more specialized classes are developed. For example, one type of vehicle is a truck. An important attribute of a truck is its cargo capacity. Thus, to create a **Truck** class, you can inherit **Vehicle**, adding an instance variable that stores the carrying capacity. In this project, you will create the **Truck** class. In the process, the instance variables in **Vehicle** will be made private, and accessor functions are provided to get their values.

Step-by-Step

1. Create a file called **TruckDemo.cpp**, and copy the last implementation of **Vehicle** from Module 8 into the file.

2. Create the **Truck** class, as shown here:

```cpp
// Use Vehicle to create a Truck specialization.
class Truck : public Vehicle {
  int cargocap; // cargo capacity in pounds
public:

  // This is a constructor for Truck.
  Truck(int p, int f,
              int m, int c) : Vehicle(p, f, m)
  {
    cargocap = c;
  }

  // Accessor function for cargocap.
  int get_cargocap() { return cargocap; }
};
```

Here, **Truck** inherits **Vehicle**, adding the **cargocap** member. Thus, **Truck** includes all of the general vehicle attributes defined by **Vehicle**. It need add only those items that are unique to its own class.

3. Here is an entire program that demonstrates the **Truck** class:

```cpp
// Create a subclass of Vehicle called Truck.

#include <iostream>
```

```cpp
using namespace std;

// Declare the Vehicle class.
class Vehicle {
  // These are private.
  int passengers; // number of passengers
  int fuelcap;    // fuel capacity in gallons
  int mpg;        // fuel consumption in miles per gallon
public:
  // This is a constructor for Vehicle.
  Vehicle(int p, int f, int m) {
    passengers = p;
    fuelcap = f;
    mpg = m;
  }

  // Compute and return the range.
  int range() { return mpg * fuelcap; }

  // Accessor functions.
  int get_passengers() { return passengers; }
  int get_fuelcap() { return fuelcap; }
  int get_mpg() { return mpg; }
};

// Use Vehicle to create a Truck specialization.
class Truck : public Vehicle {
  int cargocap; // cargo capacity in pounds
public:

  // This is a constructor for Truck.
  Truck(int p, int f,
              int m, int c) : Vehicle(p, f, m)
  {
    cargocap = c;
  }

  // Accessor function for cargocap.
  int get_cargocap() { return cargocap; }
};

int main() {

  // construct some trucks
  Truck semi(2, 200, 7, 44000);
```

10

```
Truck pickup(3, 28, 15, 2000);
int dist = 252;

cout << "Semi can carry " << semi.get_cargocap() <<
                  " pounds.\n";
cout << "It has a range of " <<
        semi.range() << " miles.\n";
cout << "To go " << dist << " miles semi needs " <<
        dist / semi.get_mpg() <<
        " gallons of fuel.\n\n";

cout << "Pickup can carry " << pickup.get_cargocap() <<
                  " pounds.\n";
cout << "It has a range of " <<
        pickup.range() << " miles.\n";
cout << "To go " << dist << " miles pickup needs " <<
        dist / pickup.get_mpg() <<
        " gallons of fuel.\n";

return 0;
}
```

4. The output from this program is shown here:

```
Semi can carry 44000 pounds.
It has a range of 1400 miles.
To go 252 miles semi needs 36 gallons of fuel.

Pickup can carry 2000 pounds.
It has a range of 420 miles.
To go 252 miles pickup needs 16 gallons of fuel.
```

5. Many other types of classes can be derived from **Vehicle**. For example, the following skeleton creates an off-road class that stores the ground clearance of the vehicle:

```
// Create an off-road vehicle class
class OffRoad : public Vehicle {
  int groundClearance; // ground clearance in inches
public:
  // ...
};
```

The key point is that once you have created a base class that defines the general aspects of an object, that base class can be inherited to form specialized classes. Each derived class simply adds its own, unique attributes. This is the essence of inheritance.

Creating a Multilevel Hierarchy

Up to this point, we have been using simple class hierarchies consisting of only a base class and a derived class. However, you can build hierarchies that contain as many layers of inheritance as you like. As mentioned, it is perfectly acceptable to use a derived class as a base class of another. For example, given three classes called **A**, **B**, and **C**, **C** can be derived from **B**, which can be derived from **A**. When this type of situation occurs, each derived class inherits all of the traits found in all of its base classes. In this case, **C** inherits all aspects of **B** and **A**.

To see how a multilevel hierarchy can be useful, consider the following program. In it, the derived class **Triangle** is used as a base class to create the derived class called **ColorTriangle**. **ColorTriangle** inherits all of the traits of **Triangle** and **TwoDShape**, and adds a field called **color**, which holds the color of the triangle.

```
// A multilevel hierarchy.

#include <iostream>
#include <cstring>
using namespace std;

// A class for two-dimensional objects.
class TwoDShape {
  // these are private
  double width;
  double height;
public:

  // Default constructor.
  TwoDShape() {
    width = height = 0.0;
  }

  // Constructor for TwoDShape.
```

10

```cpp
  TwoDShape(double w, double h) {
    width = w;
    height = h;
  }

  // Construct object with equal width and height.
  TwoDShape(double x) {
    width = height = x;
  }

  void showDim() {
    cout << "Width and height are " <<
            width << " and " << height << "\n";
  }

  // accessor functions
  double getWidth() { return width; }
  double getHeight() { return height; }
  void setWidth(double w) { width = w; }
  void setHeight(double h) { height = h; }
};

// Triangle is derived from TwoDShape.
class Triangle : public TwoDShape {
  char style[20]; // now private
public:

  /* A default constructor. This automatically invokes
     the default constructor of TwoDShape. */
  Triangle() {
    strcpy(style, "unknown");
  }

  // Constructor with three parameters.
  Triangle(char *str, double w,
           double h) : TwoDShape(w, h) {
    strcpy(style, str);
  }

  // Construct an isosceles triangle.
  Triangle(double x) : TwoDShape(x) {
    strcpy(style, "isosceles");
  }
```

```
  double area() {
    return getWidth() * getHeight() / 2;
  }

  void showStyle() {
    cout << "Triangle is " << style << "\n";
  }
};

// Extend Triangle.
class ColorTriangle : public Triangle {
  char color[20];
public:
  ColorTriangle(char *clr, char *style, double w,
                double h) : Triangle(style, w, h) {
    strcpy(color, clr);
  }

  // Display the color.
  void showColor() {
    cout << "Color is " << color << "\n";
  }
};

int main() {
  ColorTriangle t1("Blue", "right", 8.0, 12.0);
  ColorTriangle t2("Red", "isosceles", 2.0, 2.0);

  cout << "Info for t1:\n";
  t1.showStyle();
  t1.showDim();
  t1.showColor();
  cout << "Area is " << t1.area() << "\n";

  cout << "\n";

  cout << "Info for t2:\n";
  t2.showStyle();
  t2.showDim();
  t2.showColor();
  cout << "Area is " << t2.area() << "\n";

  return 0;
}
```

ColorTriangle inherits **Triangle**, which inherits **TwoDShape**.

A **ColorTriangle** object can call functions defined by itself and its base classes.

10

The output of this program is shown here:

```
Info for t1:
Triangle is right
Width and height are 8 and 12
Color is Blue
Area is 48

Info for t2:
Triangle is isosceles
Width and height are 2 and 2
Color is Red
Area is 2
```

Because of inheritance, **ColorTriangle** can make use of the previously defined classes of **Triangle** and **TwoDShape**, adding only the extra information it needs for its own, specific application. This is part of the value of inheritance; it allows the reuse of code.

This example illustrates one other important point. In a class hierarchy, if a base class constructor requires parameters, then all derived classes must pass those parameters "up the line." This is true whether or not a derived class needs parameters of its own.

Inheriting Multiple Base Classes

In C++, it is possible for a derived class to inherit two or more base classes at the same time. For example, in this short program, **D** inherits both **B1** and **B2**:

```
// An example of multiple base classes.

#include <iostream>
using namespace std;

class B1 {
protected:
  int x;
public:
  void showx() { cout << x << "\n"; }
};

class B2 {
protected:
```

```
  int y;
public:
  void showy() { cout << y << "\n"; }
};

// Inherit multiple base classes.
class D: public B1, public B2 {
public:
  /* x and y are accessible because they are
     protected in B1 and B2, not private. */
  void set(int i, int j) { x = i; y = j; }
};

int main()
{
  D ob;

  ob.set(10, 20); // provided by D
  ob.showx();     // from B1
  ob.showy();     // from B2

  return 0;
}
```

Here, **D** inherits both **B1** and **B2** at the same time.

As this example illustrates, to cause more than one base class to be inherited, you must use a comma-separated list. Further, be sure to use an access specifier for each base class inherited.

When Constructor and Destructor Functions Are Executed

Because a base class, a derived class, or both can contain constructors and/or destructors, it is important to understand the order in which they are executed. Specifically, when an object of a derived class comes into existence, in what order are the constructors called? When the object goes out of existence, in what order are the destructors called? To answer these questions, let's begin with this simple program:

```
#include <iostream>
using namespace std;
```

```
class B {
public:
  B() { cout << "Constructing base portion\n"; }
  ~B() { cout << "Destructing base portion\n"; }
};

class D: public B {
public:
  D() { cout << "Constructing derived portion\n"; }
  ~D() { cout << "Destructing derived portion\n"; }
};

int main()
{
  D ob;

  // do nothing but construct and destruct ob

  return 0;
}
```

As the comment in **main( )** indicates, this program simply constructs and then destroys an object called **ob**, which is of class **D**. When executed, this program displays

```
Constructing base portion
Constructing derived portion
Destructing derived portion
Destructing base portion
```

As the output shows, first the constructor for **B** is executed, followed by the constructor of **D**. Next (since **ob** is immediately destroyed in this program), the destructor of **D** is called, followed by that of **B**.

The results of the foregoing experiment can be generalized as follows: When an object of a derived class is created, the base class constructor is called first, followed by the constructor for the derived class. When a derived object is destroyed, its destructor is called first, followed by that of the base class. Put differently, constructors are executed in the order of their derivation. Destructors are executed in reverse order of derivation.

Ask the Expert

Question: Why are constructors called in order of derivation, and destructors called in reverse order?

Answer: If you think about it, it makes sense that constructors are executed in order of derivation. Because a base class has no knowledge of any derived class, any initialization it needs to perform is separate from, and possibly prerequisite to, any initialization performed by the derived class. Therefore, the base class constructor must be executed first.

Likewise, it is quite sensible that destructors be executed in reverse order of derivation. Since the base class underlies a derived class, the destruction of the base class implies the destruction of the derived class. Therefore, the derived destructor must be called before the object is fully destroyed.

In the case of a multilevel class hierarchy (that is, where a derived class becomes the base class for another derived class), the same general rule applies: Constructors are called in order of derivation; destructors are called in reverse order. When a class inherits more than one base class at a time, constructors are called in order from left to right as specified in the derived class' inheritance list. Destructors are called in reverse order right to left.

1-Minute Drill

10

- Can a derived class be used as a base class for another derived class?

- In a class hierarchy, in what order are the constructors called?

- In a class hierarchy, in what order are the destructors called?

- Yes, a derived class can be used as a base class for another derived class.
- Constructors are called in order of derivation.
- Destructors are called in reverse order of derivation.

Pointers to Derived Types

Before moving on to virtual functions and polymorphism, it is necessary to discuss an important aspect of pointers. Pointers to base classes and derived classes are related in ways that other types of pointers are not. In general, a pointer of one type cannot point to an object of another type. However, base class pointers and derived objects are the exceptions to this rule. In C++, a base class pointer can also be used to point to an object of any class derived from that base. For example, assume that you have a base class called **B** and a class called **D**, which is derived from **B**. Any pointer declared as a pointer to **B** can also be used to point to an object of type **D**. Therefore, given

```
B *p;    // pointer to object of type B
B B_ob; // object of type B
D D_ob; // object of type D
```

both of the following statements are perfectly valid:

```
p = &B_ob; // p points to object of type B
p = &D_ob; /* p points to object of type D,
               which is an object derived from B. */
```

A base pointer can be used to access only those parts of a derived object that were inherited from the base class. Thus, in this example, **p** can be used to access all elements of **D_ob** inherited from **B_ob**. However, elements specific to **D_ob** cannot be accessed through **p** (unless a type cast is employed).

Another point to understand is that although a base pointer can be used to point to a derived object, the reverse is not true. That is, you cannot access an object of the base type by using a derived class pointer.

As you know, a pointer is incremented and decremented relative to its base type. Therefore, when a base class pointer is pointing at a derived object, incrementing or decrementing it will *not* make it point to the next object of the derived class. Instead, it will point to (what it thinks is) the next object of the base class. Therefore, you should consider it invalid to increment or decrement a base class pointer when it is pointing to a derived object.

The fact that a pointer to a base type can be used to point to any object derived from that base is extremely important, and fundamental to C++. As you will soon learn, this flexibility is crucial to the way C++ implements runtime polymorphism.

References to Derived Types

Similar to the action of pointers just described, a base class reference can be used to refer to an object of a derived type. The most common application of this is found in function parameters. A base class reference parameter can receive objects of the base class as well as any other type derived from that base.

Virtual Functions and Polymorphism

The foundation upon which C++ builds its support for polymorphism consists of inheritance and base class pointers. The specific feature that actually implements polymorphism is the virtual function. The remainder of this module examines this important feature.

Virtual Function Fundamentals

A *virtual function* is a function that is declared as **virtual** in a base class and redefined in one or more derived classes. Thus, each derived class can have its own version of a virtual function. What makes virtual functions interesting is what happens when a base class pointer is used to call one. When a virtual function is called through a base class pointer, C++ determines which version of that function to call based upon the *type* of the object *pointed to* by the pointer. This determination is made *at runtime*. Thus, when different objects are pointed to, different versions of the virtual function are executed. In other words, it is the type of the *object* being pointed to (not the type of the pointer) that determines which version of the virtual function will be executed. Therefore, if a base class contains a virtual function and if two or more different classes are derived from that base class, then when different types of objects are pointed to through a base class pointer, different versions of the virtual function are executed.

You declare a virtual function as virtual inside a base class by preceding its declaration with the keyword **virtual**. When a virtual function is redefined by a derived class, the keyword **virtual** need not be repeated (although it is not an error to do so).

A class that includes a virtual function is called a *polymorphic class*. This term also applies to a class that inherits a base class containing a virtual function.

10

The following program demonstrates a virtual function:

```
// A short example that uses a virtual function.

#include <iostream>
using namespace std;
                                              [Declare a virtual function.]
class B {
public:
  virtual void who() { // specify a virtual function ◄──
    cout << "Base\n";
  }
};
                                        [Redefine the virtual function for D1.]
class D1 : public B {
public:
  void who() { // redefine who() for D1 ◄──
    cout << "First derivation\n";
  }
};
                                        [Redefine the virtual function
                                         a second time for D2.]
class D2 : public B {
public:
  void who() { // redefine who() for D2 ◄──
    cout << "Second derivation\n";
  }
};

int main()
{
  B base_obj;
  B *p;
  D1 D1_obj;
  D2 D2_obj;

  p = &base_obj;
  p->who();  // access B's who

  p = &D1_obj;
  p->who(); // access D1's who ◄──      [Call the virtual function
                                         through a base class pointer.]
  p = &D2_obj;
  p->who();  // access D2's who ◄──

  return 0;
}
```

This program produces the following output:

```
Base
First derivation
Second derivation
```

Let's examine the program in detail to understand how it works.

As you can see, in **B**, the function **who( )** is declared as virtual. This means that the function can be redefined by a derived class. Inside both **D1** and **D2**, **who( )** is redefined relative to each class. Inside **main( )**, four variables are declared: **base_obj**, which is an object of type **B**; **p**, which is a pointer to **B** objects; and **D1_obj** and **D2_obj**, which are objects of the two derived classes. Next, **p** is assigned the address of **base_obj**, and the **who( )** function is called. Since **who( )** is declared as virtual, C++ determines at runtime which version of **who( )** to execute based on the type of object pointed to by **p**. In this case, **p** points to an object of type **B**, so it is the version of **who( )** declared in **B** that is executed. Next, **p** is assigned the address of **D1_obj**. Recall that a base class pointer can refer to an object of any derived class. Now, when **who( )** is called, C++ again checks to see what type of object is pointed to by **p** and, based on that type, determines which version of **who( )** to call. Since **p** points to an object of type **D1**, that version of **who( )** is used. Likewise, when **p** is assigned the address of **D2_obj**, the version of **who( )** declared inside **D2** is executed.

To review: When a virtual function is called through a base class pointer, the version of a virtual function actually executed is determined at runtime by the type of object being pointed to.

Although virtual functions are normally called through base class pointers, a virtual function can also be called normally, using the standard dot operator syntax. This means that in the preceding example, it would have been syntactically correct to access **who( )** using this statement:

```
D1_obj.who();
```

However, calling a virtual function in this manner ignores its polymorphic attributes. It is only when a virtual function is accessed through a base class pointer (or reference) that runtime polymorphism is achieved.

At first, the redefinition of a virtual function in a derived class seems to be a special form of function overloading. However, this is not the case. In fact, the two processes are fundamentally different. First, an overloaded function must differ in its type and/or number of parameters, while a redefined virtual function must have exactly the same type and number of parameters. In fact, the prototypes for a virtual function and its redefinitions must be exactly the same. If the prototypes differ, then the function is simply considered to be overloaded, and its virtual nature is lost. Another restriction is that a virtual function must be a member, not a friend, of the class for which it is defined. However, a virtual function can be a friend of another class. Also, it is permissible for destructors, but not constructors, to be virtual.

Because of the restrictions and differences between overloading normal functions and redefining virtual functions, the term *overriding* is used to describe the redefinition of a virtual function.

Virtual Functions Are Inherited

Once a function is declared as virtual, it stays virtual no matter how many layers of derived classes it may pass through. For example, if **D2** is derived from **D1** instead of **B**, as shown in the next example, then **who( )** is still virtual:

```
// Derive from D1, not B.
class D2 : public D1 {
public:
  void who() { // define who() relative to second_d
    cout << "Second derivation\n";
  }
};
```

When a derived class does not override a virtual function, then the function as defined in the base class is used. For example, try this version of the preceding program. Here, **D2** does not override **who( )**:

```
#include <iostream>
using namespace std;

class B {
public:
  virtual void who() {
    cout << "Base\n";
  }
};

class D1 : public B {
public:
```

```
  void who() {
    cout << "First derivation\n";
  }
};

class D2 : public B {       ◄────── D2 does not override who( ).
// who() not defined
};

int main()
{
  B base_obj;
  B *p;
  D1 D1_obj;
  D2 D2_obj;

  p = &base_obj;
  p->who();  // access B's who()

  p = &D1_obj;
  p->who(); // access D1's who()

  p = &D2_obj;
  p->who(); /* access B's who() because    ◄──── This calls the who( )
                D2 does not redefine it */       defined by B.

  return 0;
}
```

The program now outputs the following:

```
Base
First derivation
Base
```

Because **D2** does not override **who( )**, the version of **who( )** defined in B is used instead.

Keep in mind that inherited characteristics of **virtual** are hierarchical. Therefore, if the preceding example is changed such that **D2** is derived from **D1** instead of **B**, then when **who( )** is called on an object of type **D2**, it will not be the **who( )** inside B, but the version of **who( )** declared inside **D1** that is called since it is the class closest to **D2**.

10

Why Virtual Functions?

As stated earlier, virtual functions in combination with derived types allow C++ to support runtime polymorphism. Polymorphism is essential to object-oriented programming, because it allows a generalized class to specify those functions that will be common to all derivatives of that class, while allowing a derived class to define the specific implementation of some or all of those functions. Sometimes this idea is expressed as follows: the base class dictates the general *interface* that any object derived from that class will have, but lets the derived class define the actual *method* used to implement that interface. This is why the phrase "one interface, multiple methods" is often used to describe polymorphism.

Part of the key to successfully applying polymorphism is understanding that the base and derived classes form a hierarchy, which moves from greater to lesser generalization (base to derived). When designed correctly, the base class provides all of the elements that a derived class can use directly. It also defines those functions that the derived class must implement on its own. This allows the derived class the flexibility to define its own methods, and yet still enforces a consistent interface. That is, since the form of the interface is defined by the base class, any derived class will share that common interface. Thus, the use of virtual functions makes it possible for the base class to define the generic interface that will be used by all derived classes.

At this point, you might be asking yourself why a consistent interface with multiple implementations is important. The answer, again, goes back to the central driving force behind object-oriented programming: It helps the programmer handle increasingly complex programs. For example, if you develop your program correctly, then you know that all objects you derive from a base class are accessed in the same general way, even if the specific actions vary from one derived class to the next. This means that you need to deal with only one interface, rather than several. Also, your derived class is free to use any or all of the functionality provided by the base class. You need not reinvent those elements.

The separation of interface and implementation also allows the creation of *class libraries,* which can be provided by a third party. If these libraries are implemented correctly, they will provide a common interface that you can use to derive classes of your own that meet your specific needs. For example, both the Microsoft Foundation Classes (MFC) and the newer .NET Framework Windows Forms class library support Windows programming. By using these classes, your program can inherit much of the functionality required by a

Windows program. You need add only the features unique to your application. This is a major benefit when programming complex systems.

Applying Virtual Functions

To better understand the power of virtual functions, we will apply it to the **TwoDShape** class. In the preceding examples, each class derived from **TwoDShape** defines a function called **area( )**. This suggests that it might be better to make **area( )** a virtual function of the **TwoDShape** class, allowing each derived class to override it, defining how the area is calculated for the type of shape that the class encapsulates. The following program does this. For convenience, it also adds a name field to **TwoDShape**. (This makes it easier to demonstrate the classes.)

```
// Use virtual functions and polymorphism.

#include <iostream>
#include <cstring>
using namespace std;

// A class for two-dimensional objects.
class TwoDShape {
  // these are private
  double width;
  double height;

  // add a name field
  char name[20];
public:

  // Default constructor.
  TwoDShape() {
    width = height = 0.0;
    strcpy(name, "unknown");
  }

  // Constructor for TwoDShape.
  TwoDShape(double w, double h, char *n) {
    width = w;
    height = h;
    strcpy(name, n);
```

10

```
  }

  // Construct object with equal width and height.
  TwoDShape(double x, char *n) {
    width = height = x;
    strcpy(name, n);
  }

  void showDim() {
    cout << "Width and height are " <<
            width << " and " << height << "\n";
  }

  // accessor functions
  double getWidth() { return width; }
  double getHeight() { return height; }
  void setWidth(double w) { width = w; }
  void setHeight(double h) { height = h; }
  char *getName() { return name; }

  // Add area() to TwoDShape and make it virtual.
  virtual double area() {
    cout << "Error: area() must be overridden.\n";
    return 0.0;
  }
};

// Triangle is derived from TwoDShape.
class Triangle : public TwoDShape {
  char style[20]; // now private
public:

  /* A default constructor. This automatically invokes
     the default constructor of TwoDShape. */
  Triangle() {
    strcpy(style, "unknown");
  }

  // Constructor with three parameters.
  Triangle(char *str, double w,
           double h) : TwoDShape(w, h, "triangle") {
    strcpy(style, str);
  }
```

The **area( )** function is now virtual.

```
  // Construct an isosceles triangle.
  Triangle(double x) : TwoDShape(x, "triangle") {
    strcpy(style, "isosceles");
  }

  // This now overrides area() declared in TwoDShape.
  double area() {
    return getWidth() * getHeight() / 2;
  }

  void showStyle() {
    cout << "Triangle is " << style << "\n";
  }
};
```

Override **area( )** in **Triangle**.

```
// A derived class of TwoDShape for rectangles.
class Rectangle : public TwoDShape {
public:

  // Construct a rectangle.
  Rectangle(double w, double h) :
    TwoDShape(w, h, "rectangle") { }

  // Construct a square.
  Rectangle(double x) :
    TwoDShape(x, "rectangle") { }

  bool isSquare() {
    if(getWidth() == getHeight()) return true;
    return false;
  }

  // This is another override of area().
  double area() {
    return getWidth() * getHeight();
  }
};
```

Override **area( )** again in **Rectangle**.

```
int main() {
  // declare an array of pointers to TwoDShape objects.
  TwoDShape *shapes[5];

  shapes[0] = &Triangle("right", 8.0, 12.0);
```

10

```
shapes[1] = &Rectangle(10);
shapes[2] = &Rectangle(10, 4);
shapes[3] = &Triangle(7.0);
shapes[4] = &TwoDShape(10, 20, "generic");

for(int i=0; i < 5; i++) {
  cout << "object is " <<
          shapes[i]->getName() << "\n";

  cout << "Area is " <<
          shapes[i]->area() << "\n";

  cout << "\n";
}

return 0;
}
```

The proper version of **area( )** for each object is now called.

The output from the program is shown here:

```
object is triangle
Area is 48

object is rectangle
Area is 100

object is rectangle
Area is 40

object is triangle
Area is 24.5

object is generic
Error: area() must be overridden.
Area is 0
```

Let's examine this program closely. First, **area( )** is declared as **virtual** in **TwoDShape** class and is overridden by **Triangle** and **Rectangle**. Inside **TwoDShape**, **area( )** is given a placeholder implementation that simply informs the user that this function must be overridden by a derived class. Each override of **area( )** supplies an implementation that is suitable for the type of object encapsulated by the derived class. Thus, if you were to implement an ellipse class, for example, then **area( )** would need to compute the area of an ellipse.

There is one other important feature in the preceding program. Notice in **main( )** that **shapes** is declared as an array of pointers to **TwoDShape** objects. However, the elements of this array are assigned pointers to **Triangle**, **Rectangle**, and **TwoDShape** objects. This is valid because a base class pointer can point to a derived class object. The program then cycles through the array, displaying information about each object. Although quite simple, this illustrates the power of both inheritance and virtual functions. The type of object pointed to by a base class pointer is determined at runtime and acted on accordingly. If an object is derived from **TwoDShape**, then its area can be obtained by calling **area( )**. The interface to this operation is the same no matter what type of shape is being used.

1-Minute Drill

● What is a virtual function?

● Why are virtual functions important?

● When an overridden virtual function is called through a base class pointer, which version of the function is executed?

Pure Virtual Functions and Abstract Classes

Sometimes you will want to create a base class that defines only a generalized form that will be shared by all of its derived classes, leaving it to each derived class to fill in the details. Such a class determines the nature of the functions that the derived classes must implement, but does not, itself, provide an implementation of one or more of these functions. One way this situation can occur is when a base class is unable to create a meaningful implementation for a function. This is the case with the version of **TwoDShape** used in the preceding example. The definition of **area( )** is simply a placeholder. It will not compute and display the area of any type of object.

● A virtual function is a function that is declared **virtual** in a base class and overridden in a derived class.
● Virtual functions are one way that C++ supports polymorphism.
● The version of a virtual function that is executed is determined by the type of the object pointed to at the time of the call. Thus, this determination is made at runtime.

As you will see as you create your own class libraries, it is not uncommon for a function to have no meaningful definition in the context of its base class. You can handle this situation two ways. One way, as shown in the previous example, is to simply have it report a warning message. While this approach can be useful in certain situations—such as debugging—it is not usually appropriate. You may have functions that must be overridden by the derived class in order for the derived class to have any meaning. Consider the class **Triangle**. It has no meaning if **area( )** is not defined. In this case, you want some way to ensure that a derived class does, indeed, override all necessary functions. The C++ solution to this problem is the *pure virtual function*.

A pure virtual function is a function declared in a base class that has no definition relative to the base. As a result, any derived class must define its own version—it cannot simply use the version defined in the base. To declare a pure virtual function, use this general form:

virtual *type func-name(parameter-list)* = 0;

Here, *type* is the return type of the function, and *func-name* is the name of the function.

Using a pure virtual function, you can improve the **TwoDShape** class. Since there is no meaningful concept of area for an undefined two-dimensional figure, the following version of the preceding program declares **area( )** as a pure virtual function inside **TwoDShape**. This, of course, means that all classes derived from **TwoDShape** must override **area( )**.

```
// Use a pure virtual function.

#include <iostream>
#include <cstring>
using namespace std;

// A class for two-dimensional objects.
class TwoDShape {
  // these are private
  double width;
  double height;

  // add a name field
  char name[20];
public:
```

```cpp
  // Default constructor.
  TwoDShape() {
    width = height = 0.0;
    strcpy(name, "unknown");
  }

  // Constructor for TwoDShape.
  TwoDShape(double w, double h, char *n) {
    width = w;
    height = h;
    strcpy(name, n);
  }

  // Construct object with equal width and height.
  TwoDShape(double x, char *n) {
    width = height = x;
    strcpy(name, n);
  }

  void showDim() {
    cout << "Width and height are " <<
            width << " and " << height << "\n";
  }

  // accessor functions
  double getWidth() { return width; }
  double getHeight() { return height; }
  void setWidth(double w) { width = w; }
  void setHeight(double h) { height = h; }
  char *getName() { return name; }

  // area()is now a pure virtual function
  virtual double area() = 0;

};

// Triangle is derived from TwoDShape.
class Triangle : public TwoDShape {
  char style[20]; // now private
public:

  /* A default constructor. This automatically invokes
     the default constructor of TwoDShape. */
```

area( ) is now a pure virtual function.

10

```cpp
  Triangle() {
    strcpy(style, "unknown");
  }

  // Constructor with three parameters.
  Triangle(char *str, double w,
           double h) : TwoDShape(w, h, "triangle") {
    strcpy(style, str);
  }

  // Construct an isosceles triangle.
  Triangle(double x) : TwoDShape(x, "triangle") {
    strcpy(style, "isosceles");
  }

  // This now overrides area() declared in TwoDShape.
  double area() {
    return getWidth() * getHeight() / 2;
  }

  void showStyle() {
    cout << "Triangle is " << style << "\n";
  }
};

// A derived class of TwoDShape for rectangles.
class Rectangle : public TwoDShape {
public:

  // Construct a rectangle.
  Rectangle(double w, double h) :
    TwoDShape(w, h, "rectangle") { }

  // Construct a square.
  Rectangle(double x) :
    TwoDShape(x, "rectangle") { }

  bool isSquare() {
    if(getWidth() == getHeight()) return true;
    return false;
  }

  // This is another override of area().
  double area() {
```

```
    return getWidth() * getHeight();
  }
};

int main() {
  // declare an array of pointers to TwoDShape objects.
  TwoDShape *shapes[4];

  shapes[0] = &Triangle("right", 8.0, 12.0);
  shapes[1] = &Rectangle(10);
  shapes[2] = &Rectangle(10, 4);
  shapes[3] = &Triangle(7.0);

  for(int i=0; i < 4; i++) {
    cout << "object is " <<
            shapes[i]->getName() << "\n";

    cout << "Area is " <<
            shapes[i]->area() << "\n";

    cout << "\n";
  }

  return 0;
}
```

If a class has at least one pure virtual function, then that class is said to be *abstract*. An abstract class has one important feature: there can be no objects of that class. To prove this to yourself, try removing the override of **area( )** from the **Triangle** class in the preceding program. You will receive an error when you try to create an instance of **Triangle**. Instead, an abstract class must be used only as a base that other classes will inherit. The reason that an abstract class cannot be used to declare an object is because one or more of its functions have no definition. Because of this, the **shapes** array in the preceding program has been shortened to 4, and a generic **TwoDShape** object is no longer created. As the program illustrates, even if the base class is abstract, you still can use it to declare a pointer of its type, which can be used to point to derived class objects.

10

☑ Mastery Check

1. A class that is inherited is called a _____ class. The class that does the inheriting is called a _____ class.

2. Does a base class have access to the members of a derived class? Does a derived class have access to the members of a base class?

3. Create a derived class of **TwoDShape** called **Circle**. Include an **area( )** function that computes the area of the circle.

4. How do you prevent a derived class from having access to a member of a base class?

5. Show the general form of a constructor that calls a base class constructor.

6. Given the following hierarchy:

   ```
   class Alpha { ...

   class Beta : public Alpha { ...

   Class Gamma : public Beta { ...
   ```

   in what order are the constructors for these classes called when a **Gamma** object is instantiated?

7. How can **protected** members be accessed?

8. A base class pointer can refer to a derived class object. Explain why this is important as it relates to function overriding.

9. What is a pure virtual function? What is an abstract class?

10. Can an object of an abstract class be instantiated?

11. Explain how the pure virtual function helps implement the "one interface, multiple methods" aspect of polymorphism.

Module 11

The C++ I/O System

The Goals of This Module

- Understand I/O streams
- Know the I/O class hierarchy
- Overload the << and >> operators
- Format I/O
- Use manipulators
- Create your own manipulators
- Read and write text files
- Read and write binary files
- Use random access file I/O
- Obtain I/O system status

Since the beginning of this book you have been using the C++ I/O system, but you have been doing so without much formal explanation. Since the I/O system is based upon a hierarchy of classes, it was not possible to present its theory and details without first discussing classes and inheritance. Now it is time to examine the C++ I/O system in detail.

The C++ I/O system is quite large, and it won't be possible to discuss here every class, function, or feature, but this module will introduce you to the most important and commonly used parts. Specifically, it shows how to overload the << and >> operators so that you can input or output objects of classes that you design. It describes how to format output and how to use I/O manipulators. The module ends by discussing file I/O.

Old vs. Modern C++ I/O

There are currently two versions of the C++ object-oriented I/O library in use: the older one that is based upon the original specifications for C++ and the newer one defined by Standard C++. The old I/O library is supported by the header file **<iostream.h>**. The new I/O library is supported by the header **<iostream>**. For the most part, the two libraries appear the same to the programmer. This is because the new I/O library is, in essence, simply an updated and improved version of the old one. In fact, the vast majority of differences between the two occur beneath the surface, in the way that the libraries are implemented—not in how they are used.

From the programmer's perspective, there are two main differences between the old and new C++ I/O libraries. First, the new I/O library contains a few additional features and defines some new data types. Thus, the new I/O library is essentially a superset of the old one. Nearly all programs originally written for the old library will compile without substantive changes when the new library is used. Second, the old-style I/O library was in the global namespace. The new-style library is in the **std** namespace. (Recall that the **std** namespace is used by all of the Standard C++ libraries.) Since the old-style I/O library is now obsolete, this book describes only the new I/O library, but most of the information is applicable to the old I/O library as well.

C++ Streams

The most fundamental point to understand about the C++ I/O system is that it operates on *streams*. A stream is an abstraction that either produces or consumes information. A stream is linked to a physical device by the C++ I/O system. All streams behave in the same manner, even if the actual physical devices they are linked to differ. Because all streams act the same, the same I/O functions and operators can operate on virtually any type of device. For example, the same method that you use to write to the screen can be used to write to a disk or to the printer.

In its most common form, a stream is a logical interface to a file. As C++ defines the term "file," it can refer to a disk file, the screen, the keyboard, a port, a file on tape, and so on. Although files differ in form and capabilities, all streams are the same. The advantage to this approach is that to you, the programmer, one hardware device will look much like any other. The stream provides a consistent interface.

A stream is linked to a file through an open operation. A stream is disassociated from a file through a close operation.

There are two types of streams: *text* and *binary*. A text stream is used with characters. When a text stream is being used, some character translations may take place. For example, when the newline character is output, it may be converted into a carriage return–linefeed sequence. For this reason, there might not be a one-to-one correspondence between what is sent to the stream and what is written to the file. A binary stream can be used with any type of data. No character translations will occur, and there is a one-to-one correspondence between what is sent to the stream and what is actually contained in the file.

One more concept to understand is that of the *current location*. The current location (also referred to as the *current position*) is the location in a file where the next file access will occur. For example, if a file is 100 bytes long and half the file has been read, the next read operation will occur at byte 50, which is the current location.

To summarize: In C++, I/O is performed through a logical interface called a *stream*. All streams have similar properties, and every stream is operated upon

11

by the same I/O functions, no matter what type of file it is associated with. A file is the actual physical entity that contains the data. Even though files differ, streams do not. (Of course, some devices may not support all operations, such as random-access operations, so their associated streams will not support these operations either.)

The C++ Predefined Streams

C++ contains several predefined streams that are automatically opened when your C++ program begins execution. They are **cin**, **cout**, **cerr**, and **clog**. As you know, **cin** is the stream associated with standard input, and **cout** is the stream associated with standard output. The **cerr** stream is linked to standard output, and so is **clog**. The difference between these two streams is that **clog** is buffered, but **cerr** is not. This means that any output sent to **cerr** is immediately output, but output to **clog** is written only when a buffer is full. Typically, **cerr** and **clog** are streams to which program debugging or error information is written.

C++ also opens wide (16-bit) character versions of the standard streams called **wcin**, **wcout**, **wcerr**, and **wclog**. These streams exist to support languages, such as Chinese, that require large character sets. We won't be using them in this book.

By default, the C++ standard streams are linked to the console, but they can be redirected to other devices or files by your program. They can also be redirected by the operating system.

The C++ Stream Classes

As you learned in Module 1, C++ provides support for its I/O system in **<iostream>**. In this header, a rather complicated set of class hierarchies is defined that supports I/O operations. The I/O classes begin with a system of template classes. As you will learn in Module 12, a template defines the form of a class without fully specifying the data upon which it will operate. Once a template class has been defined, specific instances of the template class can be created. As it relates to the I/O library, Standard C++ creates two specific versions of these template classes: one for 8-bit characters and another for wide characters. These specific versions act like any other classes, and no familiarity with templates is required to fully utilize the C++ I/O system.

The C++ I/O system is built upon two related, but different, template class hierarchies. The first is derived from the low-level I/O class called **basic_streambuf**. This class supplies the basic, low-level input and output operations, and provides the underlying support for the entire C++ I/O system. Unless you are doing advanced I/O programming, you will not need to use **basic_streambuf** directly. The class hierarchy that you will most commonly be working with is derived from **basic_ios**. This is a high-level I/O class that provides formatting, error-checking, and status information related to stream I/O. (A base class for **basic_ios** is called **ios_base**, which defines several traits used by **basic_ios**.) **basic_ios** is used as a base for several derived classes, including **basic_istream**, **basic_ostream**, and **basic_iostream**. These classes are used to create streams capable of input, output, and input/output, respectively.

As explained, the I/O library creates two specific versions of the I/O class hierarchies: one for 8-bit characters and one for wide characters. This book discusses only the 8-bit character classes since they are by far the most frequently used. Here is a list of the mapping of template class names to their character-based versions.

Template Class Name	Equivalent Character-Based Class Name
basic_streambuf	streambuf
basic_ios	ios
basic_istream	istream
basic_ostream	ostream
basic_iostream	iostream
basic_fstream	fstream
basic_ifstream	ifstream
basic_ofstream	ofstream

The character-based names will be used throughout the remainder of this book, since they are the names that you will use in your programs. They are also the same names that were used by the old I/O library. This is why the old and the new I/O library are compatible at the source code level.

One last point: The **ios** class contains many member functions and variables that control or monitor the fundamental operation of a stream. It will be referred to frequently. Just remember that if you include **<iostream>** in your program, you will have access to this important class.

11

1-Minute Drill

- What is a stream? What is a file?
- What stream is connected to standard output?
- C++ I/O is supported by a sophisticated set of class hierarchies. True or false?

Overloading the I/O Operators

In the preceding modules, when a program needed to output or input the data associated with a class, member functions were created whose only purpose was to output or input the class' data. While there is nothing, in itself, wrong with this approach, C++ allows a much better way of performing I/O operations on classes: by overloading the << and the >> I/O operators.

In the language of C++, the << operator is referred to as the *insertion* operator because it inserts data into a stream. Likewise, the >> operator is called the *extraction* operator because it extracts data from a stream. The operator functions that overload the insertion and extraction operators are generally called *inserters* and *extractors*, respectively.

In **<iostream>**, the insertion and extraction operators are overloaded for all of the C++ built-in types. Here you will see how to define these operators relative to classes that you create.

Creating Inserters

As a simple first example, let's create an inserter for the version of the **ThreeD** class shown here:

```
class ThreeD {
public:
  int x, y, z; // 3-D coordinates
  ThreeD(int a, int b, int c) { x = a; y = b; z = c; }
};
```

- A stream is a logical abstraction that either produces or consumes information. A file is a physical entity that contains data.
- **cout** is the stream connected to standard output.
- True, C++ I/O is supported by a sophisticated set of class hierarchies.

To create an inserter function for an object of type **ThreeD**, overload the **<<** for it. Here is one way to do this:

```
// Display X, Y, Z coordinates - ThreeD inserter.
ostream &operator<<(ostream &stream, ThreeD obj)
{
  stream << obj.x << ", ";
  stream << obj.y << ", ";
  stream << obj.z << "\n";
  return stream;  // return the stream
}
```

Let's look closely at this function, because many of its features are common to all inserter functions. First, notice that it is declared as returning a reference to an object of type **ostream**. This declaration is necessary so that several inserters of this type can be combined in a compound I/O expression. Next, the function has two parameters. The first is the reference to the stream that occurs on the left side of the **<<** operator. The second parameter is the object that occurs on the right side. (This parameter can also be a reference to the object, if you like.) Inside the function, the three values contained in an object of type **ThreeD** are output, and **stream** is returned.

Here is a short program that demonstrates the inserter:

```
// Demonstrate a custom inserter.

#include <iostream>
using namespace std;

class ThreeD {
public:
  int x, y, z; // 3-D coordinates
  ThreeD(int a, int b, int c) { x = a; y = b; z = c; }
};

// Display X, Y, Z coordinates - ThreeD inserter.
ostream &operator<<(ostream &stream, ThreeD obj)
{
  stream << obj.x << ", ";
  stream << obj.y << ", ";
  stream << obj.z << "\n";
  return stream;  // return the stream
}
```

An inserter for **ThreeD**.

11

```
}

int main()
{
  ThreeD a(1, 2, 3), b(3, 4, 5), c(5, 6, 7);

  cout << a << b << c;
```
Use **ThreeD** inserter to output coordinates.
```
  return 0;
}
```

This program displays the following output:

```
1, 2, 3
3, 4, 5
5, 6, 7
```

If you eliminate the code that is specific to the **ThreeD** class, you are left with the skeleton for an inserter function, as shown here:

```
ostream &operator<<(ostream &stream, class_type obj)
{
  // class specific code goes here
  return stream;  // return the stream
}
```

Of course, it is permissible for **obj** to be passed by reference.

Within wide boundaries, what an inserter function actually does is up to you. However, good programming practice dictates that your inserter should produce reasonable output. Just make sure that you return **stream**.

Using Friend Functions to Overload Inserters

In the preceding program, the overloaded inserter function is not a member of **ThreeD**. In fact, neither inserter nor extractor functions can be members of a class. The reason is that when an **operator** function is a member of a class, the left operand (implicitly passed using the **this** pointer) must be an object of the class that has generated the call to the **operator** function. There is no way to change this. However, when inserters are overloaded, the left operand is a stream, and the right operand is an object of the class being output. Therefore, overloaded inserters must be nonmember functions.

The fact that inserters must not be members of the class they are defined to operate on raises a serious question: How can an overloaded inserter access the private elements of a class? In the preceding program, the variables **x**, **y**, and **z** were made public so that the inserter could access them. But hiding data is an important part of OOP, and forcing all data to be public is a serious inconsistency. However, there is a solution: an inserter can be a friend of a class. As a friend of the class for which it is defined, it has access to private data. Here, the **ThreeD** class and sample program are reworked, with the overloaded inserter declared as a friend:

```
// Use a friend to overload <<.

#include <iostream>
using namespace std;

class ThreeD {
  int x, y, z; // 3-D coordinates - now private
public:
  ThreeD(int a, int b, int c) { x = a; y = b; z = c; }
  friend ostream &operator<<(ostream &stream, ThreeD obj);
};

// Display X, Y, Z coordinates - ThreeD inserter.
ostream &operator<<(ostream &stream, ThreeD obj)
{
  stream << obj.x << ", ";
  stream << obj.y << ", ";
  stream << obj.z << "\n";
  return stream;  // return the stream
}

int main()
{
  ThreeD a(1, 2, 3), b(3, 4, 5), c(5, 6, 7);

  cout << a << b << c;

  return 0;
}
```

ThreeD inserter is now a friend and has access to private data.

11

Notice that the variables **x**, **y**, and **z** are now private to **ThreeD**, but can still be directly accessed by the inserter. Making inserters (and extractors) friends of the classes for which they are defined preserves the encapsulation principle of OOP.

Overloading Extractors

To overload an extractor, use the same general approach that you use when overloading an inserter. For example, the following extractor inputs 3-D coordinates. Notice that it also prompts the user.

```
// Get three-dimensional values - ThreeD extractor.
istream &operator>>(istream &stream, ThreeD &obj)
{
  cout << "Enter X,Y,Z values: ";
  stream >> obj.x >> obj.y >> obj.z;
  return stream;
}
```

An extractor must return a reference to an object of type **istream**. Also, the first parameter must be a reference to an object of type **istream**. This is the stream that occurs on the left side of the **>>**. The second parameter is a reference to the variable that will be receiving input. Because it is a reference, the second parameter can be modified when information is input.

The skeleton of an extractor is shown here:

```
istream &operator>>(istream &stream, object_type &obj)
{
  // put your extractor code here
  return stream;
}
```

The following program demonstrates the extractor for objects of type **ThreeD**:

```
// Demonstrate a custom extractor.

#include <iostream>
using namespace std;

class ThreeD {
  int x, y, z; // 3-D coordinates
```

```
public:
  ThreeD(int a, int b, int c) { x = a; y = b; z = c; }
  friend ostream &operator<<(ostream &stream, ThreeD obj);
  friend istream &operator>>(istream &stream, ThreeD &obj);
} ;

// Display X, Y, Z coordinates - ThreeD inserter.
ostream &operator<<(ostream &stream, ThreeD obj)
{
  stream << obj.x << ", ";
  stream << obj.y << ", ";
  stream << obj.z << "\n";
  return stream; // return the stream
}

// Get three dimensional values - ThreeD extractor.
istream &operator>>(istream &stream, ThreeD &obj)
{
  cout << "Enter X,Y,Z values: ";
  stream >> obj.x >> obj.y >> obj.z;
  return stream;
}
```

Extractor for **ThreeD**

```
int main()
{
  ThreeD a(1, 2, 3);

  cout << a;

  cin >> a;
  cout << a;

  return 0;
}
```

11

Like inserters, extractor functions cannot be members of the class they are designed to operate upon. They can be friends or simply independent functions.

Except for the fact that you must return a reference to an object of type **istream**, you can do anything you like inside an extractor function. However, for the sake of structure and clarity, it is best to use extractors only for input operations.

1-Minute Drill

- What is an inserter?
- What is an extractor?
- Why are friend functions often used for inserter or extractor functions?

Formatted I/O

Up to this point, the format for inputting or outputting information has been left to the defaults provided by the C++ I/O system. However, you can precisely control the format of your data in either of two ways. The first uses member functions of the **ios** class. The second uses a special type of function called a *manipulator*. We will begin by looking at formatting using the **ios** member functions.

Formatting with the ios Member Functions

Each stream has associated with it a set of format flags that control the way information is formatted by a stream. The **ios** class declares a bitmask enumeration called **fmtflags** in which the following values are defined. (Technically, these values are defined within **ios_base**, which, as explained earlier, is a base class for **ios**.)

adjustfield	basefield	boolalpha	dec
fixed	floatfield	hex	internal
left	oct	right	scientific
showbase	showpoint	showpos	skipws
unitbuf	uppercase		

These values are used to set or clear the format flags. Some older compilers may not define the **fmtflags** enumeration type. In this case, the format flags will be encoded into a long integer.

When the **skipws** flag is set, leading whitespace characters (spaces, tabs, and newlines) are discarded when performing input on a stream. When **skipws** is cleared, whitespace characters are not discarded.

- An inserter puts data into a stream.
- An extractor removes data from a stream.
- Friend functions are often used for inserter or extractor functions because they have access to the private data of a class.

When the **left** flag is set, output is left-justified. When **right** is set, output is right-justified. When the **internal** flag is set, a numeric value is padded to fill a field by inserting spaces between any sign or base character. If none of these flags is set, output is right-justified by default.

By default, numeric values are output in decimal. However, it is possible to change the number base. Setting the **oct** flag causes output to be displayed in octal. Setting the **hex** flag causes output to be displayed in hexadecimal. To return output to decimal, set the **dec** flag.

Setting **showbase** causes the base of numeric values to be shown. For example, if the conversion base is hexadecimal, the value 1F will be displayed as 0x1F.

By default, when scientific notation is displayed, the **e** is in lowercase. Also, when a hexadecimal value is displayed, the **x** is in lowercase. When **uppercase** is set, these characters are displayed in uppercase.

Setting **showpos** causes a leading plus sign to be displayed before positive values.

Setting **showpoint** causes a decimal point and trailing zeros to be displayed for all floating-point output—whether needed or not.

By setting the **scientific** flag, floating-point numeric values are displayed using scientific notation. When **fixed** is set, floating-point values are displayed using normal notation. When neither flag is set, the compiler chooses an appropriate method.

When **unitbuf** is set, the buffer is flushed after each insertion operation.

When **boolalpha** is set, Booleans can be input or output using the keywords **true** and **false**.

Since it is common to refer to the **oct**, **dec**, and **hex** fields, they can be collectively referred to as **basefield**. Similarly, the **left**, **right**, and **internal** fields can be referred to as **adjustfield**. Finally, the **scientific** and **fixed** fields can be referenced as **floatfield**.

Setting and Clearing Format Flags

To set a flag, use the **setf( )** function. This function is a member of **ios**. Its most common form is shown here:

   fmtflags setf(fmtflags *flags*);

This function returns the previous settings of the format flags and turns on those flags specified by *flags*. For example, to turn on the **showbase** flag, you can use this statement:

```
stream.setf(ios::showbase);
```

11

Here, *stream* is the stream you want to affect. Notice the use of **ios::** to qualify **showbase**. Because **showbase** is an enumerated constant defined by the **ios** class, it must be qualified by **ios** when it is referred to. This principle applies to all of the format flags.

The following program uses **setf( )** to turn on both the **showpos** and **scientific** flags:

```
// Use setf().

#include <iostream>
using namespace std;

int main()
{
  // Turn on showpos and scientific flags.
  cout.setf(ios::showpos);
  cout.setf(ios::scientific);                 Set format flags using setf( ).

  cout << 123 << " " << 123.23 << " ";

  return 0;
}
```

The output produced by this program is shown here:

```
+123 +1.232300e+002
```

You can OR together as many flags as you like in a single call. For example, by ORing together **scientific** and **showpos**, as shown next, you can change the program so that only one call is made to **setf( )**:

```
cout.setf(ios::scientific | ios::showpos);
```

To turn off a flag, use the **unsetf( )** function, whose prototype is shown here:

void unsetf(fmtflags *flags*);

The flags specified by *flags* are cleared. (All other flags are unaffected.)

Sometimes it is useful to know the current flag settings. You can retrieve the current flag values using the **flags( )** function, whose prototype is shown here:

fmtflags flags( );

This function returns the current value of the flags relative to the invoking stream.

The following form of **flags( )** sets the flag values to those specified by *flags* and returns the previous flag values:

```
fmtflags flags(fmtflags flags);
```

The following program demonstrates **flags( )** and **unsetf( )**:

```
// Demonstrate flags() and unsetf().

#include <iostream>
using namespace std;

int main()
{
  ios::fmtflags f;

  f = cout.flags();          Get the format flags.

  if(f & ios::showpos)
    cout << "showpos is set for cout.\n";
  else
    cout << "showpos is cleared for cout.\n";

  cout << "\nSetting showpos for cout.\n";
  cout.setf(ios::showpos);

  f = cout.flags();          Set the showpos flag.

  if(f & ios::showpos)
    cout << "showpos is set for cout.\n";
  else
    cout << "showpos is cleared for cout.\n";

  cout << "\nClearing showpos for cout.\n";
  cout.unsetf(ios::showpos);

  f = cout.flags();          Clear the showpos flag.
```

11

```
   if(f & ios::showpos)
     cout << "showpos is set for cout.\n";
   else
     cout << "showpos is cleared for cout.\n";

   return 0;
}
```

The program produces this output:

```
showpos is cleared for cout.

Setting showpos for cout.
showpos is set for cout.

Clearing showpos for cout.
showpos is cleared for cout.
```

In the program, notice that the type **fmtflags** is preceded by **ios::** when **f** is declared. This is necessary since **fmtflags** is a type defined by **ios**. In general, whenever you use the name of a type or enumerated constant that is defined by a class, you must qualify it with the name of the class.

Setting the Field Width, Precision, and Fill Character

In addition to the formatting flags, there are three member functions defined by **ios** that set these additional format values: the field width, the precision, and the fill character. The functions that set these values are **width( )**, **precision( )**, and **fill( )**, respectively. Each is examined in turn.

By default, when a value is output, it occupies only as much space as the number of characters it takes to display it. However, you can specify a minimum field width by using the **width( )** function. Its prototype is shown here:

   streamsize width(streamsize *w*);

Here, *w* becomes the field width, and the previous field width is returned. In some implementations, the field width must be set before each output. If it isn't, the default field width is used. The **streamsize** type is defined as some form of integer by the compiler.

After you set a minimum field width, when a value uses less than the specified width, the field will be padded with the current fill character (space, by default) to reach the field width. If the size of the value exceeds the minimum field width, then the field will be overrun. No values are truncated.

When outputting floating-point values in scientific notation, you can determine the number of digits to be displayed after the decimal point by using the **precision( )** function. Its prototype is shown here:

```
streamsize precision(streamsize p);
```

Here, the precision is set to *p*, and the old value is returned. The default precision is 6. In some implementations, the precision must be set before each floating-point output. If you don't set it, the default precision is used.

By default, when a field needs to be filled, it is filled with spaces. You can specify the fill character by using the **fill( )** function. Its prototype is

```
char fill(char ch);
```

After a call to **fill( )**, *ch* becomes the new fill character, and the old one is returned.

Here is a program that demonstrates these three functions:

```
// Demonstrate width(), precision(), and fill().

#include <iostream>
using namespace std;

int main()
{
  cout.setf(ios::showpos);
  cout.setf(ios::scientific);
  cout << 123 << " " << 123.23 << "\n";          // Set the precision.

  cout.precision(2); // two digits after decimal point
  cout.width(10);    // in a field of 10 characters
  cout << 123 << " ";
  cout.width(10);       // set width to 10          // Set field width.
  cout << 123.23 << "\n";

  cout.fill('#');  // fill using #                  // Set the fill character.
  cout.width(10);  // in a field of 10 characters
```

11

```
cout << 123 << " ";
cout.width(10);  // set width to 10
cout << 123.23;

return 0;
}
```

The program displays this output:

```
+123 +1.232300e+002
     +123 +1.23e+002
######+123 +1.23e+002
```

In some implementations, it is necessary to reset the field width before each output operation. This is why **width( )** is called repeatedly in the preceding program.

There are overloaded forms of **width( )**, **precision( )**, and **fill( )** that obtain, but do not change, the current setting. These forms are shown here:

```
char fill( );
streamsize width( );
streamsize precision( );
```

1-Minute Drill

● What does **boolalpha** do?

● What does **setf( )** do?

● What function is used to set the fill character?

Using I/O Manipulators

The C++ I/O system includes a second way in which you can alter the format parameters of a stream. This method uses special functions, called *manipulators,* that can be included in an I/O expression. The standard manipulators are shown in Table 11-1. To use those manipulators that take arguments, you must include **<iomanip>** in your program.

● When **boolalpha** is set, Boolean values are input or output using the words **true** and **false**.

● **setf( )** sets one or more format flags.

● **fill( )** sets the fill character.

Manipulator	Purpose	Input/Output
boolalpha	Turns on **boolalpha** flag	Input/Output
dec	Turns on **dec** flag	Input/Output
endl	Outputs a newline character and flushes the stream	Output
ends	Outputs a null	Output
fixed	Turns on **fixed** flag	Output
flush	Flushes a stream	Output
hex	Turns on **hex** flag	Input/Output
internal	Turns on **internal** flag	Output
left	Turns on **left** flag	Output
noboolalpha	Turns off **boolalpha** flag	Input/Output
noshowbase	Turns off **showbase** flag	Output
noshowpoint	Turns off **showpoint** flag	Output
noshowpos	Turns off **showpos** flag	Output
noskipws	Turns off **skipws** flag	Input
nounitbuf	Turns off **unitbuf** flag	Output
nouppercase	Turns off **uppercase** flag	Output
oct	Turns on **oct** flag	Input/Output
resetiosflags (fmtflags *f*)	Turns off the flags specified in *f*	Input/Output
right	Turns on **right** flag	Output
scientific	Turns on **scientific** flag	Output
setbase(int *base*)	Sets the number base to *base*	Input/Output
setfill(int *ch*)	Sets the fill character to *ch*	Output
setiosflags(fmtflags *f*)	Turns on the flags specified in *f*	Input/Output
setprecision (int *p*)	Sets the number of digits of precision	Output
setw(int *w*)	Sets the field width to *w*	Output
showbase	Turns on **showbase** flag	Output
showpoint	Turns on **showpoint** flag	Output
showpos	Turns on **showpos** flag	Output
skipws	Turns on **skipws** flag	Input
unitbuf	Turns on **unitbuf** flag	Output
uppercase	Turns on **uppercase** flag	Output
ws	Skips leading whitespace	Input

11

Table 11-1   The C++ I/O Manipulators

A manipulator is used as part of a larger I/O expression. Here is a sample program that uses manipulators to control the format of its output:

```
// Demonstrate an I/O manipulator.

#include <iostream>
#include <iomanip>
using namespace std;

int main()
{
  cout << setprecision(2) << 1000.243 << endl;
  cout << setw(20) << "Hello there.";

  return 0;
}
```

Use I/O manipulators.

It produces this output:

```
1e+003
        Hello there.
```

Notice how the manipulators occur in the chain of I/O operations. Also, notice that when a manipulator does not take an argument, such as **endl** in the example, it is not followed by parentheses.

The following program uses **setiosflags( )** to set the **scientific** and **showpos** flags:

```
// Use setiosflags().

#include <iostream>
#include <iomanip>
using namespace std;

int main()
{
  cout << setiosflags(ios::showpos) <<
          setiosflags(ios::scientific) <<
          123 << " " << 123.23;

  return 0;
}
```

Use **setiosflags( )**.

The program shown next uses **ws** to skip any leading whitespace when inputting a string into **s**:

```
// Skip leading whitespace.

#include <iostream>
using namespace std;

int main()
{
  char s[80];

  cin >> ws >> s;
  cout << s;

  return 0;
}
```

Creating Your Own Manipulator Functions

You can create your own manipulator functions. There are two types of manipulator functions: those that take arguments and those that don't. The creation of parameterized manipulators requires the use of techniques beyond the scope of this book. However, the creation of parameterless manipulators is quite easy and is described here.

All parameterless manipulator output functions have this skeleton:

```
ostream &manip_name(ostream &stream)
{
  // your code here

  return stream;
}
```

Here, **manip_name** is the name of the manipulator. It is important to understand that even though the manipulator has as its single argument a pointer to the stream upon which it is operating, no argument is specified when the manipulator is used in an output expression.

11

The following program creates a manipulator called **setup( )** that turns on left justification, sets the field width to 10, and specifies that the dollar sign will be the fill character.

```
// Create an output manipulator.

#include <iostream>
#include <iomanip>
using namespace std;

ostream &setup(ostream &stream)          A custom output manipulator
{
  stream.setf(ios::left);
  stream << setw(10) << setfill('$');
  return stream;
}

int main()
{
  cout << 10 << " " << setup << 10;

  return 0;
}
```

Custom manipulators are useful for two reasons. First, you might need to perform an I/O operation on a device for which none of the predefined manipulators applies—a plotter, for example. In this case, creating your own manipulators will make it more convenient when outputting to the device. Second, you may find that you are repeating the same sequence of operations many times. You can consolidate these operations into a single manipulator, as the foregoing program illustrates.

All parameterless input manipulator functions have this skeleton:

```
istream &manip_name(istream &stream)
{
  // your code here

  return stream;
}
```

For example, the following program creates the **prompt( )** manipulator. It displays a prompting message and then configures input to accept hexadecimal.

```
// Create an input manipulator.

#include <iostream>
#include <iomanip>
using namespace std;

istream &prompt(istream &stream)          A custom input manipulator.
{
  cin >> hex;
  cout << "Enter number using hex format: ";

  return stream;
}

int main()
{
  int i;

  cin >> prompt >> i;
  cout << i;

  return 0;
}
```

Remember that it is crucial that your manipulator return *stream*. If this is not done, then your manipulator cannot be used in a chain of input or output operations.

1-Minute Drill

- What does **endl** do?
- What does **ws** do?
- Is an I/O manipulator used as part of a larger I/O expression?

- **endl** outputs a newline.
- **ws** skips leading whitespace on input.
- Yes, an I/O manipulator is used as part of a larger I/O expression.

File I/O

You can use the C++ I/O system to perform file I/O. To perform file I/O, you must include the header file **<fstream>** in your program. It defines several important classes and values.

Opening and Closing a File

In C++, a file is opened by linking it to a stream. As you know, there are three types of streams: input, output, and input/output. To open an input stream, you must declare the stream to be of class **ifstream**. To open an output stream, it must be declared as class **ofstream**. A stream that will be performing both input and output operations must be declared as class **fstream**. For example, this fragment creates one input stream, one output stream, and one stream capable of both input and output:

```
ifstream in;  // input
ofstream out; // output
fstream both; // input and output
```

Once you have created a stream, one way to associate it with a file is by using **open( )**. This function is a member of each of the three stream classes. The prototype for each is shown here:

```
void ifstream::open(const char *filename,
                    ios::openmode mode = ios::in);
void ofstream::open(const char *filename,
                    ios::openmode mode = ios::out | ios::trunc);
void fstream::open(const char *filename,
                   ios::openmode mode = ios::in | ios::out);
```

Here, *filename* is the name of the file; it can include a path specifier. The value of *mode* determines how the file is opened. It must be one or more of the values defined by **openmode**, which is an enumeration defined by **ios** (through its base class **ios_base**). The values are shown here:

```
ios::app
ios::ate
ios::binary
```

```
ios::in
ios::out
ios::trunc
```

You can combine two or more of these values by ORing them together.

Including **ios::app** causes all output to that file to be appended to the end. This value can be used only with files capable of output. Including **ios::ate** causes a seek to the end of the file to occur when the file is opened. Although **ios::ate** causes an initial seek to end-of-file, I/O operations can still occur anywhere within the file.

The **ios::in** value specifies that the file is capable of input. The **ios::out** value specifies that the file is capable of output.

The **ios::binary** value causes a file to be opened in binary mode. By default, all files are opened in text mode. In text mode, various character translations may take place, such as carriage return–linefeed sequences being converted into newlines. However, when a file is opened in binary mode, no such character translations will occur. Understand that any file, whether it contains formatted text or raw data, can be opened in either binary or text mode. The only difference is whether character translations take place.

The **ios::trunc** value causes the contents of a preexisting file by the same name to be destroyed, and the file to be truncated to zero length. When creating an output stream using **ofstream**, any preexisting file by that name is automatically truncated.

The following fragment opens a text file for output:

```
ofstream mystream;
mystream.open("test");
```

Since the *mode* parameter to **open( )** defaults to a value appropriate to the type of stream being opened, there is often no need to specify its value in the preceding example. (Some compilers do not default the mode parameter for **fstream::open( )** to **in | out**, so you might need to specify this explicitly.)

If **open( )** fails, the stream will evaluate to false when used in a Boolean expression. You can make use of this fact to confirm that the open operation succeeded by using a statement like this:

```
if(!mystream) {
  cout << "Cannot open file.\n";
```

11

```
   // handle error
}
```

In general, you should always check the result of a call to **open( )** before attempting to access the file.

You can also check to see if you have successfully opened a file by using the **is_open( )** function, which is a member of **fstream**, **ifstream**, and **ofstream**. It has this prototype:

bool is_open( );

It returns true if the stream is linked to an open file and false otherwise. For example, the following checks if **mystream** is currently open:

```
if(!mystream.is_open()) {
  cout << "File is not open.\n";
  // ...
```

Although it is entirely proper to use the **open( )** function for opening a file, most of the time you will not do so because the **ifstream**, **ofstream**, and **fstream** classes have constructors that automatically open the file. The constructors have the same parameters and defaults as the **open( )** function. Therefore, the most common way you will see a file opened is shown in this example:

```
ifstream mystream("myfile"); // open file for input
```

If, for some reason, the file cannot be opened, the value of the associated stream variable will evaluate to false.

To close a file, use the member function **close( )**. For example, to close the file linked to a stream called **mystream**, you would use this statement:

```
mystream.close();
```

The **close( )** function takes no parameters and returns no value.

Reading and Writing Text Files

The easiest way to read from or write to a text file is to use the << and >> operators. For example, this program writes an integer, a floating-point value, and a string to a file called **test**:

```
// Write to file.
d
#include <iostream>
#include <fstream>
using namespace std;

int main()
{
  ofstream out("test");
  if(!out) {
    cout << "Cannot open file.\n";
    return 1;
  }

  out << 10 << " " << 123.23 << "\n";
  out << "This is a short text file.";

  out.close();

  return 0;
}
```

Create and open a file called "test" for text output.

Output to the file.

Close the file.

The following program reads an integer, a **float**, a character, and a string from the file created by the previous program:

```
// Read from file.

#include <iostream>
#include <fstream>
using namespace std;

int main()
{
  char ch;
  int i;
```

11

```
float f;
char str[80];                    Open a file for text input.

ifstream in("test");
if(!in) {
   cout << "Cannot open file.\n";
   return 1;
}

in >> i;
in >> f;                         Read from the file.
in >> ch;
in >> str;

cout << i << " " << f << " " << ch << "\n";
cout << str;

in.close();                      Close the file.
return 0;
}
```

Keep in mind that when the >> operator is used for reading text files, certain character translations occur. For example, whitespace characters are omitted. If you want to prevent any character translations, you must open a file for binary access. Also remember that when >> is used to read a string, input stops when the first whitespace character is encountered.

1-Minute Drill

● What class creates an input file?

● What function opens a file?

● Can you read and write to a file using << and >>?

● To open an input file, use **ifstream**.
● To open a file, use the class' constructor, or the **open( )** function.
● Yes, you can use << and >> to read and write to a file.

Ask the Expert

Question: As you explained in Module 1, C++ is a superset of C. I know that C defines an I/O system of its own. Is the C I/O system available to C++ programmers? If so, should it be used in C++ programs?

Answer: The answer to the first question is yes. The C I/O system is available to C++ programmers. The answer to the second question is a qualified no. The C I/O system is not object-oriented. Thus, you will nearly always find the C++ I/O system more compatible with C++ programs. However, the C I/O system is still widely used and is quite streamlined, carrying little overhead. Thus, for some highly specialized programs, the C I/O system might be a good choice. Information on the C I/O system can be found in my book *C++: The Complete Reference* (Osborne/McGraw-Hill).

Unformatted and Binary I/O

While reading and writing formatted text files is very easy, it is not always the most efficient way to handle files. Also, there will be times when you need to store unformatted (raw) binary data, not text. The functions that allow you to do this are described here.

When performing binary operations on a file, be sure to open it using the **ios::binary** mode specifier. Although the unformatted file functions will work on files opened for text mode, some character translations may occur. Character translations negate the purpose of binary file operations.

In general, there are two ways to write and read unformatted binary data to or from a file. First, you can write a byte using the member function **put( )**, and read a byte using the member function **get( )**. The second way uses the block I/O functions: **read( )** and **write( )**. Each is examined here.

11

Using get( ) and put( )

The **get( )** function has many forms, but the most commonly used version is shown next, along with that of **put( )**:

```
istream &get(char &ch);
ostream &put(char ch);
```

The get( ) function reads a single character from the associated stream and puts that value in *ch*. It returns a reference to the stream. This value will be null if the end of the file is reached. The put( ) function writes *ch* to the stream and returns a reference to the stream.

The following program will display the contents of any file on the screen. It uses the get( ) function:

```
// Display a file using get().

#include <iostream>
#include <fstream>
using namespace std;

int main(int argc, char *argv[])
{
  char ch;

  if(argc!=2) {
    cout << "Usage: PR <filename>\n";
    return 1;
  }

  ifstream in(argv[1], ios::in | ios::binary);
  if(!in) {
    cout << "Cannot open file.\n";
    return 1;
  }

  while(in) { // in will be false when eof is reached
    in.get(ch);
    if(in) cout << ch;
  }

  in.close();

  return 0;
}
```

Open the file for binary operations.

Read data until the end of the file is reached.

When **in** reaches the end of the file, it will be false, causing the **while** loop to stop.

There is actually a more compact way to code the loop that reads and displays a file, as shown here:

```
while(in.get(ch))
  cout << ch;
```

This form works because **get( )** returns the stream **in**, and **in** will be false when the end of the file is encountered.

This program uses **put( )** to write a string to a file.

```
// Use put() to write to a file.

#include <iostream>
#include <fstream>
using namespace std;

int main()
{
  char *p = "hello there\n";

  ofstream out("test", ios::out | ios::binary);
  if(!out) {
    cout << "Cannot open file.\n";
    return 1;
  }

  // Write characters until the null-terminator is reached.
  while(*p) out.put(*p++);

  out.close();

  return 0;
}
```

Write a string to a file using **put( )**. No character translations will occur.

After this program executes, the file **test** will contain the string "hello there" followed by a newline character. No character translations will have taken place.

Reading and Writing Blocks of Data

To read and write blocks of binary data, use the **read( )** and **write( )** member functions. Their prototypes are shown here:

istream &read(char *buf, streamsize num);
ostream &write(const char *buf, streamsize num);

The **read( )** function reads num bytes from the associated stream and puts them in the buffer pointed to by buf. The **write( )** function writes num bytes to the associated stream from the buffer pointed to by buf. As mentioned earlier,

streamsize is some form of integer defined by the C++ library. It is capable of holding the largest number of bytes that can be transferred in any one I/O operation.

The following program writes and then reads an array of integers:

```
// Use read() and write().

#include <iostream>
#include <fstream>
using namespace std;

int main()
{
  int n[5] = {1, 2, 3, 4, 5};
  register int i;

  ofstream out("test", ios::out | ios::binary);
  if(!out) {
    cout << "Cannot open file.\n";
    return 1;
   }

  out.write((char *) &n, sizeof n);          Write a block of data.

  out.close();

  for(i=0; i<5; i++) // clear array
    n[i] = 0;

  ifstream in("test", ios::in | ios::binary);
  if(!in) {
    cout << "Cannot open file.\n";
    return 1;
  }

  in.read((char *) &n, sizeof n);            Read a block of data.

  for(i=0; i<5; i++) // show values read from file
    cout << n[i] << " ";

  in.close();

  return 0;
}
```

Note that the type casts inside the calls to **read( )** and **write( )** are necessary when operating on a buffer that is not defined as a character array.

If the end of the file is reached before *num* characters have been read, then **read( )** simply stops, and the buffer will contain as many characters as were available. You can find out how many characters have been read using another member function, called **gcount( )**, which has this prototype:

    streamsize gcount( );

gcount( ) returns the number of characters read by the last input operation.

1-Minute Drill

● To read or write binary data, you open a file using what mode specifier?
● What does **get( )** do? What does **put( )** do?
● What function reads a block of data?

More I/O Functions

The C++ I/O system defines other I/O related functions, several of which you will find useful. They are discussed here.

More Versions of get( )

In addition to the form shown earlier, the **get( )** function is overloaded in several different ways. The prototypes for the three most commonly used overloaded forms are shown here:

    istream &get(char *buf, streamsize num);
    istream &get(char *buf, streamsize num, char delim);
    int get( );

11

● To read or write binary data, use the **ios::binary** mode specifier.
● The **get( )** function reads a character. The **put( )** function writes a character.
● To read a block of data, use **read( )**.

The first form reads characters into the array pointed to by *buf* until either *num*–1 characters have been read, a newline is found, or the end of the file has been encountered. The array pointed to by *buf* will be null-terminated by **get( )**. If the newline character is encountered in the input stream, it is *not* extracted. Instead, it remains in the stream until the next input operation.

The second form reads characters into the array pointed to by *buf* until either *num*–1 characters have been read, the character specified by *delim* has been found, or the end of the file has been encountered. The array pointed to by *buf* will be null-terminated by **get( )**. If the delimiter character is encountered in the input stream, it is *not* extracted. Instead, it remains in the stream until the next input operation.

The third overloaded form of **get( )** returns the next character from the stream. It returns EOF (a value that indicates end-of-file) if the end of the file is encountered. EOF is defined by **<iostream>**.

One good use for **get( )** is to read a string that contains spaces. As you know, when you use >> to read a string, it stops reading when the first whitespace character is encountered. This makes >> useless for reading a string containing spaces. However, you can overcome this problem by using **get(buf, num)**, as illustrated in this program:

```
// Use get() to read a string that contains spaces.

#include <iostream>
#include <fstream>
using namespace std;

int main()
{
  char str[80];

  cout << "Enter your name: ";
  cin.get(str, 79);
```
Use **get( )** to read a string that contains whitespace.
```

  cout << str << '\n';

  return 0;
}
```

Here, the delimiter to **get( )** is allowed to default to a newline. This makes **get( )** act much like the standard **gets( )** function.

getline( )

Another function that performs input is **getline( )**. It is a member of each input stream class. Its prototypes are shown here:

```
istream &getline(char *buf, streamsize num);
istream &getline(char *buf, streamsize num, char delim);
```

The first form reads characters into the array pointed to by *buf* until either *num*–1 characters have been read, a newline character has been found, or the end of the file has been encountered. The array pointed to by *buf* will be null-terminated by **getline( )**. If the newline character is encountered in the input stream, it is extracted, but is not put into *buf*.

The second form reads characters into the array pointed to by *buf* until either *num*–1 characters have been read, the character specified by *delim* has been found, or the end of the file has been encountered. The array pointed to by *buf* will be null-terminated by **getline( )**. If the delimiter character is encountered in the input stream, it is extracted, but is not put into *buf*.

As you can see, the two versions of **getline( )** are virtually identical to the **get(buf, num)** and **get(buf, num, delim)** versions of **get( )**. Both read characters from input and put them into the array pointed to by *buf* until either *num*–1 characters have been read or until the delimiter character is encountered. The difference between **get( )** and **getline( )** is that **getline( )** reads and removes the delimiter from the input stream; **get( )** does not.

Detecting EOF

You can detect when the end of the file is reached by using the member function **eof( )**, which has this prototype:

```
bool eof( );
```

It returns true when the end of the file has been reached; otherwise it returns false.

11

peek( ) and putback( )

You can obtain the next character in the input stream without removing it from that stream by using **peek( )**. It has this prototype:

    int_type peek( );

peek( ) returns the next character in the stream, or **EOF** if the end of the file is encountered. (**int_type** is some form of integer that is defined by the compiler.)

You can return the last character read from a stream to that stream by using **putback( )**. Its prototype is shown here:

    istream &putback(char c);

where *c* is the last character read.

flush( )

When output is performed, data is not immediately written to the physical device linked to the stream. Instead, information is stored in an internal buffer until the buffer is full. Only then are the contents of that buffer written to disk. However, you can force the information to be physically written to disk before the buffer is full by calling **flush( )**. Its prototype is shown here:

    ostream &flush( );

Calls to **flush( )** might be warranted when a program is going to be used in adverse environments (in situations where power outages occur frequently, for example).

Note

Closing a file or terminating a program also flushes all buffers.

CompFiles.cpp

Project 11-1: A File Comparison Utility

This project develops a simple, yet useful file comparison utility. It works by opening both files to be compared and then reading and comparing each corresponding set of bytes. If a mismatch is found, the files differ. If the end of each file is reached at the same time and if no mismatches have been found, then the files are the same.

Step-by-Step

1. Create a file called **CompFiles.cpp**.

2. Begin by adding these lines to **CompFiles.cpp**:

```
/*
   Project 11-1

   Create a file comparison utility.
*/

#include <iostream>
#include <fstream>
using namespace std;

int main(int argc, char *argv[])
{
  register int i;
  int numread;

  unsigned char buf1[1024], buf2[1024];

  if(argc!=3) {
    cout << "Usage: compfiles <file1> <file2>\n";
    return 1;
  }
```

Notice that the names of the files to compare are specified on the command line.

3. Add the code that opens the files for binary input operations, as shown here:

```
ifstream f1(argv[1], ios::in | ios::binary);
if(!f1) {
  cout << "Cannot open first file.\n";
  return 1;
}
```

11

```
ifstream f2(argv[2], ios::in | ios::binary);
if(!f2) {
  cout << "Cannot open second file.\n";
  return 1;
 }
```

The files are opened for binary operations to prevent the character translations that might occur in text mode.

4. Add the code that actually compares the files, as shown next:

```
cout << "Comparing files...\n";

do {
  f1.read((char *) buf1, sizeof buf1);
  f2.read((char *) buf2, sizeof buf2);

  if(f1.gcount() != f2.gcount()) {
    cout << "Files are of differing sizes.\n";
    f1.close();
    f2.close();
    return 0;
  }

  // compare contents of buffers
  for(i=0; i<f1.gcount(); i++)
    if(buf1[i] != buf2[i]) {
      cout << "Files differ.\n";
      f1.close();
      f2.close();
      return 0;
    }

} while(!f1.eof() && !f2.eof());

cout << "Files are the same.\n";
```

This code reads one buffer at a time from each of the files using the **read( )** function. It then compares the contents of the buffers. If the contents differ, the files are closed, the "Files differ." message is displayed, and the program terminates. Otherwise, buffers continue to be read and compared until the end of one (or both) files is reached. Because less than a full buffer may be read at the end of a file, the program uses the **gcount( )** function to determine precisely how many characters are in the buffers. If one of the files is shorter than the other, the values returned by **gcount( )** will differ when the end of one of the files is reached. In this case, the message "Files are of differing sizes." will be displayed. Finally, if the files are the same, then when the end of one file is reached, the other will also have been reached. This is confirmed by calling **eof( )** on each stream. If the files compare equal in all regards, then they are reported as equal.

5. Finish the program by closing the files, as shown here:

```
f1.close();
f2.close();

return 0;
}
```

6. The entire **FileComp.cpp** program is shown here:

```
/*
   Project 11-1

   Create a file comparison utility.
*/

#include <iostream>
#include <fstream>
using namespace std;

int main(int argc, char *argv[])
{
  register int i;
  int numread;

  unsigned char buf1[1024], buf2[1024];

  if(argc!=3) {
    cout << "Usage: compfiles <file1> <file2>\n";
    return 1;
  }
```

```
ifstream f1(argv[1], ios::in | ios::binary);
if(!f1) {
  cout << "Cannot open first file.\n";
  return 1;
}
ifstream f2(argv[2], ios::in | ios::binary);
if(!f2) {
  cout << "Cannot open second file.\n";
  return 1;
 }

cout << "Comparing files...\n";

do {
  f1.read((char *) buf1, sizeof buf1);
  f2.read((char *) buf2, sizeof buf2);

  if(f1.gcount() != f2.gcount()) {
    cout << "Files are of differing sizes.\n";
    f1.close();
    f2.close();
    return 0;
  }

  // compare contents of buffers
  for(i=0; i<f1.gcount(); i++)
    if(buf1[i] != buf2[i]) {
      cout << "Files differ.\n";
      f1.close();
      f2.close();
      return 0;
    }

} while(!f1.eof() && !f2.eof());

cout << "Files are the same.\n";

f1.close();
f2.close();

return 0;
}
```

7. To try **CompFiles**, first copy **CompFiles.cpp** to a file called **temp.txt**. Then, try this command line:

```
CompFiles CompFiles.temp txt
```

The program will report that the files are the same. Next, compare **CompFiles.cpp** to a different file, such as one of the other program files from this module. You will see that **CompFiles** reports that the files differ.

8. On your own, try enhancing **CompFiles** with various options. For example, add an option that ignores the case of letters. Another idea is to have **CompFiles** display the position within the file where the files differ.

Random Access

So far, files have been read or written sequentially. But you can also access a file in random order. In C++'s I/O system, you perform random access using the **seekg( )** and **seekp( )** functions. Their most common forms are shown here:

```
istream &seekg(off_type offset, seekdir origin);
ostream &seekp(off_type offset, seekdir origin);
```

Here, **off_type** is an integer type defined by **ios** that is capable of containing the largest valid value that *offset* can have. **seekdir** is an enumeration that has these values:

Value	Meaning
ios::beg	Beginning of file
ios::cur	Current location
ios::end	End of file

The C++ I/O system manages two pointers associated with a file. One is the *get pointer*, which specifies where in the file the next input operation will occur. The other is the *put pointer*, which specifies where in the file the next output operation will occur. Each time an input or an output operation takes place, the appropriate pointer is automatically advanced. Using the **seekg( )** and **seekp( )** functions, it is possible to move this pointer and access the file in a non-sequential fashion.

11

The **seekg( )** function moves the associated file's current get pointer *offset* number of bytes from the specified *origin*. The **seekp( )** function moves the associated file's current put pointer *offset* number of bytes from the specified *origin*.

Generally, random access I/O should be performed only on those files opened for binary operations. The character translations that may occur on text files could cause a position request to be out of sync with the actual contents of the file.

The following program demonstrates the **seekp( )** function. It allows you to specify a filename on the command line, followed by the specific byte that you want to change in the file. The program then writes an **X** at the specified location. Notice that the file must be opened for read/write operations.

```
// Demonstrate random access.

#include <iostream>
#include <fstream>
#include <cstdlib>
using namespace std;

int main(int argc, char *argv[])
{
  if(argc!=3) {
    cout << "Usage: CHANGE <filename> <byte>\n";
    return 1;
  }

  fstream out(argv[1], ios::in | ios::out | ios::binary);
  if(!out) {
    cout << "Cannot open file.\n";
    return 1;
  }

  out.seekp(atoi(argv[2]), ios::beg);

  out.put('X');
  out.close();

  return 0;
}
```

Seek to a specific byte within the file. This moves the put pointer.

The next program uses **seekg( )**. It displays the contents of a file, beginning
with the location you specify on the command line.

```cpp
// Display a file from a given starting point.

#include <iostream>
#include <fstream>
#include <cstdlib>
using namespace std;

int main(int argc, char *argv[])
{
  char ch;

  if(argc!=3) {
    cout << "Usage: NAME <filename> <starting location>\n";
    return 1;
  }

  ifstream in(argv[1], ios::in | ios::binary);
  if(!in) {
    cout << "Cannot open file.\n";
    return 1;
  }

  in.seekg(atoi(argv[2]), ios::beg);    This moves the get pointer.

  while(in.get(ch))
    cout << ch;

  return 0;
}
```

11

You can determine the current position of each file pointer using these functions:

```cpp
pos_type tellg( );
pos_type tellp( );
```

Here, **pos_type** is a type defined by **ios** that is capable of holding the largest
value that either function can return.

There are overloaded versions of **seekg( )** and **seekp( )** that move the file pointers to the location specified by the return values of **tellg( )** and **tellp( )**. Their prototypes are shown here:

```
istream &seekg(pos_type position);
ostream &seekp(pos_type position);
```

1-Minute Drill

● What function detects the end of the file?

● What does **getline( )** do?

● What functions handle random access position requests?

Checking I/O Status

The C++ I/O system maintains status information about the outcome of each I/O operation. The current status of an I/O stream is described in an object of type **iostate**, which is an enumeration defined by **ios** that includes these members.

Name	Meaning
ios::goodbit	No error bits set
ios::eofbit	1 when end-of-file is encountered; 0 otherwise
ios::failbit	1 when a (possibly) nonfatal I/O error has occurred; 0 otherwise
ios::badbit	1 when a fatal I/O error has occurred; 0 otherwise

There are two ways in which you can obtain I/O status information. First, you can call the **rdstate( )** function. It has this prototype:

```
iostate rdstate( );
```

● **eof( )** is the function that detects the end of the file.
● **getline( )** reads a line of text.
● To handle random access position requests, use **seekg( )** and **seekp( )**.

It returns the current status of the error flags. As you can probably guess from looking at the preceding list of flags, **rdstate( )** returns **goodbit** when no error has occurred. Otherwise, an error flag is turned on.

The other way you can determine if an error has occurred is by using one or more of these **ios** member functions:

```
bool bad( );
bool eof( );
bool fail( );
bool good( );
```

The **eof( )** function was discussed earlier. The **bad( )** function returns true if **badbit** is set. The **fail( )** function returns true if **failbit** is set. The **good( )** function returns true if there are no errors. Otherwise they return false.

Once an error has occurred, it may need to be cleared before your program continues. To do this, use the **ios** member function **clear( )**, whose prototype is shown here:

```
void clear(iostate flags = ios::goodbit);
```

If *flags* is **goodbit** (as it is by default), all error flags are cleared. Otherwise, set *flags* to the settings you desire.

Before moving on, you might want to experiment with using these status-reporting functions to add extended error-checking to the preceding file examples.

11

☑ *Mastery Check*

1. What are the four predefined streams called?

2. Does C++ define both 8-bit and wide-character streams?

3. Show the general form for overloading an inserter.

4. What does **ios::scientific** do?

5. What does **width( )** do?

6. An I/O manipulator is used within an I/O expression. True or false?

7. Show how to open a file for reading text input.

8. Show how to open a file for writing text output.

9. What does **ios::binary** do?

10. When the end of the file is reached, the stream variable will evaluate as false. True or false?

11. Assuming a file is associated with an input stream called **strm**, show how to read to the end of the file.

12. Write a program that copies a file. Allow the user to specify the name of the input and output file on the command line. Make sure that your program can copy both text and binary files.

13. Write a program that merges two text files. Have the user specify the names of the two files on the command line in the order they should appear in the output file. Also, have the user specify the name of the output file. Thus, if the program is called **merge**, then the following command line will merge the files MyFile1.txt and MyFile2.txt into Target.txt:

```
merge MyFile1.txt MyFile2.txt Target.txt
```

14. Show how the **seekg( )** statement will seek to the 300th byte in a stream called **MyStrm**.

Module 12

Exceptions, Templates, and Other Advanced Topics

The Goals of This Module

- Know the fundamentals of exception handling
- Monitor code for errors using try and catch
- Learn to throw and rethrow exceptions
- Use the new and delete dynamic allocation operators
- Create template functions
- Create template classes
- Apply namespaces
- Use static class members
- Obtain runtime type information
- Know the additional cast operators

Y ou have come a long way since the start of this book. In this, the final module, you will examine several important, advanced C++ topics, including exception handling, templates, dynamic allocation, and namespaces. Runtime type ID and the casting operators are also covered. Keep in mind that C++ is a large, sophisticated, professional programming language, and it is not possible to cover every advanced feature, specialized technique, or programming nuance in this beginner's guide. When you finish this module, however, you will have mastered the core elements of the language and will be able to begin writing real-world programs.

Exception Handling

An exception is an error that occurs at runtime. Using C++'s exception handling subsystem, you can, in a structured and controlled manner, handle runtime errors. When exception handling is employed, your program automatically invokes an error-handling routine when an exception occurs. The principal advantage of exception handling is that it automates much of the error-handling code that previously had to be entered "by hand" into any large program.

Exception Handling Fundamentals

C++ exception handling is built upon three keywords: **try**, **catch**, and **throw**. In the most general terms, program statements that you want to monitor for exceptions are contained in a **try** block. If an exception (that is, an error) occurs within the **try** block, it is thrown (using **throw**). The exception is caught, using **catch**, and processed. The following discussion elaborates upon this general description.

Code that you want to monitor for exceptions must have been executed from within a **try** block. (A function called from within a **try** block is also monitored.) Exceptions that can be thrown by the monitored code are caught by a **catch** statement that immediately follows the **try** statement in which the exception was thrown. The general form of **try** and **catch** are shown here:

```
try {
  // try block
}
catch (type1 arg) {
  // catch block
}
```

```
catch (type2 arg) {
  // catch block
}
catch (type3 arg) {
  // catch block
}
// ...
catch (typeN arg) {
  // catch block
}
```

The **try** block must contain the portion of your program that you want to monitor for errors. This section can be as short as a few statements within one function, or as all-encompassing as a **try** block that encloses the **main( )** function code (which would, in effect, cause the entire program to be monitored).

When an exception is thrown, it is caught by its corresponding **catch** statement, which then processes the exception. There can be more than one **catch** statement associated with a **try**. The type of the exception determines which **catch** statement is used. That is, if the data type specified by a **catch** statement matches that of the exception, then that **catch** statement is executed (and all others are bypassed). When an exception is caught, *arg* will receive its value. Any type of data can be caught, including classes that you create.

The general form of the **throw** statement is shown here:

throw *exception*;

throw generates the exception specified by *exception*. If this exception is to be caught, then **throw** must be executed either from within a **try** block itself, or from any function called from within the **try** block (directly or indirectly).

If you throw an exception for which there is no applicable **catch** statement, an abnormal program termination will occur. That is, your program will stop abruptly in an uncontrolled manner. Thus, you will want to catch all exceptions that will be thrown.

Here is a simple example that shows how C++ exception handling operates:

```
// A simple exception handling example.

#include <iostream>
using namespace std;

int main()
{
```

12

```
cout << "start\n";

try { // start a try block
  cout << "Inside try block\n";
  throw 99; // throw an error
  cout << "This will not execute";
}
catch (int i) { // catch an error
  cout << "Caught an exception -- value is: ";
  cout << i << "\n";
}

cout << "end";

return 0;
}
```

Begin a **try** block.

Throw an exception.

Catch the exception.

This program displays the following output:

```
start
Inside try block
Caught an exception -- value is: 99
end
```

Look carefully at this program. As you can see, there is a **try** block containing three statements and a **catch(int i)** statement that processes an integer exception. Within the **try** block, only two of the three statements will execute: the first **cout** statement and the **throw**. Once an exception has been thrown, control passes to the **catch** expression, and the **try** block is terminated. That is, **catch** is *not* called. Rather, program execution is transferred to it. (The program's stack is automatically reset, as necessary, to accomplish this.) Thus, the **cout** statement following the **throw** will never execute.

Usually, the code within a **catch** statement attempts to remedy an error by taking appropriate action. If the error can be fixed, then execution will continue with the statements following the **catch**. Otherwise, program execution should be terminated in a controlled manner.

As mentioned earlier, the type of the exception must match the type specified in a **catch** statement. For example, in the preceding program, if you change the type in the **catch** statement to **double**, then the exception will not be caught and abnormal termination will occur. This change is shown here:

```
// This example will not work.

#include <iostream>
using namespace std;

int main()
{
  cout << "start\n";

  try { // start a try block
    cout << "Inside try block\n";
    throw 99; // throw an error
    cout << "This will not execute";
  }
  catch (double i) { // won't work for an int exception
    cout << "Caught an exception -- value is: ";
    cout << i << "\n";
  }

  cout << "end";

  return 0;
}
```

This can't catch
an **int** exception!

This program produces the following output because the integer exception will not be caught by the **catch(double i)** statement. Of course, the final message indicating abnormal termination will vary from compiler to compiler.

```
start
Inside try block
Abnormal program termination
```

An exception thrown by a function called from within a **try** block can be caught by that **try** block. For example, this is a valid program:

```
/* Throwing an exception from a function called
   from within a try block. */

#include <iostream>
using namespace std;

void Xtest(int test)
{
  cout << "Inside Xtest, test is: " << test << "\n";
```

12

```
    if(test) throw test;
}

int main()
{
  cout << "start\n";

  try { // start a try block
    cout << "Inside try block\n";
    Xtest(0);
    Xtest(1);
    Xtest(2);
  }
  catch (int i) { // catch an error
    cout << "Caught an exception -- value is: ";
    cout << i << "\n";
  }

  cout << "end";

  return 0;
}
```

This exception is caught by the **catch** statement in **main( )**.

Because **Xtest( )** is called from within a **try** block, its code is also monitored for errors.

This program produces the following output:

```
start
Inside try block
Inside Xtest, test is: 0
Inside Xtest, test is: 1
Caught an exception -- value is: 1
end
```

As the output confirms, the exception thrown in **Xtest( )** was caught by the exception handler in **main( )**.

A **try** block can be localized to a function. When this is the case, each time the function is entered, the exception handling relative to that function is reset. Examine this sample program:

```
// A try block can be localized to a function.

#include <iostream>
using namespace std;

// A try/catch is reset each time a function is entered.
void Xhandler(int test)
{
```

```
   try{                          This try block is local to Xhandler( ).
     if(test) throw test;
   }
   catch(int i) {
     cout << "Caught One!  Ex. #: " << i << '\n';
   }
}

int main()
{
  cout << "start\n";

  Xhandler(1);
  Xhandler(2);
  Xhandler(0);
  Xhandler(3);

  cout << "end";

  return 0;
}
```

This program displays the following output:

```
start
Caught One!  Ex. #: 1
Caught One!  Ex. #: 2
Caught One!  Ex. #: 3
end
```

In this example, three exceptions are thrown. After each exception, the function returns. When the function is called again, the exception handling is reset.

In general, a **try** block is reset each time it is entered. Thus, a **try** block that is part of a loop will be reset each time the loop repeats.

1-Minute Drill

● In the language of C++, what is an exception?

● Exception handling is based on what three keywords?

● An exception is caught based on its type. True or false?

● An exception is a runtime error.
● Exception handling is based on **try**, **catch**, and **throw**.
● True, an exception is caught based on its type.

Using Multiple catch Statements

As stated earlier, you can associate more than one **catch** statement with a **try**. In fact, it is common to do so. However, each **catch** must catch a different type of exception. For example, the program shown here catches both integers and character pointers:

```
// Use multiple catch statements.

#include <iostream>
using namespace std;

// Different types of exceptions can be caught.
void Xhandler(int test)
{
  try{
    if(test) throw test; // throw int
    else throw "Value is zero"; // throw char *
  }
  catch(int i) {                                    ┌─────────────────┐
    cout << "Caught One!  Ex. #: " << i << '\n';    │ This catches    │
  }                                                 │ int exceptions. │
  catch(char *str) {                                └─────────────────┘
    cout << "Caught a string: ";      ┌──────────────────────────────────┐
    cout << str << '\n';              │ This catches char * exceptions.  │
  }                                   └──────────────────────────────────┘
}

int main()
{
  cout << "start\n";

  Xhandler(1);
  Xhandler(2);
  Xhandler(0);
  Xhandler(3);

  cout << "end";

  return 0;
}
```

This program produces the following output:

```
start
Caught One!  Ex. #: 1
Caught One!  Ex. #: 2
```

```
Caught a string: Value is zero
Caught One!  Ex. #: 3
end
```

As you can see, each **catch** statement responds only to its own type.

In general, **catch** expressions are checked in the order in which they occur in a program. Only a matching statement is executed. All other **catch** blocks are ignored.

Catching Base Class Exceptions

There is one important point about multiple **catch** statements that relates to derived classes. A **catch** clause for a base class will also match any class derived from that base. Thus, if you want to catch exceptions of both a base class type and a derived class type, put the derived class first in the **catch** sequence. If you don't, the base class **catch** will also catch all derived classes. For example, consider the following program:

```
// Catching derived classes. This program is wrong!

#include <iostream>
using namespace std;

class B {
};

class D: public B {
};

int main()
{
  D derived;

  try {
    throw derived;
  }
  catch(B b) {                                    This catch list is in the
    cout << "Caught a base class.\n";             wrong order! You must
  }                                               catch derived classes before
  catch(D d) {                                    base classes.
    cout << "This won't execute.\n";
  }

  return 0;
}
```

12

Here, because **derived** is an object that has **B** as a base class, it will be caught by the first catch clause, and the second clause will never execute. Some compilers will flag this condition with a warning message. Others may issue an error message and stop compilation. Either way, to fix this condition, reverse the order of the **catch** clauses.

Catching All Exceptions

In some circumstances, you will want an exception handler to catch all exceptions instead of just a certain type. To do this, use this form of **catch**:

```
catch(...) {
    // process all exceptions
}
```

Here, the ellipsis matches any type of data.

The following program illustrates **catch(...)**:

```cpp
// This example catches all exceptions.

#include <iostream>
using namespace std;

void Xhandler(int test)
{
  try{
    if(test==0) throw test; // throw int
    if(test==1) throw 'a'; // throw char
    if(test==2) throw 123.23; // throw double
  }
  catch(...) { // catch all exceptions    ◄——————  Catch all exceptions.
    cout << "Caught One!\n";
  }
}

int main()
{
  cout << "start\n";

  Xhandler(0);
  Xhandler(1);
  Xhandler(2);

  cout << "end";

  return 0;
}
```

This program displays the following output:

```
start
Caught One!
Caught One!
Caught One!
end
```

Xhandler( ) throws three types of exceptions: **int**, **char**, and **double**. All are caught using the **catch(...)** statement.

One very good use for **catch(...)** is as the last **catch** of a cluster of catches. In this capacity, it provides a useful default or "catch all" statement. Using **catch(...)** as a default is a good way to catch all exceptions that you don't want to handle explicitly. Also, by catching all exceptions, you prevent an unhandled exception from causing an abnormal program termination.

Specifying Exceptions Thrown by a Function

You can specify the type of exceptions that a function can throw outside of itself. In fact, you can also prevent a function from throwing any exceptions whatsoever. To accomplish these restrictions, you must add a **throw** clause to a function definition. The general form of this clause is

```
ret-type func-name(arg-list) throw(type-list)
{
    // ...
}
```

Here, only those data types contained in the comma-separated *type-list* can be thrown by the function. Throwing any other type of expression will cause abnormal program termination. If you don't want a function to be able to throw *any* exceptions, then use an empty list.

12

Note

At the time of this writing, Visual C++ does not actually prevent a function from throwing an exception type that is not specified in the **throw** clause. This is nonstandard behavior. You can still specify a **throw** clause, but such a clause is informational only.

The following program shows how to specify the types of exceptions that can be thrown from a function:

```
// Restricting function throw types.

#include <iostream>
using namespace std;

// This function can only throw ints, chars, and doubles.
void Xhandler(int test) throw(int, char, double)
{
  if(test==0) throw test;    // throw int
  if(test==1) throw 'a';     // throw char
  if(test==2) throw 123.23; // throw double
}

int main()
{
  cout << "start\n";

  try{
    Xhandler(0); // also, try passing 1 and 2 to Xhandler()
  }
  catch(int i) {
    cout << "Caught int\n";
  }
  catch(char c) {
    cout << "Caught char\n";
  }
  catch(double d) {
    cout << "Caught double\n";
  }

  cout << "end";

  return 0;
}
```

Specify the exceptions that can be thrown by **Xhandler( )**.

In this program, the function **Xhandler( )** can only throw integer, character, and **double** exceptions. If it attempts to throw any other type of exception, then an abnormal program termination will occur. To see an example of this, remove **int** from the list and retry the program. An error will result. (As mentioned, currently Visual C++ does not restrict the exceptions that a function can throw.)

It is important to understand that a function can only be restricted in what types of exceptions it throws back to the **try** block that has called it. That is, a

try block *within* a function can throw any type of exception, as long as the exception is caught *within* that function. The restriction applies only when throwing an exception outside of the function.

Rethrowing an Exception

You can rethrow an exception from within an exception handler by calling **throw** by itself, with no exception. This causes the current exception to be passed on to an outer **try/catch** sequence. The most likely reason for calling **throw** this way is to allow multiple handlers access to the exception. For example, perhaps one exception handler manages one aspect of an exception, and a second handler copes with another aspect. An exception can only be rethrown from within a **catch** block (or from any function called from within that block). When you rethrow an exception, it will not be recaught by the same **catch** statement. It will propagate to the next **catch** statement. The following program illustrates rethrowing an exception. It rethrows a **char** * exception.

```
// Example of "rethrowing" an exception.

#include <iostream>
using namespace std;

void Xhandler()
{
  try {
    throw "hello"; // throw a char *
  }
  catch(char *) { // catch a char *
    cout << "Caught char * inside Xhandler\n";
    throw ; // rethrow char * out of function        Rethrow an exception.
  }
}

int main()
{
  cout << "start\n";

  try{
    Xhandler();
  }
  catch(char *) {
    cout << "Caught char * inside main\n";
  }
```

12

```
   cout << "end";

   return 0;
}
```

This program displays the following output:

```
start
Caught char * inside Xhandler
Caught char * inside main
end
```

1-Minute Drill

● Show how to catch all exceptions.

● How do you specify the type of exceptions that can be thrown out of a function?

● How do you rethrow an exception?

Ask the Expert

Question: It seems that there are two ways for a function to report an error: to throw an exception or to return an error code. In general, when should I use each approach?

Answer: You are correct, there are two general approaches to reporting errors: throwing exceptions and returning error codes. Today, language experts favor exceptions rather than error codes. For example, both the Java and C# languages rely heavily on exceptions, using them to report most types of common errors, such as an error opening a file or an arithmetic overflow. Because C++ is derived from C, it uses a blend of error codes and exceptions to report errors. Thus, many error conditions that relate to C++ library functions are reported using error return codes. However, in new code that you write, you should consider using exceptions to report errors. It is the way modern code is being written.

● To catch all exceptions, use **catch(...)**.

● To specify the type of exceptions that can be thrown out of a function, use a **throw** clause.

● To rethrow an exception, specify **throw** without a value.

Templates

The template is one of C++'s most sophisticated and high-powered features. Although not part of the original specification for C++, it was added several years ago and is supported by all modern C++ compilers. Templates help you achieve one of the most elusive goals in programming: the creation of reusable code.

Using templates, it is possible to create generic functions and classes. In a generic function or class, the type of data upon which the function or class operates is specified as a parameter. Thus, you can use one function or class with several different types of data without having to explicitly recode specific versions for each data type. Both generic functions and generic classes are introduced here.

Generic Functions

A generic function defines a general set of operations that will be applied to various types of data. The type of data that the function will operate upon is passed to it as a parameter. Through a generic function, a single general procedure can be applied to a wide range of data. As you probably know, many algorithms are logically the same no matter what type of data is being operated upon. For example, the Quicksort sorting algorithm is the same whether it is applied to an array of integers or an array of floats. It is just that the type of data being sorted is different. By creating a generic function, you can define the nature of the algorithm, independent of any data. Once you have done this, the compiler will automatically generate the correct code for the type of data that is actually used when you execute the function. In essence, when you create a generic function, you are creating a function that can automatically overload itself.

A generic function is created using the keyword **template**. The normal meaning of the word "template" accurately reflects its use in C++. It is used to create a template (or framework) that describes what a function will do, leaving it to the compiler to fill in the details as needed. The general form of a generic function definition is shown here:

```
template <class Ttype> ret-type func-name(parameter list)
{
    // body of function
}
```

Here, *Ttype* is a placeholder name for a data type. This name is then used within the function definition to declare the type of data upon which the function

12

operates. The compiler will automatically replace *Ttype* with an actual data type when it creates a specific version of the function. Although the use of the keyword **class** to specify a generic type in a **template** declaration is traditional, you may also use the keyword **typename**.

The following example creates a generic function that swaps the values of the two variables with which it is called. Because the process of exchanging two values is independent of the type of the variables, it is a good candidate for being made into a generic function.

```
// Function template example.

#include <iostream>
using namespace std;

// This is a function template.
template <class X> void swapargs(X &a, X &b)
{
  X temp;

  temp = a;
  a = b;
  b = temp;
}

int main()
{
  int i=10, j=20;
  float x=10.1, y=23.3;
  char a='x', b='z';

  cout << "Original i, j: " << i << ' ' << j << '\n';
  cout << "Original x, y: " << x << ' ' << y << '\n';
  cout << "Original a, b: " << a << ' ' << b << '\n';

  swapargs(i, j); // swap integers
  swapargs(x, y); // swap floats
  swapargs(a, b); // swap chars

  cout << "Swapped i, j: " << i << ' ' << j << '\n';
  cout << "Swapped x, y: " << x << ' ' << y << '\n';
  cout << "Swapped a, b: " << a << ' ' << b << '\n';

  return 0;
}
```

A generic function that exchanges the values of its arguments. Here, **X** is the generic data type.

The compiler automatically creates versions of **swapargs( )** that use the type of data specified by its arguments.

Let's look closely at this program. The line

```
template <class X> void swapargs(X &a, X &b)
```

tells the compiler two things: that a template is being created and that a generic definition is beginning. Here, **X** is a generic type that is used as a placeholder. After the **template** portion, the function **swapargs( )** is declared, using **X** as the data type of the values that will be swapped. In **main( )**, the **swapargs( )** function is called using three different types of data: **int**s, **float**s, and **char**s. Because **swapargs( )** is a generic function, the compiler automatically creates three versions of **swapargs( )**: one that will exchange integer values, one that will exchange floating-point values, and one that will swap characters. Thus, the same generic **swap( )** function can be used to exchange arguments of any type of data.

Here are some important terms related to templates. First, a generic function (that is, a function definition preceded by a **template** statement) is also called a *template function*. Both terms are used interchangeably in this book. When the compiler creates a specific version of this function, it is said to have created a *specialization*. This is also called a *generated function*. The act of generating a function is referred to as *instantiating* it. Put differently, a generated function is a specific instance of a template function.

A Function with Two Generic Types

You can define more than one generic data type in the **template** statement by using a comma-separated list. For example, this program creates a template function that has two generic types:

```
#include <iostream>
using namespace std;

template <class Type1, class Type2>◄——————[ Two generic types ]
  void myfunc(Type1 x, Type2 y)
{
  cout << x << ' ' << y << '\n';
}

int main()
{
  myfunc(10, "hi");
```

12

```
    myfunc(0.23, 10L);

    return 0;
}
```

In this example, the placeholder types **Type1** and **Type2** are replaced by the compiler with the data types **int** and **char ***, and **double** and **long**, respectively, when the compiler generates the specific instances of **myfunc( )** within **main( )**.

Explicitly Overloading a Generic Function

Even though a generic function overloads itself as needed, you can explicitly overload one, too. This is formally called *explicit specialization*. If you overload a generic function, then that overloaded function overrides (or "hides") the generic function relative to that specific version. For example, consider the following, revised version of the argument-swapping example shown earlier:

```
// Specializing a template function.

#include <iostream>
using namespace std;

template <class X> void swapargs(X &a, X &b)
{
  X temp;

  temp = a;
  a = b;
  b = temp;
  cout << "Inside template swapargs.\n";
}

// This overrides the generic version of swapargs() for ints.
void swapargs(int &a, int &b)
{
  int temp;

  temp = a;
  a = b;
  b = temp;
  cout << "Inside swapargs int specialization.\n";
}

int main()
{
```

Explicit overload of **swapargs( )**

```
  int i=10, j=20;
  float x=10.1, y=23.3;
  char a='x', b='z';

  cout << "Original i, j: " << i << ' ' << j << '\n';
  cout << "Original x, y: " << x << ' ' << y << '\n';
  cout << "Original a, b: " << a << ' ' << b << '\n';

  swapargs(i, j); // calls explicitly overloaded swapargs()
  swapargs(x, y); // calls generic swapargs()
  swapargs(a, b); // calls generic swapargs()

  cout << "Swapped i, j: " << i << ' ' << j << '\n';
  cout << "Swapped x, y: " << x << ' ' << y << '\n';
  cout << "Swapped a, b: " << a << ' ' << b << '\n';

  return 0;
}
```

This calls the explicit overload of **swapargs( )**.

This program displays the following output:

```
Original i, j: 10 20
Original x, y: 10.1 23.3
Original a, b: x z
Inside swapargs int specialization.
Inside template swapargs.
Inside template swapargs.
Swapped i, j: 20 10
Swapped x, y: 23.3 10.1
Swapped a, b: z x
```

As the comments inside the program indicate, when **swapargs(i, j)** is called, it invokes the explicitly overloaded version of **swapargs( )** defined in the program. Thus, the compiler does not generate this version of the generic **swapargs( )** function, because the generic function is overridden by the explicit overloading.

Relatively recently, an alternative syntax was introduced to denote the explicit specialization of a function. This newer approach uses the **template** keyword. For example, using the newer specialization syntax, the overloaded **swapargs( )** function from the preceding program looks like this:

```
// Use the newer-style specialization syntax.
template<> void swapargs<int>(int &a, int &b)
{
```

12

```
int temp;

temp = a;
a = b;
b = temp;
cout << "Inside swapargs int specialization.\n";
}
```

As you can see, the new-style syntax uses the **template<>** construct to indicate specialization. The type of data for which the specialization is being created is placed inside the angle brackets following the function name. This same syntax is used to specialize any type of generic function. While there is no advantage to using one specialization syntax over the other at this time, the new-style syntax is probably a better approach for the long term.

Explicit specialization of a template allows you to tailor a version of a generic function to accommodate a unique situation—perhaps to take advantage of some performance boost that applies to only one type of data, for example. However, as a general rule, if you need to have different versions of a function for different data types, you should use overloaded functions rather than templates.

Generic Classes

In addition to using generic functions, you can also define a generic class. When you do this, you create a class that defines all the algorithms used by that class; however, the actual type of data being manipulated will be specified as a parameter when objects of that class are created.

Generic classes are useful when a class uses logic that can be generalized. For example, the same algorithm that maintains a queue of integers will also work for a queue of characters, and the same mechanism that maintains a linked list of mailing addresses will also maintain a linked list of auto-part information. When you create a generic class, it can perform the operation you define, such as maintaining a queue or a linked list, for any type of data. The compiler will automatically generate the correct type of object, based upon the type you specify when the object is created.

The general form of a generic class declaration is shown here:

```
template <class Ttype> class class-name {
   // body of class
}
```

Here, *Ttype* is the placeholder type name, which will be specified when a class is instantiated. If necessary, you can define more than one generic data type using a comma-separated list.

Once you have created a generic class, you create a specific instance of that class using the following general form:

   class-name <type> ob;

Here, *type* is the type name of the data that the class will be operating upon. Member functions of a generic class are, themselves, automatically generic. You need not use **template** to explicitly specify them as such.

Here is a simple example of a generic class:

```
// A simple generic class.

#include <iostream>
using namespace std;

template <class T> class MyClass {      Declare a generic class.
  T x, y;                               Here, T is the generic type.
public:
  MyClass(T a, T b) {
    x = a;
    y = b;
  }
  T div() { return x/y; }
};
                                        Create a specific instance
int main()                              of a generic class.
{
  // Create a version of MyClass for doubles.
  MyClass<double> d_ob(10.0, 3.0 );
  cout << "double division: " << d_ob.div() << "\n";

  // Create a version of MyClass for ints.
  MyClass<int> i_ob(10, 3);
  cout << "integer division: " << i_ob.div() << "\n";

  return 0;
}
```

The output is shown here:

```
double division: 3.33333
integer division: 3
```

12

As the output shows, the **double** object performed a floating-point division, and the **int** object performed an integer division.

When a specific instance of **MyClass** is declared, the compiler automatically generates versions of the **div( )** function, and **x** and **y** variables necessary for handling the actual data. In this example, two different types of objects are declared. The first, **d_ob**, operates on **double** data. This means that **x** and **y** are **double** values, and the outcome of the division—and thus the return type of **div( )**—is **double**. The second, **i_ob**, operates on type **int**. Thus, **x**, **y**, and the return type of **div( )** are **int**. Pay special attention to these declarations:

```
MyClass<double> d_ob(10.0, 3.0);
MyClass<int> i_ob(10, 3);
```

Notice how the desired data type is passed inside the angle brackets. By changing the type of data specified when **MyClass** objects are created, you can change the type of data operated upon by **MyClass**.

A template class can have more than one generic data type. Simply declare all the data types required by the class in a comma-separated list within the **template** specification. For instance, the following example creates a class that uses two generic data types:

```
/* This example uses two generic data types in a
   class definition. */
#include <iostream>
using namespace std;

template <class T1, class T2> class MyClass
{
  T1 i;
  T2 j;
public:
  MyClass(T1 a, T2 b) { i = a; j = b; }
  void show() { cout << i << ' ' << j << '\n'; }
};

int main()
{
  MyClass<int, double> ob1(10, 0.23);
  MyClass<char, char *> ob2('X', "This is a test");

  ob1.show(); // show int, double
```

```
  ob2.show(); // show char, char *

  return 0;
}
```

This program produces the following output:

```
10 0.23
X This is a test
```

The program declares two types of objects. **ob1** uses **int** and **double** data. **ob2** uses a character and a character pointer. For both cases, the compiler automatically generates the appropriate data and functions to accommodate the way the objects are created.

Explicit Class Specializations

As with template functions, you can create a specialization of a generic class. To do so, use the **template<>** construct as you did when creating explicit function specializations. For example:

```
// Demonstrate class specialization.

#include <iostream>
using namespace std;

template <class T> class MyClass {
  T x;
public:
  MyClass(T a) {
    cout << "Inside generic MyClass\n";
    x = a;
  }
  T getx() { return x; }
};

// Explicit specialization for int.
template <> class MyClass<int> {          This is an explicit
  int x;                                  specialization of **MyClass**.
public:
  MyClass(int a) {
    cout << "Inside MyClass<int> specialization\n";
    x = a * a;
  }
```

12

```
    int getx() { return x; }
};

int main()
{
  MyClass<double> d(10.1);
  cout << "double: " << d.getx() << "\n\n";

  MyClass<int> i(5);
  cout << "int: " << i.getx() << "\n";

  return 0;
}
```

> This uses the explicit specialization of **MyClass**.

This program displays the following output:

```
Inside generic MyClass
double: 10.1

Inside MyClass<int> specialization
int: 25
```

In the program, pay close attention to this line:

```
template <> class MyClass<int> {
```

It tells the compiler that an explicit integer specialization of **MyClass** is being created. This same general syntax is used for any type of class specialization.

Explicit class specialization expands the utility of generic classes because it lets you easily handle one or two special cases while allowing all others to be automatically processed by the compiler. Of course, if you find that you are creating too many specializations, then you are probably better off not using a template class in the first place.

1-Minute Drill

● What keyword is used to declare a generic function or class?

● Can a generic function be explicitly overloaded?

● In a generic class, are all of its member functions also automatically generic?

● To declare a generic function or class, use the keyword **template**.
● Yes, a generic function can be explicitly overloaded.
● Yes, in a generic class, all of its member functions are also automatically generic.

GenericQ.cpp

Project 12-1: Creating a Generic Queue Class

In Project 8-2, you created a **Queue** class that maintained a queue of characters. In this project, you will convert **Queue** into a generic class that can operate on any type of data. **Queue** is a good choice for conversion to a generic class, because its logic is separate from the data upon which it functions. The same mechanism that stores integers, for example, can also store floating-point values, or even objects of classes that you create. Once you have defined a generic **Queue** class, you can use it whenever you need a queue.

Step-by-Step

1. Begin by copying the **Queue** class from Project 8-2 into a file called **GenericQ.cpp**.

2. Change the **Queue** declaration into a template, as shown here:

```
template <class QType> class Queue {
```

Here, the generic data type is called **QType**.

3. Change the data type of the **q** array to **QType**, as shown next:

```
QType q[maxQsize]; // this array holds the queue
```

Because **q** is now generic, it can be used to hold whatever type of data an object of **Queue** declares.

4. Change the data type of the parameter to the **put( )** function to **QType**, as shown here:

```
// Put a data into the queue.
void put(QType data) {
  if(putloc == size) {
    cout << " -- Queue is full.\n";
    return;
  }

  putloc++;
  q[putloc] = data;
}
```

5. Change the return type of **get( )** to **QType**, as shown next:

```
// Get data from the queue.
QType get() {
```

12

```
   if(getloc == putloc) {
     cout << " -- Queue is empty.\n";
     return 0;
   }

   getloc++;
   return q[getloc];
}
```

6. The entire generic **Queue** class is shown here along with a **main( )** function
to demonstrate its use:

```
/*
   Project 12-1

   A template queue class.
*/
#include <iostream>
using namespace std;

const int maxQsize = 100;

// This creates a generic queue class.
template <class QType> class Queue {
  QType q[maxQsize]; // this array holds the queue
  int size; // maximum number of elements that the queue can store
  int putloc, getloc; // the put and get indices
public:

  // Construct a queue of a specific length.
  Queue(int len) {
    // Queue must be less than max and positive.
    if(len > maxQsize) len = maxQsize;
    else if(len <= 0) len = 1;

    size = len;
    putloc = getloc = 0;
  }

  // Put data into the queue.
  void put(QType data) {
    if(putloc == size) {
      cout << " -- Queue is full.\n";
      return;
```

```
    }

    putloc++;
    q[putloc] = data;
  }

  // Get data from the queue.
  QType get() {
    if(getloc == putloc) {
      cout << " -- Queue is empty.\n";
      return 0;
    }

    getloc++;
    return q[getloc];
  }
};

// Demonstrate the generic Queue.
int main()
{
  Queue<int> iQa(10), iQb(10);  // create two integer queues

  iQa.put(1);
  iQa.put(2);
  iQa.put(3);

  iQb.put(10);
  iQb.put(20);
  iQb.put(30);

  cout << "Contents of integer queue iQa: ";
  for(int i=0; i < 3; i++)
    cout << iQa.get() << " ";
  cout << endl;

  cout << "Contents of integer queue iQb: ";
  for(int i=0; i < 3; i++)
    cout << iQb.get() << " ";
  cout << endl;

  Queue<double> dQa(10), dQb(10);  // create two double queues

  dQa.put(1.01);
  dQa.put(2.02);
  dQa.put(3.03);
```

12

```
    dQb.put(10.01);
    dQb.put(20.02);
    dQb.put(30.03);

    cout << "Contents of double queue dQa: ";
    for(int i=0; i < 3; i++)
      cout << dQa.get() << " ";
    cout << endl;

    cout << "Contents of double queue dQb: ";
    for(int i=0; i < 3; i++)
      cout << dQb.get() << " ";
    cout << endl;

    return 0;
}
```

The output is shown here:

```
Contents of integer queue iQa: 1 2 3
Contents of integer queue iQb: 10 20 30
Contents of double queue dQa: 1.01 2.02 3.03
Contents of double queue dQb: 10.01 20.02 30.03
```

7. As the **Queue** class illustrates, generic functions and classes are powerful tools that you can use to maximize your programming efforts, because they allow you to define the general form of an object that can then be used with any type of data. You are saved from the tedium of creating separate implementations for each data type for which you want the algorithm to work. The compiler automatically creates the specific versions of the class for you.

Dynamic Allocation

There are two primary ways in which a C++ program can store information in the main memory of the computer. The first is through the use of variables. The storage provided by variables is fixed at compile time and cannot be altered during the execution of a program. The second way information can be stored is through the use of C++'s *dynamic allocation* system. In this method, storage for data is allocated as needed from the free memory area that lies between your program (and its permanent storage area) and the stack. This region is called the *heap*. (Figure 12-1 shows conceptually how a C++ program appears in memory.)

Dynamically allocated storage is determined at runtime. Thus, dynamic allocation makes it possible for your program to create variables that it needs during

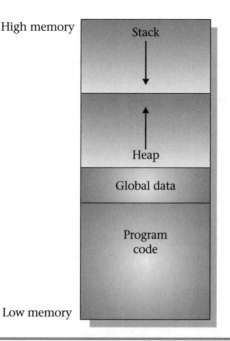

Figure 12-1   A conceptual view of memory usage in a C++ program

its execution. It can create as many or as few variables as required, depending upon the situation. Dynamic allocation is often used to support such data structures as linked lists, binary trees, and sparse arrays. Of course, you are free to use dynamic allocation wherever you determine it to be of value. Dynamic allocation for one purpose or another is an important part of nearly all real-world programs.

Memory to satisfy a dynamic allocation request is taken from the heap. As you might guess, it is possible, under fairly extreme cases, for free memory to become exhausted. Therefore, while dynamic allocation offers greater flexibility, it too is finite.

C++ provides two dynamic allocation operators: **new** and **delete**. The **new** operator allocates memory and returns a pointer to the start of it. The **delete** operator frees memory previously allocated using **new**. The general forms of **new** and **delete** are shown here:

p_var = new *type*;
delete *p_var*;

Here, *p_var* is a pointer variable that receives a pointer to memory that is large enough to hold an item of type *type*.

12

Since the heap is finite, it can become exhausted. If there is insufficient available memory to fill an allocation request, then **new** will fail and a **bad_alloc** exception will be generated. This exception is defined in the header **<new>**. Your program should handle this exception and take appropriate action if a failure occurs. If this exception is not handled by your program, then your program will be terminated.

The actions of **new** on failure as just described are specified by Standard C++. The trouble is that some older compilers will implement **new** in a different way. When C++ was first invented, **new** returned a null pointer on failure. Later, this was changed so that **new** throws an exception on failure, as just described. If you are using an older compiler, check your compiler's documentation to see precisely how it implements **new**.

Since Standard C++ specifies that **new** generates an exception on failure, this is the way the code in this book is written. If your compiler handles an allocation failure differently, then you will need to make the appropriate changes.

Here is a program that allocates memory to hold an integer:

```
// Demonstrate new and delete.

#include <iostream>
#include <new>
using namespace std;

int main()
{
  int *p;

  try {
    p = new int; // allocate space for an int
  } catch (bad_alloc xa) {
    cout << "Allocation Failure\n";
    return 1;
  }

  *p = 100;

  cout << "At " << p << " ";
  cout << "is the value " << *p << "\n";

  delete p;

  return 0;
}
```

Allocate an **int**.

Watch for an allocation failure.

Release the allocated memory.

Ask the Expert

Question: I have seen some C++ code that uses the functions malloc( ) and free( ) to handle dynamic allocation. What are these functions?

Answer: The C language does not support the **new** and **delete** operators. Instead, C uses the functions **malloc( )** and **free( )** for dynamic allocation. **malloc( )** allocates memory and **free( )** releases it. C++ also supports these functions, and you will sometimes see **malloc( )** and **free( )** used in C++ code. This is especially true if that code has been updated from older C code. However, you should use **new** and **delete** in your code. Not only do **new** and **delete** offer a more convenient method of handling dynamic allocation, but they also prevent several types of errors that are common when working with **malloc( )** and **free( )**. One other point: Although there is no formal rule that states this, it is best not to mix **new** and **delete** with **malloc( )** and **free( )** in the same program. There is no guarantee that they are mutually compatible.

This program assigns to **p** an address in the heap that is large enough to hold an integer. It then assigns that memory the value 100 and displays the contents of the memory on the screen. Finally, it frees the dynamically allocated memory.

The **delete** operator must be used only with a valid pointer previously allocated by using **new**. Using any other type of pointer with **delete** is undefined and will almost certainly cause serious problems, such as a system crash.

Initializing Allocated Memory

You can initialize allocated memory to some known value by putting an initializer after the type name in the **new** statement. Here is the general form of **new** when an initialization is included:

```
p_var = new var_type (initializer);
```

Of course, the type of the initializer must be compatible with the type of data for which memory is being allocated.

12

This program gives the allocated integer an initial value of 87:

```
// Initialize memory.

#include <iostream>
#include <new>
using namespace std;

int main()
{
  int *p;

  try {
    p = new int (87); // initialize to 87    ← Initialize allocated memory.
  } catch (bad_alloc xa) {
    cout << "Allocation Failure\n";
    return 1;
  }

  cout << "At " << p << " ";
  cout << "is the value " << *p << "\n";

  delete p;

  return 0;
}
```

Allocating Arrays

You can allocate arrays using **new** by using this general form:

   p_var = new *array_type* [*size*];

Here, *size* specifies the number of elements in the array.
   To free an array, use this form of **delete**:

   delete [ ] *p_var*;

Here, the [ ] informs **delete** that an array is being released.
   For example, the next program allocates a ten-element integer array:

```
// Allocate an array.

#include <iostream>
```

```
#include <new>
using namespace std;

int main()
{
  int *p, i;

  try {                                    ┌─────────────────────────┐
    p = new int [10]; // allocate 10 integer array ◄──┘ Allocate an array of int.
  } catch (bad_alloc xa) {                 └─────────────────────────┘
    cout << "Allocation Failure\n";
    return 1;
  }

  for(i=0; i<10; i++ )
    p[i] = i;

  for(i=0; i<10; i++)
    cout << p[i] << " ";
                                           ┌──────────────────┐
  delete [] p; // release the array ◄──────┤ Release the array. │
                                           └──────────────────┘
  return 0;
}
```

Notice the **delete** statement. As just mentioned, when an array allocated by **new** is released, **delete** must be made aware that an array is being freed by using the [ ]. (As you will see in the next section, this is especially important when you are allocating arrays of objects.)

One restriction applies to allocating arrays: They may not be given initial values. That is, you may not specify an initializer when allocating arrays.

Allocating Objects

You can allocate objects dynamically by using **new**. When you do this, an object is created, and a pointer is returned to it. The dynamically created object acts just like any other object. When it is created, its constructor (if it has one) is called. When the object is freed, its destructor is executed.

Here is a program that creates a class called **Rectangle** that encapsulates the width and height of a rectangle. Inside **main( )**, an object of type **Rectangle** is created dynamically. This object is destroyed when the program ends.

12

```
// Allocate an object.

#include <iostream>
```

```
#include <new>
using namespace std;

class Rectangle {
  int width;
  int height;
public:
  Rectangle(int w, int h) {
    width = w;
    height = h;
    cout << "Constructing " << width <<
         " by " << height << " rectangle.\n";
  }

  ~Rectangle() {
    cout << "Destructing " << width <<
         " by " << height << " rectangle.\n";
  }

  int area() {
    return width * height;
  }
};

int main()
{
  Rectangle *p;

  try {
    p = new Rectangle(10, 8);
  } catch (bad_alloc xa) {
    cout << "Allocation Failure\n";
    return 1;
  }

  cout << "Area is " << p->area();

  cout << "\n";

  delete p;

  return 0;
}
```

Allocate a **Rectangle** object. This calls the **Rectangle** constructor.

Release the object. This calls the **Rectangle** destructor.

The output is shown here:

```
Constructing 10 by 8 rectangle.
Area is 80
Destructing 10 by 8 rectangle.
```

Notice that the arguments to the object's constructor are specified after the type name, just as in other sorts of initializations. Also, because **p** contains a pointer to an object, the arrow operator (rather than the dot operator) is used to call **area( )**.

You can allocate arrays of objects, but there is one catch. Since no array allocated by **new** can have an initializer, you must make sure that if the class defines constructors, one will be parameterless. If you don't, the C++ compiler will not find a matching constructor when you attempt to allocate the array and will not compile your program.

In this version of the preceding program, a parameterless constructor is added so that an array of **Rectangle** objects can be allocated. Also added is the function **set( )**, which sets the dimensions of each rectangle.

```
// Allocate an array of objects.

#include <iostream>
#include <new>
using namespace std;

class Rectangle {
  int width;
  int height;
public:
  Rectangle() {  ◄──────────── Add a parameterless constructor.
    width = height = 0;
    cout << "Constructing " << width <<
         " by " << height << " rectangle.\n";
  }

  Rectangle(int w, int h) {
    width = w;
    height = h;
    cout << "Constructing " << width <<
         " by " << height << " rectangle.\n";
  }

  ~Rectangle() {
    cout << "Destructing " << width <<
         " by " << height << " rectangle.\n";
```

12

```
  }

  void set(int w, int h) {              ← Add the set( ) function.
    width = w;
    height = h;
  }

  int area() {
    return width * height;
  }
};

int main()
{
  Rectangle *p;

  try {
    p = new Rectangle [3];
  } catch (bad_alloc xa) {
    cout << "Allocation Failure\n";
    return 1;
  }

  cout << "\n";

  p[0].set(3, 4);
  p[1].set(10, 8);
  p[2].set(5, 6);

  for(int i=0; i < 3; i++)
    cout << "Area is " << p[i].area() << endl;

  cout << "\n";

  delete [] p;              ← This calls the destructor for
                              each object in the array.

  return 0;
}
```

The output from this program is shown here:

```
Constructing 0 by 0 rectangle.
Constructing 0 by 0 rectangle.
Constructing 0 by 0 rectangle.
```

```
Area is 12
Area is 80
Area is 30

Destructing 5 by 6 rectangle.
Destructing 10 by 8 rectangle.
Destructing 3 by 4 rectangle.
```

Because the pointer **p** is released using **delete** [ ], the destructor for each object in the array is executed, as the output shows. Also, notice that because **p** is indexed as an array, the dot operator is used to access members of **Rectangle**.

1-Minute Drill

● What operator allocates memory? What operator releases memory?

● What happens if an allocation request cannot be fulfilled?

● Can memory be initialized when it is allocated?

Namespaces

Namespaces were briefly described in Module 1. Here they are examined in detail. The purpose of a namespace is to localize the names of identifiers to avoid name collisions. In the C++ programming environment, there has been an explosion of variable, function, and class names. Prior to the invention of namespaces, all of these names competed for slots in the global namespace and many conflicts arose. For example, if your program defined a function called **toupper( )**, it could (depending upon its parameter list) override the standard library function **toupper( )**, because both names would be stored in the global namespace. Name collision problems were compounded when two or more third-party libraries were used by the same program. In this case, it was possible—even likely—that a name defined by one library would conflict with the same name defined by the other library. The situation can be particularly troublesome for class names. For example, if your program defines a class call **Stack** and a library used by your program defines a class by the same name, a conflict will arise.

12

● The **new** operator allocates memory. The **delete** operator releases memory.
● If an allocation request cannot be fulfilled, a **bad_alloc** exception is thrown.
● Yes, memory can be initialized when it is allocated.

The creation of the **namespace** keyword was a response to these problems. Because it localizes the visibility of names declared within it, a namespace allows the same name to be used in different contexts without conflicts arising. Perhaps the most noticeable beneficiary of **namespace** is the C++ standard library. Prior to **namespace**, the entire C++ library was defined within the global namespace (which was, of course, the only namespace). Since the addition of **namespace**, the C++ library is now defined within its own namespace, called **std**, which reduces the chance of name collisions. You can also create your own namespaces within your program to localize the visibility of any names that you think may cause conflicts. This is especially important if you are creating class or function libraries.

Namespace Fundamentals

The **namespace** keyword allows you to partition the global namespace by creating a declarative region. In essence, a **namespace** defines a scope. The general form of **namespace** is shown here:

```
namespace name {
  // declarations
}
```

Anything defined within a **namespace** statement is within the scope of that namespace.

Here is an example of a **namespace**. It localizes the names used to implement a simple countdown counter class. In the namespace are defined the **counter** class, which implements the counter, and the variables **upperbound** and **lowerbound**, which contain the upper and lower bounds that apply to all counters.

```
// Demonstrate a namespace.

namespace CounterNameSpace {          Create a namespace called
  int upperbound;                     CounterNameSpace.
  int lowerbound;

  class counter {
    int count;
  public:
    counter(int n) {
      if(n <= upperbound) count = n;
      else count = upperbound;
```

```
   }

   void reset(int n) {
     if(n <= upperbound) count = n;
   }

   int run() {
     if(count > lowerbound) return count--;
     else return lowerbound;
   }
 };
}
```

Here, **upperbound**, **lowerbound**, and the class **counter** are part of the scope defined by the **CounterNameSpace** namespace.

Inside a namespace, identifiers declared within that namespace can be referred to directly, without any namespace qualification. For example, within **CounterNameSpace**, the **run( )** function can refer directly to **lowerbound** in the statement

```
if(count > lowerbound) return count--;
```

However, since **namespace** defines a scope, you need to use the scope resolution operator to refer to objects declared within a namespace from outside that namespace. For example, to assign the value 10 to **upperbound** from code outside **CounterNameSpace**, you must use this statement:

```
CounterNameSpace::upperbound = 10;
```

Or, to declare an object of type **counter** from outside **CounterNameSpace**, you will use a statement like this:

```
CounterNameSpace::counter ob;
```

12

In general, to access a member of a namespace from outside its namespace, precede the member's name with the name of the namespace followed by the scope resolution operator.

Here is a program that demonstrates the use of the **CounterNameSpace**:

```
// Demonstrate a namespace.

#include <iostream>
```

```
using namespace std;

namespace CounterNameSpace {
  int upperbound;
  int lowerbound;

  class counter {
    int count;
  public:
    counter(int n) {
      if(n <= upperbound) count = n;
      else count = upperbound;
    }

    void reset(int n) {
      if(n <= upperbound) count = n;
    }

    int run() {
      if(count > lowerbound) return count--;
      else return lowerbound;
    }
  };
}

int main()
{
  CounterNameSpace::upperbound = 100;
  CounterNameSpace::lowerbound = 0;

  CounterNameSpace::counter ob1(10);

  int i;

  do {
    i = ob1.run();
    cout << i << " ";
  } while(i > CounterNameSpace::lowerbound);
  cout << endl;

  CounterNameSpace::counter ob2(20);

  do {
    i = ob2.run();
    cout << i << " ";
  } while(i > CounterNameSpace::lowerbound);
  cout << endl;
```

> Explicitly refer to members of **CounterNameSpace**. Note the use of the scope resolution operator.

```
  ob2.reset(100);
  CounterNameSpace::lowerbound = 90;
  do {
    i = ob2.run();
    cout << i << " ";
  } while(i > CounterNameSpace::lowerbound);

  return 0;
}
```

Notice that the declaration of a **counter** object and the references to **upperbound** and **lowerbound** are qualified by **CounterNameSpace**. However, once an object of type **counter** has been declared, it is not necessary to further qualify it or any of its members. Thus, **ob1.run( )** can be called directly; the namespace has already been resolved.

There can be more than one namespace declaration of the same name. In this case, the namespaces are additive. This allows a namespace to be split over several files or even separated within the same file. For example:

```
namespace NS {
  int i;
}

// ...

namespace NS {
  int j;
}
```

Here, **NS** is split into two pieces, but the contents of each piece are still within the same namespace, that is, **NS**.

One last point: Namespaces can be nested. That is, one namespace can be declared within another.

using

If your program includes frequent references to the members of a namespace, having to specify the namespace and the scope resolution operator each time you need to refer to one quickly becomes tedious. The **using** statement was invented to alleviate this problem. The **using** statement has these two general forms:

using namespace *name*;

using *name::member*;

In the first form, *name* specifies the name of the namespace you want to access. All of the members defined within the specified namespace are brought into view (that is, they become part of the current namespace) and may be used without qualification. In the second form, only a specific member of the namespace is made visible. For example, assuming **CounterNameSpace** as just shown, the following **using** statements and assignments are valid:

```
using CounterNameSpace::lowerbound; // only lowerbound is visible
lowerbound = 10; // OK because lowerbound is visible

using namespace CounterNameSpace; // all members are visible
upperbound = 100; // OK because all members are now visible
```

The following program illustrates **using** by reworking the counter example from the previous section:

```
// Demonstrate using.

#include <iostream>
using namespace std;

namespace CounterNameSpace {
  int upperbound;
  int lowerbound;

  class counter {
    int count;
  public:
    counter(int n) {
      if(n <= upperbound) count = n;
      else count = upperbound;
    }

    void reset(int n) {
      if(n <= upperbound) count = n;
    }

    int run() {
      if(count > lowerbound) return count--;
      else return lowerbound;
    }
  };
}

int main()
```

```
{
    // use only upperbound from CounterNameSpace
    using CounterNameSpace::upperbound;
```
Use a specific member of **CounterNameSpace**.

```
    // now, no qualification needed to set upperbound
    upperbound = 100;

    // qualification still needed for lowerbound, etc.
    CounterNameSpace::lowerbound = 0;

    CounterNameSpace::counter ob1(10);
    int i;

do {
    i = ob1.run();
    cout << i << " ";
} while(i > CounterNameSpace::lowerbound);
cout << endl;

    // Now, use entire CounterNameSpace
    using namespace CounterNameSpace;
```
Use the entire **CounterNameSpace**.

```
    counter ob2(20);

    do {
      i = ob2.run();
      cout << i << " ";
    } while(i > lowerbound);
    cout << endl;

    ob2.reset(100);
    lowerbound = 90;
    do {
      i = ob2.run();
      cout << i << " ";
    } while(i > lowerbound);

    return 0;
}
```

12

The program illustrates one other important point: using one namespace does not override another. When you bring a namespace into view, it simply adds its names to whatever other namespaces are currently in effect. Thus, by the end of the program, both **std** and **CounterNameSpace** have been added to the global namespace.

Anonymous Namespaces

There is a special type of namespace, called an *unnamed namespace,* that allows you to create identifiers that are unique within a file. It has this general form:

```
namespace {
  // declarations
}
```

Unnamed namespaces allow you to establish unique identifiers that are known only within the scope of a single file. That is, within the file that contains the unnamed namespace, the members of that namespace may be used directly, without qualification. But outside the file, the identifiers are unknown.

As mentioned earlier in this book, one way to restrict the scope of a global name to the file in which it is declared, is to declare it as **static**. While the use of **static** global declarations is still allowed in C++, a better way to accomplish this is to use an unnamed namespace.

The std Namespace

Standard C++ defines its entire library in its own namespace called **std**. This is the reason that most of the programs in this book have included the following statement:

```
using namespace std;
```

This causes the **std** namespace to be brought into the current namespace, which gives you direct access to the names of the functions and classes defined within the library without having to qualify each one with **std::**.

Of course, you can explicitly qualify each name with **std::** if you like. For example, you could explicitly qualify **cout** like this:

```
std::cout << "Explicitly qualify cout with std.";
```

You may not want to bring the standard C++ library into the global namespace if your program will be making only limited use of it, or if doing so will cause name conflicts. However, if your program contains hundreds of references to library names, then including **std** in the current namespace is far easier than qualifying each name individually.

1-Minute Drill

● What is a namespace? What keyword creates one?

● Are namespaces additive?

● What does **using** do?

static Class Members

You learned about the keyword **static** in Module 7 when it was used to modify local and global variable declarations. In addition to those uses, **static** can be applied to members of a class. Both variables and function members can be declared **static**. Each is described here.

static Member Variables

When you precede a member variable's declaration with **static**, you are telling the compiler that only one copy of that variable will exist and that all objects of the class will share that variable. Unlike regular data members, individual copies of a **static** member variable are not made for each object. No matter how many objects of a class are created, only one copy of a **static** data member exists. Thus, all objects of that class use that same variable. All **static** variables are initialized to zero when the first object is created.

When you declare a **static** data member within a class, you are *not* defining it. Instead, you must provide a global definition for it elsewhere, outside the class. This is done by redeclaring the **static** variable using the scope resolution operator to identify which class it belongs to. This causes storage to be allocated for the **static** variable.

12

● A namespace is a declarative region that defines a scope. It is created by the keyword **namespace**.

● Yes, namespaces are additive.

● **using** brings the members of a namespace into view.

Here is an example that uses a **static** member:

```
// Use a static instance variable.

#include <iostream>
using namespace std;

class ShareVar {
  static int num;            Declare a static data member. It will be
public:                      shared by all instances of ShareVar.
  void setnum(int i) { num = i; };
  void shownum() { cout << num << " "; }
};

int ShareVar::num; // define num    Define the static data member.

int main()
{
  ShareVar a, b;

  a.shownum(); // prints 0
  b.shownum(); // prints 0

  a.setnum(10); // set static num to 10

  a.shownum(); // prints 10
  b.shownum(); // also prints 10

  return 0;
}
```

The output is shown here:

```
0 0 10 10
```

In the program, notice that the **static** integer **num** is both declared inside the
ShareVar class and defined as a global variable. As stated earlier, this is necessary
because the declaration of **num** inside **ShareVar** does *not* allocate storage for the
variable. C++ initializes **num** to 0 since no other initialization is given. This is
why the first calls to **shownum( )** both display 0. Next, object **a** sets **num** to 10.
Then both **a** and **b** use **shownum( )** to display its value. Because there is only one
copy of **num** shared by **a** and **b**, both calls to **shownum( )** display 10.

When a static variable is public, it can be referred to directly through its
class name, without reference to any specific object. It can also be referred to
through an object. For example:

```
// Refer to static variable through its class name.

#include <iostream>
using namespace std;

class Test {
public:
  static int num;
  void shownum() { cout << num << endl; }
};

int Test::num; // define num

int main()
{
  Test a, b;

  // Set num through its class name.
  Test::num = 100;  ◄─────────────────   Refer to num through its
                                          class name Test.

  a.shownum(); // prints 100
  b.shownum(); // prints 100

  // Set num through an object.
  a.num = 200;  ◄─────────────────────   Refer to num through
                                          an object.

  a.shownum(); // prints 200
  b.shownum(); // prints 200

  return 0;
}
```

Notice how the value of **num** is set using its class name in this line:

```
Test::num = 100;
```

It is also accessible through an object, as in this line:

```
a.num = 200;
```

Either approach is valid.

12

static Member Functions

It is also possible for a member function to be declared as static, but this usage is not common. A member function declared as **static** can access only other static members of its class. (Of course, a **static** member function may access non-**static** global data and functions.) A **static** member function does not have a **this** pointer. Virtual **static** member functions are not allowed. Also, they cannot be declared as **const** or **volatile**.

A **static** member function can be invoked by an object of its class, or it can be called independent of any object, using the class name and the scope resolution operator. For example, consider this program. It defines a **static** variable called **count** that keeps count of the number of objects currently in existence.

```cpp
// Demonstrate a static member function.

#include <iostream>
using namespace std;

class Test {
  static int count;
public:

  Test() {
    count++;
    cout << "Constructing object " <<
            count << endl;
  }

  ~Test() {
    cout << "Destroying object " <<
            count << endl;
    count--;
  }

  static int numObjects() { return count; }   ← A **static** member function
};

int Test::count;

int main() {
  Test a, b, c;

  cout << "There are now " <<
          Test::numObjects() <<
```

```
                " in existence.\n\n";

  Test *p = new Test();

  cout << "After allocating a Test object, " <<
          "there are now " <<
          Test::numObjects() <<
          " in existence.\n\n";

  delete p;

  cout << "After deleting an object, " <<
          " there are now " <<
          a.numObjects() <<
          " in existence.\n\n";

  return 0;
}
```

The output from the program is shown here:

```
Constructing object 1
Constructing object 2
Constructing object 3
There are now 3 in existence.

Constructing object 4
After allocating a Test object, there are now 4 in existence.

Destroying object 4
After deleting an object,  there are now 3 in existence.

Destroying object 3
Destroying object 2
Destroying object 1
```

In the program, notice how the **static** function **numObjects( )** is called. In the first two calls, it is called through its class name using this syntax:

```
Test::numObjects()
```

In the third call, it is invoked using the normal, dot operator syntax on an object.

Runtime Type Identification (RTTI)

Runtime type information may be new to you because it is not found in non-polymorphic languages, such as C or traditional BASIC. In non-polymorphic languages there is no need for runtime type information, because the type of each object is known at compile time (that is, when the program is written). However, in polymorphic languages such as C++, there can be situations in which the type of an object is unknown at compile time because the precise nature of that object is not determined until the program is executed. As you know, C++ implements polymorphism through the use of class hierarchies, virtual functions, and base class pointers. A base class pointer can be used to point to objects of the base class or to *any object derived from that base.* Thus, it is not always possible to know in advance what type of object will be pointed to by a base pointer at any given moment. This determination must be made at runtime, using runtime type identification.

To obtain an object's type, use **typeid**. You must include the header **<typeinfo>** in order to use **typeid**. Its most commonly used form is shown here:

typeid(*object*)

Here, *object* is the object whose type you will be obtaining. It may be of any type, including the built-in types and class types that you create. **typeid** returns a reference to an object of type **type_info** that describes the type of *object*.

The **type_info** class defines the following public members:

```
bool operator==(const type_info &ob);
bool operator!=(const type_info &ob);
bool before(const type_info &ob);
const char *name( );
```

The overloaded == and != provide for the comparison of types. The **before( )** function returns true if the invoking object is before the object used as a parameter in collation order. (This function is mostly for internal use only. Its return value has nothing to do with inheritance or class hierarchies.) The **name( )** function returns a pointer to the name of the type.

Here is a simple example that uses **typeid**:

```
// A simple example that uses typeid.

#include <iostream>
```

```
#include <typeinfo>
using namespace std;

class MyClass {
  // ...
};

int main()
{
  int i, j;
  float f;
  MyClass ob;

  cout << "The type of i is: " << typeid(i).name();
  cout << endl;
  cout << "The type of f is: " << typeid(f).name();
  cout << endl;
  cout << "The type of ob is: " << typeid(ob).name();
  cout << "\n\n";

  if(typeid(i) == typeid(j))
    cout << "The types of i and j are the same\n";

  if(typeid(i) != typeid(f))
    cout << "The types of i and f are not the same\n";

  return 0;
}
```

Use **typeid** to obtain the type of an object at runtime.

The output produced by this program is shown here:

```
The type of i is: int
The type of f is: float
The type of ob is: class MyClass

The types of i and j are the same
The types of i and f are not the same
```

12

Perhaps the most important use of **typeid** occurs when it is applied through a pointer of a polymorphic base class (that is, a class that includes at least one virtual function). In this case, it will automatically return the type of the actual object being pointed to, which may be a base class object or an object derived from that base. (Remember, a base class pointer can point to objects of the base class or of any class derived from that base.) Thus, using **typeid**, you can determine at runtime the type of the object that is being pointed to by a base class pointer. The following program demonstrates this principle:

```
// An example that uses typeid on a polymorphic class hierarchy.

#include <iostream>
#include <typeinfo>
using namespace std;

class Base {
  virtual void f() {}; // make Base polymorphic
  // ...
};

class Derived1: public Base {
  // ...
};

class Derived2: public Base {
  // ...
};

int main()
{
  Base *p, baseob;
  Derived1 ob1;
  Derived2 ob2;

  p = &baseob;
  cout << "p is pointing to an object of type ";
  cout << typeid(*p).name() << endl;

  p = &ob1;
  cout << "p is pointing to an object of type ";
  cout << typeid(*p).name() << endl;

  p = &ob2;
  cout << "p is pointing to an object of type ";
  cout << typeid(*p).name() << endl;

  return 0;
}
```

The output produced by this program is shown here:

```
p is pointing to an object of type class Base
p is pointing to an object of type class Derived1
p is pointing to an object of type class Derived2
```

When **typeid** is applied to a base class pointer of a polymorphic type, the type of object pointed to will be determined at runtime, as the output shows.

In all cases, when **typeid** is applied to a pointer of a non-polymorphic class hierarchy, then the base type of the pointer is obtained. That is, no determination of what that pointer is actually pointing to is made. As an experiment, comment-out the virtual function **f( )** in **Base** and observe the results. As you will see, the type of each object will be **Base** because that is the type of the pointer.

Since **typeid** is commonly applied to a dereferenced pointer (that is, one to which the * operator has been applied), a special exception has been created to handle the situation in which the pointer being dereferenced is null. In this case, **typeid** throws a **bad_typeid** exception.

References to an object of a polymorphic class hierarchy work the same as pointers. When **typeid** is applied to a reference to an object of a polymorphic class, it will return the type of the object actually being referred to, which may be of a derived type. The circumstance where you will most often make use of this feature is when objects are passed to functions by reference.

There is a second form of **typeid** that takes a type name as its argument. This form is shown here:

typeid(*type-name*)

For example, the following statement is perfectly acceptable:

```
cout << typeid(int).name();
```

The main use of this form of **typeid** is to obtain a **type_info** object that describes the specified type so that it can be used in a type comparison statement.

1-Minute Drill

- What makes a **static** member variable unique?
- What does **typeid** do?
- What type of object does **typeid** return?

12

- A **static** member variable is shared by all objects of its class.
- **typeid** determines at runtime the type of an object.
- **typeid** returns an object of type **type_info**.

The Casting Operators

C++ defines five casting operators. The first is the traditional-style cast described earlier in this book. It has been part of C++ from the start. The remaining four were added a few years ago. They are **dynamic_cast**, **const_cast**, **reinterpret_cast**, and **static_cast**. These operators give you additional control over how casting takes place. Each is examined briefly here.

dynamic_cast

Perhaps the most important of the additional casting operators is the **dynamic_cast**. The **dynamic_cast** performs a runtime cast that verifies the validity of a cast. If at the time **dynamic_cast** is executed, the cast is invalid, then the cast fails. The general form of **dynamic_cast** is shown here:

dynamic_cast<*target-type*> (*expr*)

Here, *target-type* specifies the target type of the cast, and *expr* is the expression being cast into the new type. The target type must be a pointer or reference type, and the expression being cast must evaluate to a pointer or reference. Thus, **dynamic_cast** can be used to cast one type of pointer into another or one type of reference into another.

The purpose of **dynamic_cast** is to perform casts on polymorphic types. For example, given two polymorphic classes B and D, with D derived from B, a **dynamic_cast** can always cast a D* pointer into a B* pointer. This is because a base pointer can always point to a derived object. But a **dynamic_cast** can cast a B* pointer into a D* pointer only if the object being pointed to *actually is* a D object. In general, **dynamic_cast** will succeed if the pointer (or reference) being cast is pointing to (or referring to) either an object of the target type or an object derived from the target type. Otherwise, the cast will fail. If the cast fails, then **dynamic_cast** evaluates to null if the cast involves pointers. If a **dynamic_cast** on reference types fails, a **bad_cast** exception is thrown.

Here is a simple example. Assume that **Base** is a polymorphic class and that **Derived** is derived from **Base**.

```
Base *bp, b_ob;
Derived *dp, d_ob;

bp = &d_ob; // base pointer points to Derived object
dp = dynamic_cast<Derived *> (bp); // cast to derived pointer OK
if(dp) cout << "Cast OK";
```

Here, the cast from the base pointer **bp** to the derived pointer **dp** works because **bp** is actually pointing to a **Derived** object. Thus, this fragment displays **Cast OK**. But in the next fragment, the cast fails because **bp** is pointing to a **Base** object, and it is illegal to cast a base object into a derived object.

```
bp = &b_ob; // base pointer points to Base object
dp = dynamic_cast<Derived *> (bp); // error
if(!dp) cout << "Cast Fails";
```

Because the cast fails, this fragment displays **Cast Fails**.

const_cast

The **const_cast** operator is used to explicitly override **const** and/or **volatile** in a cast. The target type must be the same as the source type, except for the alteration of its **const** or **volatile** attributes. The most common use of **const_cast** is to remove **const**-ness. The general form of **const_cast** is shown here:

const_cast<*type*> (*expr*)

Here, *type* specifies the target type of the cast, and *expr* is the expression being cast into the new type. It must be stressed that the use of **const_cast** to cast away **const**-ness is a potentially dangerous feature. Use it with care.

One other point: Only **const_cast** can cast away **const**-ness. That is, **dynamic_cast**, **static_cast**, and **reinterpret_cast** cannot alter the **const**-ness of an object.

static_cast

The **static_cast** operator performs a non-polymorphic cast. It can be used for any standard conversion. No runtime checks are performed. Thus, the **static_cast** operator is essentially a substitute for the original cast operator.

Its general form is

static_cast<*type*> (*expr*)

Here, *type* specifies the target type of the cast, and *expr* is the expression being cast into the new type.

reinterpret_cast

The **reinterpret_cast** operator converts one type into a fundamentally different type. For example, it can change a pointer into an integer and an integer into a

12

pointer. It can also be used for casting inherently incompatible pointer types. Its general form is

reinterpret_cast<*type*> (*expr*)

Here, *type* specifies the target type of the cast, and *expr* is the expression being cast into the new type.

What Next?

The purpose of this book is to teach the core elements of the language. These are the features and techniques of C++ that are used in everyday programming. With the knowledge you now have, you can begin writing real-world, professional-quality programs. However, C++ is a very rich language, and it contains many advanced features that you will still want to master, including:

- The Standard Template Library (STL)

- Explicit constructors

- Conversion functions

- **const** member functions and the **mutable** keyword

- The **asm** keyword

- Overloading the array indexing operator [ ], the function call operator ( ), and the dynamic allocation operators, **new** and **delete**

Of the preceding, perhaps the most important is the Standard Template Library. It is a library of template classes that provide off-the-shelf solutions to a variety of common data-storage tasks. For example, the STL defines generic data structures, such as queues, stacks, and lists, which you can use in your programs.

You will also want to study the C++ function library. It contains a wide array of routines that will simplify the creation of your programs.

To continue your study of C++, I suggest reading my book *C++: The Complete Reference*, published by Osborne/McGraw-Hill, Berkeley, California. It covers all of the preceding, and much, much more. You now have sufficient knowledge to make full use of this in-depth C++ guide.

☑ *Mastery Check*

1. Explain how **try**, **catch**, and **throw** work together to support exception handling.

2. How must the **catch** list be organized when catching exceptions of both base and derived classes?

3. Show how to specify that a **MyExcpt** exception can be thrown out of a function called **func( )** that returns **void**.

4. Define an exception for the generic **Queue** class shown in Project 12-1. Have **Queue** throw this exception when an overflow or underflow occurs. Demonstrate its use.

5. What is a generic function, and what keyword is used to create one?

6. Create generic versions of the **quicksort( )** and **qs( )** functions shown in Project 5-1. Demonstrate their use.

7. Using the **Sample** class shown here, create a queue of three **Sample** objects using the generic **Queue** shown in Project 12-1:

```
class Sample {
  int id;
public:
  Sample() { id = 0; }
  Sample(int x) { id = x; }
  void show() { cout << id << endl; }
};
```

8. Rework your answer to question 7 so that the **Sample** objects stored in the queue are dynamically allocated.

9. Show how to declare a namespace called **RobotMotion**.

10. What namespace contains the C++ standard library?

11. Can a **static** member function access the non-**static** data of a class?

12. What operator obtains the type of an object at runtime?

12

☑ Mastery Check

13. To determine the validity of a polymorphic cast at runtime, what casting operator do you use?

14. What does **const_cast** do?

15. On your own, try putting the **Queue** class from Project 12-1 in its own namespace called **QueueCode**, and into its own file called **Queue.cpp**. Then rework the **main( )** function so that it uses a **using** statement to bring **QueueCode** into view.

16. Continue to learn about C++. It is the most powerful computer language currently available. Mastering it puts you in an elite league of programmers.

Appendix A

Answers to Mastery Checks

Module 1: C++ Fundamentals

1. C++ is at the center of modern programming because it was derived from C and is the parent of Java and C#. These are the four most important programming languages.

2. True, a C++ compiler produces code that can be directly executed by the computer.

3. Encapsulation, polymorphism, and inheritance are the three guiding principles of OOP.

4. C++ programs begin execution at **main( )**.

5. A header contains information used by the program.

6. **<iostream>** is the header the supports I/O. The statement includes the **<iostream>** header in a program.

7. A namespace is a declarative region in which various program elements can be placed. Elements declared in one namespace are separate from elements declared in another.

8. A variable is a named memory location. The contents of a variable can be changed during the execution of a program.

9. The invalid variables are d and e. Variable names cannot begin with a digit or be the same as a C++ keyword.

10. A single-line comment begins with // and ends at the end of the line. A multiline comment begins with /* and ends with */.

11. The general form of the **if**:
    if(*condition*) *statement*;

    The general form of the **for**:
    for(*initialization*; *condition*; *increment*) *statement*;

12. A block of code is started with a { and ended with a }.

13. ```
    // Show a table of Earth to Moon weights.

    #include <iostream>
    using namespace std;
    ```
    ```

```cpp
int main() {
  double earthweight; // weight on earth
  double moonweight;  // weight on moon
  int counter;

  counter = 0;
  for(earthweight = 1.0; earthweight <= 100.0; earthweight++) {
    moonweight = earthweight * 0.17;
    cout << earthweight << " earth-pounds is equivalent to " <<
                     moonweight << " moon-pounds.\n";
    counter++;
    if(counter == 25) {
       cout << "\n";
       counter = 0;
    }
  }

  return 0;
}
```

14.
```cpp
// Convert Jovian years to Earth years.

#include <iostream>
using namespace std;

int main() {
  double e_years; // earth years
  double j_years;  // Jovian years

  cout << "Enter number of Jovian years: ";
  cin >> j_years;

  e_years = j_years * 12.0;

  cout << "Equivalent Earth years: " << e_years;

  return 0;
}
```

15. When a function is called, program control transfers to that function.

16.
```cpp
// Average the absolute values of 5 numbers.

#include <iostream>
#include <cstdlib>
using namespace std;
```

A

```
int main()
{
  int i;
  double avg, val;

  avg = 0.0;

  for(i=0; i<5; i++) {
    cout << "Enter a value: ";
    cin >> val;

    avg = avg + abs(val);
  }
  avg = avg / 5;


  cout << "Average of absolute values: " << avg;

  return 0;
}
```

Module 2: Introducing Data Types and Operators

1. The C++ integer types are

int	short int	long int
unsigned int	unsigned short int	unsigned long int
signed int	signed short int	signed long int

The type **char** can also be used as an integer type.

2. 12.2 is type **double**.

3. A **bool** variable can be either **true** or **false**.

4. The long integer type is **long int**, or just **long**.

5. The \t sequence represents a tab. The \b rings the bell.

6. True, a string is surrounded by double quotes.

7. The hexadecimal digits are 0, 1, 2, 3, 4, 5, 6, 7, 8, 9, A, B, C, D, E, F.

8. To initialize a variable, use this general form:

> *type var = value;*

9. The % is the modulus operator. It returns the remainder of an integer division. It cannot be used on floating-point values.

10. When the increment operator precedes its operand, C++ will perform the corresponding operation prior to obtaining the operand's value for use by the rest of the expression. If the operator follows its operand, then C++ will obtain the operand's value before incrementing.

11. A, C, and E

12. x += 12;

13. A cast is an explicit type conversion.

14. Here is one way to find the primes between 1 and 100. There are, of course, other solutions.

```
// Find prime numbers between 1 and 100.

#include <iostream>
using namespace std;

int main() {
  int i, j;
  bool isprime;

  for(i=1; i < 100; i++) {
    isprime = true;

    // see if the number is evenly divisible
    for(j=2; j <= i/2; j++)
      // if it is, then it is not prime
      if((i%j) == 0) isprime = false;

    if(isprime)
      cout << i << " is prime.\n";
  }

  return 0;
}
```

A

Module 3: Program Control Statements

1.
```cpp
// Count periods.

#include <iostream>
using namespace std;

int main() {
  char ch;
  int periods = 0;

  cout << "Enter a $ to stop.\n";

  do {
    cin >> ch;
    if(ch == '.') periods++;
  } while(ch != '$');

  cout << "Periods: " << periods << "\n";

  return 0;
}
```

2. Yes. If there is no **break** statement concluding a **case** sequence, then execution will continue on into the next **case**. A **break** statement prevents this from happening.

3. if(*condition*)
   statement;
else if(*condition*)
   statement;
else if(*condition*)
   statement;

   .

   .

   .

else
   statement;

4. The last **else** associates with the outer **if**, which is the nearest **if** at the same level as the **else**.

5. for(int i = 1000; i >= 0; i -= 2) // ...

6. No. According to the ANSI/ISO C++ Standard, **i** is not known outside of the **for** loop in which it is declared. (Note that some compilers may handle this differently.)

7. A **break** causes termination of its immediately enclosing loop or **switch** statement.

8. After **break** executes, "after while" is displayed.

9. 0 1
2 3
4 5
6 7
8 9

10.
```
/*
    Use a for loop to generate the progression

      1 2 4 8 16, ...
*/

#include <iostream>
using namespace std;

int main() {

  for(int i = 1; i < 100; i += i)
    cout << i << " ";

  cout << "\n";

  return 0;
}
```

11.
```
// Change case.

#include <iostream>
using namespace std;

int main() {
  char ch;
  int changes = 0;

  cout << "Enter period to stop.\n";

  do {
```

```
    cin >> ch;
    if(ch >= 'a' && ch <= 'z') {
      ch -= (char) 32;
      changes++;
      cout << ch;
    }
    else if(ch >= 'A' && ch <= 'Z') {
      ch += (char) 32;
      changes++;
      cout << ch;
    }
  } while(ch != '.');

  cout << "\nCase changes: " << changes << "\n";

  return 0;
}
```

12. C++'s unconditional jump statement is the **goto**.

Module 4: Arrays, Strings, and Pointers

1. `short int hightemps[31];`

2. zero

3.
```
// Find duplicates

#include <iostream>
using namespace std;

int main()
{
  int nums[] = {1, 1, 2, 3, 4, 2, 5, 4, 7, 7};

  for(int i=0; i < 10; i++)
    for(int j=i+1; j < 10; j++)
      if(nums[i] == nums[j])
        cout << "Duplicate: " << nums[i] << "\n";

  return 0;
}
```

4. A null-terminated string is an array of characters that ends with a null.

5. `// Ignore case when comparing strings.`

```
#include <iostream>
#include <cctype>
using namespace std;

int main()
{
  char str1[80];
  char str2[80];
  char *p1, *p2;

  cout << "Enter first string: ";
  cin >> str1;
  cout << "Enter second string: ";
  cin >> str2;

  p1 = str1;
  p2 = str2;

  // loop as long as p1 and p2 point to non-null characters
  while(*p1 && *p2) {
    if(tolower(*p1) != tolower(*p2)) break;
    else {
      p1++;
      p2++;
    }
  }

  /* strings are the same if both p1 and p2 point
     to the null terminator.
  */
  if(!*p1 && !*p2)
    cout << "Strings are the same except for " <<
         "possible case differences.\n";
  else
    cout << "Strings differ\n";

  return 0;
}
```

A

6. When using **strcat( )**, the recipient array must be large enough to hold the contents of both strings.

7. In a multidimensional array, each index is specified within its own set of brackets.

8. `int nums[] = {5, 66, 88};`

9. An unsized array declaration ensures that an initialized array is always large enough to hold the initializers being specified.

10. A pointer is an object that contains a memory address. The pointer operators are & and *.

11. Yes, a pointer can be indexed like an array. Yes, an array can be accessed through a pointer.

12.
```cpp
// Count uppercase letters.
#include <iostream>
#include <cstring>
#include <cctype>
using namespace std;

int main()
{
  char str[80];
  int i;
  int count;

  strcpy(str, "This Is A Test");

  count = 0;
  for(i=0; str[i]; i++)
    if(isupper(str[i])) count++;

  cout << str << " contains " << count << " uppercase letters.";

  return 0;
}
```

13. *Multiple indirection* is the term used for the situation in which one pointer points to another.

14. By convention, a null pointer is assumed to be unused.

Module 5: Introducing Functions

1. The general form of a function is

```
return-type name(parameter list)
{
  // body of function
}
```

2.
```cpp
#include <iostream>
#include <cmath>
using namespace std;

double hypot(double a, double b);

int main() {

  cout << "Hypotenuse of a 3 by 4 right triangle: ";
  cout << hypot(3.0, 4.0) << "\n";

  return 0;
}

double hypot(double a, double b)
{
  return sqrt((a*a) + (b*b));
}
```

3. Yes, a function can return a pointer. No, a function cannot return an array.

4.
```cpp
// A custom version of strlen().
#include <iostream>
using namespace std;

int mystrlen(char *str);

int main()
{
  cout << "Length of Hello There is: ";
  cout << mystrlen("Hello There");

  return 0;
}

// A custom version of strlen().
int mystrlen(char *str)
{
  int i;

  for(i=0; str[i]; i++) ; // find the end of the string

  return i;
}
```

5. No, a local variable's value is lost when its function returns. (Or, more generally, its value is lost when its block is exited.)

A

6. The main advantages to global variables are that they are available to all other functions in the program and that they stay in existence during the entire lifetime of the program. Their main disadvantages are that they take up memory the entire time the program is executing, using a global where a local variable will do makes a function less general, and using a large number of global variables can lead to unanticipated side effects.

7.
```cpp
#include <iostream>
using namespace std;

int seriesnum = 0;

int byThrees();
void reset();

int main() {

  for(int i=0; i < 10; i++)
    cout << byThrees() << " ";

  cout << "\n";

  reset();

  for(int i=0; i < 10; i++)
    cout << byThrees() << " ";

  cout << "\n";

  return 0;
}


int byThrees()
{
  int t;

  t = seriesnum;
  seriesnum += 3;

  return t;
}

void reset()
```

```
{
  seriesnum = 0;
}
```

8.
```cpp
#include <iostream>
#include <cstring>
using namespace std;

int main(int argc, char *argv[])
{
  if(argc != 2) {
    cout << "Password required!\n";
    return 0;
  }

  if(!strcmp("mypassword", argv[1]))
    cout << "Access permitted.\n";
  else
    cout << "Access denied.\n";

  return 0;
}
```

9. True. A prototype prevents a function from being called with the improper number of arguments.

10.
```cpp
#include <iostream>
using namespace std;

void printnum(int n);

int main()
{
  printnum(10);

  return 0;
}

void printnum(int n)
{
  if(n > 1) printnum(n-1);
  cout << n << " ";
}
```

A

Module 6: A Closer Look at Functions

1. An argument can be passed to a subroutine using call-by-value or call-by-reference.

2. A reference is an implicit pointer. A reference parameter is created by preceding the parameter name with an **&**.

3. `f(ch, &i);`

4.
```cpp
#include <iostream>
#include <cmath>
using namespace std;

void round(double &num);

int main()
{
  double i = 100.4;

  cout << i << " rounded is ";
  round(i);
  cout << i << "\n";

  i = -10.9;
  cout << i << " rounded is ";
  round(i);
  cout << i << "\n";

  return 0;
}

void round(double &num)
{
  double frac;
  double val;

  // decompose num into whole and fractional parts
  frac =  modf(num, &val);

  if(frac < 0.5) num = val;
  else num = val+1.0;
}
```

5. ```cpp
#include <iostream>
using namespace std;

// Swap args and return minimum.
int & min_swap(int &x, int &y);

int main()
{
  int i, j, min;

  i = 10;
  j = 20;

  cout << "Initial values of i and j: ";
  cout << i << ' ' << j << '\n';

  min = min_swap(j, i);

  cout << "Swapped values of i and j: ";
  cout << i << ' ' << j << '\n';

  cout << "Minimum value is " << min << "\n";
  return 0;
}

// Swap args and return minimum.
int &min_swap(int &x, int &y)
{
  int temp;

  // use references to exchange the values of the arguments
  temp = x;
  x = y;
  y = temp;

  // return reference to minimum arg
  if(x < y) return x;
  else return y;
}
```

**6.** A function should not return a reference to a local variable, because that variable will go out-of-scope (that is, cease to exist) when the function returns.

A
```

7. Overloaded functions must differ in the type and/or number of their parameters.

8.
```cpp
/*
    Project 6-1 -- updated for Mastery Check

    Create overloaded println() functions
    that display various types of data.

    This version includes an indentation parameter.
*/

#include <iostream>
using namespace std;

// These output a newline.
void println(bool b, int ident=0);
void println(int i, int ident=0);
void println(long i, int ident=0);
void println(char ch, int ident=0);
void println(char *str, int ident=0);
void println(double d, int ident=0);

// These functions do not output a newline.
void print(bool b, int ident=0);
void print(int i, int ident=0);
void print(long i, int ident=0);
void print(char ch, int ident=0);
void print(char *str, int ident=0);
void print(double d, int ident=0);

int main()
{
  println(true, 10);
  println(10, 5);
  println("This is a test");
  println('x');
  println(99L, 10);
  println(123.23, 10);

  print("Here are some values: ");
  print(false);
  print(88, 3);
  print(100000L, 3);
  print(100.01);
```

```cpp
    println(" Done!");

    return 0;
}

// Here are the println() functions.
void println(bool b, int ident)
{
  if(ident)
    for(int i=0; i < ident; i++) cout << ' ';

  if(b) cout << "true\n";
  else cout << "false\n";
}

void println(int i, int ident)
{
  if(ident)
    for(int i=0; i < ident; i++) cout << ' ';

  cout << i << "\n";
}

void println(long i, int ident)
{
  if(ident)
    for(int i=0; i < ident; i++) cout << ' ';

  cout << i << "\n";
}

void println(char ch, int ident)
{
  if(ident)
    for(int i=0; i < ident; i++) cout << ' ';

  cout << ch << "\n";
}

void println(char *str, int ident)
{
  if(ident)
    for(int i=0; i < ident; i++) cout << ' ';

  cout << str << "\n";
```

A

```cpp
}

void println(double d, int ident)
{
  if(ident)
    for(int i=0; i < ident; i++) cout << ' ';

  cout << d << "\n";
}

// Here are the print() functions.
void print(bool b, int ident)
{
  if(ident)
    for(int i=0; i < ident; i++) cout << ' ';

  if(b) cout << "true";
  else cout << "false";
}

void print(int i, int ident)
{
  if(ident)
    for(int i=0; i < ident; i++) cout << ' ';

  cout << i;
}

void print(long i, int ident)
{
  if(ident)
    for(int i=0; i < ident; i++) cout << ' ';

  cout << i;
}

void print(char ch, int ident)
{
  if(ident)
    for(int i=0; i < ident; i++) cout << ' ';

  cout << ch;
}

void print(char *str, int ident)
{
```

```
  if(ident)
    for(int i=0; i < ident; i++) cout << ' ';

  cout << str;
}

void print(double d, int ident)
{
  if(ident)
    for(int i=0; i < ident; i++) cout << ' ';

  cout << d;
}
```

9. ```
myfunc('x');
myfunc('x', 19);
myfunc('x', 19, 35);
```

10. Function overloading can introduce ambiguity when the compiler cannot decide which version of the function to call. This can occur when automatic type conversions are involved and when default arguments are used.

# Module 7: More Data Types and Operators

1. `static int test = 100;`

2. True. The **volatile** specifier tells the compiler that a variable might be changed by forces outside the program.

3. In a multifile project, to tell one file about a global variable declared in another file, use **extern**.

4. The most important attribute of a **static** local variable is that it holds its value between function calls.

5. ```
// Use static to count function invocations.

#include <iostream>
using namespace std;

int counter();

int main()
{
```

A

```
    int result;

    for(int i=0; i<10; i++)
      result = counter();

    cout << "Function called " <<
          result << " times." << "\n";

    return 0;
}

int counter()
{
  static count = 0;

  count++;

  return count;
}
```

6. Specifying **x** as register will have the most impact on performance, followed by **y**, and then **z**. The reason is that **x** is accessed most frequently within the loop, **y** the second most, and **z** is used only when the loop is initialized.

7. The **&** is a bitwise operator that acts on the individual bits within a value. **&&** is a logical operator that acts on true/false values.

8. The statement multiplies the current value of **x** by 10 and assigns that result to **x**. It is the same as

```
x = x * 10;
```

9. `// Use rotations to encode a message.`

```
#include <iostream>
#include <cstring>
using namespace std;

unsigned char rrotate(unsigned char val, int n);
unsigned char lrotate(unsigned char val, int n);
void show_binary(unsigned int u);

int main()
{
  char msg[] = "This is a test.";
  char *key = "xanadu";
  int klen = strlen(key);
```

```cpp
  int rotnum;

  cout << "Original message: " << msg << "\n";

  // Encode the message by left-rotating.
  for(int i = 0 ; i < strlen(msg); i++) {
    /* Left-rotate each letter by a value
       derived from the key string. */
    rotnum = key[i%klen] % 8;
    msg[i] = lrotate(msg[i], rotnum);
  }

  cout << "Encoded message: " << msg << "\n";

  // Decode the message by right-rotating.
  for(int i = 0 ; i < strlen(msg); i++) {
    /* Right-rotate each letter by a value
       derived from the key string. */
    rotnum = key[i%klen] % 8;

    msg[i] = rrotate(msg[i], rotnum);
  }

  cout << "Decoded message: " << msg << "\n";

  return 0;
}

// Left-rotate a byte n places.
unsigned char lrotate(unsigned char val, int n)
{
  unsigned int t;

  t = val;

  for(int i=0; i < n; i++) {
    t = t << 1;

    /* If a bit shifts out, it will be in bit 8
       of the integer t. If this is the case,
       put that bit on the right side. */
    if(t & 256)
      t = t | 1; // put a 1 on the right end
  }

  return t; // return the lower 8 bits.
}
```

A

```
// Right-rotate a byte n places.
unsigned char rrotate(unsigned char val, int n)
{
  unsigned int t;

  t = val;

  // First, move the value 8 bits higher.
  t = t << 8;

  for(int i=0; i < n; i++) {
    t = t >> 1;

    /* If a bit shifts out, it will be in bit 7
       of the integer t. If this is the case,
       put that bit on the left side. */
    if(t & 128)
      t = t | 32768; // put a 1 on left end
  }

  /* Finally, move the result back to the
     lower 8 bits of t. */
  t = t >> 8;

  return t;
}

// Display the bits within a byte.
void show_binary(unsigned int u)
{
  int t;

  for(t=128; t>0; t = t/2)
    if(u & t) cout << "1 ";
    else cout << "0 ";

  cout << "\n";
}
```

Module 8: Classes and Objects

1. A class is a logical construct that defines the form of an object. An object is an instance of a class. Thus, an object has physical reality within memory.

2. To define a class, use the **class** keyword.

3. Each object has its own copy of the member variables of a class.

4.
```
class Test {
    int count;
    int max;
    // ...
}
```

5. A constructor has the same name as its class. A destructor has the same name as its class except that it is preceded by a ~.

6. Here are three ways to create an object that initializes **i** to 10:

```
Sample ob(10);
Sample ob = 10;
Sample ob = Sample(10);
```

7. When a member function is declared within a class, it is automatically inlined, if possible.

8.
```
// Create a Triangle class.

#include <iostream>
#include <cmath>
using namespace std;

class Triangle {
  double height;
  double base;
public:
  Triangle(double h, double b) {
    height = h;
    base = b;
  }

  double hypot() {
    return sqrt(height*height + base*base);
  }

  double area() {
    return base * height / 2.0;
  }
};

int main()
{
  Triangle t1(3.0, 4.0);
```

A

```
    Triangle t2(4.5, 6.75);

    cout << "Hypotenuse of t1: " <<
      t1.hypot() << "\n";
    cout << "Area of t1: " <<
      t1.area() << "\n";

    cout << "Hypotenuse of t2: " <<
      t2.hypot() << "\n";
    cout << "Area of t2: " <<
      t2.area() << "\n";

    return 0;
  }
```

9.
```
/*
    Enhanced Project 8-1

    Add user ID to Help class.
*/

#include <iostream>
using namespace std;

// A class that encapsulates a help system.
class Help {
  int userID;
public:
  Help(int id) { userID = id; }

  ~Help() { cout << "Terminating help for #" <<
            userID << ".\n"; }

  int getID() { return userID; }

  void helpon(char what);
  void showmenu();
  bool isvalid(char ch);
};

// Display help information.
void Help::helpon(char what) {
  switch(what) {
    case '1':
      cout << "The if:\n\n";
      cout << "if(condition) statement;\n";
      cout << "else statement;\n";
```

```
      break;
    case '2':
      cout << "The switch:\n\n";
      cout << "switch(expression) {\n";
      cout << "  case constant:\n";
      cout << "    statement sequence\n";
      cout << "    break;\n";
      cout << "  // ...\n";
      cout << "}\n";
      break;
    case '3':
      cout << "The for:\n\n";
      cout << "for(init; condition; iteration)";
      cout << " statement;\n";
      break;
    case '4':
      cout << "The while:\n\n";
      cout << "while(condition) statement;\n";
      break;
    case '5':
      cout << "The do-while:\n\n";
      cout << "do {\n";
      cout << "  statement;\n";
      cout << "} while (condition);\n";
      break;
    case '6':
      cout << "The break:\n\n";
      cout << "break;\n";
      break;
    case '7':
      cout << "The continue:\n\n";
      cout << "continue;\n";
      break;
    case '8':
      cout << "The goto:\n\n";
      cout << "goto label;\n";
      break;
  }
  cout << "\n";
}

// Show the help menu.
void Help::showmenu() {
  cout << "Help on:\n";
  cout << "  1. if\n";
  cout << "  2. switch\n";
  cout << "  3. for\n";
```

A

```
    cout << "  4. while\n";
    cout << "  5. do-while\n";
    cout << "  6. break\n";
    cout << "  7. continue\n";
    cout << "  8. goto\n";
    cout << "Choose one (q to quit): ";
  }

  // Return true if a selection is valid.
  bool Help::isvalid(char ch) {
    if(ch < '1' || ch > '8' && ch != 'q')
      return false;
    else
      return true;
  }

  int main()
  {
    char choice;
    Help hlpob(27); // create an instance of the Help class.

    cout << "User ID is " << hlpob.getID() <<
            ".\n";

    // Use the Help object to display information.
    for(;;) {
      do {
        hlpob.showmenu();
        cin >> choice;
      } while(!hlpob.isvalid(choice));

      if(choice == 'q') break;
      cout << "\n";

      hlpob.helpon(choice);
    }

    return 0;
  }
```

Module 9: A Closer Look at Classes

1. A copy constructor makes a copy of an object. It is called when one object initializes another. Here is the general form:

```
classname (const classname &obj) {
  // body of constructor
}
```

2. When an object is returned by a function, a temporary object is created as the return value. This object is destroyed by the object's destructor after the value has been returned.

3.
```
int sum() {
   return this.i + this.j;
}
```

4. A structure is a class in which members are public by default. A union is a class in which all data members share the same memory. Union members are also public by default.

5. *this** refers to the object on which the function was called.

6. A **friend** function is a nonmember function that is granted access to the private members of the class for which it is a friend.

7.
```
type classname::operator#(type op2)
{
  // left operand passed via "this"
}
```

8. To allow operations between a class type and a built-in type, you must use two **friend** operator functions, one with the class type as the first parameter, and one with the built-in type as the first parameter.

9. No, the **?** cannot be overloaded. No, you cannot change the precedence of an operator.

10.
```
// Determine if one set is a subset of another.
bool Set::operator <(Set ob2) {
  if(len > ob2.len) return false; // ob1 has more elements

  for(int i=0; i < len; i++)
    if(ob2.find(members[i]) == -1) return false;
  return true;
}

// Determine if one set is a superset of another.
bool Set::operator >(Set ob2) {
  if(len < ob2.len) return false; // ob1 has fewer elements
```

A

```
    for(int i=0; i < ob2.len; i++)
      if(find(ob2.members[i]) == -1) return false;
    return true;
  }
```

11.
```
// Set intersection.
Set Set::operator &(Set ob2) {
  Set newset;

  // Add elements common to both sets.
  for(int i=0; i < len; i++)
    if(ob2.find(members[i]) != -1) // add if element in both sets
      newset = newset + members[i];

  return newset; // return set
}
```

Module 10: Inheritance, Virtual Functions, and Polymorphism

1. A class that is inherited is called a <u>base</u> class. The class that does the inheriting is called a <u>derived</u> class.

2. A base class does *not* have access to the members of derived classes, because a base class has no knowledge of derived classes. A derived class *does* have access to the non-private members of its base class(es).

3.
```
// A circle class.
class Circle : public TwoDShape {
public:
  Circle(double r) : TwoDShape(r) { } // specify radius

  double area() {
    return getWidth() * getWidth() * 3.1416;
  }
};
```

4. To prevent a derived class from having access to a member of a base class, declare that member as private in the base class.

5. Here is the general form of a derived class constructor that calls a base class constructor:

derived-class( ) : base-class( ) { // ...

6. Constructors are always called in order of derivation. Thus, when a **Gamma** object is created, the constructors are called in this order: **Alpha**, **Beta**, **Gamma**.

7. A **protected** member in a base class can be accessed by its own class and by derived classes. It is private, otherwise.

8. When a virtual function is called through a base class pointer, it is the type of the object being pointed to that determines which version of the function will be called.

9. A pure virtual function is a function that has no body inside its base class. Thus, a pure virtual function must be overridden by derived classes. An abstract class is a class that contains at least one pure virtual function.

10. No, an abstract class cannot be used to create an object.

11. A pure virtual function represents a generic description that all implementations of that function must adhere to. Thus, in the phrase "one interface, multiple methods," the pure virtual function represents the *interface,* and the individual implementations represent the *methods.*

Module 11: The C++ I/O System

1. The predefined streams are **cin**, **cout**, **cerr**, and **clog**.

2. Yes, C++ defines both 8-bit and wide-character streams.

3. The general form for overloading an inserter is shown here:

```
ostream &operator<<(ostream &stream, class_type obj)
{
  // class specific code goes here
  return stream;  // return the stream
}
```

4. **ios::scientific** causes numeric output to be displayed in scientific notation.

5. The **width( )** function sets the field width.

6. True, an I/O manipulator is used within an I/O expression.

7. Here is one way to open a file for text input:

```
ifstream in("test");
if(!in) {
```

A

```
   cout << "Cannot open file.\n";
   return 1;
 }
```

8. Here is one way to open a file for text output:

```
ofstream out("test");
if(!out) {
  cout << "Cannot open file.\n";
  return 1;
}
```

9. ios::binary specifies that a file be opened for binary rather than text-based I/O.

10. True, at end-of-file, the stream variable will evaluate as false.

11. `while(strm.get(ch)) // ...`

12. There are many solutions. The following shows just one way:

```
// Copy a file.

#include <iostream>
#include <fstream>
using namespace std;

int main(int argc, char *argv[])
{
  char ch;

  if(argc!=3) {
    cout << "Usage: copy <source> <target>\n";
    return 1;
  }

  ifstream src(argv[1], ios::in | ios::binary);
  if(!src) {
    cout << "Cannot open source file.\n";
    return 1;
  }

  ofstream targ(argv[2], ios::out | ios::binary);
  if(!targ) {
    cout << "Cannot open target file.\n";
    return 1;
  }

  do {
```

```
      src.get(ch);
      if(!src.eof()) targ.put(ch);
    } while(!src.eof());

    src.close();
    targ.close();

    return 0;
  }
```

13. There are many solutions. The following shows one simple way:

```
// Merge two files.

#include <iostream>
#include <fstream>
using namespace std;

int main(int argc, char *argv[])
{
  char ch;

  if(argc != 4) {
    cout << "Usage: merge <source1> <source2> <target>\n";
    return 1;
  }

  ifstream src1(argv[1], ios::in | ios::binary);
  if(!src1) {
    cout << "Cannot open 1st source file.\n";
    return 1;
  }

  ifstream src2(argv[2], ios::in | ios::binary);
  if(!src2) {
    cout << "Cannot open 2nd source file.\n";
    return 1;
  }

  ofstream targ(argv[3], ios::out | ios::binary);
  if(!targ) {
    cout << "Cannot open target file.\n";
    return 1;
  }

  // Copy first source file.
```

A

```
  do {
    src1.get(ch);
    if(!src1.eof()) targ.put(ch);
  } while(!src1.eof());

  // Copy second source file.
  do {
    src2.get(ch);
    if(!src2.eof()) targ.put(ch);
  } while(!src2.eof());

  src1.close();
  src2.close();
  targ.close();

  return 0;
}
```

14. `MyStrm.seekg(300, ios::beg);`

Module 12: Exceptions, Templates, and Other Advanced Topics

1. C++ exception handling is built upon three keywords: **try**, **catch**, and **throw**. In the most general terms, program statements that you want to monitor for exceptions are contained in a **try** block. If an exception (that is, an error) occurs within the **try** block, it is thrown (using **throw**). The exception is caught, using **catch**, and processed.

2. When catching exceptions of both base and derived classes, the derived classes must precede the base class in a **catch** list.

3. `void func() throw(MyExcpt)`

4. Here is one way to add an exception to **Queue**. It is one of many solutions.

```
/*
   Add an exception to Project 12-1

   A template queue class.
*/
#include <iostream>
#include <cstring>
using namespace std;

// This is the exception thrown by Queue on error.
```

```
class QExcpt {
public:
  char msg[80];
};

const int maxQsize = 100;

// This creates a generic queue class.
template <class QType> class Queue {
  QType q[maxQsize]; // this array holds the queue
  int size; // maximum number of elements that the queue can store
  int putloc, getloc; // the put and get indices
  QExcpt Qerr; // add an exception field
public:

  // Construct a queue of a specific length.
  Queue(int len) {
    // Queue must be less than max and positive.
    if(len > maxQsize) len = maxQsize;
    else if(len <= 0) len = 1;

    size = len;
    putloc = getloc = 0;
  }

  // Put data into the queue.
  void put(QType data) {
    if(putloc == size) {
      strcpy(Qerr.msg, "Queue is full.\n");
      throw Qerr;
    }

    putloc++;
    q[putloc] = data;
  }

  // Get data from the queue.
  QType get() {
    if(getloc == putloc) {
      strcpy(Qerr.msg, "Queue is empty.\n");
      throw Qerr;
    }

    getloc++;
    return q[getloc];
  }
};

// Demonstrate the generic Queue.
int main()
{
  // notice that iQa is only 2 elements long
```

A

```
Queue<int> iQa(2), iQb(10);

try {
  iQa.put(1);
  iQa.put(2);
  iQa.put(3); // this will overflow!

  iQb.put(10);
  iQb.put(20);
  iQb.put(30);

  cout << "Contents of integer queue iQa: ";
  for(int i=0; i < 3; i++) // this will underflow!
    cout << iQa.get() << " ";
  cout << endl;

  cout << "Contents of integer queue iQb: ";
  for(int i=0; i < 3; i++)
    cout << iQb.get() << " ";
  cout << endl;

  Queue<double> dQa(10), dQb(10);  // create two double queues

  dQa.put(1.01);
  dQa.put(2.02);
  dQa.put(3.03);

  dQb.put(10.01);
  dQb.put(20.02);
  dQb.put(30.03);

  cout << "Contents of double queue dQa: ";
  for(int i=0; i < 3; i++)
    cout << dQa.get() << " ";
  cout << endl;

  cout << "Contents of double queue dQb: ";
  for(int i=0; i < 3; i++)
    cout << dQb.get() << " ";
  cout << endl;
} catch(QExcpt exc) {
  cout << exc.msg;
}

return 0;
}
```

5. A generic function defines the general form of a routine, but does not specify the precise type of data upon which it operates. It is created using the keyword **template**.

6. Here is one way to make **quicksort( )** and **qs( )** into generic functions:

```
// A generic Quicksort.

#include <iostream>
#include <cstring>

using namespace std;


// Set up a call to the actual sorting function.
template <class X> void quicksort(X *items, int len)
{
  qs(items, 0, len-1);
}

// A generic version of Quicksort.
template <class X> void qs(X *items, int left, int right)
{
  int i, j;
  X x, y;

  i = left; j = right;
  x = items[( left+right) / 2 ];

  do {
    while((items[i] < x) && (i < right)) i++;
    while((x < items[j]) && (j > left)) j--;

    if(i <= j) {
      y = items[i];
      items[i] = items[j];
      items[j] = y;
      i++; j--;
    }
  } while(i <= j);

  if(left < j) qs(items, left, j);
  if(i < right) qs(items, i, right);
}

int main() {

  // sort characters.
  char str[] = "jfmckldoelazlkper";
  int i;
```

A

```
    cout << "Original order: " << str << "\n";

    quicksort(str, strlen(str));

    cout << "Sorted order: " << str << "\n";

    // sort integers
    int nums[] = { 4, 3, 7, 5, 9, 8, 1, 3, 5, 4 };

    cout << "Original order: ";
    for(int i=0; i < 10; i++)
      cout << nums[i] << " ";
    cout << endl;

    quicksort(nums, 10);

    cout << "Sorted order: ";
    for(int i=0; i < 10; i++)
      cout << nums[i] << " ";
    cout << endl;


    return 0;
  }
```

7. Here is one way to store **Sample** objects in a **Queue**:

```
/*
   Use Project 12-1 to store Sample objects.

   A template queue class.
*/
#include <iostream>
using namespace std;

class Sample {
  int id;
public:
  Sample() { id = 0; }
  Sample(int x) { id = x; }
  void show() { cout << id << endl; }
};

const int maxQsize = 100;

// This creates a generic queue class.
template <class QType> class Queue {
```

```
    QType q[maxQsize]; // this array holds the queue
    int size; // maximum number of elements that the queue can store
    int putloc, getloc; // the put and get indices
  public:

    // Construct a queue of a specific length.
    Queue(int len) {
      // Queue must be less than max and positive.
      if(len > maxQsize) len = maxQsize;
      else if(len <= 0) len = 1;

      size = len;
      putloc = getloc = 0;
    }

    // Put data into the queue.
    void put(QType data) {
      if(putloc == size) {
        cout << " -- Queue is full.\n";
        return;
      }

      putloc++;
      q[putloc] = data;
    }

    // Get data from the queue.
    QType get() {
      if(getloc == putloc) {
        cout << " -- Queue is empty.\n";
        return 0;
      }

      getloc++;
      return q[getloc];
    }
};

// Demonstrate the generic Queue.
int main()
{
  Queue<Sample> sampQ(3);

  Sample o1(1), o2(2), o3(3);

  sampQ.put(o1);
```

```
    sampQ.put(o2);
    sampQ.put(o3);

    cout << "Contents of sampQ:\n";
    for(int i=0; i < 3; i++)
      sampQ.get().show();
    cout << endl;

    return 0;
  }
```

8. Here, the **Sample** objects are allocated:

```
/*
    Use Project 12-1 to store Sample objects.

    Allocate the Sample objects dynamically.

    A template queue class.
*/
#include <iostream>
using namespace std;

class Sample {
  int id;
public:
  Sample() { id = 0; }
  Sample(int x) { id = x; }
  void show() { cout << id << endl; }
};

const int maxQsize = 100;

// This creates a generic queue class.
template <class QType> class Queue {
  QType q[maxQsize]; // this array holds the queue
  int size; // maximum number of elements that the queue can store
  int putloc, getloc; // the put and get indices
public:

  // Construct a queue of a specific length.
  Queue(int len) {
    // Queue must be less than max and positive.
    if(len > maxQsize) len = maxQsize;
    else if(len <= 0) len = 1;
```

```cpp
    size = len;
    putloc = getloc = 0;
  }

  // Put data into the queue.
  void put(QType data) {
    if(putloc == size) {
      cout << " -- Queue is full.\n";
      return;
    }

    putloc++;
    q[putloc] = data;
  }

  // Get data from the queue.
  QType get() {
    if(getloc == putloc) {
      cout << " -- Queue is empty.\n";
      return 0;
    }

    getloc++;
    return q[getloc];
  }
};

// Demonstrate the generic Queue.
int main()
{
  Queue<Sample> sampQ(3);

  Sample *p1, *p2, *p3;

  p1 = new Sample(1);
  p2 = new Sample(2);
  p3 = new Sample(3);

  sampQ.put(*p1);
  sampQ.put(*p2);
  sampQ.put(*p3);

  cout << "Contents of sampQ:\n";
  for(int i=0; i < 3; i++)
    sampQ.get().show();
```

```
    cout << endl;

    delete(p1);
    delete(p2);
    delete(p3);

    return 0;
}
```

9. To declare a namespace called **RobotMotion** use:

```
namespace RobotMotion {
  // ...
}
```

10. The C++ standard library is contained in the **std** namespace.

11. No, a **static** member function cannot access the non-**static** data of a class.

12. The **typeid** operator obtains the type of an object at runtime.

13. To determine the validity of a polymorphic cast at runtime, use **dynamic_cast**.

14. **const_cast** overrides **const** or **volatile** in a cast.

Appendix B

The Preprocessor

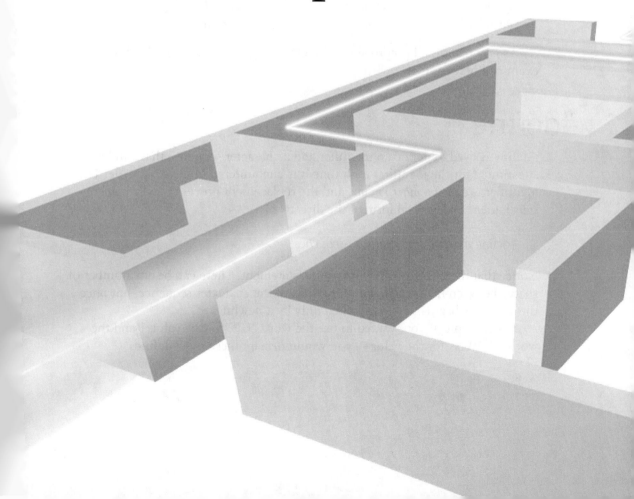

The *preprocessor* is that part of the compiler that performs various text manipulations on your program prior to the actual translation of your source code into object code. You can give text manipulation commands to the preprocessor. These commands are called *preprocessor directives*, and although not technically part of the C++ language, they expand the scope of its programming environment.

The preprocessor is a holdover from C and is not as important to C++ as it is to C. Also, some preprocessor features have been rendered redundant by newer and better C++ language elements. However, since many programmers still use the preprocessor, and because it is still part of the C++ language environment, it is briefly discussed here.

The C++ preprocessor contains the following directives:

#define	#error	#include
#if	#else	#elif
#endif	#ifdef	#ifndef
#undef	#line	#pragma

As is apparent, all preprocessor directives begin with a # sign. Each will be examined here in turn.

#define

#define is used to define an identifier and a character sequence that will be substituted for the identifier each time it is encountered in the source file. The identifier is called a *macro name,* and the replacement process is called *macro substitution*. The general form of the directive is

#define *macro-name character-sequence*

Notice that there is no semicolon in this statement. There can be any number of spaces between the identifier and the start of the character sequence, but once the sequence begins, it is terminated only by a newline.

For example, if you wanted to use the word "UP" for the value 1 and the word "DOWN" for the value 0, you would declare these two **#define**s:

```
#define UP 1
#define DOWN 0
```

These statements will cause the compiler to substitute a 1 or a 0 each time the name **UP** or **DOWN** is encountered in your source file. For example, the following will print **1 0 2** on the screen:

```
cout << UP << ' ' << DOWN << ' ' << UP + UP;
```

It is important to understand that the macro substitution is simply the replacing of an identifier with its associated string. Therefore, if you want to define a standard message, you might write something like this:

```
#define GETFILE "Enter File Name"
// ...
cout << GETFILE;
```

C++ will substitute the string "Enter File Name" when the macro name **GETFILE** is encountered. To the compiler, the **cout** statement will actually appear to be

```
cout << "Enter File Name";
```

No text substitutions will occur if the macro name occurs within a quoted string. For example,

```
#define GETFILE "Enter File Name"
// ...
cout << "GETFILE is a macro name\n";
```

will not print

```
Enter File Name is a macro name
```

but rather will print

```
GETFILE is a macro name
```

If the string is longer than one line, you can continue it on the next by placing a backslash at the end of the line, as shown in this example:

```
#define LONG_STRING "this is a very long \
string that is used as an example"
```

B

It is common practice among C++ programmers to use capital letters for macro names. This convention helps anyone reading the program know at a glance that a macro substitution will take place. Also, it is best to put all **#defines** at the start of the file, or perhaps in a separate include file, rather than sprinkling them throughout the program.

One last point: C++ provides a better way of defining constants than by using **#define**. This is to use the **const** specifier. However, many C++ programmers migrated from C, where **#define** is commonly used for this purpose. Thus, you will likely see it frequently in C++ code, too.

Function-Like Macros

The **#define** directive has another feature: The macro name can have arguments. Each time the macro name is encountered, the arguments associated with it are replaced by the actual arguments found in the program. This creates a *function-like* macro. Here is an example:

```cpp
// Use a function-like macro.

#include <iostream>
using namespace std;

#define MIN(a,b)  (((a)<(b)) ? a : b)

int main()
{
  int x, y;

  x = 10;
  y = 20;
  cout << "The minimum is " << MIN(x, y);

  return 0;
}
```

When this program is compiled, the expression defined by **MIN(a,b)** will be substituted, except that x and y will be used as the operands. That is, the **cout** statement will be substituted to look like this:

```cpp
cout << "The minimum is: " << ((x)<(y)) ? x : y);
```

In essence, the function-like macro is a way to define a function that has its code expanded inline rather than called.

The apparently redundant parentheses surrounding the **MIN** macro are necessary to ensure proper evaluation of the substituted expression because of the relative precedence of the operators. In fact, the extra parentheses should be applied in virtually all function-like macros. Otherwise, there can be surprising results. For example, consider this short program, which uses a macro to determine whether a value is even or odd:

```
// This program will give the wrong answer.

#include <iostream>
using namespace std;

#define EVEN(a) a%2==0 ? 1 : 0

int main()
{
  if(EVEN(9+1)) cout << "is even";
  else cout << "is odd";

  return 0;
}
```

This program will not work correctly because of the way the macro substitution is made. When compiled, the **EVEN(9+1)** is expanded to

```
9+1%2==0 ? 1 : 0
```

As you should recall, the % (modulus) operator has higher precedence than the plus operator. This means that the % operation is first performed on the 1 and that the result is added to 9, which (of course) does not equal 0. To fix the problem, there must be parentheses around **a** in the macro definition of **EVEN**, as is shown in this corrected version of the program:

```
// This program is now fixed.

#include <iostream>
using namespace std;
```

B

```
#define EVEN(a) (a)%2==0 ? 1 : 0

int main()
{
  if(EVEN(9+1)) cout << "is even";
  else cout << "is odd";

  return 0;
}
```

Now, the **9+1** is evaluated prior to the modulus operation. In general, it is a good idea to surround macro parameters with parentheses to avoid unforeseen troubles like the one just described.

The use of macro substitutions in place of real functions has one major benefit: Because macro substitution code is expanded inline, no overhead of a function call is incurred, so the speed of your program increases. However, this increased speed might be paid for with an increase in the size of the program, due to duplicated code.

Although still commonly seen in C++ code, the use of function-like macros has been rendered completely redundant by the **inline** specifier, which accomplishes the same goal better and more safely. (Remember, **inline** causes a function to be expanded inline rather than called.) Also, **inline** functions do not require the extra parentheses needed by most function-like macros. However, function-like macros will almost certainly continue to be a part of C++ programs for some time to come, because many former C programmers continue to use them out of habit.

#error

When the **#error** directive is encountered, it forces the compiler to stop compilation. This directive is used primarily for debugging. The general form of the directive is

#error *error-message*

Notice that the *error-message* is not between double quotes. When the compiler encounters this directive, it displays the error message and other information and terminates compilation. Your implementation determines what information will actually be displayed. (You might want to experiment with your compiler to see what is displayed.)

#include

The **#include** preprocessor directive instructs the compiler to include either a standard header or another source file into the file that contains the **#include** directive. The name of the standard headers should be enclosed between angle brackets, as shown in the programs throughout this book. For example,

```
#include <fstream>
```

includes the standard header for file I/O.

When including another source file, its name can be enclosed between double quotes or angle brackets. For example, the following two directives both instruct C++ to read and compile a file called **sample.h**:

```
#include <sample.h>
#include "sample.h"
```

When including a file, whether the filename is enclosed by quotes or angle brackets determines how the search for the specified file is conducted. If the filename is enclosed between angle brackets, the compiler searches for it in one or more implementation-defined directories. If the filename is enclosed between quotes, then the compiler searches for it in some other implementation-defined directory, which is typically the current working directory. If the file is not found in this directory, the search is restarted as if the filename had been enclosed between angle brackets. Since the search path is implementation defined, you will need to check your compiler's user manual for details.

Conditional Compilation Directives

There are several directives that allow you to selectively compile portions of your program's source code. This process, called *conditional compilation,* is widely used by commercial software houses that provide and maintain many customized versions of one program.

#if, #else, #elif, and #endif

The general idea behind the **#if** directive is that if the constant expression following the **#if** is true, then the code between it and an **#endif** will be compiled; otherwise, the code will be skipped over. **#endif** is used to mark the end of an **#if** block.

B

The general form of **#if** is

```
#if constant-expression
    statement sequence
#endif
```

If the constant expression is true, the block of code will be compiled; otherwise, it will be skipped. For example:

```cpp
// A simple #if example.

#include <iostream>
using namespace std;

#define MAX 100

int main()
{
#if MAX>10
  cout << "Extra memory required.\n";
#endif

  // ...
  return 0;
}
```

This program will display the message on the screen because, as defined in the program, **MAX** is greater than 10. This example illustrates an important point. The expression that follows the **#if** is *evaluated at compile time.* Therefore, it must contain only identifiers that have been previously defined and constants. No variables can be used.

The **#else** directive works in much the same way as the **else** statement that forms part of the C++ language: it establishes an alternative if the **#if** directive fails. The previous example can be expanded to include the **#else** directive, as shown here:

```cpp
// A simple #if/#else example.

#include <iostream>
using namespace std;

#define MAX 6
```

```
int main()
{
#if MAX>10
  cout << "Extra memory required.\n");
#else
  cout << "Current memory OK.\n";
#endif

  // ...

  return 0;
}
```

In this program, **MAX** is defined to be less than 10, so the **#if** portion of the code is not compiled, but the **#else** alternative is. Therefore, the message **Current memory OK.** is displayed.

Notice that the **#else** is used to mark both the end of the **#if** block and the beginning of the **#else** block. This is necessary because there can only be one **#endif** associated with any **#if**.

The **#elif** means "else if" and is used to establish an if-else-if ladder for multiple compilation options. The **#elif** is followed by a constant expression. If the expression is true, then that block of code is compiled, and no other **#elif** expressions are tested or compiled. Otherwise, the next in the series is checked. The general form is

```
#if expression
    statement sequence
#elif expression 1
    statement sequence
#elif expression 2
    statement sequence
#elif expression 3
    statement sequence
// ...
#elif expression N
    statement sequence
#endif
```

For example, this fragment uses the value of **COMPILED_BY** to define who compiled the program:

```
#define JOHN 0
#define BOB 1
```

```
#define TOM 2

#define COMPILED_BY JOHN

#if COMPILED_BY == JOHN
  char who[] = "John";
#elif COMPILED_BY == BOB
  char who[] = "Bob";
#else
  char who[] = "Tom";
#endif
```

#ifs and **#elif**s can be nested. In this case, the **#endif**, **#else**, or **#elif** associate with the nearest **#if** or **#elif**. For example, the following is perfectly valid:

```
#if COMPILED_BY == BOB
   #if DEBUG == FULL
      int port = 198;
   #elif DEBUG == PARTIAL
      int port = 200;
   #endif
#else
   cout << "Bob must compile for debug output.\n";
#endif
```

#ifdef and #ifndef

Another method of conditional compilation uses the directives **#ifdef** and **#ifndef**, which mean "if defined" and "if not defined," respectively, and refer to macro names.

The general form of **#ifdef** is

```
#ifdef macro-name
   statement sequence
#endif
```

If the *macro-name* has been previously defined in a **#define** statement, the statement sequence between the **#ifdef** and **#endif** will be compiled.

The general form of **#ifndef** is

```
#ifndef macro-name
   statement sequence
#endif
```

If *macro-name* is currently undefined by a **#define** statement, then the block of code is compiled. Both the **#ifdef** and **#ifndef** can use an **#else** or **#elif** statement. **Also**, you can nest **#ifdef**s and **#ifndef**s in the same way as **#if**s.

#undef

The **#undef** directive is used to remove a previously defined definition of a macro name. The general form is

    #undef *macro-name*

Consider this example:

```
#define TIMEOUT 100
#define WAIT 0
// ...
#undef TIMEOUT
#undef WAIT
```

Here, both **TIMEOUT** and **WAIT** are defined until the **#undef** statements are encountered. The principal use of **#undef** is to allow macro names to be localized to only those sections of code that need them.

Using defined

In addition to **#ifdef**, there is a second way to determine if a macro name is defined. You can use the **#if** directive in conjunction with the **defined** compile-time operator. For example, to determine if the macro **MYFILE** is defined, you can use either of these two preprocessing commands:

```
#if defined MYFILE
```

or

```
#ifdef MYFILE
```

You can also precede **defined** with the ! to reverse the condition. For example, the following fragment is compiled only if **DEBUG** is not defined:

```
#if !defined DEBUG
  cout << "Final version!\n";
#endif
```

B

#line

The **#line** directive is used to change the contents of _ _LINE_ _ and _ _FILE_ _, which are predefined macro names. _ _LINE_ _ contains the line number of the line currently being compiled, and _ _FILE_ _ contains the name of the file being compiled. The basic form of the **#line** command is

> #line *number "filename"*

Here *number* is any positive integer, and the optional *filename* is any valid file identifier. The line number becomes the number of the current source line, and the filename becomes the name of the source file. **#line** is primarily used for debugging purposes and for special applications.

#pragma

The **#pragma** directive is an implementation-defined directive that allows various instructions, defined by the compiler's creator, to be given to the compiler. The general form of the **#pragma** directive is

> #pragma *name*

Here, *name* is the name of the **#pragma** you want. If the *name* is unrecognized by the compiler, then the **#pragma** directive is simply ignored and no error results.

To see what pragmas your compiler supports, check its documentation. You might find some that are valuable to your programming efforts. Typical **#pragma**s include those that determine what compiler warning messages are issued, how code is generated, and what library is linked.

The # and ## Preprocessor Operators

C++ supports two preprocessor operators: **#** and **##**. These operators are used in conjunction with **#define**. The **#** operator causes the argument it precedes to become a quoted string. For example, consider this program:

```
#include <iostream>
using namespace std;
```

```
#define mkstr(s)  # s

int main()
{
  cout << mkstr(I like C++);

  return 0;
}
```

The C++ preprocessor turns the line

```
cout << mkstr(I like C++);
```

into

```
cout << "I like C++";
```

The ## operator is used to concatenate two tokens. Here is an example:

```
#include <iostream>
using namespace std;

#define concat(a, b)  a ## b

int main()
{
  int xy = 10;

  cout << concat(x, y);

  return 0;
}
```

The preprocessor transforms

```
cout << concat(x, y);
```

into

```
cout << xy;
```

If these operators seem strange to you, keep in mind that they are not needed or used in most programs. They exist primarily to allow some special cases to be handled by the preprocessor.

B

Predefined Macro Names

C++ specifies six built-in predefined macro names. They are

```
_ _LINE_ _
_ _FILE_ _
_ _DATE_ _
_ _TIME_ _
_ _STDC_ _
_ _cplusplus
```

The _ _LINE_ _ and _ _FILE_ _ macros were described in the discussion of **#line**. Briefly, they contain the current line number and filename of the program when it is being compiled.

The _ _DATE_ _ macro contains a string of the form *month/day/year* that is the date of the translation of the source file into object code.

The _ _TIME_ _ macro contains the time at which the program was compiled. The time is represented in a string having the form *hour:minute:second*.

The meaning of _ _STDC_ _ is implementation-defined. Generally, if _ _STDC_ _ is defined, then the compiler will accept only standard C/C++ code that does not contain any nonstandard extensions.

A compiler conforming to ANSI/ISO Standard C++ will define_ _cplusplus as a value containing at least six digits. Nonconforming compilers will use a value with five or fewer digits.

Appendix C

Working with an Older C++ Compiler

I f you are using a modern compiler, then you had no trouble compiling the programs in this book. If this is the case, you won't need the information presented in this appendix. Simply use the programs exactly as they are shown. As explained, the programs in this book fully conform to the ANSI/ISO Standard for C++ and can be compiled by nearly any modern C++ compiler, including Microsoft's Visual C++ and Borland's C++ Builder.

However, if you are using a compiler that was created several years ago, then it might report a number of errors when you try to compile the examples, because it does not recognize a few of C++'s newer features. If this is the case, don't worry—only minor changes are required to modify most of the example programs so that they will work with old compilers. Most often, the differences between old-style and modern code involve the use of two features: new-style headers and the **namespace** statement. Each is examined here.

As explained in Module 1, the **#include** statement includes a header into your program. For early versions of C++, all headers were files that used the file extension **.h**. For example, in an old-style program you would use a statement like this to include the **iostream** header:

```
#include <iostream.h>
```

This caused the file **iostream.h** to be included in your program. Thus, in an old-style program, when you included a header, you specified its filename, which had the **.h** extension. This is not the case today.

Modern C++ uses a new kind of header, which was developed when the ANSI/ISO Standard for C++ was created. The new-style headers *do not* specify filenames. Instead, they simply specify standard identifiers, which may be mapped to files by the compiler, but need not be. The new-style C++ headers are an abstraction that simply guarantees that the appropriate information required by your program is included.

Since the new-style headers are not filenames, they do not have a **.h** extension. They consist solely of the header name contained between angle brackets. For example, here are two of the new-style headers supported by Standard C++:

```
<iostream>
<fstream>
```

To convert these new-style headers into old-style header files, simply add a **.h** extension.

When you include a modern header in your program, the contents of that header are contained in the **std** namespace. As explained, a namespace is simply a declarative region. Its purpose is to localize the names of identifiers to avoid name collisions. Older versions of C++ put the names of library functions, and so on, into the global namespace, not the **std** namespace used by modern compilers. Thus, when working with an old-style compiler, there is no need for this statement:

```
using namespace std;
```

In fact, most older compilers won't even accept the **using** statement.

Two Simple Changes

If your compiler does not support namespaces and modern-style headers, then it will report one or more errors when it tries to compile the first few lines of the sample programs in this book. If this is the case, you need only make two simple changes: use an old-style header and delete the **namespace** statement. For example, just replace

```
#include <iostream>
using namespace std;
```

with

```
#include <iostream.h>
```

This change transforms a modern program into an old-style one. Since the old-style header reads all of its contents into the global namespace, there is no need for a **namespace** statement. After making these changes, the sample program can be compiled by an older compiler.

There is one other change that you will occasionally need to make. C++ inherits a few headers from the C language. The C language does not support the new-style headers. To allow for backward compatibility, Standard C++ still supports the C-style header files. However, Standard C++ also defines new-style

C

headers that you can use in place of the C header files. The C++ versions of the C standard headers simply add a *c* prefix to the C filename and drop the **.h**. For example, the C++ new-style header for **math.h** is **<cmath>**. The one for **string.h** is **<cstring>**. Although it is currently permissible to include a C-style header file, this approach is not recommended by Standard C++. For this reason, this book uses new-style C++ headers in all **#include** statements. If your compiler does not support new-style headers for the C headers, then simply substitute the old-style header files.

Index

INTERNATIONAL CONTACT INFORMATION

AUSTRALIA
McGraw-Hill Book Company Australia Pty. Ltd.
TEL +61-2-9417-9899
FAX +61-2-9417-5687
http://www.mcgraw-hill.com.au
books-it_sydney@mcgraw-hill.com

CANADA
McGraw-Hill Ryerson Ltd.
TEL +905-430-5000
FAX +905-430-5020
http://www.mcgrawhill.ca

GREECE, MIDDLE EAST, NORTHERN AFRICA
McGraw-Hill Hellas
TEL +30-1-656-0990-3-4
FAX +30-1-654-5525

MEXICO (Also serving Latin America)
McGraw-Hill Interamericana Editores S.A. de C.V.
TEL +525-117-1583
FAX +525-117-1589
http://www.mcgraw-hill.com.mx
fernando_castellanos@mcgraw-hill.com

SINGAPORE (Serving Asia)
McGraw-Hill Book Company
TEL +65-863-1580
FAX +65-862-3354
http://www.mcgraw-hill.com.sg
mghasia@mcgraw-hill.com

SOUTH AFRICA
McGraw-Hill South Africa
TEL +27-11-622-7512
FAX +27-11-622-9045
robyn_swanepoel@mcgraw-hill.com

UNITED KINGDOM & EUROPE (Excluding Southern Europe)
McGraw-Hill Education Europe
TEL +44-1-628-502500
FAX +44-1-628-770224
http://www.mcgraw-hill.co.uk
computing_neurope@mcgraw-hill.com

ALL OTHER INQUIRIES Contact:
Osborne/McGraw-Hill
TEL +1-510-549-6600
FAX +1-510-883-7600
http://www.osborne.com
omg_international@mcgraw-hill.com